Mental Health, Disability, and Combating Marginalization in Education

Nareadi Tlakale Phasha
University of South Africa, South Africa

IGI Global
Scientific Publishing
Publishing Tomorrow's Research Today

Vice President of Editorial	Melissa Wagner
Director of Acquisitions	Mikaela Felty
Director of Book Development	Jocelynn Hessler
Production Manager	Mike Brehm
Cover Design	Jose Rosado

Published in the United States of America by
IGI Global Scientific Publishing
701 East Chocolate Avenue
Hershey, PA, 17033, USA
Tel: 717-533-8845 | Fax: 717-533-7115
Website: https://www.igi-global.com E-mail: cust@igi-global.com

Library of Congress Cataloging-in-Publication Data

LCCN: 2025004513 (CIP Data Pending)
ISBN13: 9798337371634
Isbn13Softcover: 9798337371641
EISBN13: 9798337371658
British Cataloguing in Publication Data
A Cataloguing in Publication record for this book is available from the British Library.

Table of Contents

Detailed Table of Contents

Kenya's legal frameworks uphold the rights of children with disabilities, ensuring dignity, safety, education, and inclusion. However, barriers such as stigma, poverty, and inadequate resources, particularly for children with intellectual disabilities in rural areas, exacerbate their vulnerability. This study explored challenges faced by learners with mild intellectual disabilities in rural southwestern Kenya, focusing on their safety, inclusion, and access to services. Using a qualitative descriptive design, the study conducted focus group discussions and interviews with 24 teachers and 35 learners from three special schools, employing English, Swahili, and Ekegusii to enhance inclusivity. Braun and Clarke's thematic framework guided data analysis, validated via participant transcript reviews and expert feedback. Key findings revealed: (a) institutions' failure to meet learners' specific needs; (b) poverty and stigma limiting families' support capacity; and (c) societal attitudes and policies shaping their experiences. Systemic reforms are essential to ensure learners' safety.

Disability issues have been a serious subject of discourse in Nigeria as a result of human rights abuses, stigma, discrimination, and negative attitudes at family, community, and societal levels. These problems contribute to people with disabilities' limited access to services and exclusion in various settings in Nigeria, a situation that resulted in advocacy calls and inclusion of people with disabilities all over the country. This chapter collected data through documentaries and content analysis to explore factors limiting access to support services by people with disabilities in Nigeria and their effects on the well-being of disabled persons. The paper recommended amongst others that the government as a matter of urgency should put in place machinery to enforce the domestication and implementation of the Discrimination against Persons with Disabilities (Prohibition) Act for enhanced well-being of People with disabilities.

The aim of this chapter is to discuss the misconceptions about leaners living with bipolar mood disorder (BMD). The lack of lived experience with BMD can result in a number of critical misconceptions, with opinions abounding as to those of who live with BMD. Often, the commentaries concerned are written by those who do not understand the bipolar experience. Therefore, a scholarly and academic attempt was made to review the relevant literature critically with a view to presenting a balanced attempt to dismiss the stereotypes and the stigma perpetuated against learners living with BMD. The derogatory language used against such learners, which often leads to exclusionary practices, was explored.

This chapter aims to focus on the misconceptions concerning learners living with HIV/AIDS. False rumors about how HIV is spread in our country remains a problem despite the education and awareness campaigns that are taking place. Knowing about the myths regarding HIV is extremely important for everyone – whether you are living with HIV or not. At the end of the day, HIV affects us all and we have a responsibility to learn more about it so that we can protect each other from infection, stereotypes and stigma. Myths about HIV contribute to stigmatization of the topic. Stigma and stereotypes around HIV prevent more people from being tested and, consequently, prevent more people from getting treatment. It also increases the risk of judgment and discrimination.

Creating learning environments that accommodate all students, regardless of their skills or limitations, is the fundamental goal of inclusion. This method is very important for students who have autism spectrum disorders. The complex developmental disorder known as autism spectrum disorders (ASD) has an impact on social relationships, behavior, and communication. Students with autism spectrum disorders confront particular difficulties that call for specialised approaches that encourage empathy and cooperation from peers, teachers, and the larger society. This chapter will explore the core ideas of Ubuntu, a Southern African philosophy that emphasises relationships within the community and mutual care. Ubuntu encourages African communities to view an individual's identity through the collective well-being of the community, advocating for empathy, compassion, and shared humanity. By implementing Ubuntu principles in educational settings, African communities can redefine inclusion as a shared responsibility that enable students with autism spectrum disorders to thrive.

This chapter investigated the society's conceptions of hearing impairment and the strategies for including learners with hearing impairment is schools. People with hearing impairment often struggle to integrate with the public. The study examines how hearing impairment is viewed and labelled, and the impact of using Afrocentric approaches on teaching and learning in schools. Open-ended interviews with members of the community and the teachers for these learners were used to gain insights into conceptions of hearing impairment. Of interest was how the conceptions about hearing impairment were transferred to schools that constituted these learners. Data was analysed by using content analysis. The findings of the study indicate that individuals with hearing impairment are generally viewed as requiring assistance to access various facilities, including access to education. They are often labelled as 'those ones' and are frequently marginalised. The study concluded that the community and the teachers showed appreciation of the importance of embracing individuals with hearing impairment.

Chapter 7

This chapter interrogates stigma and attitudes towards persons with disabilities, as these are obstacles to the successful implementation of inclusive education. Important aspects are the stigmas and attitudes towards realising inclusive education without discrimination, the impact of stereotypes on inclusive education, and best inclusion practices to mitigate those stigmas, attitudes and stereotypes towards persons with disabilities. South African policies and principles promote inclusive education for learner diversity. The promise to make provision for inclusive education in South African policies was part of a shift from the divided education system under apartheid to a diverse society that breaks down economic and public barriers. The ideal of inclusive education in South Africa holds that all learners, irrespective of capability, have the right to education and equal learning opportunities.

Chapter 8

Education worldwide has seen significant shifts, requiring teachers to adapt to diverse student needs. In the UAE, numerous professional development sessions were organized to promote inclusive teaching practices. However, many teachers struggled to fully grasp the concept of inclusive education and lacked the skills to implement it effectively. This study explored teachers' experiences after completing a six-month professional development program on inclusive education. Using a qualitative approach, fourteen teachers from eight UAE schools were interviewed. The findings revealed that, despite initial challenges, participants experienced transformative growth, gaining the skills necessary to implement inclusive teaching. The study concluded that professional development is essential in enabling teachers to teach inclusively.

This chapter explores the critical issue of mental health challenges in academia, which focus on the impacts of excessive workloads, competition, gender inequality, and the COVID-19 pandemic. The findings highlight how heightened expectations, institutional pressures, and the online learning during the pandemic exacerbated anxiety, depression, and burnout. Female academics and students are particularly vulnerable, facing additional stress from societal and institutional gender biases. The chapter adopts a qualitative autoethnographic approach, integrating personal narratives with thematic analysis, which deeply relates academic responsibilities and psychological well-being. It emphasizes the role of socio-economic factors and educational policies in worsening mental health conditions. Recommendations include creating inclusive, flexible learning environments and advancing mental health interventions such as counseling and support systems. This chapter urgently mentions mental health in education to foster a more sustainable, balanced, and effective academic culture.

This chapter provides a comprehensive cross-cultural analysis of educational inclusion practices in Poland, Israel, and Arab-Israeli contexts. Following the landmark Salamanca Statement, we focus on the formative period of 1994-2014. We examine the evolution toward inclusive educational frameworks while exposing unique challenges shaped by cultural, social, and political settings. Poland's late adoption of inclusion practices highlights the gap between theoretical acceptance and practical application, particularly for students with intellectual disabilities. In Israel, the 'Shiluv' law facilitates inclusive education yet reveals disparities among various educational sectors, with limited success for students with severe disabilities.

Preface

As the editor, it is my privilege to introduce this volume, *Mental Health, Disability, and Combating Marginalization in Education*. This book emerges at a critical time when questions of equity, access, and inclusion are being re-examined within educational contexts across the globe. Too often, persons with disabilities and those facing mental health challenges are pushed to the margins of society through stigma, policy gaps, and structural barriers. My intention with this collection is to amplify scholarly voices, highlight lived realities, and advance knowledge that can contribute to dismantling those barriers.

The chapters assembled in this book address a wide range of issues—from intellectual disabilities in rural Kenya, to discrimination in Nigeria, to inclusive education debates in South Africa, the UAE, and beyond. While the settings and conditions differ, the shared reality is one of persistent struggle for dignity, recognition, and access to educational opportunities. It is my hope that readers will not only encounter research findings and theoretical insights here, but also a call to action: to imagine and build more inclusive systems that honor diversity in all its forms.

Equally important, this book highlights the interconnectedness of mental health and disability with broader social, cultural, and policy contexts. Each contribution illustrates that marginalization does not arise in isolation, but rather through intersecting dynamics of poverty, stigma, inadequate policy implementation, and systemic neglect. To combat these forces requires collaborative commitment among educators, policymakers, communities, and scholars. This volume aspires to be a resource for that ongoing work.

CHAPTER OVERVIEW

Chapter 1 by *Nareadi Phasha and Doris Nyokang'i* examines safety, inclusion, and access for learners with intellectual disabilities in rural Kenya, revealing how stigma, poverty, and systemic barriers leave children vulnerable, despite existing legal frameworks.

Chapter 2 by *Paulinus Okah, Chinwe Nnama-Okechukwu, Nkemdilim Anazonwu, and Chinyere Onalu* explores the social and institutional discrimination faced by persons with disabilities in Nigeria, calling for full enforcement of protective legislation.

Chapter 3 by *Andile Mdikana* critically analyzes misconceptions about learners with bipolar mood disorder, highlighting the exclusionary practices that arise from stigma and stereotypes.

Chapter 4, also by *Andile Mdikana*, addresses the stigmatization of learners living with HIV/AIDS, demonstrating how myths about transmission contribute to discrimination and exclusion in schools.

Chapter 5 by *Jabulani Mpofu and Maximus Sefotho* applies the philosophy of Ubuntu to the inclusion of learners with autism spectrum disorders, promoting empathy, shared responsibility, and collective well-being in educational contexts.

Chapter 6 by *Gaone Molapisi* investigates societal conceptions of hearing impairment and their influence on classroom inclusion practices, emphasizing the importance of Afrocentric approaches to education.

Chapter 7 by *Marubini Sadiki* interrogates stigmas, stereotypes, and attitudes that hinder inclusive education in South Africa, while highlighting best practices that can help overcome these challenges.

Chapter 8 by *Lawrence Meda, Laila Mohebi, and Areej ElSayary* presents teachers' experiences in an inclusive education professional development program in the UAE, showing how structured training can transform classroom practice.

Chapter 9 by *Thi Win, Jahid Siraz Chowdhury, Zulkarnain Hatta, Nor Solehatun Mohd Shakri, Noor Atieka Binti Azmi, and Bilkis Bilkis* explores the impact of stressors such as workload, gender inequality, and the COVID-19 pandemic on the mental health of educators and students in academia.

Chapter 10 by *Enas Majadley, Islam Ismail, Jihan Aloshi, and Alaviyya Nuri* provides a cross-cultural analysis of inclusive education policies and practices in Poland, Israel, and Arab-Israeli contexts, exposing gaps between policy and practice.

Chapter 11 by *Anisha Arora* surveys innovations in mental health treatment, including digital health technologies and psychotherapeutic interventions, while stressing the importance of addressing stigma and cultural context.

CONCLUSION

As this book demonstrates, the work of inclusion is both deeply contextual and universally urgent. The chapters span different continents, educational systems, and cultural realities, yet all reveal how disability and mental health remain entwined with structures of inequality. Collectively, they show that no society can claim true progress until all learners, regardless of ability or differences, are granted equal dignity and opportunity.

The findings presented here offer not only clear articulation of the challenges but also hopeful pathways forward. Whether through embracing philosophies like Ubuntu, implementing targeted professional development for teachers, or enforcing legal frameworks designed to protect the rights of persons with disabilities, the solutions are both practical and attainable. What remains is the collective will to prioritize them.

I close this preface by inviting readers—researchers, educators, policymakers, and advocates alike—to engage with these chapters critically and reflectively. Let this book serve as a tool not only for understanding but for transformation. The goal is a world where education is not a site of exclusion or marginalization, but rather a space of belonging, empowerment, and shared humanity.

Chapter 1
Safety, Inclusion, and Access to Services for Learners With Intellectual Disabilities in Southeastern, Kenya:
Intellectual Disability at a Rural County in Kenya

Nareadi Phasha
https://orcid.org/0000-0002-4763-2668
University of South Africa, South Africa

Doris Nyangoge Nyokang'i
Independent Researcher, Kenya

ABSTRACT

Kenya's legal frameworks uphold the rights of children with disabilities, ensuring dignity, safety, education, and inclusion. However, barriers such as stigma, poverty, and inadequate resources, particularly for children with intellectual disabilities in rural areas, exacerbate their vulnerability. This study explored challenges faced by learners with mild intellectual disabilities in rural southwestern Kenya, focusing on their safety, inclusion, and access to services. Using a qualitative descriptive design, the study conducted focus group discussions and interviews with 24 teachers and 35 learners from three special schools, employing English, Swahili, and Ekegusii to enhance inclusivity. Braun and Clarke's thematic framework guided data analysis, validated via participant transcript reviews and expert feedback. Key findings

DOI: 10.4018/979-8-3373-7163-4.ch001

revealed: (a) institutions' failure to meet learners' specific needs; (b) poverty and stigma limiting families' support capacity; and (c) societal attitudes and policies shaping their experiences. Systemic reforms are essential to ensure learners' safety.

INTRODUCTION

Kenya's commitment to protecting children with disabilities is enshrined in several legal provisions. For example, Chapter 4 of the Constitution of Kenya (Republic of Kenya, 2010) guarantees the rights and freedom of all individuals, explicitly including those with disabilities. Article 37(a) of the Constitution prohibits torture and any form of cruel, inhuman or degrading treatment, therefore, affirming every child's right to protection against abuse, neglect and all harmful practices. Furthermore, Section 54(3) upholds the dignity of persons with disabilities, mandating respect and the provision of assistive materials or devices to address their unique needs.

The Children's Act (Republic of Kenya, 2001) strengthens these constitutional protection by addressing issues of economic exploitation, health, and education. In particular, sections 10 and 12 of this Act prioritise the provision of appropriate care and education, specifically requiring that children with disabilities be treated with dignity and granted access to necessary medical treatment, special care, and tailored education services, preferably free or at a reduced cost. Section 18 of the same Act extends this protection by explicitly prohibiting violence, including torture or other cruel forms of treatment. Complementary to these legal provisions, the Ministry of Education, Science, and Technology (Republic of Kenya, 2012) emphasises providing educational opportunities to vulnerable groups and eliminating cultural practices that hinder access to education. Additionally, the Sex Offences Bill (Republic of Kenya, 2006) provides a legal shields against sexual abuse and exploitation, further enhancing the protective measures of this group.

Despite these clear legal frameworks, significant challenges remain in ensuring the safety, inclusion and educational opportunities for children with disabilities. The nation's commitment to create safer, accessible and inclusive learning and living environments for all, as well as achieving gender equity by 2030, necessitates an urgent focus on the situation of teen learners with mild intellectual disabilities. These individuals may require substantial support to understand complex information and cope independently (WHO, 2011), as they navigate the development and identity formation, which can involve increased risks taking behaviours. Without adequate services and with pervasive negative perceptions about disability, their rights to safety and inclusion are at risk, particularly in communities where such support is scarce.

Cultural and sociological dynamics significantly shape parents' ability to protect children with disabilities, as persistent societal stigma surrounding disabilities often breeds feelings of shame and rejection. In Kenya, these challenges are deeply rooted in cultural beliefs, where disabilities are frequently associated with witchcraft, taboos, and curses (Gona et al., 2015; Bunning et al., 2017; Ogechi & Ruto, 2002; Aley 2016). According to Bunning et al. (2017), such perceptions rarely attribute disabilities to natural elements, God's will, or biological factors. Similarly, Baffoe (2013) observed that these beliefs are fraught with fear, misunderstanding, and stereotypes. This stigma discourages many parents from advocating for their children, Couple with limited education and a lack of awareness about disability rights, the stigma prevents families from seeking essential resources or support (Koszela, 2013).

Poverty further exacerbates these challenges, as families struggling with economic hardships may view children with disabilities as burdens, leading to anger, a problem that often leads to rejection, or even abandonment (Black, 2000; Koszela, 2013; Shannon & Agorastou, 2006). In some regions, such as Kissi in Kenya, women can even be chased away from their matrimonial homes if they give birth to a child with a disability (National Gender and Equality Commission {NGEC}, 2016). In some cases, families resort to secrecy or concealment of the child's condition (Ngo et al., 2012). Societal pressure may also prompt families to place their children in orphanages or boarding facilities, mistakenly believing these institutions provide better care (Disability Rights International, 2018; Stopler, 2001). Tragically, extreme stigma can lead to harmful actions or abandonment (Rodriques, Bradshaw et al., 2018).

The interplay of gender roles and caregiving expectations further complicates these dynamics, especially in patriarchal societies where caregiving responsibilities often fall disproportionately on mother, who may face overwhelming stress without adequate support (Koszela, 2013). This can result in inadequate protection for children with disabilities. Moreover, intergenerational attitudes within families such as older relatives prioritising traditional beliefs over modern disability rights can hinder proactive care.

This study investigates the key challenges faced by learners with intellectual disabilities in rural Southwestern Kenya, focusing on issues of safety, inclusion, and access to essential services, and their impact on educational and personal development. It examines factors driving these issues and investigates potential educational and community-based interventions that can promote safer, inclusive, and equitable environments for these learners. Through this investigation, the research aims to contribute to the broader national goal of achieving gender equity and inclusive education by 2030.

Research in Africa shows that children with disabilities face heightened risks of abuse and neglect in various settings, including homes, schools, and institutional care (Crowley, 2016; Zermatten & McCallum, 2011; Save the Children, 2011). They are two to five times more likely to be abused than children who do not have a disability, and those classified as having an intellectual disability are three to eight times more likely to be abused (African Child Policy Forum 2014). Internationally, these children are at least three times more likely to experience abuse and four to five times more likely to face sexual victimisation compared to their peers without disabilities (Jones et al., 2012; The American Academy of Pediatrics, 2001). Studies in Kenya, Ghana, and other African countries reveal severe neglect and abuse, including physical violence, starvation, and abandonment (Were et al., 2016; Phasha & Myaka, 2013; Kassah, Kassah, & Abota, 2012). For instance, children with disabilities in Kenya may be hidden away, chained, or subjected to derogatory treatment (Rodriquez, Bradshaw et al., 2018). Similar issues are reported in other African nations, where children with disabilities face extreme neglect and abuse (Boersma, 2008; Stopler, 2007; Banks et al., 2017; Hodgson & Khumalo, 2016). Incidences of being looked are in a degrading manner and called derogatory names were reported (Aldersey et al., 2018; Haihambo and Lightfood, 2010).

In educational settings, children with disabilities often face significant barriers that hinder learning experiences and opportunities. These challenges are rooted in inadequate resources, negative attitudes from teachers, and poor learning environments are common issues (du Toit, 1996; Engelbrecht, 2006; Human Rights Watch, 2015; Mwoma, 2017). Cultural norms and prejudices further exacerbate these barriers by perpetuating exclusions and discouraging parental engagement, particularly in rural areas where such attitudes may be more deeply entrenched.

These challenges are particularly pronounced in special schools in Kenya, where insufficient materials and facilities compound the difficulties faced by learners with disabilities (Wanjohi, 2019; Mburu, 2017). As a result, these conditions contributes to low enrolment and participation rates, particularly in rural areas where resources and support are even scarcer (Moyi, 2017).

Investigating abuse, neglect and exclusions faced by learners with intellectual disabilities is crucial, as existing studies in Kenya have largely overlooked their specific experiences. The majority of studies tend to focus, often on broader categories of disability, which obscure the unique challenges faced by those with intellectual disabilities. The limited research available does not adequately capture the extent of their vulnerability, particularly in rural areas where access to resources and educational opportunities is even more constrained. Consequently, there is a pressing need for more focused research that highlights the distinct experiences of learners with intellectual disabilities, enabling the development of targeted interventions that address their specific needs and promote inclusion.

The social model of disability provides a critical lens through which this issue was investigated. From this perspective, disability is framed as a social justice matter and the responsibility of removing barriers and creating inclusive environments is placed squarely with the society (Shakespeare, 2013). Thus, the focus shifts away from individual limitations to the systematic factors such as stigma, discrimination and inadequate services, which perpetuate exclusion (Loewen & Pollard, 2010). This transformative approach advocates for dignity, respect and equal opportunities for persons with disabilities (Terzi, 2014; Shakespeare & Watson, 2002), aligning closely with Kenya's legal commitments and aspirations for inclusion and gender equity.

In the context of learners with mild intellectual disabilities, the social model highlights how societal barriers, rather than the disabilities themselves, create obstacles to their safety, inclusion and development. Therefore, the social model as used in this chapter will facilitate the identification and challenge the societal and structural inequities hat hinder progress, while advocating for intervention that promote accessible and equitable educational and living environments. Through this lens (of the social model), this investigation will move beyond individual experiences and uncover the broader systemic changes necessary to ensure that children with disabilities are not only protected by also empowered. The transformative principles of this model serve as a foundation for redefining disability as an integral part of human diversity and advancing Kenya's broader goals of inclusion and equity.

METHODS

This study employed a qualitative descriptive design, a method not anchored in any particular disciplinary tradition or methodological framework (Lambert & Lambert, 2012). This approach is particularly well-suited for research where the aim is to gather information directly from individuals experiencing the phenomenon under investigation (Bradshaw, Atkinson & Doody, 2017). The decision to use this design was influenced by the limited research in this area, the sensitive nature of the topic, and societal perceptions of disability. The design provided flexibility in exploring various issues and allowed participants the freedom to express their views in their own unique ways.

The study was conducted in a rural county in southwestern Kenya, following ethical clearance from the National Commission for Science, Technology, and Innovation, and obtaining permission from the relevant education districts, three special schools, and parents or legal guardians, as well as committees representing them. Also, ethical clearance at the authors' institution in South Africa was obtained. Among the participating schools, two catered specifically to learners with intellectual disabilities, while the third served both deaf learners and those with intellectual disabilities. All three schools provided boarding facilities, although some learners commuted daily to and from school.

SAMPLE

Purposive sampling was employed to identify participants, including both learners and teachers. This strategy enabled the selection of individuals whose characteristics or experiences were particularly relevant to the study's objectives (Bradshaw, Atkinson, & Doody, 2017; Babbie & Mouton, 2009). Teachers were invited to an initial meeting where the study was explained in detail. This included discussions on data collection methods, research ethics, audio recording of interviews, and the availability of psychological support. Teachers were provided with a brief version of the research proposal to review, allowing them to seek clarification before voluntarily expressing their interest in participating. Once teachers expressed interest, they were asked to sign a consent form. Selection criteria for teachers were based on two key factors: (a) having received a disclosure of abuse or neglect from a learner, and (b) having supported a learner suspected or reported to have experienced abuse or neglect.

Learners were recruited with the assistance of teachers appointed by the school principals, based on their roles in managing learner challenges or their qualifications in Guidance and Counselling. Four criteria guided the selection of learners: (a) the ability to express themselves with a reasonable degree of clarity; (b) being between 16 and 21 years old; (c) a willingness to participate without coercion; and (d) written permission from parents or legal guardians. The second author explained the study and relevant research ethics to the learners in a mix of Swahili, English, and the local language. This explanation was repeated individually for each learner after they indicated interest in participating. Throughout the study, the learners' rights to participate voluntarily and withdraw at any time without negative consequences were emphasised. The principles of confidentiality, anonymity, and the absence of payment for participation were also stressed. Learners were encouraged to ask questions, which they did.

The final sample consisted of 24 teachers (8 males and 16 females) and 35 learners (24 girls and 11 boys) with mild intellectual disabilities. Of the learners, 22 (15 girls and 7 boys) resided in the school hostels, while 13 (9 girls and 4 boys) were day learners.

DATA COLLECTION

Data collection was conducted through focus group discussions (FGDs) and individual interviews. These two strategies permitted a comprehensive understanding of the topic from both collective and individual perspective. FGDs were particularly useful in gathering group opinions and uncovering shared experiences, as they encouraged dynamic exchange of ideas and facilitated the expression of diverse perspectives on the topic under investigation (Denscombe, 2008). The group setting also enabled participants to build on each other's contributions, therefore providing a a richer data that might not have emerged in isolation.

In contrast, individual interviews offered a more private and less intimidating space for participants to share personal experiences, that include sensitive or 'stigmatised" information that they might have been reluctant to share in a group. This method provided an opportunity for a deeper exploration of perspectives as participants were able to express themselves openly without fear of judgement. Both FGDs and individual interviews uses open-ended questions to encourage detailed responses. Additional probing helped to obtain clarity on specific issues.

Data collection sessions were strategically held at the school as this was a familiar and accessible environments for participants. Sessions were scheduled during lunch breaks or after school to reduce disruption to daily routines, with each session lasting between 45 and 60 minutes. This timing ensured that participants could contribute without feeling rushed or overburdened,

The interviews were conducted in English, Swahili, and Ekegusii, depending on the participants' preferences. This was to ensure inclusivity and to accommodate different levels of language proficiency. This approach enhanced communication and created a comfortable atmosphere for participants to express themselves in the language they felt most confident using.

Participants' responses were documented both manually and via audio recordings, with their consent obtained beforehand to ensure ethical compliance and transparency. The use of audio recording allowed for the capturing of nuanced responses, while manual note taking facilitated real-time documentation of key issues. At the conclusion of each session, a summary of the key points discussed was provided to participants to ensure accuracy. This also offered an opportunity to clarify or elaborate on any issues. Additionally, participants were reminded about the availability of psychological support if needed.

FOCUS GROUP DISCUSSIONS WITH TEACHERS

We organised three groups of teachers, each comprising 6 to 10 members, with one group from each participating school. This structure allowed for diverse perspectives to be captured from various educational environments. Two groups consented to audio recordings of their discussions. The third group expressed discomfort with being recorded, but agreed to allow note-taking. To ensure accuracy, these notes were later shared with them for confirmation and validation. This encouraged a collaborative approach to data integrity.

The discussions were facilitated by the first author, who led them in English to maintain clarity and structure, while the second author provided support by taking notes and interpreting words spoken in Swahili and Ekegusii, as needed. Dual facilitation ensured effective communication and inclusivity and allowed all participants to express themselves in the language of their choice.

The focus of the discussion was carefully framed around two key areas: a) Teachers' views on the general treatment of learners with disabilities in comparison to their peers or relatives without disabilities. b) Observations of neglect and/or abuse directed towards learners with disabilities, as well as any incidents that had been reported within the school environment.

FOCUS GROUP DISCUSSIONS WITH LEARNERS

We conducted focus group discussions (FGDs) with three groups of learners, each consisting of 6 to 10 members, with one group from each participating school. This setup ensured a diverse range of perspectives that reflects the experiences of learners across educational environments. The discussions were facilitated by the second author, who used a combination of English, Swahili, and Ekegusii to ensure clear communication and inclusivity. This advance an open and participatory atmosphere. The first author took notes and documented the learners' gestures and non-verbal cues as a way to capture the full breadth of their interactions.

To create a safe and supportive environment, learners were informed at the outset that there were no right or wrong answers. They were encouraged to seek clarification if they did not understand a question or needed further guidance during the discussions. Additionally, they were reminded of their right to withdraw from the study at any time or to refrain from answering questions if they felt uncomfortable. Learners were also asked to speak one at a time to ensure that everyone had an opportunity to contribute.

Each group participated in two sessions of FGDs. The decision to conduct two sessions was deliberate, as it provided an opportunity for learners to become more comfortable and familiar with the process. It was observed that most participants became more engaged and forthcoming in the second session, probably due to the rapport established during the initial meeting. This progression indicated the importance of building trust and advancing a sense of security among participants.

The discussions focused on the following questions: a) How would you describe the way you are treated at home, at school, and within your community? b) How would you explain that treatment, particularly in relation to how others, such as family members and community members, are treated?

INDIVIDUAL INTERVIEWS WITH PRINCIPALS

The three principals of the participating schools, along with five learners who felt uncomfortable participating in the FGDs, were interviewed individually. This provided an alternative method for gathering data valuable from individuals who might otherwise opted out of the study. The principals were unable to join the FGDs with the teachers due to their demanding work schedules. Their insights offered leadership perspective on the challenges faced by learners with disabilities. The first author conducted the interviews with the principals in English to maintain consistency and clarity in communication.

For the learner interviews, the second author facilitated discussions with learners using a mix of English, Swahili, and Ekegusii to ensure clarity and comfort. During the individual interviews with learners, some were able to share personal experiences, including instances of sexual abuse, which they felt more comfortable discussing in a private setting. The topics explored in these interviews were similar to those discussed during the FGDs, allowing for consistency in the information gathered across different methods of data collection.

DATA ANALYSIS

Thematic data analysis, which commenced during fieldwork, followed the steps outlined by Braun and Clarke (2006). The process included the following steps: (a) listening to audio recordings:(b) identifying initial codes; (c) searching for themes and sub-themes; (d) refining and naming themes; and (e) writing up the narrative. Both authors conducted the analysis independently to minimise bias. The second author, fluent in Swahili and the local languages, translated the non-English portions of the data.

To enhance the credibility of the findings, a series of validation measures were implemented. Transcripts were cross-checked with teachers, who reviewed them alongside the notes taken during the interviews. For the learners, the second author read their transcripts back to them for verification and corrections where necessary. Additionally, both authors exchanged their individual analyses and engaged in a discussion to identify gaps, validate thematic patterns and refine interpretations. These sessions were complemented by critical feedback from two experienced researchers, whose external perspectives further ensured rigorous evaluation of the thematic analysis. The first experienced researcher was a disability strategist who brought a rights-based perspective an in-depth knowledge of systemic barriers to inclusion; while the second researcher, with a deep understanding of sociocultural dynamics in rural Kenya, provided invaluable contextual insights.

RESULTS

Several issues emerged in relation to the learners with intellectual disabilities' safety, inclusion and access to essential services. Their implication on the learners' educational and personal development were also noted. To facilitate an understanding, the issues are organised under three main areas: (a) the failure of the educational institutions to adequately address the needs of learners with intellectual disabilities; (b) the impact of poverty and stigma on the families' ability to support learners with intellectual disabilities; and (c) community attitudes and policies in shaping the experiences of persons with disabilities.

EDUCATIONAL INSTITUTIONS' FAILURE TO ADEQUATELY ADDRESS THE NEEDS OF LEARNERS WITH INTELLECTUAL DISABILITIES

The provision of a supportive and effective educational environment for learners with intellectual disabilities emerged as a pressing concern throughout the discussions. Participants described how inadequate infrastructure, insufficient resources, and poor safety measures jeopardise not only the quality of education but also the overall well-being of the leaners. This issue was highlighted by nine participants, who mentioned the problem of overcrowding in special schools, largely attributed to limited government funding. Principals shared similar accounts of how these infrastructure constraints negatively affect the schools. Principal A noted:

> *"Last year we were forced to partition one class to create a dormitory because of an accommodation problem. The problem is that government funding to special schools is too limited. At this point we cannot even feed these children, hence we are looking for donation."*

This reality paints a clear picture of schools struggling with insufficient space, leaving them unable to provide the necessary facilities for proper learning and living arrangements. The repurposing of spaces, such as turning classrooms or computer labs into dormitories, reflects the dire compromises that institutions are forced to make in the face of insufficient support. In some instances, learners were reported to share beds, indicating the strain placed on the already overcrowded facilities.

Principal C detailed the negative effects of this space shortage when describing the lack of proper playing fields for learners and the unfortunate politics that frustrated plans to relocate the school to a more suitable site. He particularly lamented that the problem has left learners "*squeezed up in classes and dormitories*" with little room for essential developmental activities. The principal pointed to a small locked room containing 50 unused computers, which was donated two years ago, but yet to be used due to the lack of a designated space for them. He also mentioned that:

"This situation affects our learners badly because they are missing out on the opportunity to learn computer skills".

He also added that these missed opportunities highlight not just the immediate struggles of overcrowding but also the long-term impacts on learners' development and future prospects.

In addition to the lack of infrastructure, the lack of fencing and the absence of security guards on school premises was also highlighted as compromising the safety of learners. With great concern, Principal B, noted:

"Madam, we used to have a watchman until December 2012. Then the government reduced funding. The watchman was never paid, and so he resigned. As you can see there is no fence. Anyone get access from any side of the school.

The principal's frustration was noticeable as he described the interim measure of installing strong grilled doors in dormitories to offer learners some form of protection during the night. He expressed:

Learners are not safe, and there is nothing we can do. When funds are available, we will construct the fence. For now, we have put a strong grill doors in their dormitories where they sleep."

This solution indicates the broader issue of resource scarcity that forces schools to prioritise urgent needs at the expense of comprehensive safety measures.

A pressing matter raised by 12 participants relates to bathroom facilities. They noted the absence of bathroom or their presence, but lacking doors and/or windows. This creates not only a lack of privacy, but also exposes learners, especially girls, to unwelcome behaviours from their male peers. Lydia, one of the learners, recounted:

"Some windows are broken and boys come in our dormitories at night. Some bathrooms do not have windows and doors, and so boys peep through when we bath. Sometimes they come to our bathrooms to touch our breasts and laugh at us." [Lydia]

Lydia's words provide an account of the vulnerabilities faced by young girls in these environments. This indicates the urgent need for intervention to address both infrastructural and behavioural concerns.

THE IMPACT OF POVERTY AND STIGMA ON THE FAMILY ABILITY TO SUPPORT LEARNERS WITH INTELLECTUAL DISABILITIES

Learners shared emotionally charged accounts of financial neglect and limited provisions for basic needs, such as travel fares, hygiene products, and lunch money. These challenges are particularly acute for day learners, with five female participants highlighting how financial difficulties force them to make arduous commutes or consider dropping out of school entirely. Maya, an 18-year-old learner, lamented:

"I either have to walk that distance or drop out from school because I do not get money from home."

This choice highlights the systemic failure to address the vulnerabilities faced by these learners. Hloni, aged 17, added:

"I walk to school during cold or hot days. I do so even ... eh... even when it is rainy. My mom does not have money for transport. That is why I am always tired in class."

Hloni's words clearly illustrate the physical and emotional toll on learners whose families struggle to provide even the most basic resources.

Boarding learners also shared their plight, with 14 learners reporting the lack of essential hygiene products, such as toiletries and sanitary towels. Rhoda, a 16-year-old participant, offered this account:

"Usually, I don't have sanitary towels since my mother never buys for me. She always says that she has no money. So ekero amanyinga agocha (when my menstruation comes), I remain in bed and pretend to be sick because I don't have anything to use and I can't go to the classes."

This excerpt highlights how the lack of support profoundly impacts educational participation and dignity. Teachers noted the correlation between these issues and absenteeism, as learners often skipped classes to manage hygiene needs privately.

The role of stigma emerged as a central theme in the unequal distribution of responsibilities and resources within families. Nine learners described being treated unfairly compared to their siblings, often burdened with heavy chores or denied allowances provided to their brothers and sisters. Guluba explained:

"I do not rest when I am at home. I do all the heavy jobs, and they ask me to go anywhere and at any time without asking [me] whether I am tired or not (sighs)."

Similarly, Kubibi shared feelings of alienation, stating:

"I do everything that my sisters and brothers do not do. Sometimes I feel as if I am being punished."

Zodike's experience revealed neglect of educational priorities:

"My parents give money to my sister, but to me, they just say you can walk to school or stay at home. Since I take my schooling seriously, I walk."

These accounts reflect deep-rooted biases and the devaluation of learners with intellectual disabilities within their own families.

Isolation from family contact emerged as another recurring issue, with 15 learners and 14 teachers emphasising the lack of visitation or communication from families while children reside in hostels. Most learners are collected only at the end of the academic year, with few experiencing visits or family interaction during school terms. Mashele poignantly shared:

"My parents think it is best if I stay here because the school will look after me. They promise to visit, but that does not happen. I no longer ask."

Jappie corroborated:

"Some go home after some months, but otherwise ... most of us go home at the end of year, just for Christmas. It is like that every year."

Teachers viewed these situations as symptomatic of families offloading caregiving responsibilities onto schools. Teacher Johannes remarked:

"Relatives drop them at school when we reopen and collect them at the end of the term. Before the new rule, some children used to be left at special schools over the holidays because they were never collected. However, with the new law all parents must collect their children, or they get arrested for neglect."

Despite this improvement, the limited contact continues to impact learners' emotional well-being, potentially destroying family relationships and hindering emotional development.

The issue of addressing violations involving learners with intellectual disabilities revealed troubling patterns of familial inaction and corruption. Teachers noted that many families settle cases out of court, often accepting bribes in exchange for silence. Teacher Masindi highlighted:

"Madam, abaibori nigo bakobwata chibesa, nobokima batagete, kobua abana babo (parents take bribes, they want food). Even if we try to advise them to follow the cases against the perpetrators, they are hesitant."

Martha, a learner, disclosed her painful experience of being silenced:

"The man who forced himself on me gave my parents money to keep quiet. I know that some meetings took place between him, my father, and my uncle, and later he brought some parcels and money to my father. They later informed me that the matter was resolved and that I must never talk about it to anybody."

These revelations do not only demonstrate how poverty and stigma contribute to neglect of learners with disabilities, but they also indicate how they actively undermine justice for victims by perpetuating cycles of abuse and marginalisation. These systemic failures reveal an urgent need for holistic interventions to address educational barriers, promote equity, and ensure justice, while empowering families to promote inclusive and supportive environments.

COMMUNITY ATTITUDES AND POLICIES INFLUENCE THE EXPERIENCES OF PWDs

Community attitudes and policies play a pivotal role in influencing the experiences of persons with disabilities (PwDs), particularly learners with intellectual disabilities. As they travel to and from school, these learners face heightened vulnerability to exploitation and abuse, often at the hands of individuals who prey on their circumstances. Perpetrators exploit their need for basic necessities, such as transportation or food by using coercion or enticement to manipulate them into compromising situations. This vulnerability is compounded by the absence of protective measures and support systems, leaving learners exposed to repeated harm. Teacher Joseph shared a distressing account:

"We have received reports from our students about abuses as they travel to and from school. They give in for sex with the matatu (taxi) or motorbike, just to get a ride to school or home. At times they are hungry, and so people deceive them for sex, in return for as little as ten shillings. Last year we had such a case where two of our girls fell for this trap. They were abused and exploited after being convinced with only a cup of tea and mandazi (fried cakes), because they were hungry."

This reality signifies the intersection of poverty and exploitation, where basic needs become tools for manipulation. Teacher Majuba added:

"It also happens to boys. Last year we had a boy who reported that he frequently had sexual encounters with a barber in exchange for shaving his head."

These accounts reveal the pervasive nature of abuse, affecting both male and female learners, and highlight the urgent need for community-driven interventions to address these vulnerabilities.

Learners themselves corroborated these experiences, shedding light on the emotional toll of such encounters. Josephine shared:

"As I walk to and from school, it is like every man wants to talk to me. If I just pass them, both young and old men call me, whistle, laugh, and call me names that I do not like. They call me mpumbavu (less intelligent)."

These words reflect not only the harassment faced by learners but also the stigma attached to intellectual disabilities, which further isolates them and diminishes their sense of self-worth.

The systemic failure to protect learners with intellectual disabilities extends beyond community interactions to the legal system. When cases involving these learners reach court, they are often prolonged and dismissed due to manipulation or lack of evidence, which may have been lost over time. Teacher Laurens recounted:

"The case of a boy who was sexually molested by the barber went on for almost two and a half years. They ended up saying that there was no strong evidence to convict the alleged perpetrator because the boy forgot some information."

This highlights the challenges faced by learners with intellectual disabilities in recalling and articulating their experiences, which perpetrators exploit to evade accountability.

Teacher Sekonko emphasised the role of corruption and systemic bias in perpetuating these injustices:

"Incidents involving people with good relations with the police or who have money are thrown out very easily. They would be recalled and recalled, and at the end, they will come up with some story. That is why some perpetrators repeat the crimes, because they know how to manipulate the system to their advantage. Unfortunately, it is the children who suffer... The police fail them."

These observations reveal a troubling pattern where wealth and influence shield perpetrators from consequences, leaving vulnerable learners without recourse or justice.

The exploitation and systemic neglect of learners with intellectual disabilities expose critical gaps in community safety and legal protections. These failures not only undermine trust in the justice system but also perpetuate cycles of abuse and marginalisation. Addressing these issues requires a multifaceted approach, including strengthening legal frameworks, enhancing community awareness, and implementing vigorous protective measures to safeguard the rights and dignity of PwDs. The narratives shared by teachers and learners call for the urgency of these interventions. They highlight the need for systemic change to break the cycle of exploitation and neglect.

DISCUSSION

The findings of this study support UNICEF's (2018) observation that persons with disabilities are largely invisible in society; and they are frequently overlooked by government services, denied access to education, and compelled to live in unsafe conditions (Zermatten & McCallum, 2011). They often face isolation from their families and communities, rendering them vulnerable to neglect and abuse from an early age (Barriga, Buchanan, Ceremovic, et al., 2017; Save the Children, 2011).

The finding about severe inadequacies in educational and boarding facilities for learners with intellectual disabilities is in alignment with studies conducted in Kenya such as Wanjohi (2019); Mburu (2017); Mwoma (2017). The problem highlights critical challenges concerning safety, inclusion, and access to services. Safety is paramount in educational environments, particularly for these vulnerable learners who may be more susceptible to exploitation and harm. Unfenced and unguarded buildings create direct risks, making learners targets for abuse by passerby. In addition, poorly maintained facilities, such as bathrooms lacking basic privacy and sanitation, compromise physical safety and learners' dignity and self-esteem. The constant threat of harm can lead to anxiety and fear that may interfere with the learner's ability to focus on learning. Similarly, overcrowded classrooms and inadequate facilities can complicate classroom management and hinder the ability to tailor instruction to meet diverse needs. This could breed a cycle of exclusion, leaving learners without the necessary support to integrate into society. This finding reflects a deeper reluctance by governments to invest in the education of children with disabilities, possibly driven by outdated beliefs that they are incapable of success (NGEC, 2016; Opoku et al., 2020). Marginalisation runs deep, with ineffective policies, underfunding, and a lack of enforcement exacerbating the problem (Stopler, 2007).

Without proper resources or safe environments, learners with disabilities remain marginalised, denied the rights and protections outlined in the CRC (1988) and impeding global goals for equity in education. Therefore, the need to address the shortage of facilities in schools for learners with intellectual disability cannot be overstated, as that is necessary to encourage an environment where they can thrive. By doing so, governments and school would not only be fulfilling their legal and ethical obligations, but also contribute to building a more equitable society that recognises and nurtures the potential of every individual.

Families also have their own share in contributing to the children's safety, inclusion and access to facilities. Though placing children in boarding facilities could be attributable to various reasons. In some instances, families choose to send these children to boarding facilities as a way to cope with societal stigma or to alleviate the stress associated with community perceptions of disability (Koszela, 2013; Ngo et al., 2012). In some instances, it could be motivated by lack of community schools that cater for such learners as specialised schools tend to be centralised for facility sharing. This decision can also enable families to focus on the needs of other children and maintain stability at home, while simultaneously allowing unemployed parents to seek employment (Opoku et al., 2017; Badu, 2016). Whatever reason may be, the decision to place children in boarding school can inadvertently isolate children from essential familial support and emotional connections (Koszela, 2013; Ngo et al., 2012). If they stay in boarding facilities for longer periods without familial contact, their self-worth could be diminished as they may internalise the belief that they are less valued than their siblings. This can heighten their vulnerability to exploitation by individuals who offer affection and attention that the learners lack at home. This emotional void poses significant risks to their social and psychological development.

Deprivation of basic needs and disparities in allocation of resources can exacerbate the challenges faced by learners with intellectual disabilities. As revealed in this study, families experiencing financial strain may prioritise the needs of non-disabled siblings, leaving their children with disabilities without essential resources such as food, clothing, and educational support (Banks et al., 2017; Stopler, 2007). This imbalance can lead to feelings of neglect and further isolate these children from their peers. In addition, societal misconceptions about the capabilities of children with disabilities can result in them being burdened with excessive responsibilities. The challenge is that when society fails to recognise their rights and needs, it perpetuates cycles of inequity and exploitation that are difficult to break (Phasha & Myaka, 2014). Such misconceptions undermine their rights and dignity.

Parents' reliance on traditional justice systems rather than formal legal channels could further complicate the safety of learners with intellectual disability. Local mediation may provide quicker resolutions; however, it often prioritises community reputation over the rights and needs of victims (Muigus, 2017). This can leave children feeling powerless and unaware of the proceedings surrounding incidents of violence against them. When families accept settlements without consulting the affected child, it can create a deep sense of betrayal and erode trust in caregivers (Stopler, 2007).

Traveling to and from school presents significant safety risks for learners with intellectual disabilities, who are often vulnerable to exploitation in the forms of sexual abuse and being called derogatory name-calling. This vulnerability is shaped by a complex interplay of social, economic, and cultural factors that are compounded by a lack of awareness, empathy, and institutional safeguards. The perception of persons with intellectual disabilities as inferior with limited ability to advocate for their own rights or defend themselves often breeds an environment where they become easy targets for exploitation. Perpetrators feel emboldened by the assumption that learners with disabilities cannot report or resist the abuse. In the same vein, abusers frequently exploit the child's inherent trust and limited understanding of complex situations, preying on their dependency. They may offer basic necessities that the child's family cannot afford, in exchange for sexual favours. Their need for attention and affection can be exploited by perpetrators who shower them with gifts or promises of care. Lacking the emotional or cognitive capacity to recognise inappropriate behaviour, the child becomes an easy target for coercion, as the abuser exploits their emotional vulnerability to manipulate them into sexual acts.

Delays in the prosecution of crimes against learners/children with intellectual disability due to corruption within the legal system further threaten their safety. Studies, including those by Stopler (2006), Aley (2016), and Shumba (2006), have documented a troubling tendency for some officials to accept bribes from perpetrators. Such practices not only compromise the integrity of the judicial process but also cultivate widespread distrust in the justice system. Victims and their families may become disillusioned, fearing that reporting abuse will lead to inaction or further victimisation, thereby perpetuating a cycle of abuse. This systemic failure to protect vulnerable populations constitutes a violation of their fundamental rights, leaving them in precarious situations that heighten their susceptibility to further exploitation.

CONCLUSION

The findings of this study point to the urgent need for systemic reforms across multiple sectors to ensure that children with intellectual disabilities are afforded their fundamental rights to safety, education, and inclusion. Firstly, the significant inadequacies in educational facilities such as overcrowded classrooms, unsafe infrastructure, and lack of specialised support suggests the need for immediate investment in accessible and inclusive educational environments. The government must prioritise funding for specialised schools, ensure proper teacher training, and improve the safety of educational facilities to ensure an environment where children with intellectual disabilities can thrive academically and socially. This includes fencing, secure buildings, clean and private sanitation facilities, and specialised classrooms tailored to diverse needs. Schools should introduce comprehensive safety protocols, including regular monitoring of facilities, professional child protection officers, and advocacy workshops to empower learners to identify inappropriate behaviour.

Integrating inclusive education in teacher training programs and providing ongoing professional development for educators would enable institutions to address the barriers faced by learners with disabilities effectively. Inclusive curricula should also focus on encouraging understanding and empathy among peers to create supportive learning environments. This would not only fulfil legal obligations under international conventions such as the Convention on the Rights of the Child (CRC, 1989) but also contribute to broader goals of educational equity and social justice. Importantly, if governments should consider incentivising community schools to provide inclusive education as that would go a long way in reducing the burden on families and ensuring local access to quality education.

The emotional isolation and vulnerability experienced by children in boarding schools accentuates the damaging impact of societal stigma. These challenges can be effectively addressed through community education and awareness campaigns aimed at reshaping societal attitudes and reducing discrimination. Partnerships with non-governmental organisations (NGOs) could amplify these efforts by leveraging their expertise and resources. Such initiatives are key for encouraging inclusive environments where children with intellectual disabilities feel supported, accepted and valued. They could help integrate children into everyday social structures and in reducing their marginalisation. Importantly, these efforts also contribute to the development of support systems that lessen reliance on institutional care, such as boarding schools. Through this collaborative approach, socio-cultural and economic barriers can be addressed comprehensively. When children receive care within their communities, their well-being could also improve.

Reforming the legal system is essential to protect the rights and well-being of children with intellectual disabilities and to ensure cases of reported abuse and exploitation are addressed with the urgency and sensitivity they deserve. The government must play a leading role by introducing accountability measures to enforce policies effectively and tackle corruption, which continues to undermine judicial processes. Also, establishing transparent reporting systems could ensure that cases are handled ethically and efficiently, while dedicated oversight committees can provide an additional layer of accountability. These measures are essential for restoring public trust in legal institutions. Collectively, they would create a legal environment that prioritises justice and safeguards the most vulnerable members of society.

In addition to these reforms, judicial systems must adopt measures that strengthen their overall capacity to handle disability-related cases effectively. This include training law enforcement officials to handle cases involving persons with disabilities as that would encourage sensitivity and professionalism in addressing the unique challenges these cases may present. Additionally, awareness campaigns targeted at families can empower them about their legal rights and build confidence in pursuing justice. Similarly, developing disability-specific legal frameworks and accessible reporting mechanisms would give victims and their families the tools to seek justice more effectively. These should occur alongside victim support initiatives tailored to the needs of children with disabilities such as psychological and rehabilitation services, and specialised shelters. Partnerships between community policing and local organisations would further increase vigilance and responsiveness at the grassroots level. This multifaceted approach would not only reform the legal system but also promote systemic change across societal structures and ensure that children with intellectual disabilities are comprehensively protected and included.

REFERENCES

African Child Policy Forum. (2014). *The African report on children with disabilities: Promising starts and persisting challenges*. Central Printing Press.

Aldersey, H. M., Kavira, S., Kiasmbua, J., Lokako, W., Miaka, P., & Monte, L. (2018). Stigma experienced by families with members with intellectual disabilities in Kinshasa, Democratic Republic of the Congo. *Intervention (Amstelveen, Netherlands)*, *16*(2), 119–128.

Aley, R. (2016). *An assessment of the social, cultural and institutional factors contributing to the sexual abuse of persons with disabilities in East Africa*. Advantage Africa.

Babbie, E., & Mouton, J. (2009). *The practice of social research*. Oxford University Press.

Badu, E. (2016). Experiences of children with intellectual disabilities in the Ashanti Region of Ghana. *Journal of Social Inclusion*, *7*(1), 20–30.

Baffoe, M. (2013). Stigma, discrimination and marginalisation: Gateway to oppression of persons with disabilities in Ghana, West Africa. *Journal of Educational and Social Research*, *3*(1), 187–193.

Banks, L. M., Kelly, S. A., & Kyegombe, N.. (2017). If he could speak, he would be able to point out who does those things to him: Experiences of violence against children with disabilities in Uganda and Malawi. *PLoS One*, *12*(9), e0183736. PMID: 28926598

Black, M. (2000). The roots of child neglect. In Reece, R. M. (Ed.), *Treatment of child abuse: Common ground for mental health, medical, and legal practitioners* (pp. 157–164). Johns Hopkins University Press.

Boersma, J. M. F. (2008). *Violence against Ethiopian children with disabilities: The stories and perspectives of children* (Unpublished PhD thesis). University of Amsterdam, Netherlands. Retrieved from https://www.dcdd.nl

Bradshaw, C., Atkinson, S., & Doody, O. (2017). Employing a qualitative descriptive approach in health care research. *Global Qualitative Nursing Research*, *4*(1), 1–8. PMID: 29204457

Bunning, K., Gona, J. K., Newton, C. R., & Hartley, S. (2017). The perception of disability by community groups: Stories of local understanding, beliefs and challenges in a rural part of Kenya. *PLoS One*, *12*(8), e0182214. PMID: 28771637

Crowley, P. E. (2016). Preventing abuse and neglect in the lives of children with disabilities. In Crowley, P. E. (Ed.), *Preventing abuse and neglect in the lives of children with disabilities* (pp. 239–266). Springer.

Denscombe, M. (2008). *The Good Research Guide for small-scale social research projects* (3rd ed.). Open University Press.

Du Toit, L. (1996). An introduction to specialised education. In Engelbrecht, P., Kriegler, S. M., & Booysen, M. I. (Eds.), *Perspectives on learning difficulties: International concerns and South African realities* (pp. 5–19). Van Schaik.

Engelbrecht, P. (2006). The implementation of inclusive education in South Africa after ten years of democracy. *European Journal of Psychology of Education*, *21*(3), 253–264.

Gona, J. K., Newton, C. R., & Rimba, K.. (2015). Parents' and professionals' perceptions on causes and treatment options for autism spectrum disorders in a multicultural context on the Kenyan coast. *PLoS One*, *12*(1), e0132729. PMID: 26267668

Haihambo, C., & Lightfoot, E. (2010). Cultural beliefs about disability in Namibia: Implications for inclusion of people with disabilities. *International Journal of Special Education*, *25*(3), 76–87.

Hodgson, T. F., & Khumalo, S. (2016). Too many children left behind: Exclusion in the South African inclusive education system, with a focus on the Umkhanyakude District, KwaZulu-Natal. *A Section 27 Report*. Retrieved March 17, 2024, from www.section27.org.za

Human Rights Watch. (2015). *Complicit in exclusion: South Africa's failure to guarantee an inclusive education for children with disabilities*. Human Rights Watch.

Jones, L., Bellis, M. A., Wood, S., Hughes, K., McCoy, E., Eckley, L., Bates, G., Mikton, C., Shakespeare, T., & Officer, A. (2012). Prevalence and risk of violence against children with disabilities: A systematic review and meta-analysis of observational studies. *Lancet*, *380*(9845), 899–907. DOI: 10.1016/S0140-6736(12)60692-8 PMID: 22795511

Kassah, K. A., Kassah, B., & Abota, K. (2012). Abuse of disabled children in Ghana. *Disability & Society*, *25*(5), 1–13.

Koszela, K. (2013). The stigmatisation of disabilities in Africa and the developmental effects. *Independent Study Project (ISP) collection 1639*. University of Texas at Austin, US, Summer.

Lambert, V. A., & Lambert, C. E. (2012). Qualitative descriptive research: An acceptable design. *Pacific Rim International Journal of Nursing*, *16*(4), 255–256.

Loewen, G., & Pollard, W. (2010). The social justice perspective. *Journal of Post-secondary Education and Disability*, *23*(1), 5–18.

Mburu, S. (2017). Challenges faced by schools for disabled children in Kenya. *Kenyaplex*, *15*(October), 3.

Moyi, P. (2017). School enrolment and attendance for children with disabilities in Kenya: An examination of household survey data. *Forum of International Research in Education*, *4*(2), 1–21.

Mwoma, T. (2017). Education for children with special needs in Kenya: A review of related literature. *Journal of Education and Practice*, *8*(28), 188–200.

Ngo, H., Shin, J. Y., Nhan, N. V., & Yang, L. H. (2012). Stigma and restriction on the social life of families of children with intellectual disabilities in Vietnam. *Singapore Medical Journal*, *53*(7), 451–457. PMID: 22815013

Ogechi, N. O., & Ruto, S. J. (2002). Portrayal of disability through personal names and proverbs in Kenya: Evidence from Ekegusii and Nandi. *Stichproben. Wiener Zeitschrift für Kritische Afrikastudien, 3*(2).

Opoku, M. P., Nketsia, W., Banye, M. A., Mprah, W. K., Dogbe, J. A., & Badu, E. (2020). Caregiving experiences and expectations of parents with in-school children with intellectual disability in Ghana. *Research in Developmental Disabilities*, *96*. Advance online publication. DOI: 10.1016/j.ridd.2019.103524 PMID: 31739195

Phasha, T. N., & Myaka, L. D. (2014). Sexuality and sexual abuse involving teenagers with intellectual disability: Community conceptions in a rural village of KwaZulu-Natal, South Africa. *Sexuality and Disability*, *32*(2), 153–165.

Republic of Kenya. (2001). *The Children's Act (No. 8)*. Nairobi: The National Council for Law Reporting with the Authority of the Attorney General. Retrieved from www.kenyalaw.org

Republic of Kenya. (2006). *The Sexual Offences Act (No. 3)*. Nairobi: The National Council for Law Reporting with the Authority of the Attorney General. Retrieved from www.kenyalaw.org

Republic of Kenya. (2010). *The Constitution*. Nairobi, Kenya: The National Council for Law Reporting with the Authority of the Attorney General. Retrieved from www.kenyalaw.org

Republic of Kenya. (2012). *The Task Force on the Re-alignment of the Education Sector to the Constitution of Kenya, 2010: Towards a globally competitive quality education for sustainable development.* Report of the Task Force. Nairobi: The National Council for Law Reporting with the Authority of the Attorney General. Retrieved from www.kenyalaw.org

Save the Children. (2011). *Out of the shadows: Sexual violence against children with disabilities.* Save the Children.

Shakespeare, T. (2013). The social model of disability. In Davis, L. J. (Ed.), *The Disability Studies Reader* (4th ed., pp. 214–221). Routledge.

Shakespeare, T., & Watson, N. (2002). The social model of disability: An outdated ideology. *Research in Social Science and Disability*, *2*, 9–28.

Shannon, P., & Agorastou, M. (2006). Identifying children with developmental disability receiving child protection services: A national survey of child welfare administrators. *Families in Society*, *87*(3), 351–357.

Shumba, A. (2006). Child abuse in schools and the law in Zimbabwe: Current issues and challenges in the new millennium. *Child Abuse and Neglect Research in South Africa*, *7*(4), 48–60.

Stopler, L. (2007). *Hidden shame: Violence against children with disabilities in East Africa.* Terres des Hommes Nederlands.

UNICEF. (2018). *In focus: Including children with disabilities.* UNICEF Europe and Central Asia Regional Office. Retrieved from www.unicef.org/eca

Wanjohi, A. M. (2019). Challenges facing inclusive education in Kenya. *Schools Net Kenya*, *3*(January), 1.

Were, A. R., Kioli, N. F., & Kurgat, S. G. (2016). Hidden shame: Sexual abuse against children with physical disabilities in rural Kenya. *International Journal of Sociology*, *4*(3), 82–87.

World Health Organisation. (2011). *World report on disability.* WHO/World Bank.

Zermatten, J., & McCallum, R. (2011). Foreword. *Out from the Shadows: Sexual Violence against Children with Disabilities.* Handicap International: Save the Children, London.

ADDITIONAL READING

Abeid, M., & Muganyinzi, P., Olsson, et al. (2014). Community perceptions of rape and child sexual abuse: A qualitative study in rural Tanzania. *BMC International Health and Human Rights, 14*(23). Advance online publication. DOI: 10.1186/1472-698X-14-23 PMID: 25132543

Boat, T. F., & Wu, J. (2015). Poverty and childhood disability. In Boat, T. F., & Wu, J. T. (Eds.), *Mental disorders and disabilities amongst low-income children* (pp. 105–148). Academies Press.

Greco, D., & Dawgert, S. (2007). *Poverty and sexual violence: Building prevention and intervention responses.* Pennsylvania Coalition Against Rape (PCAR). Retrieved from www.pcar.org

Kiru, E. W. (2018). Special education in Kenya - global perspective. *Intervention in School and Clinic*, •••, 1–8.

Njelesani, J., Hashemi, G., & Cameron, C.. (2018). From the day they are born: A qualitative study exploring violence against children with disabilities in West Africa. *BMJ Public Health, 18*(1), 153. PMID: 29343234

Reilly, J. M., & Gravdal, J. A. (2012). An ecological model for family violence prevention across the life-cycle. *Journal of Family Medicine*, *44*(5), 332–332. PMID: 23027115

Rohwerder, B. (2018). *Disability stigma in developing countries. K4D Helpdesk Report.* Institute of Development Studies.

Rosenthal, E., & Szeli, E. (2003). *Not on the agenda: Human rights of people with mental disabilities in Kosovo*. Report. Mental Disability Rights International, Washington, DC, August.

Thomas, P. (2005). *Disability, poverty and the Millennium Development Goals: Relevance, challenges and opportunities for DFID*. Report. Disability Knowledge and Research Programme (KAR), UK, September.

UNESCO. (2008). *Inclusion education: The way of the future*. Paper prepared for the International Conference on Education, UNESCO, Geneva, November.

UNICEF. (2005). Violence against disabled children. *UN Secretary General's Report on Violence Against Children - Thematic Group on Violence Against Disabled Children: Findings and Recommendations*. United Nations, New York, July.

UNICEF-MENARO. (2005). *Violence in schools in the Middle East and North Africa: Features, causes, interventions and prevention*. UNICEF.

Van der Mark, E. J., Conradie, I., Dedding, W. M., & Broerse, J. W. E. (2019). We create our own small world: Daily realities of mothers of disabled children in South African urban settlement. *Disability & Society*, *34*(1), 95–120.

Winters, N., Langer, L., & Geniets, A. (2017). Physical, psychological, sexual and systematic abuse of children with disabilities in East Africa: Mapping the evidence. *PLoS One*, *12*(19), e1184541. PMID: 28892508

Chapter 2
Factors Limiting Access to Support Services by Persons with Disabilities (PWDs) in Nigeria

Paulinus S. Okah
https://orcid.org/0000-0003-4768-3526
Department of Social Work, University of Nigeria, Nsukka, Nigeria

Chinwe U. Nnama-Okechukwu
Department of Social Work, University of Nigeria, Nsukka, Nigeria

Nkemdilim P. Anazonwu
Department of Social Work, University of Nigeria, Nsukka, Nigeria

Chinyere E. Onalu
https://orcid.org/0000-0001-8883-2458
Department of Social Work, University of Nigeria, Nsukka, Nigeria

ABSTRACT

Disability issues have been a serious subject of discourse in Nigeria as a result of human rights abuses, stigma, discrimination, and negative attitudes at family, community, and societal levels. These problems contribute to people with disabilities' limited access to services and exclusion in various settings in Nigeria, a situation that resulted in advocacy calls and inclusion of people with disabilities all over the country. This chapter collected data through documentaries and content analysis to explore factors limiting access to support services by people with disabilities in Nigeria and their effects on the well-being of disabled persons. The

DOI: 10.4018/979-8-3373-7163-4.ch002

paper recommended amongst others that the government as a matter of urgency should put in place machinery to enforce the domestication and implementation of the Discrimination against Persons with Disabilities (Prohibition) Act for enhanced well-being of People with disabilities.

INTRODUCTION

Globally, about one billion people, representing 15% of the world's population are living with disabilities with about 80% of these people living in low and middle-income countries (LMICs) including Nigeria (Clemente et al., 2022; World Bank, 2020; World Health Organization [WHO], 2021). Nigeria, with its diverse and sizable population, includes a significant number of People with Disabilities (PWDs) and is one of the countries in Africa with the largest number of people with disabilities. About 25 million Nigerians, according to the 2021 National Handicap Survey, live with one form of disability or the other. While there is no clear estimation of the number of people with disabilities in Nigeria, data from the 2018 Nigeria Demographic and Health Survey (NDHS, 2018) revealed that an estimated 7% of household members above the age of 5 as well as 9% of those aged 60 and above experience some level of difficulty in at least one functional domain such as seeing, hearing, communication, cognition, walking or self-care. This high rate of disability is caused by frequent road accidents and outbreaks of infectious diseases, war, drug abuse, unchecked chronic infirmity, conflicts, and natural disasters, which incapacitate people and affect their functioning capabilities.

PWDs are individuals with physical, developmental, and intellectual dysfunctions who may not be privileged to access support services and may be hindered from full involvement in society and unable to perform certain roles (Ajuwon et al., 2008). Disability issues have been the subject of discourse in Nigeria as a result of human rights challenges, stigma, discrimination, and negative attitudes at family and community levels. In Nigeria, disability is often accompanied by institutional neglect and societal stigma and discrimination, which compound the challenges faced by PWDs. The way disabilities are viewed and dealt with is frequently influenced by cultural values and customs. Disabilities are sometimes seen as a result of superstition, bad luck, or curse rather than as a condition that calls for integration and care. PWDs have poorer health access, lower educational achievements, less social and economic participation, and lower rates of income than persons without disabilities (Sedeto & Dar, 2019). This is because they experience barriers in accessing support services including health, education, employment, transport, and information as well as rehabilitation. These include challenges of accessibility to physical structures, exclusion in employment/programs, challenges in social relationships, public misconceptions around disabilities, lack of support services, stigmatization, societal abuse, poor health care service delivery, unavailability of educational training facilities, exclusion and lack of an institutional framework to address the plight of PWDs.

The negative attitude of employers toward people with disabilities is unreasonable and a reflection of the poor social status of PWDs in the country. Compared to the general population, PWDs are significantly excluded from several social metrics, including relationships, opportunities, and community involvement (McCausland et al., 2021; Xiao & O'Neil 2021), thus are at risk of poorer well-being and lower quality of life [QOL]. The welfare of PWDs is left to the sympathy of government, and non-governmental organizations and not as dictated by the law, hence, the rights of PWDs are constantly violated. PWDs across age groups feel lonely, and socially isolated, do not engage in formal or informal social networks, lack access to leisure activities, and decreased social participation (Bonsang & Klein 2012; Holt-Lundstad 2017; Iwuagwu & Kalu, 2021). The limited accessibility possessed by persons with disabilities, such as difficulties in carrying out social activities, work activities, household activities, and daily activities makes persons with disabilities underestimated by the surrounding community because they are considered unproductive and unable to carry out their full duties and responsibilities (Destyani, 2019). This results in persons with disabilities feeling inclined to be ignored (Irwanto et al., 2010); and this can affect the psychological well-being of persons with disabilities, such as a more unstable emotional attitude, self-confidence and self-acceptance, moody, feeling insignificant, withdrawing from social situations, tend to blame themselves and the social environment (Sayyidah, 2015).

A significant stride in creating a legal framework to assist PWDs has been made by the Nigerian government. The National Policy on Disability, enacted in 2009, and the Discrimination Against Persons with Disabilities, DAPPA (Prohibition) Act of 2018 are essential in promoting the rights and well-being of PWDs. These legislative tools aim to eradicate discrimination and ensure equal opportunities in various sectors, including public services, employment, and education. However, due to poor institutional support, low public awareness, lack of political will, and inadequate implementation of these legislations or non-functional national policies on disability, many PWDs continue to face barriers in accessing support services as they are constantly excluded from social, economic, and political spheres of life (Anazonwu et al., 2022). Protecting the rights of PWDs and ensuring their inclusion begins with creating access to public structures, and that ramps, special conveniences, and easy access way to public buildings are adequately provided. Such provisions will make PWDs feel belong to society and can integrate properly and contribute to societal development (Akinola, 2021; Arimori, 2021; Etieyibo, 2020; Nnama-Okechukwu et al., 2020). This study identifies and discusses factors limiting access to support services by PWDs in various sectors in Nigeria and their effect on the well-being of disabled persons. It also demonstrates how discrimination practices influence service provision in various sectors and perpetuates the exclusion of PWDs in society. This will help suggest strategies to overcome obstacles faced by PWDs in Nigeria and ease their challenges in accessing quality education, institutional buildings, and transport systems.

THE CONCEPTS OF DISABILITY AND SUPPORT SERVICES

Disability refers to different kinds of impairments and deformities that restrict people's ability to cope in society (Onalu & Nwafor, 2021). The term disability encompasses a variety of impairments, activity restrictions, and participation limitations. Disability is an umbrella term convening impairment, activity limitation, and participation restrictions and is an outcome of an interaction between impairment and negative environmental impact. Disability may be physical, cognitive, mental, sensory, emotional developmental, or some combination of these and may be present from birth or occur during a person's life. Disability is not just a health problem or attribute of individuals but reflects the problems persons with disabilities (PWDs) experience in their interaction with society and physical movements (Kuvalekar et al., 2015). The challenges faced by PWDs in the areas of exclusion and stigmatization cut across every region of Nigeria, especially with a lack of operational support services. This is because there are no integrated and functional formal support services as the majority of the well-recognized support services either do not exist or have become obsolete (Okah et al., 2023a). For instance, persons with disabilities in Nigeria are confronted with the challenges of difficult access to structural buildings because most of the public buildings do not have access ways for PWDs.

Most public buildings in Nigeria such as schools, hospitals, government buildings, company buildings, shopping malls even churches/mosques were structured without considering the plight of PWDs, and this poses great challenges for PWDs who would need to access such facilities (Akande, 2019). With a lack of access to public buildings and facilities because of physical impediments, PWDs are structurally excluded from benefiting from public utilities (Bumma et al., 2020). The effects might lead to total or partial dependency on other people to help out with carrying out tasks that ordinarily such individuals can accomplish. Dependence often introduces barriers in social relationships and other aspects of life for PWDs. Such barriers may hinder effective participation in society on an equal basis with others who are without disabilities thereby creating both visible and invisible interpersonal relationship gaps in social, economic, and other kinds of living arrangements. This may thus necessitate public and private intervention through laws, policies, and programs that will address challenges for more inclusive participation.

PWDs require a range of support services to be integrated into their communities, to participate in activities that are meaningful and necessary, and to have access, on an equal basis to persons without disabilities, to community living (Hunt et al., 2022). PWDs who account for upwards of 15% of the global population are often considered key beneficiaries in national and international social protection strategies (World Bank, 2020). They may be targeted for inclusion in social protection due to high levels of economic and multidimensional poverty, as well as frequent social exclusion and marginalization (Gentilini & Omamo, 2011; United Nations 2015). Support services refer to the psychological and material resources provided by a social network to help individuals cope with stress. These support services, some of which are distinctive to persons with disabilities, exist in various life domains, such as communication, decision-making, self-care, mobility, and housing.

The support services fall under the umbrella of community support, the services and/or assistance necessary to support living and inclusion in the community, and to prevent isolation or segregation from the community, for persons with disabilities (Swartz & Marchetti-Mercer, 2019). Community support can be provided formally by governments or private sector providers or informally by unpaid family members or peers. Support services are provided by the government, NGOs, family members, philanthropists, and community members to help vulnerable groups like PWDs function better in society. Across Nigeria, social welfare services are provided and delivered by the government through its agencies (Agba et al., 2020; Okpa et al., 2020). The services cover every range of welfare services, including personal and social services, educational services, housing and community development efforts, environmental and general health matters, and general infrastructure provisions, among others (Alao et al., 2015). Support services emphasize the relationship with whom that provides support and the availability of support resources when needed, and create mutual obligations, in which, an individual feels loved, cared for, and valued (Zaki, 2009).

The psychosocial benefit of support services among persons with disabilities may be due to its effects on their mental evaluation of pressure factors, choosing effective coping methods, improving self-esteem, personal skills, better social life, and empowering them for help in the process of social development (Obst & Stafurik, 2010). Support services assist people in dealing with various life challenges and can be emotional, physical, instrumental, or informational; and aid in the reduction of psychological stress, improvement of quality of life, attainment of social inclusion, and participation in community and national development. This is because, having a social relationship and being aware that help is readily available can have a positive effect on the individual's health and overall well-being, while lack of support services has great consequences for people with life-threatening/challenging situations. Ayide (2021) noted the need to make provisions for persons with disabilities in areas such as adequate access ramps, reserved parking in the appropriate locations, and special conveniences. With such provisions, PWDs can relate more with able-bodied persons in their day-to-day interactions which may reduce some societal misconceptions and public perception about disability.

Although people with disabilities are frequently targeted as key beneficiaries of social protection, little is known about their access to existing programs. According to Adebisi et al. (2014), lack of equal access to school, work, healthcare, and legal support, has led to the poverty, marginalization, and social exclusion of PWDs. This lack of access and exclusion continue to fester not minding the existence of support services and policies meant to improve the quality of lives of PWDs. Therefore, for people with disabilities to partake in any of the intended benefits of social protection, they must first be able to access programs (Banks et al., 2019).

THE CONCEPT OF DISCRIMINATION

Despite efforts to integrate society, PWD still experiences considerable discrimination (Lee et al., 2022), which is linked with poorer well-being cross-sectionally (Hackett et al., 2020). Discrimination is one of the major obstacles to achieving social integration and can be defined as the unfair or biased treatment of particular individuals or groups (Thomsen, 2017). It can also be defined as unwanted, exploitative, or abusive conduct against disabled people, which violates their dignity and security or creates an intimidating or offensive environment (Equality and Human Rights Commission., 2011). Disability discrimination involves any kind of behavior, policy, or practice that either directly or indirectly, intentionally or unintentionally, disadvantages a person or a group of people because of their disability. This can happen in numerous settings, such as employment, education, access to goods and services, or housing (Hulatt & Freitas, 2024). It can also happen on the street, in the workplace, and public venues such as shops or pubs (Skyes et al, 2011).

Those with multiple and specific disabilities (physical or psychological disabilities) have been found to face barriers to accessing healthcare and importantly, experiencing a barrier to healthcare is associated with low levels of trust in health professionals and perceptions of discrimination in healthcare settings (Temple & Williams, 2018). Temple and Kelaher (2018) show that experiencing discrimination or avoidance due to disability is associated with deleterious mental health through psychological distress. Empirical studies show people who experience disability discrimination are less likely to utilize health services, less likely to access preventative health services, delay or fail to fill prescriptions, and delay or avoid treatment

(Burgess et al., 2008; Moscoso-Porras & Alvarado, 2018). This avoidance behavior can contribute to the development of undiagnosed comorbidities, further increasing the burden of poor physical and mental health upon the individual, community, and economy (Moscoso-Porras & Alvarado, 2018). The challenges confronting PWDs further put them in precarious and disadvantaged conditions as the social and behavioral construct of disability tend to perpetuate injustice on PWDs in Nigeria leading to exclusion despite various inclusive laws and policies that advocate for the rights of persons with disabilities. According to Hulatt and Freitas (2024) and Temple et al. (2018), direct discrimination occurs when someone is treated less favorably than another person in a similar situation, because of their disability. This form of discrimination is usually easy to spot because the unfavorable treatment is explicit and based solely on the person's disability. Indirect discrimination, on the other hand, occurs when there is a policy, practice, procedure, or workplace rule which applies to all workers, but particularly disadvantages people with a certain disability. Unlike direct discrimination, indirect discrimination is not always obvious and can often be unintentional.

RELATIONSHIP BETWEEN DISABILITY AND THEORETICAL FRAMEWORK

This study is anchored on the social model of disability because of its relevance to the study. The model was first put forth in the United Kingdom in a 1976 statement by the Union of the Physically Impaired Against Segregation (UPIAS, 1976). It was later discussed in detail by Corker (2000), Finkelstein (1980), and Oliver (1996). According to the social model, disability encompasses all factors that impose restrictions on people with disabilities, ranging from negative social attitudes to institutional discrimination, from inaccessible public buildings to unusable transport systems, from segregated education to exclusion in work arrangements, and so on. The model seeks to redefine disability to refer to the restrictions caused by society when it does not give equitable social and structural support according to disabled peoples' structural needs (Paley, 2002).

In Nigeria, most PWDs do not have access to basic services of life because of exclusion from social, political, health, economic, and cultural activities. This exclusion is orchestrated by negative perception, stigma, discrimination, and weak institutional policies on disability. Most PWDs do not live in a conducive environment, and lack access to equal education, infrastructure-including lecture rooms, special transportation arrangements, or vehicles with assistive aids, despite the expiration of the five-year transitional period of the DAPPA Act. The social model of disability identifies systemic barriers, derogatory attitudes, and social exclusion, which make it difficult or impossible for disabled people to attain their valued functioning. For example, if a person is unable to climb stairs, the social model tries to make stair-climbing unnecessary, such as by making society adapt to their needs and assisting them by replacing the stairs with a wheelchair-accessible ramp.

According to the model, the person remains disabled concerning climbing stairs, but the disability is negligible and no longer disabling in that scenario because the person can get to the same locations without climbing any stairs (Winter, 2003). Essentially, the social model says that individual limitations are not the cause of disability; rather, it is society's failure to provide appropriate services and adequately ensure that the needs of disabled people are taken into account in societal organization. This model perceived the constraints and limitations of disabled persons as resulting from barriers within society and do not arise from their impairments. These barriers include prevailing attitudes and preconceptions, leading to underestimation; the policies, practices, and procedures of a local and national government; the structure of health, welfare, and education systems; lack of access to buildings, transport, and the whole range of community resources available to the rest of the population; and the impact of poverty deprivation on the community as a whole and more specifically on persons with disabilities and their families (Digest, 2007).

The model, therefore, emphasizes the role of government, civil societies, and helping professions like social work in removing the obstacles faced by PWDs in Nigeria to enable them to become active participants in society through the provision and implementation of PWD-friendly policies like the DAPPA Act (2018). This involves ensuring that transportation systems, public buildings, and other necessary facilities are accessible to PWDs. The government and private sectors should work together to put universal design principles into practice and make sure that accessibility features are included in new developments. Also, awareness creation and community engagement are important for changing societal attitudes and reducing stigma and discrimination. Public attitudes can be influenced by initiatives that showcase the abilities of PWDs and foster positive images of disability.

STATE OF PWDs IN NIGERIA

Globally, PWDs face several difficulties, such as institutional, environmental, and attitude barriers that prevent them from fully participating in all facets of life (Bonsang & Klein, 2012). Compared to the general population, they are significantly excluded from several social metrics, including relationships, opportunities, and community involvement (McCausland et al., 2021), and are at risk of poorer well-being and lower quality of life. PWDs experience high levels of multidimensional poverty, such as malnutrition and lower levels of health, barriers to accessing education and healthcare, and exclusion from decent work and social participation (Hume-Nixon & Kuper, 2018; Mitra et al., 2013; Mizunoya & Mitra, 2013; Mizunoya et al., 2018). PWDs across age groups feel lonely, and socially isolated, do not engage in formal or informal social networks, lack access to leisure activities, and decreased social participation (Bonsang & Klein 2012; Holt-Lundstad 2017; Iwuagwu & Kalu 2021). Social discrimination against PWDs also takes various forms, including public attitude and lack of accessible physical environment and transportation. In Nigeria, people with disabilities face stigma, marginalization, discrimination, and obstacles to accessing essential social services and employment possibilities (Bello, 2020).

The Discrimination against Persons with Disabilities (Prohibition) Act, 2018 prohibits disability discrimination and imposes penalties for violations (Institute of Development Studies [IDS], 2020). It gave PWDs new hope by aiming to reintegrate them fully into society. Unfortunately, due to a lack of political will and a clear legal framework for its implementation, PWDs in Nigeria have continued to face many challenges, ranging from stigma and discrimination to difficulties in accessing basic services, limited education, and inadequate social infrastructure (Amadasun, 2020; Lang & Upah, 2008). Though it is the traditional responsibility of families, friends, and societies to take care of the needy like PWDs, modernization, and globalization have created a shift in this responsibility; thus, making them dependent on assistance from others, which compounds their woes. Their living condition is very bad because the government is not taking care of them as they should.

The government does not employ or provide aid to PWDs. They do not care about their welfare, education, health, social engagements, etc. as they (PWDs) are allowed to struggle to live under their conditions. As a result, so many of them resort to street begging just to feed. The condition of disabled persons in Nigeria is very pathetic because they are easily stigmatized. They also lack government attention coupled with the shortage of humanitarian assistance from fellow citizens, which in turn contributes to the myriad of woes faced by PWDs. In advanced countries, they are being taken good care of by the government, but here, proper provisions are not meant for them. No employment, no social security, no education, and so on, as they only beg for survival-with some dying of preventable diseases because of lack of funds to access healthcare as they live on unfulfilled promises from the government. A study by Okah et al. (2023a) found that the only time the government, some NGOs, and philanthropists remember PWDs and distribute some assistive devices to them is during electioneering campaigns, festive periods, and the International Day of PWDs. To survive, most PWDs have turned to begging, farming, and hawking.

The growing public perception views PWDs as those to be pitied, helped, and supported, and those who do not have any meaningful thing to contribute to society. These "ill mindsets" of the society have unfortunately spelled how PWDs are treated in their families and various communities; as they are viewed in many localities as bad luck, misfortunes, and a curse from the gods (Baffoe, 2013; Uromi & Mazagwa, 2014). In addition, many PWDs are deep into poverty, and with a lack of education, employment, and income-generating ventures, they live in worse housing conditions, poor diets, and poor health conditions with little or no access to quality healthcare (Agbo, 2020; Uromi & Mazagwa, 2014; WHO, 2018). The PWDs in a bid to survive the economic hardship often engage in street begging and other means of appealing to the sympathy of members of society. In most cases, families of PWDs use them as a symbol of pity to beg for alms from the public, and this has become a big source of income for the families.

GOVERNMENT RESPONSE TO DISABILITY CHALLENGES IN NIGERIA

Government welfare or support services include areas like health, education, housing, transportation, and social security as handicapped individuals and groups are dependent on the government for protection, care, and survival (Ekpe & Mamah, 1997). Onalu and Nwafor (2021) asserted that through support services, problems are minimized and peoples' social, psychological, emotional, economic, and political well-being are positively affected. The federal government of Nigeria has at various times made substantial contributions in terms of regulatory commitment and legislative policy on disability matters. For instance, the Nigerian with Disability Decree, 1993, the Physically Challenged Persons Social Health Insurance Programme (PCPSHIP), the National Policy on Education (NPE, 2004), and the DAPPA Act 2018, all of which have specific provisions for PWDs.

In particular, the DAPPA Act 2018 amongst others prohibits discrimination based on disability and imposes sanctions including fines and prison sentences on those who contravene it (IDS, 2020). The Act 2018 stipulates that all public buildings must be accessible to people with disabilities and outlaws all types of discrimination based on disability (Federal Republic of Nigeria [FRN], 2020). The act stipulates a five-year transitional period for modifying public buildings, structures, and automobiles to make them accessible and usable for people with disabilities. It mandates that a government or government agency, body, or individual responsible for the approval of building plans shall not approve the plan of a public building if the plan does not make provision for accessibility facilities in line with the new building code (Sholanke, 2019).

To ensure strict implementation, the law provides clear and comprehensive legal protection and security for Nigerians with disabilities as well as establishes standards for enforcement of the rights and privileges guaranteed under other laws applicable to PWDs in the Federal Republic of Nigeria. This was to support and protect the human rights and fundamental freedoms of PWDs without any form of discrimination (Ogundipe, 2019). The DAPPA Act was also designed to provide for the full integration of PWDs into society and establish the National Commission for People with Disabilities (NCPD), whose responsibilities were the education, health care, social, economic, civil rights, and related matters of the PWDs (Anazonwu et al, 2022). The Act brought new hope for those affected with disabilities as it aimed at reintegrating them fully into society (The Guardian, 2019).

As a signatory member of the United Nations, the Nigerian government also signed and ratified the United Nations Convention on the Rights of Persons with Disabilities [UNCRPD] in 2007 (Agha et al., 2024); however, the ratification was more like paying lip services to it as there was no concrete effort to domesticate the convention in the country until 2018 (Christian Blind Commission [CBM], 2019). Furthermore, several organizations provide support services to PWDs in Nigeria, with most of these organizations (private and public) in the non-profit making sector (Amadasun, 2020). The public establishment in charge of support service delivery to PWDs in Nigeria is the Ministry of Women Affairs and Social Development within the federal and various state governments. Other sources of support services to PWDs include private organizations ranging from Non-Governmental Organizations (NGOs), Faith Based Organizations (FBOs), Civil Society Organizations (CSOs), and Disabled Persons Organizations (DPOs) like the Joint National Association for People with Disabilities (JONAPWD). Also, social workers in collaboration with other professionals, and governmental and nongovernmental agencies provide support services to PWDs to ensure the demolition of structural and societal barriers that impede their well-being.

Despite various legislative efforts aimed at enhancing their quality of life, PWDs continue to face substantial barriers to accessing essential services ranging from physical inaccessibility to socio-economic difficulties and discriminatory practices, which collectively prevent them from participating fully in society. PWDs in Nigeria are still being excluded from social, economic, and political spheres of life due to the non-functional national policy on disability (Anazonwu et al, 2022). The World Bank (2020) reports that there is no existing documentation of progress made or lessons learned from the implementation of these laws in Nigeria.

FACTORS LIMITING ACCESS TO SUPPORT SERVICES BY PWDs

The challenges faced by persons with disabilities in accessing support services can vary depending on the types of services and the nature of the barriers that a person faces (Coleman, 2024). The absence or presence of some features in social and physical environments constitute challenges to PWDs in accessing support services. They include inaccessible physical environment, lack of relevant assistive devices, negative attitudes towards people with disability, poor healthcare system, public perception of disability, and lack of transport or mobile facilities, etc. Barriers to full social and economic inclusion of persons with disabilities include inaccessible physical environments and transportation, the unavailability of assistive devices and technologies, non-adapted means of communication, gaps in service delivery, and discriminatory prejudice and stigma in society (Kim et al., 2022; World Bank, 2020). Factors limiting access to support services by PWDs in Nigeria include but are not limited to inaccessible healthcare services, inaccessible physical structures, lack of specialized means of transportation, lack of a specialized educational program, cultural belief, stigma and discrimination, poverty, and economic challenges, lack of support services or lack of knowledge of existing services, feelings of shame and desire to maintain one's dignity, societal attitude and perception of disability, lack of political will to implement and domesticate disability policies and programs, lack of assistive technologies, weak employment policy, lack of housing program, and non-involvement of social workers in formulation and implementation of disability policies.

INACCESSIBLE HEALTHCARE SERVICES

PWDs generally experience greater barriers in accessing healthcare services than the general population, especially those in rural areas where there are few or no health clinics. Healthcare services in Nigeria are often inaccessible to PWDs due to a lack of specialized care and facilities. Many healthcare professionals are not trained to handle the unique needs of PWDs, leading to inadequate support and care. The unavailability of accessible hospitals and staff, who are aware of and skilled in disability inclusion and providing services for people with disabilities, frequently restricts access to proper health services for people with disabilities (Faronbi et al., 2019). Furthermore, accessibility features are frequently absent from healthcare facilities thereby making it difficult for PWDs to access medical services. Evidence indicates that people with disabilities have greater health needs than people without disabilities and that these needs are generally not met.

Furthermore, PWDs, especially those in low-and-middle-income countries like Nigeria face worse levels of access to health services and worse health outcomes. Potential challenges faced in accessing health care include discrimination, physical inaccessibility, information inaccessibility, and unavailability (Clemente et al., 2022). The existing health services lack policies to accommodate the needs of PWDs, resulting in prejudice, stigma, and discrimination by health service providers and other health facility personnel (WHO, 2021). The concentration of health facilities in the urban areas and the long distance of most of the facilities constitute a challenge to PWDs. Because of the long distance and lack of funds for transportation, and pay for expensive drugs, PWDs seek alternatives by patronizing nearby private clinics, pharmacies, or patent-medicine stores, with far-reaching implications on their health and medical bills (Okah et al., 2023b). Even the PWDs who registered with the PCPSHIP complain of delays in generating the secondary billing code, which is now a requirement for the collection of prescribed drugs and conducting recommended medical examinations. Due to the delays in generating the code, most enrollees end up not getting the needed healthcare when they need it most. Some enrollees stayed days waiting for the confirmation of secondary codes from their HMOs, while some others waited for hours before getting theirs. In a similar study elsewhere, it was reported that delays in generating the secondary code and service forms by the patients because of centralization of the process, and non-availability of some prescribed drugs in NHIS pharmacies affect the utilization of the scheme by the enrollees (Okpanachi & Vambe, 2020). The frustration faced by enrollees because of the delays in generating the secondary code has forced some of them to seek healthcare through other means, other than the NHIS, including the out-of-pocket payment method (Okah et al., 2023b).

INACCESSIBLE PHYSICAL STRUCTURES

Physical restrictions are among the most obvious and immediate challenges faced by PWDs in Nigeria. Accessibility components that are necessary for many public buildings, such as government offices, schools, churches, mosques, malls, banks, companies, recreational centers, and healthcare institutions, are missing. Accessible restrooms, elevators, and ramps are frequently absent or insufficient, making it challenging for people with mobility disabilities to use these areas. A previous study by Bumma et al. (2020) decried the poor accessibility of public buildings and the need to make the environment and public spaces in LMICs, Nigeria inclusive, and disability-friendly. Anazonwu et al. (2022) stated that ramps are a critical need for PWDs, especially for people using wheelchairs. Wheelchair users and other mobility device users should not have difficulties entering doors as this denies them opportunities and social activities (Sambo, 2016). Participation in physical and social activities aids in the restoration of people with disabilities' physical and mental health as well as the improvement of their social cohesion and social support (Crawford et al., 2008; Fiorilli et al., 2013; Kim et al., 2021). However, compared to non-disabled people, disabled people may have a smaller geographic area in which to participate in activities, take longer on average to go out, and face greater spatial and temporal constraints (Farber & Páez, 2010; Sur et al., 2022). They most times spend more of their leisure time indoors doing passive activities such as reading, sleeping, or watching television and less time participating in cultural or outdoor activities (Meyer & Mok, 2019; Pagán-Rodríguez, 2014). As a result, people living with disabilities are less likely to meet physical activity guidelines and are at higher risk of serious health problems related to inactivity than people without disabilities (Jaarsma et al., 2014; Martin Ginis et al., 2021).

LACK OF SPECIALIZED MEANS OF TRANSPORT FOR PWDs

Also, public transportation presents another important challenge. It is common for buses, taxis, and trains to be devoid of accommodations for PWDs, including audio-visual announcements or low-floor buses. This lack of accessibility limits their ability to healthcare, education, or travel for work, which further isolates them from vital services and necessities of life. According to Okah et al. (2023a), many PWDs find it difficult to move around for their business because there are no accessible or special transportation arrangements or vehicles with assistive aids for them. The Nigerian public transportation system is insensitive to the plight of PWDs, and no social inclusion project or program is planned (Umeh & Adeola, 2013). People with disabilities rely greatly on public transportation, and road transportation because many of them do not own a car. The most popular means of public road transportation in Nigeria are buses, taxis, motorcycles, and tricycles. Ipingbemi (2015) noted that the attitudes of bus drivers toward people with disabilities are a concern as they do not stop for them and do not give them time to get on and off the bus. This will no doubt constitute a big challenge to the movement of PWDs in search of daily bread.

LACK OF SPECIAL EDUCATION PROGRAMS

While there has been a gradual move toward inclusion of students with disabilities in Nigeria promoted by the National Policy on Education as well as policies emerging from the United Nations Educational, Scientific, and Cultural Organisation [UNESCO, 2009], the infrastructure and resources to make inclusion materialize are generally lacking (Obiakor & Offor, 2011; Barrio, et al., 2018). The implementation of these laws and policies has stalled due to constraints such as a lack of resources and trained teachers (Fakolade, et al., 2009; Garuba, 2003). Available literature revealed that apart from a few dilapidated special education centers and the provision of scholarship programs to some PWDs by the government, some NGOs, and philanthropists, there are no other special arrangements by the government for educating PWDs (Okah et al., 2023a). Regrettably, the few tertiary institutions that prepare special educators, rehabilitation specialists, and social workers are yet to infuse into their curricula the competency needed to assist families and caregivers in terms of how to cope effectively with disabling conditions in children, youth, and adults (Haruna, 2017). Furthermore, there is a lack of commitment by the government to provide the necessary human and other resources to ensure the functioning of these centers (Ofuani, 2011).

Furthermore, Nigerian educational institutions usually lack the facilities and resources necessary to serve students with disabilities. Many schools lack the specialized equipment and staff needed to serve students with a range of needs. Due to this, there is a large educational gap, making it difficult for many PWDs to get a good education or finish their studies. For example, pupils/students with visual or hearing impairments most often, do not have access to braille textbooks or sign language interpreters, limiting their learning opportunities. Even at the tertiary level, many student-PWDs are frustrated with their programs or perform poorly because of the nonexistence of support services, including ramps for those in wheelchairs (Eleweke & Ebenso, 2016; Martinez &Vemuru, 2020). Moreover, PWDs face the challenge of mass illiteracy as some of them do not attend formal education due to a lack of special education centers within their locations. Ahmed et al. (2014) opined that in Nigeria, people with disabilities have been denied access to education, which is supposed to be their greatest asset, to enable them to benefit from the opportunities in the country and give them independence.

POVERTY/ECONOMIC CHALLENGES

In Nigeria, economic disparities significantly affect PWDs. Many PWDs experience high unemployment rates and few job opportunities, which are made worse by the high cost of specialized healthcare and assistive devices. Most often, the ability of these persons to obtain the necessary equipment, such as wheelchairs, reading or hearing aids is restricted due to a lack of financial resources. The economic barriers being faced by PWs highlight the need for targeted financial support and employment initiatives. Many PWDs have been trained over the years in shoe making, fashion designing, hairdressing, hair cutting, and soap making, among others but they do not have the capital to rent shops to start a business. There is a connection between poverty and disability and many PWDs in Nigeria live under worse living conditions with no basic income, housing, or gainful employment (Krahn, 2011; Uromi &Mazagwa, 2014; WHO, 2011). Most PWDs are left in the streets begging for alms to be able to survive; and in some cases, the families of the PWDs exploit them further by using them as a means of earning money. Families of PWDs use them as objects of pity while begging to solicit support from well-spirited Nigerians who are willing to undertake an act of charity. Begging therefore by PWDs and their families is now a common sight with many PWDs living and working on the street, especially in major car terminals, churches, financial institutions, busy marketplaces, and shopping malls.

CULTURAL BELIEF, STIGMA, AND DISCRIMINATION

Cultural myths and beliefs in Nigeria can have a significant influence on social attitudes toward PWDs. PWDs are frequently excluded and marginalized as a result of stigma and negative perceptions. These persons may be discouraged from obtaining essential services or engaging in community events due to negative perceptions. Cultural narratives that portray disability as a personal shortcoming or a heavenly retribution help to perpetrate this stigma and stigmatization. Social discrimination against people with disabilities takes various forms, including public attitude and lack of accessible physical environment, social services, and transportation. In Nigeria, people with disabilities face stigma, marginalization, discrimination, and obstacles to accessing essential support services and employment possibilities (Bello, 2020). Despite the DAPPA Act 2018 and other international directives to support the rights of persons with disabilities to participate in society and live with dignity, and countries' responsibilities to them, persons with disabilities experience significant unmet support needs (Berthé, et al., 2013; de Andrade & de Andrade, 2018; Vasquez et al., 2021), particularly in LMICs. In these settings, formal community support services for persons with disabilities are underdeveloped, under-resourced, or do not exist, leaving persons with disabilities to rely primarily on family members to have their needs met (United Nations, 2006; Vasquez, 2021).

Also, it is evident that, compared to non-disabled persons, people with disability have lesser legal protection, live in extreme poverty and poor health, as well as poor educational achievement, and are rarely involved in social, cultural, and political participation (Haruna, 2017). The government does not employ them the way they employ people without disabilities. Even in their very homes, they are being regarded as liabilities who cannot contribute meaningfully to society, not minding the fact that some of the PWDs can do better if given the opportunity. They are often stigmatized as handicapped and incapacitated to contribute to national development hence the non-inclusion of PWDs in national and economic development. This results in infringements of the rights of persons with disabilities, restrictions in choices, high disability-related costs, and opportunity costs for those providing support (Vasquez et al, 2021).

LACK OF EXISTING SERVICES/KNOWLEDGE OF EXISTING SERVICES

Owing to a lack of functional formal support services, persons with disabilities [PWDs] face numerous challenges in daily living in Nigeria (Okah et al., 2023a). Generally, there are no support services specifically made for PWDs in Nigeria, apart from a few laws and policies like the DAPPA Act 2018. Despite the enactment of this Act that aimed to improve the living conditions of PWDs in the country, implementation has stalled because of a lack of political will, corruption, lack of funds, and operational legal framework. Also, most PWDs, especially those in rural areas are not even aware of the few existing services like occasional training and distribution of mobile aids. They are not always aware of such skeletal services because most of them live in rural areas where electronic gadgets that disseminate information are absent. Even those who own mobile cell phones sometimes find it difficult to charge them because of lack of electricity.

FEELINGS OF SHAME AND DESIRE TO MAINTAIN ONE'S DIGNITY

Because of the public perception of PWDs as beggars who depend on others for survival, some disabled persons choose to live in difficult conditions and maintain their dignity rather than beg or depend on the government for survival. They continue to struggle for survival on their own rather than sourcing for assistance of any kind. Recent research carried out with wheelchair users and providers in Kenya has shown that, although the functionality of assistive technologies is important, considerations around identity, self-expression, and presentation might play an even bigger role in assistive technologies' choices (Barbareschi et al., 2020). The negative attitudes of the public towards PWDs are not helping matters. Sometimes, the politicians and the government, especially during electioneering campaigns make promises they will not fulfill to the people including PWDs. Such empty promises have negative effects on the mindsets of the people. In this case, PWDs may decide not to honor any other invitation from the government for assistance as they already believe that nothing good would come out of such an invitation except another empty promise. Therefore, they will choose to manage their lives and have their respect intact rather than going for assistance which always brings public disgrace and time-wasting.

SOCIETAL ATTITUDE AND PUBLIC PERCEPTION OF DISABILITY

According to the Department for International Development (DFID, 2015), attitudinal barriers find expression in those unsubstantiated yet pervasive beliefs and ideas about the causes of disability, in which PWDs are viewed as justifiably suffering the consequences of their actions in their previous life. Public perception around disability in Nigeria is often built around the misconception that persons with disabilities are people in need rather than valuable members of society with the capabilities to contribute to national discourse and development. Society looks down on people with disabilities and does not see them as normal human beings capable of doing anything for themselves and society because of their conditions. They rather see them as people who should not belong to the society and should not be equated with the able-bodied persons in the society. Some people even believe that PWDs are disabled because of their wickedness or curse from God or the land. The public sees PWDs as unfortunate members of society who have nothing to offer for the progress and development of society leading to their being deserted. They are not given the same respect and dignity given to those without disability as some of them who are employed only work in the physically challenged related offices-like rehabilitation centers despite their good educational qualifications and extraordinary talents. People’s knowledge of the disability and their contact with individuals with disabilities are the main influential factors in public attitudes towards persons with disabilities (Wang et al., 2021). Evidence showed that negative public attitudes have been indicated as a barrier to the participation of individuals with disabilities in several demands such as physical activity, fitness, and education settings (Rimmer et al., 2004). Public attitudes towards disabled people not only affect their integration into the community and access to public services (Verdonschot et al., 2009; Scior, 2011) but also influence their daily lives and social participation (Findley et al., 2007), such as employment Burge & Ouellette-KuntzHln, 2007). Thus, public perceptions and attitudes toward PWDs based on societal misconceptions are often manifested in marginalization, stigmatization, and discriminatory practices.

LACK OF POLITICAL WILL TO IMPLEMENT DISABILITY POLICIES AND PROGRAMS

Disability rights remain weak in Nigeria. Even with the protective law in place PWDs still find it difficult to obtain their rights and support services due to bureaucratic obstacles and institutional support structures' lack of willingness or competence to make the required adjustments (Onalu et al., 2023). Lack of interest and political will from the government and stakeholders are hindering the whole exercise because the government did not see it as a priority. The government is also showing indifference to the act. On January 23, 2019, President Muhammadu Buhari signed into law the Discrimination Against Persons with Disabilities (Prohibition) Act, 2018. The law amongst other things prohibits discrimination based on disability and imposes sanctions including fines and prison sentences on those who contravene it (IDS, 2020). The Act brought new hope for those affected with disabilities and probably for all the citizens, as the over 25 million persons living with disabilities in Nigeria were happy with the law aimed at reintegrating them fully back into society (The Guardian, 2019). However, like most previous laws in Nigeria, implementation of the Act may not happen soon because of a lack of political will and legal frameworks. According to the Centre for Citizens with Disabilities (CCD, 2021), it is only when legal frameworks are provided to protect them that they will be able to maximize their potential. Similarly, Umoh and Unaka (2019) noted that though the Discrimination Against Persons with Disabilities (Prohibition) Act 2018 has been signed into law, an implementation agency with persons with disabilities to drive the process is yet to be set up. Having a law without an implementation agency to drive it means that people with disabilities remain subjected to daily human rights abuses because of the barriers they encounter every day.

LACK OF ASSISTIVE TECHNOLOGIES

One of the challenges facing PWDs in Nigeria is the unavailability of assistive aids. Assistive technology maintains or improves an individual's functioning and independence to facilitate participation and enhance overall well-being (Rohweder, 2018; Tangcharoensathien et al., 2018). Many persons with disabilities rely on assistive technology services to carry out their daily activities because they have huge potential to reduce difficulties faced by PWDs in their day-to-day lives (Brandt et al., 2020; Thapaliya, 2016). Assistive products maintain or improve an individual's functioning and independence, thereby promoting their well-being. Hearing aids, wheelchairs, communication aids, spectacles, prostheses, pill organizers, and memory aids are all examples of assistive products (WHO, 2021). Assistive technology enables people to live healthy, productive, independent, and dignified lives, and to participate in education, the labor market, and civic life. The device reduces the need for formal health and support services, long-term care, and the work of caregivers. However, assistive technologies are not being utilized adequately in Nigeria (Yusuf et al., 2012), as they are expensive and not easily available, which limits mobility and access to technology for PWDs. Moreover, some individuals might choose not to use assistive technologies to avoid attracting unnecessary attention. According to Barbareschi et al. (2021), assistive technologies can work as a constantly visible mark of disability that can attract unwanted attention and occasionally be seen as more important than the person with disability who is using them. A recent study suggests that the presence of assistive devices may modify the stereotypical judgments that people without disabilities confer on people with disabilities, seeing them as incompetent (Meyer & Asbrock, 2018). As a result, PWDs are often excluded, isolated, and locked into poverty, thereby increasing the impact of disease and disability on a person, their family, and society (WHO, 2020).

WEAK EMPLOYMENT POLICY

Despite legislation on diversity in the workplace, people with disabilities still do not experience the same access to work opportunities as their counterparts without disabilities. In other words, there are no known coordinated efforts or policies to recruit PWDs into the public sector except the yet-to-be-implemented and domesticated DAPPA Act. Many employers have been shown to harbor sincere yet ill-founded views about the work-related abilities of people with disabilities; these negative views are often a result of interrelated concerns that permeate the entire employment cycle (Bonaccio et al., 2020). Even when they have been educated and met the requirements for employment, they are often denied employment opportunities because of their disability. This means that having a good education does not overcome employment discrimination because many employers are concerned with productivity and are influenced by negative stereotypes about PWDs and their ability to perform their roles (Ofuani, 2011). Consequently, they have to depend on family members, well-wishers, and charity groups for assistance to sustain themselves as they have no source of income for their livelihood. Including PWDs in the labor market also reduces stigma and promotes inclusion, as gainful employment can have a significant impact on feelings of worth, ability, and self-determination, as well as increasing their social and civic interaction (Lamichhane, 2015).

HOUSING PROBLEM

Many PWDs do not have a conducive living environment because there are no housing schemes for them. They live in unconducive and unsanitary houses with most of them sleeping on the streets after begging for alms for the day. They lack the resources to build or acquire good houses. Moreover, physically disabled persons who have good buildings or whose relatives, parents, or children have good houses still find it difficult to access such buildings because they lack ramps for those in wheelchairs. Although appropriate accessible housing enables independent living, research shows that people with disabilities often lack suitable housing, are more likely to experience an increased likelihood of living in unaffordable, insecure, and/or poor-quality housing, and are at a higher risk of experiencing homelessness (Lindsay et al., 2024; Beer et al., 2011; Aitken et al., 2019; Kavanagh et al., 2015). People with disabilities often encounter barriers and stigma/discrimination in finding appropriate housing, including learning about available accessible units, securing appointments, and receiving reasonable modification requests (Aranda, 2015). Additionally, home builders often lack an understanding of the basic needs of people with disabilities and are reluctant to innovate or increase costs by customizing accessible homes (Tucker et al., 2022). Interventions to enhance the accessibility of homes such as home modifications, creating space to accommodate mobility devices, and implementing accessible designs can have positive health and social impacts, like reduced depression, mortality rates, and falls or injuries, in addition to enhanced social participation (Cho et al., 2016; Carnemolla & Bridge, 2018), and improve independence, safety, privacy, and self-confidence for people with disabilities (Goodwin et al., 2022).

NON-INVOLVEMENT OF SOCIAL WELFARE PROFESSIONALS

The challenges experienced by persons with disabilities (PWDs) are real and profound, requiring the attention of social workers (Amadasun, 2020). Social workers collaborate with other professionals, the government, and NGOs to ensure the demolition of structural and societal barriers that impede PWDs' well-being (Okah et al., 2023a). The non-inclusion of professional service providers and welfare specialists like social workers in the formulation, implementation, and domestication of policies meant to benefit PWDs constitutes challenges in accessing services by PWDs. Social workers are trained professionals who help people, especially vulnerable groups overcome their life challenges and lead a better life in society. They act as motivators, facilitators, enablers, teachers, and advocates for the less-privileged members of the society. In particular, social workers can advocate on behalf of PWDs so that the government and other agencies working in partnership with PWDs should be abreast of the challenges facing this vulnerable group, and try to provide them with some essential services. The aim is to help them function better. Since they are trained for service delivery, they should be included in the formulation and implementation of policies and programs aimed at improving the living conditions of PWDs. The absence of trained social workers in the formulation and implementation of policies and programs for PWDs has led to the abysmal performance of these policies, thus worsening the pitiable conditions of PWDs in Nigeria.

RELEVANCE OF SOCIAL WORK PRACTICE IN DISABILITY DISCOURSE

Social work is a professional category that possesses enough competence to carry out work that aims at the well-being of families from the perspective of guaranteeing rights since it is qualified to deal with families that are in social vulnerability (Rahim, 2024). Underpinned by theories of social work, social sciences, humanities, and indigenous knowledge, social work engages people and structures to address life challenges and enhance well-being (International Federation of Social Work [IFSW], 2014). They contribute skills and expertise to help communities, families, and persons with disabilities with strategy formulation and administration, as well as individual case management, planning, consulting, and coordination. The role of social workers in disability services is dynamic and unique. Some specialize in helping individuals with learning disabilities; some primarily work with the aging population; and others care for individuals who have life-altering physical disabilities such as vision loss, hearing loss, and or acute mobility issues (Korndoerfer, 2023). Social workers play a vital role in supporting individuals with intellectual and developmental disabilities, advocating for their rights, promoting inclusion, and enhancing their overall well-being. Their dedication, expertise, and compassionate approach make a profound difference in the lives of those they serve and contribute to building a more inclusive and supportive society for all (East, 2024).

As revealed in this study, most PWDs face a lot of environmental, educational, socioeconomic, and even employment challenges. This serves as a wake-up call for social workers. There is a dire need for professionals like social workers and NGOs, well-meaning individuals, and humanitarian service providers to advocate for the domestication and implementation of policies that improve the welfare of PWDs. Social workers collaborate with other professionals, the government, and NGOs to ensure the demolition of structural and societal barriers that impede PWDs' well-being. Social workers play an important role in advocacy, policy formulation and implementation. There is a need for social workers to be part of advocacy visits to the legislators to ensure that the welfare of PWDs is being captured. Social workers should advocate for the right of these persons to education, and the right to be employed after graduating from school. Additionally, social workers' advocacy roles and skills are needed to coordinate the efforts of JONAPWD and other stakeholders to get the government and concerned bodies to push for the implementation of policies for PWDs.

Social workers should intensify action for the domestication and implementation of the Act through awareness creation, advocacy, lobbying, and interface with, relevant stakeholders, among others (Anazonwu et al., 2022). Additionally, social workers should educate the public on the importance of creating movable or improvised ramps in already-built structures to create an inclusive environment for all people. Creating equal opportunities and justice for people with disabilities, as well as others who have been oppressed, is at the heart of social work practice and is identified as a grand challenge for the future (Calvo et al., 2018). Social work's commitment to social justice compels those in the profession to advocate for nondiscriminatory laws, policies, and practices that promote the well-being of people with disabilities. Social justice promotes the participation of individuals with disabilities in decision-making about their care, as well as ensures that social service systems have those with varying abilities in authoritative positions with decision-making power. Awareness creation by social service providers, including social workers, on the concept of disability to change the mindset of the public and negative stereotypes of the populace would be of help.

CONCLUSION

The subject matter of disability and the need for making available support services to assist PWDs should be the responsibility of everyone including the governmental and nongovernmental agencies. This chapter demonstrated how discrimination influences service provision in various sectors and perpetuates the exclusion of PWDs in society. Making support services available and accessible to PWDs should be a continuous discourse until the majority if not all PWDs in Nigeria begin to feel the impacts of such services. Accessing support services without much hindrances is vital for ensuring adequate utilization and improvement of the living conditions of PWDs. This would also help PWDs feel belonging and a sense of worth, as well as reduce the burden faced by their family members in taking care of them. The study exposed that there are some support services available to PWDs in Nigeria. However, some factors were highlighted to be limiting access to the accessibility of such available support services. Based on the above militating factors, the study recommended strategies for surmounting them to make the services more accessible to PWDs.

RECOMMENDATIONS

The study suggests that the conditions of PWDs in Nigeria especially about access to support services have not improved despite the enactment of the DAPPA Act. Therefore, to increase access to support services by PWDs and improve their living conditions, the government and concerned bodies should:

1. Provide more organized support services to improve the welfare and independence of PWDS. The government should ensure that the physical and social environments are made accessible to PWDs to enable them to access support services.
2. Create a disability unit in the Ministry of Women's Affairs and Social Development to take full responsibility for the needs of PWDs. This unit should be manned or headed by a person with a disability for more effective functioning.
3. Ensure more public awareness campaigns emphasizing the importance of coordinating efforts to provide functional support services to PWDs, regular sensitization programs for PWDs on available services, and the need for them to access such services.
4. Create room for empowerment of PWDs through the provision of permanent job opportunities, skills acquisition, assistive technologies, and soft loans and grants for small-scale businesses.
5. Ensure the implementation and domestication of the DAPPA Act for the inclusion of PWDs in society and the abolition of discriminatory practices.
6. Awareness creation by social service providers, including social workers, on the concept of disability to change the mindset of the public and negative stereotypes of the populace.
7. Acknowledge the importance of social work by the government and society, and involve them in the planning and implementation of policies and programs meant to better the living conditions of PWDs to add value to the struggle for total inclusion of PWDs in all facets of life.
8. Encourage social workers to intensify efforts through advocacy, sensitization, lobbying, and interface with relevant stakeholders to ensure that policies and programs strive to eradicate factors limiting access to support services by PWDs for their mutual benefit and well-being.

REFERENCES

Adebisi, R., Jerry, J., Rasaki, S., & Igwe, E. (2014). Barriers to special needs education in Nigeria. *International Journal of Education and Research, 2*(11), 451–462. https:// www.ijern.com/journal/2014/November-2014/36.pdf

Agba, A. M. O., Okpa, J. T., & Ogar, J. A. (2020). Amnesty programme and skills training among ex-militants in Nigeria. *FWU Journal of Social Sciences, 14*(3), 14–26. DOI: 10.51709/FW1272J/fall2020/2

Agbo, C. (2020). COVID-19 and persons with disabilities in Nigeria. Qualitative Magazine. http://www.qualitativemagazine/ com/?p=4179

Agha, A. A., Nnama-Okechukwu, C. U., Onalu, C. E., Okah, P. S., Anazonwu, N. P., Iwuagwu, A. O., Chukwu, N. E., & Okoye, U. O. (2024). Stakeholders Perspectives on the Rights of Persons with Disabilities in Abia and Imo States, Southeast Nigeria: A Multi-sectorial Approach. *Journal of Human Rights and Social Work.* Advance online publication. DOI: 10.1007/s41134-023-00289-6

Ahmed, A., Awad, Z. A., & Yaacob, N. M. (2014). The response of accessibility infrastructures for PWD to national disability policies in higher institutions of developing countries: Case study of Ahmadu Bello University, Zaria and University of Malaya, Kuala Lumpur. *Journal of Surveying* [JSCP]. *Construction and Property, 5*(1), 1–16. DOI: 10.22452/jscp/vol5no1.1

Aitken, Z., Baker, E., Badland, H., Mason, K., Bentley, R., Beer, A., & Kavanagh, A. (2019). Precariously placed: Housing affordability, quality and satisfaction of Australians with disabilities. *Disability & Society, 34*(1). Advance online publication. DOI: 10.1080/09687599.2018.1521333

Ajuwon, M. P. (2008). Inclusive education for students with disabilities in Nigeria: Benefits, challenges and policy implications. *International Journal of Special Education, 23*(3), 12–17. https://www.scirp.org/reference/referencespapers?referenceid=1338523

Akande, A. (2019). The need for access: Is Nigeria failing persons living with disabilities? Nigeria Health Watch. https:// nigeriahealthwatch.com/the-need-for-access-is-nigeria-failingpersons-living-with-disabilities/

Akinola, O. B. (2021). Protection and enforcement of disability rights in Nigeria: Opportunities and challenges. http://dspace.run.edu. ng:8080/jspui/handle/123456789/2324

Alao, D. O., Osakede, K. O., & Owolabi, T. Y. (2015). Challenges of local government administration in Nigeria: Lessons from comparative analysis. *International Journal of Development and Economic Sustainability*, *3*(4), 61–79. https://www.eajournals.org/wp-content/uploads/Challenges-of-Local-Government-Administration-in-Nigeria.pdf

Amadasun, S. (2020). Social work services for persons with disabilities in Nigeria: A qualitative inquiry. *International Journal of Social Sciences Perspectives*, *6*(2), 59–67. DOI: 10.33094/7.2017.2020.62.59.67

Anazonwu, N., Okah, P., Chukwu, N., Agha, A., Iwuagwu, A., Onalu, C., Nnama-Okechukwu, C., & Okoye, U. (2022). Barriers to domestication and implementation of the Disability Act in Southeast Nigeria. *Journal of Social Work in Developing Societies*, *4*(1), 33–50. https://journals.aphriapub.com/index.php/JSWDS/article/view/1532/1459

Aranda, C. L. (2015). Targeting disability discrimination: Findings and reflections from the national study on housing discrimination against people who are deaf and people who use wheelchairs. *Cityscape: A Journal of Policy Development and Research, 17*(3), 103-122. https://www.jstor.org/stable/26326963

Baffoe, M. (2013). Stigma, discrimination & marginalization: Gateways to oppression of persons with disabilities in Ghana, West Africa. *Journal of Educational and Social Research*, *3*(1). Advance online publication. DOI: 10.5901/jesr.2013.v3n1p187

Banks, L. M., Walsham, M., Neupane, S., Pradhananga, Y., Maharjan, M., Blanchet, K., & Kuper, H. (2019). Access to Social Protection Among People with Disabilities: Mixed Methods Research from Tanahun, Nepal. *European Journal of Development Research, 31*, 929–956. DOI: 10.1057/s41287-019-0194-3

Barbareschi, G., Carew, M. T., Johnson, E. A., Kopi, N., & Holloway, C. (2021). "When They See a Wheelchair, They've Not Even Seen Me"-Factors Shaping the Experience of Disability Stigma and Discrimination in Kenya. *International Journal of Environmental Research and Public Health*, *18*(8), 4272. DOI: 10.3390/ijerph18084272

Barbareschi, G., & Holloway, C. (2020). Understanding independent wheelchair transfers. Perspectives from stakeholders. *Disability and Rehabilitation. Assistive Technology*, *15*(5), 545–552. DOI: 10.1080/17483107.2019.1594407

Barrio, B., Miller, D., Ojeme, C., & Tamakloe, D. (2018). Teachers' and parents' knowledge about disabilities inclusion in Nigeria. *Journal of International Special Needs Education*, *22*(1), 14–24. https://files.eric.ed.gov/fulltext/EJ1222118.pdf

Beer, A., Faulkner, C., Paris, C., & Clower, T. (2011). *Housing transitions through the life course: Aspirations, needs and policy*. Policy Press., DOI: 10.2307/j.ctt9qgq1p

Bello, O. S. (2020). *The accusation of elderly women as witches in Nigeria. A project submitted in partial fulfilment of the requirements for obtaining the degree of Master of Arts in Development Studies*. International Institute of Social Studies.

Berthé, A., Berthé-Sanou, L., Konaté, B., Hien, H., Tou, F., Somda, S., Bamba, I., Drabo, M., Badini-Kinda, F., & Macq, J. (2013). The unmet needs of the elderly living with functional disabilities in Bobo-Dioulasso (Burkina Faso) Rev. *D'epidemiol. Sante Publique*, *61*, 531–537. DOI: 10.1016/j.respe.2013.07.682

Bonaccio, S., Connelly, C. E., Gellatly, I. R., Jetha, A., & Martin-Ginis, K. A. (2020). The participation of people with disabilities in the workplace across the employment cycle: Employer concerns and research evidence. *Journal of Business and Psychology*, *35*(2), 135–158. DOI: 10.1007/s10869-018-9602-5

Bonsang, E., & Klein, T. J. (2012). Retirement and subjective well-being. *Journal of Economic Behaviour and Organization, 83(3),* 311-329. https://doi.org/. 06.002DOI: 10.1016/j.jebo.2012

Brandt, A., Hansen, E. M., & Christensen, J. R. (2020). The effects of assistive technology service delivery processes and factors associated with positive outcomes-A systematic review. *Disability and Rehabilitation. Assistive Technology*, *15*(5), 590–603. DOI: 10.1080/17483107.2019.1682067

Bumma, F. N., Ayagere, S. A., Amakiri-Whyte, B. H., & Ubani, P. (2020). Urban public buildings and accessibility challenges in Nigeria. *International Journal of Research and Scientific Innovation*, *7*(5), 209–215. https://rsisinternational.org/journals/ijrsi/digital-library/volume-7-issue-5/209-215.pdf

Burge, P., Ouellette-Kuntz, H., & Lysaght, R. (2007). Public views on employment of people with intellectual disabilities. *Journal of Vocational Rehabilitation*, *26*(1), 29–37. DOI: 10.3233/JVR-2007-00360

Burgess, D., Ding, Y., Hargreaves, M., van Ryn, M., & Phelan, S. (2008). The association between perceived discrimination and underutilization of needed medical and mental healthcare in a multi-ethnic community sample. *Journal of Health Care for the Poor and Underserved,* 19:894-911.https://www.ncbi.nlm.nih.gov/nlmcatalog?term=%22J+Health+Care+Poor+ Underserved%22%5BTitle+Abbreviation%5D

Calvo, R., Teasley, M., Goldback, J., McRoy, R., & Padilla, Y. (2018). Achieve equal opportunity and justice. In Fong, R., Lubben, J., & Barth, R. (Eds.), *Grand challenges for social work and society* (pp. 239–272). Oxford University Press.

Carnemolla, P., & Bridge, C. (2018). A scoping review of home modification interventions: Mapping the evidence base. *Indoor and Built Environment, 29*(3), 299–310. DOI: 10.1177/1420326X18761112

Centre for Citizens with Disabilities. (2021). Peoples with disabilities want domestication of Disability Act in all states. *The Guardian, March 17.* m.guardian.ng>news>pwds-want-dom... Cho, H., MacLachlan, M., Clarke, M., & Mannan, H. (2016). Accessible home environments for people with functional limitations: A systematic review. *International Journal of Environmental Research and Public Health, 13*(8), 826; https://doi.org/DOI: 10.3390/ ijerph13080826

Christian Blind Mission. (2019). *Lessons from disability audit of Northeast Nigeria Transition to Development (NENTAD) humanitarian response. Nigeria briefing.* https://www.cbmuk.org.uk/wp-content/uploads/2019/07/Lessons-from-Disability -Audit-of-North-East-Nigeria-NENTAD-humanitarian-response.pdf

Clemente, K.A.P., Silva, S.V.D., Vieira, G.I., Bortoli, M.C., Toma, T.S., & Ramos, V.D., Brito, & C.M.M. (2022). Barriers to the access of people with disabilities to health services: A scoping review. *Revista de Saude Publica, 56*, 64. DOI: 10.11606/ s1518-8787.2022056003893

Coleman, C. (2024). Challenges faced by people with disabilities. https://lordslibrary .parliament.uk/ challenges-faced-by-people-with-disabilities/?cf_chl_f_tk=6laY-Ca7Ceh9HoiDp0EC_fK4a_rtsSK. wGQ7 kv64uPV0-1729728839-1.0.1.1-DhWQx8FNf771FdVJ9pleh14KU0.sQLtpF14Yu7c.7Tw

Corker, M. (2000). The U.K. Disability Discrimination Act: Disabling language, justifying inequitable social participation. In Francis, L. P., & Silvers, A. (Eds.), *Americans with disabilities: Exploring implications of the law for individuals and institutions* (pp. 357–370). Routledge.

Crawford, A., Hollingsworth, H. H., Morgan, K., & Gray, D. B. (2008). People with mobility impairments: Physical activity and quality of participation. *Disability and Health Journal, 1*, 7–13. https://pubmed.ncbi.nlm.nih.gov/21122706/

de Andrade, T. B., & de Andrade, F. B. (2018). Unmet need for assistance with activities of daily life among older adults in Brazil. *Revista de Saude Publica, 52*, 75. DOI: 10.11606/S1518-8787.2018052000463

Destyani, A. R., Ghazali, A. F., Harizta, A. D., & Nashori, H. F. (2019). Social support, gratitude and psychological wellbeing of persons with disabilities. ICRMH, September 18-19, Jakarta, Indonesia. https://doi: DOI: 10.4108/eai.18-9-2019.2293369

Digest, I. (2007). https:www.unicef-irc.org/publications

East, M. (2024). The vital role of social workers in supporting individuals with intellectual and developmental disabilities. https://www.linkedin.com/pulse/vital-role-social-workers-supporting-individuals-matt-east-rfmnc

Ekpe, C., & Mamah, S. (1997). *Social Work in Nigeria: A colonial heritage*. Unik Oriental Prints Ltd.

Eleweke, C., & Ebenso, J. (2016). Barriers to accessing services by people with disabilities in Nigeria: Insights from a qualitative study. *Journal of Educational and Social Research*, *6*(2), 113–123. DOI: 10.5901/jear.2016.v6n2p113

Equality and Human Rights Commission. (2011). Hidden in plain sight: inquiry into disability-related harassment. https://www.equalityhumanrights.com/en/publication-download/ hiddenplain-sight- inquiry- disability- related- harassment.

Etieyibo, E. (2020). Rights of persons with disabilities in Nigeria. *Afrika Focus*, *33*(1), 59–81. DOI: 10.1163/2031356X-03301005

Fakolade, O., Adeniyi, S., & Tella, A. (2009). Attitude of teachers towards the inclusion of special need children in general education classroom: The case of teachers in some selected schools in Nigeria. *International Electronic Journal of Elementary Education*, *1*(3), 155–169. https://files.eric.ed.gov/fulltext/EJ1052033.pdf

Farber, S., & Páez, A. (2010). Employment status and commute distance of Canadians with disabilities. *Transportation*, *37*(6), 931–952. DOI: 10.1007/s11116-010-9268-y

Faronbi, J. O., Faronbi, G. O., Ayamolowo, S. J., & Olaogun, A. A. (2019). Caring for the seniors with chronic illness: The lived experience of caregivers of older adults. *Archives of Gerontology and Geriatrics* 82: 8-14. https://doi.org/. archger.2019.01.013DOI: 10.1016/j

Federal Republic of Nigeria. (2020). National Policy on Aging. https://fmic. gov.ng/fg-approves-national-policy-on-ageing-for-older-persons-in-nigeria/

Findley, M., Smith, S., Gorski, J., & O'neil, M. (2007). Safety climate differences among job positions in a nuclear decommissioning and demolition industry: Employees' self-reported safety attitudes and perceptions. *Safety Science*, *45*(8), 875–889. DOI: 10.1016/ j.ssci.2006.08.027

Finkelstein, V. (1980). *Attitudes and disabled people*. World Rehabilitation Fund.

Fiorilli, G., Iuliano, E., Aquino, G., Battaglia, C., Giombini, A., Calcagno, G., & de Cagno, A. (2013). Mental health and social participation skills of wheelchair basketball players: A controlled study. *Research in Developmental Disabilities*, *34*(11), 3679–3685.

Garuba, A. (2003). Inclusive education in the 21st century: Challenges and opportunities for Nigeria. *Asia Pacific Disability Rehabilitation Journal, 14*, 191–200.

Gentilini, U., & Omamo, S. W. (2011). Social protection: Exploring issues, evidence and debates in a globalizing world. *Food Policy, 36*, 329–340. https://www.sciencedirect.com/science/article/pii/S0306-9192(11)00046-7

Goodwin, I., Davis, E., Winkler, D., Douglas, J., Wellecke, C., D'Cruz, K., Mulherin, P., & Liddicoat, S. (2022). Making homes more accessible for people with mobility impairment: A lived experience perspective. *The Australian Journal of Social Issues, 57*(4), 956–969. DOI: 10.1002/ajs4.214

Hackett, R. A., Steptoe, A., Lang, R. P., & Jackson, S. E. (2020). Disability discrimination and well-being in the United Kingdom: A prospective cohort study. *BMJ Open, 10*(3), e035714. DOI: 10.1136/bmjopen-2019-035714

Haruna, M. A. (2017). The problems of living with disability in Nigeria. *Journal of Law, Policy andGlobalization, 6(5),* 103-113. https://iiste.org/Journals/index.php/JLPG /article/view/3902 7.

Holt-Lundstad, J. (2017). The potential public health relevance of social isolation and loneliness: Prevalence, Epidemiology, and risk factors. *The Public Policy and Aging Report, 27*(4), 127–130. DOI: 10.1093/ppar/prx030

Hulatt, L., & Freitas, G. (2024). Disability discrimination: Act, causes and effects. https://www.studysmarter.co.uk/explanations/social-studies/stratification-and-differentiation/disability-discrimination/

Hume-Nixon, M., & Kuper, H. (2018). The association between malnutrition and childhood disability in low- and middle-income countries: Systematic review and meta-analysis of observational studies. *Tropical Medicine & International Health, 23*(11), 1158–1175. DOI: 10.1111/tmi.13139

Hunt, X., Bradshaw, M., Vogel, S. L., Encalada, A. V., Eksteen, S., Schneider, M., Chunga, K., & Swartz, L. (2022). Community Support for Persons with Disabilities in Low- and Middle-Income Countries: A Scoping Review. *International Journal of Environmental Research and Public Health, 19*(14), 8269. DOI: 10.3390/ijerph19148269

Institute of Development Studies. (2020). *Nigeria Situational Analysis Version II.* https://opendocs.ids.ac.uk/opendocs/bitstream/handle/20.500.12413/15561/DID%20SITAN%20Nigeria%20V2%20July%202020.pdf?sequence=1&isAllowed=y

Ipingbemi, O. (2015). Mobility challenges and transport safety of people with disabilities in Ibadan, Nigeria. *African Journal for the Psychological Study of Social Issues, 18*(3), 15–28. https://www.ajol.info/index.php/ajpssi/article/view/136989

Irwanto, Kasim, E.R., Fransiska, A., Lusli, M., & Siradj, O. (2010). Analisis situasi penyandang disabilitas di Indonesia: Sebuah desk-review. *Pusat Kajian Disabilitas Fisip UI*

Iwuagwu, A. O., & Kalu, M. E. (2021). Covid-19 and older adults: The paradox of physical distancing. *Ace Journal of Public Health and Community Medicine, 1(1)* 8-9. https://www.researchgate.net/publication/349992131_COVID-19_and_Nigerian_Older_Adults_The_Paradox_of_Physical_Distancing#fullTextFileContent

Jaarsma, E. A., Dijkstra, P. U., Geertzen, J. H. B., & Dekker, R. (2014). Barriers to and facilitators of sports participation for people with physical disabilities: A systematic review. *Scandinavian Journal of Medicine & Science in Sports*, (6), 871–881. DOI: 10.1111/sms.12218

Kavanagh, A., Krnjacki, L., Aitken, Z., LaMontagne, A., Beer, A., Baker, E., & Bentley, R. (2015). Intersections between disability, type of impairment, gender and socio-economic disadvantage in a nationally representative sample of 33,101 working-aged Australians. *Disability and Health Journal*, *8*(2), 191–199. DOI: 10.1016/j.dhjo.2014.08.008

Kim, H. Jang, S, & Lim, J. (2022). Service Demand for and Awareness of a Primary Healthcare Pilot Project for People with Disabilities. *J Korean Med Sci. 1;37(30)*:e241https://doi. org/DOI: 10.3346/ jkms.2022.37.e241

Kim, J., Kim, J., Kim, Y., Han, A., & Nguyen, M. C. (2021). The contribution of physical and social activity participation to social support and happiness among people with physical disabilities. *Disability and Health Journal*, *1*, 100974. DOI: 10.1016/j.dhjo.2020.100974

Korndoerfer, K. M. (2023). What Does a Social Worker for Disability Services Do? https://www.google.com/search?q=What+Does+a+Social+Worker+for+Disability+Services+Do%3F&oq=What+Does+a+Social+Worker+for+Disability+Services+Do%3F&gs_lcrp=EgZjaHJvbWUyBggAEEUYOTIHCAEQIRiPAtIBCDEzNTZqMGo3qAIIsAIB8QVCdxFwWM2_2g&sourceid=chrome&ie=UTF-8

Krahn, G. L. (2011). WHO World Report on Disability: A review. *Disability and Health Journal*, *4*(3), 141–142. DOI: 10.1016/j.dhjo.2011.05.001

Kuvalekar, K., Kamath, R., Ashok, L., Shetty, B., Mayya, S., & Chandrasekaran, V. (2015). Quality of life among persons with physical disability in Udupi Taluk: A cross sectional study. *Journal of Family Medicine and Primary Care*, *4*(1), 69–73. DOI: 10.4103/2249-4863.152258

Lamichhane, K. (2015). *Disability, education and employment in developing countries: From charity to investment.* University Press.

Lang, R., & Upah, L. (2008). Scoping study: Disability issues in Nigeria. https://studylib.net/doc/13390397/scoping-study--disability-issues-in-nigeria-final-report

Lee, H. J., Jeong, W., Chon, D., Kim, J. H., & Moon, J. Y. (2022). The Association between perceived discrimination and mental health of wage workers with disabilities: Findings from the panel survey of employment for the disabled 2016-2018. *International Journal of Environmental Research and Public Health*, *19*(14), 8541. DOI: 10.3390/ijerph1914 8541

Lindsay, S., Fuentes, K., Ragunathan, S., Li, Y., & Ross, T. (2024). Accessible independent housing for people with disabilities: A scoping review of promising practices, policies and interventions. *PLoS One*, *19*(1), e0291228. DOI: 10.1371/journal.pone.0291228

Martin Ginis, K. A., van der Ploeg, H. P., Foster, C., Lai, B., McBride, C. B., Ng, K., Pratt, M., Shirazipour, C. H., Smith, B., Vásquez, P. M., & Heath, G. W. (2021). Participation of people living with disabilities in physical activity: A global perspective. *Lancet*, *398*(10298), 443–455. DOI: 10.1016/S0140-6736(21)01164-8

Martinez, R., & Vemuru, V. (2020). Social inclusion of persons with disabilities in Nigeria: Challenges and opportunities. https://blogs.worldbank.org/nasikiliza/social-inclusion-persons-disabilities-nigeria-challenges-and-opportunities

McCausland, D., McCallion, P., Carroll, R., & McCarron, M. (2021). The nature and quality of friendship for older adults with an intellectual disability in Ireland. *Journal of Applied Research in Intellectual Disabilities*, *34*, 763–776. DOI: 10.1111/jar.12851

Meyer, B., & Asbrock, F. (2018). Disabled or cyborg? How bionics affect stereotypes toward people with physical disabilities. *Frontiers in Psychology*, *9*, 2251. DOI: 10.3389/ fpsyg.2018.02251

Meyer, B. D., & Mok, W. K. C. (2019). Disability, earnings, income and consumption. *Journal of Public Economics*, *171*(C), 51–69. DOI: 10.1016/j.jpubeco.2018.06.011

Mitra, S., Posarac, A. & Vick, B. (2013). Disability and poverty in developing countries: A multidimensional study. *World Development* 41: 1-18. https://doi.org/ . 2012.05.024DOI: 10.1016/j.worlddev

Mizunoya, S., & Mitra, S. (2013). Is there a disability gap in employment rates in developing countries? *World Development, 42*, 28–43. DOI: 10.1016/j.world-dev.2012.05.037

Mizunoya, S., Mitra, S., & Yamasaki, I. (2018). Disability and school attendance in 15 low- and middle-income countries. *World Development,* Elsevier, 104(C), 388-403. https://doi: : 388-403.DOI: 10.1016/j.worlddev.2017.12.001 104

Moscoso-Porras, M., & Alvarado, G. (2018). Association between perceived discrimination and healthcare-seeking behaviour in people with a disability. *Disability and Health Journal,11*(1), 93-8. https://www.ncbi.nlm.nih.gov/nlmcatalog?term=%22Disabil+Health +J%22%5BTitle+Abbreviation%5D

Nigeria Demographic and Health Survey. (2018). *2018 DHS key findings*. https://www.microdata.worldbank.org>...>DHS

Nnama-Okechukwu, C. U., Chukwuka, P. N., & Okoye, U. O. (2020). Challenges with institutional support services for undergraduate students with visual impairment in University of Nigeria, Nsukka. *Evidence-Informed Social Work, 17*(6), 677–695.

Obiakor, F., & Offor, M. (2011). Special education provision in Nigeria: Analysing contexts, problems and prospects. *International Journal of Special Education, 26*(1), 25–32. https://www.academia.edu/59362328/Special_Education_Provision_in_Nigeria_Analyzing_Contexts_Problems_and_Prospects

Obst, P., & Stafurik, J. (2010). Online we are all able bodied: Online psychological sense of community and social support found through membership of disability-specific websites promotes well-being for people living with a physical disability. *Journal of Community & Applied Social Psychology, 20*(6), 525–531. DOI: 10.1002/casp.1067

Ofuani, A. (2011). The right to economic empowerment of persons with disabilities in Nigeria: How enabled? *African Human Rights Law Journal, 11(2),* 639-658. https://www.ahrlj.up.ac. za /ofuani-ai-2011

Ogundipe, S. (2019). Buhari signs law banning discrimination against persons with disability. https://www.premiumtimesng.com/news/headlines/307474-buhari-signs-law-banning-discrimination-against-persons-with-disability.html?tztc=1

Okah, P., Chukwu, N., Agha, A., Onalu, C., Nnama-Okechukwu, C., Iwuagwu, A., Anazonwu, N., & Okoye, U. (2023a). Formal support services for People living With Disabilities (PWDs) in Southeast Nigeria. *Journal of Social Work in Developing Societies*, *5*(2), 50–64. https://journals.aphriapub.com/index.php/JSWDS/article/view/2315

Okah, P., Onalu, C., & Okoye, U. (2023b). National Health Insurance Scheme in Nigeria: Exploring limitations to utilisation by adult enrollees. *Journal of Social Service Research*, *49*(6), 715–730. DOI: 10.1080/01488376.2023.2265417

Okpa, J. T., Ilupeju, A. A., & Eshiotse, E. (2020). Cybercrime and socio-economic development of corporate organisations in Cross River State, Nigeria. *Asian Journal of Scientific Research*, *13*(3), 205–213. DOI: 10.3923/ajsr.2020.205.213

Oliver, M. (1996). *Understanding disability: From theory to practice*. Macmillan.

Onalu, C., Chukwu, N., Nnama-Okechukwu, C. U., Iwuagwu, A., Agha, A., Okah, P., Anazonwu, P., & Okoye, U. (2023). An exploratory study of the situation of persons with disabilities in Nigeria: Practice consideration for social workers. *Journal of Evidence-Based Social Work*. Advance online publication. DOI: 10.1080/26408066.2023.2265920

Onalu, C., & Nwafor, N. (2021). Social supports available to persons with disabilities in Nigeria. https://www.doi: DOI: 10.5772/intechopen.97790

Pagán-Rodríguez, R. (2014). How do disabled individuals spend their leisure time? *Disability and Health Journal*, *7*(2), 196–205. DOI: 10.1016/j.dhjo.2014.01.001

Paley, J. (2002). The Cartesian melodrama in nursing. *Nursing Philosophy*, *3*(3), 189–192. DOI: 10. 1046/j.1466-769X.2002.00113.x

Rahim, R. (2024). Social workers' role in the provision of services for families with children and youth with disabilities in Latvia, Slovakia, and Portugal. SHS Web of Conferences 184, 01007. *Int. Conf. Society Health Welfare*. https://doi.org/DOI: 10.1051/shsconf/202418401007

Rimmer, J. H., Riley, B., Wang, E., Rauworth, A., & Jurkowski, J. (2004). Physical activity participation among persons with disabilities: Barriers and facilitators. *American Journal of Preventive Medicine*, *26*(5), 419–425. DOI: 10.1016/j.amepre.2004.02.002

Sambo, A. (2016). Physically challenged students and their information needs. Library Philosophy and Practice (E-Journal), 1461. https://www.researchgate.net/publication/313615123

Sayyidah, A. N. (2015). Dinamika penyesuaian diri penyandang disabilitas di tempat magang kerja (studi deskriptif di balai rehabilitas terpadu penyandang disabilitas (BRTPD) Yogyakarta). *INKLUSI*, *2*(1), 64–86. DOI: 10.14421/ijds.020104

Scior, K. (2011). Public awareness, attitudes and beliefs regarding intellectual disability: A systematic review. *Research in Developmental Disabilities*, *32*(6), 2164–2182. DOI: 10.1016/j.ridd.2011.07.005

Sedeto, M. H., & Dar, M. J. (2019). Socio-economic challenges of persons with disabilities: A Case Study of Ethiopia. *Global Journal of Human-Social Science: C Sociology & Culture, 19* (1), 1-9. https://globaljournals.org/GJHSS_Volume19/3-Socio-Economic-Challenges-of-Persons.pd

Sholanke, A. B. (2019). Compliance of academic buildings of selected universities in Ogun State, Nigeria with universal design parameters. Unpublished Ph.D Thesis, Covenant University, Ota, Ogun State, Nigeria. https://www.academia.edu/113763853/Compliance_of_High_rise_Buildings_Vertical_Accessibility_Components_with_Universal_Design_Strategies_A_Case_Study_of_Covenant_University_Ota_Nigeria

Sur, M. H., Jung, J., & Shapiro, D. R. (2022). Theory of planned behavior to promote physical activity of adults with physical disabilities: Meta-analytic structural equation modeling. *Disability and Health Journal*, *15*(1), 101199. DOI: 10.1016/j.dhjo.2021.101199

Swartz, L., & Marchetti-Mercer, M. (2019). Migration, technology and care: What happens to the body? *Disability & Society*, *34*, 407–420. DOI: 10.1080/09687599.2018.1519409

Tangcharoensathien, V., Witthayapipopsakul, W., Viriyathorn, S., & Patcharanarumol, W. (2018). Improving access to assistive technologies: Challenges and solutions in low- and middle-income countries. *WHO South-East Asia Journal of Public Health*, *7*(2), 84–89. DOI: 10.4103/2224-3151.239419

Temple, J., & Kelaher, M. (2018). Is disability exclusion associated with psychological distress? Australian evidence from a national cross-sectional survey. *BMJ Open*, *8*, e020829. DOI: 10.1136/bmjopen-2017-020829

Temple, J., & Williams, R. (2018). Financial wellbeing of older Australians with multiple health conditions. *Australasian Journal on Ageing*. Advance online publication. DOI: 10.1111/ajag.12497

Temple, J. B., Kelaher, M., & Williams, R. (2018). Discrimination and avoidance due to disability in Australia: Evidence from a national cross-sectional survey. *BMC Public Health*, *18*, 1347. DOI: 10.1186/s12889-018-6234-7

Thapaliya, M. A. (2016). Report on disability in Nepal. Sydney (Australia): Australian Himalayan Foundation (AHF), 1-24. https://www.australianhimalayanfoundation .org.au/wp-content/uploads/2017/08/2016_Nepal_Disability_Report.pdf

The Guardian. (2019). Next level for disability law in Nigeria, July 11. M.guardian.ng>opinion.next-level-for... Thomsen, F. K. (2017). *Discrimination: Oxford research encyclopedia of politics*. Oxford University Press; Oxford, UK. https://oxfordre.com/politics/display/10.1093/acrefore/ 9780190228637.001.0001/acrefore-9780190228637-e-202?d=%2F10.1093% 2Facrefore%2F9780190228637.001.0001%2Facrefore-9780190228637-e-202&p= emailAG4hUJ.qDxj6E

Tucker, R., Kelly, D., Johnson, L., De, J. U., & Watchorn, V. (2022). Housing at the fulcrum: A systems approach to uncovering built environment obstacles to city scale accessibility and inclusion. *Journal of Housing and the Built Environment*, *37*, 1179–1197. https://hdl.handle. net/ 10536/DRO/DU:30154331

Umeh, N., & Adeola, R. (2013). Country Reports: Nigeria. In: Ngwena, C., Plessis, H., Combrinck, H., & Kamga, S. (Eds.), *African Disability Rights Yearbook*. 1. https://www. adry.up.ac.za/images/adry/volume1_2013/adry_2013_1_full_text.pdf

Umoh, E., & Unaka, D. (2019). What needs to be done to enhance disability rights in Nigeria. Report on human rights violations based on real or perceived sexual orientation and gender identity in Nigeria, pp. 48-50. https://theinitiativeforequalrights .org/wp-content/uploads/2019/12/2019-Human-Rights-Violations-Reports-Based-on-SOGI.pdf

United Nations. (2006). *Conventions on the rights of persons with disabilities*. United Nations Department of Economic and Social Affairs.

United Nations. (2015). *Report of the Special Rapporteur on the rights of persons with disabilities. A/70/297*. United Nations.

United Nations Educational Scientific and Cultural Organisation. (2009). Policy guidelines on inclusion in education. https://unesdoc.unesco.org/ark:/48223/ pf0000177849

UPIAS. (1976). Fundamental principles of disability. London: Union of the Physically Impaired Against Segregation. https://books.google.com.ng/books/about/Fundamental_Principles_ of_Disability.html?id=rS5BPQAACAAJ&redir_esc=y
Uromi, S., & Mazagwa, M. (2014). Challenges facing people with disabilities and possible solutions in Tanzania. Journal of Educational Policy and Entrepreneurial Research, 1(2), 158-165. https://core.ac.uk/download/pdf/234698127.pdf

Vasquez, E. A. (2021). How can we best provide community supports in low- and middle-income countries? https://inclusive-policy.org/forum/how-can-we-best -provide-community-supports-in-low-and-middle-income-countries

Verdonschot, M. M., de Witte, L. P., Reichrath, E., Buntinx, W. H., & Curfs, L. M. (2009). Impact of environmental factors on community participation of persons with an intellectual disability: A systematic review. *Journal of Intellectual Disability Research, 53*(1), 54–64. DOI: 10.1111/j.1365-2788.2008.01128.x

Wang, Z., Xu, X., Han, Q., Chen, Y., Jiang, J., & Ni, G. X. (2021). Factors associated with public attitudes towards persons with disabilities: A systematic review. *BMC Public Health, 21*(1), 1058. DOI: 10.1186/s12889-021-11139-3

Winter, J. A. (2003). The development of the disability rights movement as a social problem solver. *Disability Studies Quarterly, 23*(1). Advance online publication. DOI: 10.18061/dsq.v23i1.399.S2CID1429869 57

World Bank. (2020). *Disability inclusion.* https://www.worldbank.org/en/topic/disability#1

World Health Organisation. (2021). *Disability and Health.* https://www.who.int/news-room/fact-sheets/detail/disability-and-health

World Health Organization. (2018). *Improving access to assistive technology report by the director-general seventy-first world health assembly.* World Health Organization.

Xiao, J. J., & O'Neill, B. (2021). Disability type, financial capability, and Risky asset holding. *Journal of Disability Policy Studies, 32*(4). Advance online publication. DOI: 10.1177/1044207320981781

Yusuf, M., Fakomogbon, M., & Issa, A. (2012). Availability of assistive technologies in Nigerian educational institutions. *International Journal of Social Sciences and Education, 2*(1), 44–55. http://ijsse.com/sites/default/files/issues/2012/volume%202 %20issue%201%20Jan%202012/paper%204/paper-04.pdf

Zaki, M. (2009). Validity and reliability of social support scale at the student of Isfahan Universities. *Majallah-i Ravanpizishki va Ravanshinasi-i Balini-i Iran, 14*(4), 439–446. https://core.ac.uk/download/pdf/33096621.pdf

ADDITIONAL READING

Adaka, T. A., & Uji, V. I. (2018). Service delivery to persons with disabilities. In T. A., Adaka & E. W. Obiozor (eds). *Issues in education: Theory and practice,* 91-104. https://www.researchgate.net/profile/Adaka-Ahon/publication/358229332_Service_Delivery_to_Persons_with_Disabilities/links/61f6fd3e11a1090a79c0e14b/Service-Delivery-to-Persons-with-Disabilities.pdf

Arimoro, A. (2019). Are they not Nigerians? The obligation of the state to end discriminatory practices against persons with disabilities. *International Journal of Discrimination and the Law, 19 (2),* 89-109. https://journals.sagepub.com/doi/abs/10.1177/13582291198 4676427

Barrio, B., Miller, D., Ojeme, C., & Tamakloe, D. (2018). Teachers' and parents' knowledge about disabilities inclusion in Nigeria. *Journal of International Special Needs Education, 22*(1), 14–24. https://files.eric.ed.gov/fulltext/EJ1222118.pdf

Buettgen, A., & Zubrow, E. (2024). Nothing without us: Disability critical thought and social change in a globalizing world. In M. H. Rioux, A. Buettgen, E, Zubrow & Viera (eds). *Handbook of Disability.* 9-18. https://link.springer.com/referencework/10.1007/978-981-19-6056-7?page=4#toc

Etieyibo, E., & Omiegbe, O. (2017). *Disabilities in Nigeria: Attitudes, reactions, and remediation.* https://rowman.com/ISBN/9780761869061/Disabilities-in-Nigeria-Attitudes-Reactions-and-Remediation

Fefoame, G. O., & Loryman, H. (2024). Towards a rights-based policy environment for the employment of persons with disabilities (eds). In M. H. Rioux, A. Buettgen, E, Zubrow & Viera (eds). *Handbook of Disability.* 1055-1069. https://link.springer.com/referencework/10.1007/978-981-19-6056-7?page=4#toc

Idris, Z., & Adaka, T. A. (2023). Family Engagement and Service Delivery to People with Disabilities in Nigeria (2023). DOI: . https://www.igi-global.com/chapter/family-engagement-and-service-delivery-to-people-with-disabilities-in-nigeria/329463DOI: 10.4018/978-1-6684-8651-1.ch014

Löve, L. E., & Traustadóttir, R. (2024). Disabled people's mobilization around a human rights approach to enhance their participation in law and policy making in Iceland. In M. H. Rioux, A. Buettgen, E, Zubrow & Viera (eds). *Handbook of Disability.* 183-194. https://link.springer.com/referencework/10.1007/978-981-19-6056-7?page=4#toc

Martinez, R., & Vemuru, V. (2020). Social inclusion of persons with disabilities in Nigeria: Challenges and opportunities. https://blogs.worldbank.org/nasikiliza/social-inclusion-persons-disabilities-nigeria-challenges-and-opportunities

Onalu, C., & Nwafor, N. (2021). Social supports available to persons with disabilities in Nigeria. In R. Morese, V. Auriemma, & S. Palemo (eds). *Evolutionary Psychology Meets Social Neuroscience*. https://www.intechopen.com/chapters/76704

Series, L. (2020). Disability and human rights. In N. Watson, A. Roulstone, & C. Thomas (2nd Ed). Routledge *Handbook of Disability Studies*. 72-87. https://routledge.com/Routledge-Handbook-of-Disability-Studies/Watson-Roulstone-Thomas/p/book/9781032376189? srsltid=AfmBOooK70y_waOIlhupVPXeu_W_ad1gxxnu-mIlRSl1Vc71dSM0227sL

KEY TERMS AND DEFINITIONS

Access: This is the ability to get services meant for improved living conditions without difficulties or discrimination.

Disability: This means an impediment that affects one's functioning or prevents him or her from functioning well like those without any form of disabilities.

Discrimination: This is the deliberate attempt or act of scheming people out or exhibiting prejudice in the provision of services in society.

Factors: These mean obstacles or challenges that prevent PWDs from fully accessing available support services aimed at improving their living conditions.

People with Disabilities: These are people with one or more forms of disabilities or impairments that limit their full functioning in society. These disabilities which could be physical, mental, or psychological prevent these people (PWDs) from carrying out some functions required of them or needed to sustain a healthy living. They therefore need assistance to carry out some activities that they would have carried out independently if not for disability.

Social work: Social work is a professional discipline that seeks to help individuals, especially vulnerable groups overcome most, if not all the challenges confronting their lives. It is a profession that helps people to help themselves in dealing with life challenges.

Support services: These are assistance provided for PWDs and other vulnerable groups by either the government, family and friends, society, organizations, or spirited individuals to help the concerned persons cope with the challenges of life.

Chapter 3
Misconceptions Against the Learners With Bipolar Mood Disorder and Implications for Inclusive Education in Schools and Society

Andile Alred Mdikana
https://orcid.org/0000-0002-6968-8945
University of South Africa, South Africa

ABSTRACT

The aim of this chapter is to discuss the misconceptions about leaners living with bipolar mood disorder (BMD). The lack of lived experience with BMD can result in a number of critical misconceptions, with opinions abounding as to those of who live with BMD. Often, the commentaries concerned are written by those who do not understand the bipolar experience. Therefore, a scholarly and academic attempt was made to review the relevant literature critically with a view to presenting a balanced attempt to dismiss the stereotypes and the stigma perpetuated against learners living with BMD. The derogatory language used against such learners, which often leads to exclusionary practices, was explored.

DOI: 10.4018/979-8-3373-7163-4.ch003

INTRODUCTION

Complex mental health conditions, such as bipolar mood disorder (BMD), are deeply misunderstood (Youngstrom et al., 2005). Whether due to a general lack of understanding, or to a belief in damaging stereotypes, many people who live with BMD have had to face discrimination, bullying, isolation, or, at its worst, violence, throughout their life (Berk & Dodd, 2005). While the media is currently doing a better job of depicting bipolar mood disorder (BMD) than it did before, many misconceptions still exist when it comes to understanding this mood disorder (Goodwin & Jamison, 2007). All of us have some form of challenge with which we have to cope, but for people with BMD, the peaks and valleys are much more severe, ranging from the highs of mania to the lows of depression (Healy, 2006). Unlike typical mood swings that pass quickly, BMD features cycles or episodes that can last anything from weeks to months (Sachs, 2004). Since BMD often worsens without treatment, it is essential to learn what the symptoms look like, so as to reduce the associated stigma and so as to encourage those with BMD to seek help for the disorder (Ghaemi et al., 2008).

In the United States of America (USA), BMD is not confined to those of a certain age or race, with people from all racial and age groups having been negatively affected (Kowatch, 2005). This is despite the medical and research advances that are taking place in that country, with, in addition, those affected still showing unwillingness to reveal the nature of their illness to others (Neighbours et al., 2007), due to the myths, stigmas and stereotypes that are associated with the condition. The treatment of BMD is made problematic by the issue of culture and assessment. Despite the USA being such a developed and advanced country, some Americans still believe that, if one is attacked by BMD, a cure is only possible through the performance of certain cultural rites, so that they might refuse to undergo psychological and/or psychiatric assessment (Mackin et al., 2006).

The United Kingdom (UK) is one of the most progressive countries in the world in terms of the fight against, and the treatment of, mental health problems like BMD (The Lancet Editorial, 2016), which it has declared is a mental health crisis requiring urgent intervention and attention. The seriousness with which it deals with the matter explains why the UK is able to manage and contain the condition so effectively (Rossler, 2016), so that the impact of the disorder is felt minimally in the country concerned. Widespread education, awareness, advocacy and information sharing occur in both the print and the social media against the myths, stereotypes, stigmas and misconceptions associated with the disorder (Forde, 2020), affecting its consequent impact (Greenstein, 2017).

The fight against the incorrect and harmful misperception of BMD should be regarded as a national emergency, so as to minimise the impact of BMD-related stigma on seeking out, and participating in, mental health care programmes and treatment (Corrigan et al., 2014). Overcoming the stigma of BMD is possible, through those affected taking the right treatment, living in a stress-free environment and abstaining from alcohol (Mayo Clinic Staff, 2017).

The health authorities in the UK have focused on perceptions, knowledge and proof (Pescosolido, 2013), which all entail active involvement in problem-solving processes. Any health intervention that involves human life should be well thought out, with the primary attention being given to critical intervention. In addition, the intervention should be based on the currently held body of knowledge, which usually consists of empirical research regarding the BMD. Finally, the focus should be on proof. The BMD is an age-old treatable condition, with which one can live a long and meaningful life, due to the progress that has been made in terms of medical and psychological research, with the associated stigma, myths and stereotypes no longer being a barrier to recovery (Oexle et al., 2017).

India is a country that is deeply divided along both cultural and religious lines. In some Indian communities, the existence of BMD is given a cultural and religious meaning, with it usually having a negative connotation and being regarded as a subjective burden on the spouse and family concerned, as well as on the other members of the extended family (Kumari et al., 2009). The situation has been acerbated by health inequalities, with those from the poverty-stricken communities lacking adequate and quality mental health care, education and information (Ngui, 2010). The inadequacies of the situation make the understanding of BMD and its impact of stigma difficult to understand in relation to those living with BMD (Corrigan & Watson, 2002). Srinivasa and Trivedi (1982), in providing a solution to the problem, argue that having knowledge about, and adopting an attitude change towards, mental disease are vital in dealing with misconceptions about people and children living with BMD. Wig et al. (1980) argue that community reactions to mental disorders like BMD need to be considered for successful interventions to take place against the disorder.

Since 2013, Australia has been embarking on aggressive initiatives in the fight against stigma, myths, stereotypes and misconceptions in relation to BMD (SANE Australia, 2013), with positive results. The initiatives have yielded good results, with the Australians becoming aware of the psychological dangers that are associated with misconceptions. The manifestation of stigmatising attitudes towards people with mental disorders is regarded as a violation of human rights (Reavley & Jorm, 2012). In Australia, the stigma of mental illness, such as BMD, has been done away with (Sheehan et al., 2017). The fight against misconceptions relating to people with BMD should not be limited to Australia, but it should, rather, be regarded as part of a global pattern of countering experienced and anticipated discrimination against people with BMD (Thornicroft et al., 2009). The fight against the misconception should be taken seriously, with there being a reported link between mental health-related discrimination and suicidality (Farrelly et al., 2015). The mental health professionals or caregivers should focus on teaching recovery from a lived experience perspective (Byrne et al., 2013).

In the Saharan region, mental illness is largely influenced by stigma and ethno cultural beliefs, values and norms (Abdullah & Brown, 2011). Such influence complicates the interventions that are aimed at preventing and treating BMD. Furthermore, what complicates the intervention and treatment activities is the economic burden of caregiving for persons with severe mental illness in sub-Saharan Africa (Addo et al., 2018). Resultantly, mental health treatment tends to be rendered to the select few who have access to economic resources. In South Africa, for instance, the state-owned mental institutions tend to be poorly resourced, with, as a result, such institutions failing to provide quality health care services (Herman et al., 2009). An alternative view is that it is simplistic to confine interventions to cultural and economic aspects alone, with the role of the mental health care giver being critical to the management of BMD.

ADOPTING THE HUMAN RIGHTS APPROACH

For the current study, the human rights approach was preferred, because of its emphasis on the rights of marginalised groups. Learners with BMD are generally considered to be part of a marginalised community, including those who face discrimination and social exclusion. Accordingly, BMD is considered to be a human rights issue, with learners living with BMD often finding their rights relegated to the periphery of societal and political concerns (Katsui & Kumpuvuori, 2008). Learners with BMD often find themselves subject to abuse, which violates their human rights.

The human rights approach seeks to empower learners living with BMD, and encourages the development of an attitude of self-respect, as well as enabling them to fight for their own rights (Bollard, 2009). The approach calls on all those who are responsible for enforcing their rights to do so in a manner that reinforces their sense of accountability and responsibility, in terms of respecting, safeguarding and realising them (Venkatapuram, 2014). Civil society should help to initiate empowerment support programmes for those who are living with BMD, as participating in such programmes would enable them to play a meaningful role in decisions affecting themselves. Such participation can be used to inform the policies affecting learners living with BMD.

The human rights approach is guided by principles of participation, accountability, non-discrimination and equality, as well as empowerment and legality. The participation of the individual in the self-management of their disorder means that they are free to engage in activities affecting their daily life (Bollard, 2009), as well as having the freedom to decide what rights they wish to enjoy. Such involvement also concerns the concept of accessibility to health care and social services, education and training opportunities, housing and the criminal justice system, as well as freedom of expression (Bollard, 2009). Learners with BMD often find themselves excluded from community-based activities, due to a lack of active participation in them. In relation to care, people with BMD need to have a say in the care and support that they receive (Venkatapuram, 2014).

COUNTERING MYTHS ABOUT LEARNERS WITH BMD

In South Africa, the scant knowledge that is available about childhood BMD often results in misdiagnosis, and in relatively few people seeking treatment for the disorder (Pinfold et al., 2005). BMD is highly stigmatised and stereotyped in South Africa (Kakuma, 2010), with those who have to live with the condition most of the time being regarded as social outcasts, which situation is complicated by the myths that are associated with the disorder (Thornicroft et al., 2008). The concepts of stigma, stereotype, prejudice, discrimination and myths impact on one another (Bayer, 2008). The following section discusses the common myths and facts that exist in relation to BMD.

Myth: There is no hope for people with mental health problems. Once a friend or family member develops mental health problems, he or she will never recover from them.

Fact: Studies (Deacon, 2006; Sartorius, 1998) show that people with mental health problems improve, and that many recover completely. Recovery refers to the process by which people with problems are able, once more, to learn to live, work, learn and participate fully in their communities. Currently, there are more treatments, services and community support systems than ever before, which have all proved to be effective in their own way.

Myth: Therapy and self-help are a waste of time. Why bother to make the effort when you can just take a pill?

Fact: Treatment for mental health problems varies, depending on the individual concerned, with it including medication, therapy or both (Phelan et al., 2008). Many individuals function with a support system during the healing and recovery process.

Myth: I can do nothing for a person with a mental health problem.

Fact: Friends and loved ones can make a big difference in helping to support someone who lives with a mental health problem. Research shows that, only 20% of adults receive any mental health treatment, including the 10% who receive counselling and/or therapy from a professional. Friends and family can be important influences on helping someone receive the treatment and services that they require (Corrigan et al., 2005).

Myth: Prevention does not work. It is impossible to prevent mental illness.

Fact: Prevention of mental, emotional and behavioural disorders focuses on addressing known risk factors, like exposure to trauma, which can lead to children, youths and young adults developing mental health problems. Promoting the social-emotional well-being of children and youth can contribute to the well-being of a person living with mental illness, like BMD (Rüsch et al., 2005). The other members of the family can serve as the support structure, when they are informed and educated about the condition. In some cases, family members may be encouraged to attend relevant support groups, where they can share their experiences of living with someone with BMD.

ADDRESSING STIGMAS AND STEREOTYPES ASSOCIATED WITH BIPOLAR MOOD DISORDER AMONG LEARNERS IN SOUTH AFRICA

Over half of those living with mental illness do not receive help for their mental disorders (Keusch et al., 2006). Often, those with BMD avoid or delay seeking treatment, due to the concerns that they have about being treated differently, or due to fears related to losing their job and livelihood (Kahng & Mowbray, 2005). Stigma, prejudice and discrimination against people with mental illness, which is still very much a problem, can be either subtle or obvious, but, no matter its magnitude, it can lead to harm (Link & Phelan, 2006). People with mental illness are marginalised and discriminated against in various ways, but understanding what it feels like, and how to address and eradicate the problem, can help. Stigma often comes either from lack of understanding or from fear. Inaccurate or misleading media representations of mental illness contribute to both such elements. A review of studies on stigma shows that, while the public might accept the medical or genetic nature of a mental health disorder and the need for treatment, many people still have a negative view of those with a mental problem (Corrigan & Shapiro, 2010; Parle, 2012<<AUTHOR: Please add the publication details of this source to your reference list. Thank you.>>; Scambler, 1998). The following South African strategies are proposed to address the difficulties caused by the stigmas, the stereotypes and the marginalisation of learners living with BMD at school: school-orientated strategies and parent- and family-oriented strategies.

School-Oriented Strategies For Supporting Learners with BMD

School-oriented strategies should target the learners, the teachers, the school management teams, the parents and the support staff. A child is a member of the school community, which means that, if he or she is living with BMD, this should be of concern to all the members of the community, including the parents. Within the context of the school, programmes and strategies that are aimed at caring for and supporting the child who is living with BMD are usually led by the school-based support team (SBST). This structure has the primary responsibility for training and empowering teachers and parents on such issues as the prevention and early identification of stigmas and stereotypes, the awareness of children with living with BMD, and the reporting and referral of learners with symptoms of BMD, before they are ostracised and discriminated against by those learners and teachers who have little understanding of BMD. Since such support teams usually have expertise, they can also provide sexuality education and basic counselling, as well as being in a position to facilitate awareness and advocacy campaigns. The activities of the SBST are expected to result in informed and capacitated school and parent communities that are aware of the struggle against BMD in relation to the myths, stigmas and stereotypes that are associated with the disorder. It is also imperative for the structure to formulate school-based policies on matters relating to BMD. The policy framework should be well placed, so as to be able to guide the practice of quality care and support with which the learners with BMD should be provided.

Parent- and Family-Oriented Strategies for Supporting Learners with BMD

Parents are an important and critical stakeholder in the education and health of any child, with parental involvement and engagement requiring to be enhanced for the purpose of quality care and support provision. Therefore, the school is not only responsible for providing quality care, support and protection for the child living with BMD, but also for supporting their parents and families. Collaboration between the school and the family becomes critical, with the parents involved being trained by the SBST to prevent, identify and support the learner with BMD, and being in a position to manage the BMD problem without prejudice, and up until the learner is referred to the health authorities for quality care and support.

Involvement of the Department of Education in Supporting Learners with BMD

The Department of Education in South Africa manages schools through its District Offices. Within each district is an established structure called a district-based support team (DBST), whose main responsibility is to ensure that the SBSTs are equipped to provide quality care and support, which it monitors. The DBST should also be in a position to provide strategic training and development on all aspects of health, including BMD. BMD can affect all children, including those with intellectual disabilities. The DBST runs awareness and parental training sessions to complement and strengthen the work of schools. The increased involvement of the DBST should lead to the improved implementation of care and support services and to the development of a conscientised parental and school community in the fight against BMD. Finally, the recruitment and retention of competent DBST staff who are knowledgeable about children living with BMD would go a long way towards the early identification, prevention and management of BMD in children.

Involvement in the Department of Social Development in Supporting Learners with BMD

The presence of BMD in learners, which can be a traumatic experience, can manifest as emotional and behavioural complications requiring counselling and psychotherapy. It is imperative for the Department of Social Development to be involved with the school in such a timely manner that it can employ professional social workers who can take care of the counselling needs and the challenges of learners living with BMD. Social workers, who are trained in understanding and intervening in social problems that result from BMD, are often invited by schools to train members of the school community and parents regarding how to identify and manage responses. Most social workers, at school level, work with children with health and psychosocial problems. The increased role of the Department of Social Development should result in the empowerment of parents, learners and the school community.

Involvement of the Department of Children, Women and People with Disabilities in Supporting Learners with BMD

The Department of Children, Women and People with Disabilities, which is a custodian of children's rights, is a critical and strategic stakeholder. Children living with BMD have rights, including the right not to be subjected to discrimination, myths, stigmas and stereotypes. Schools should be encouraged to work closely with the Department for policy and legislative guidance, as it formulates policies at national level. Schools are encouraged to work with the Department, as they can benefit from its advocacy and ability to organise awareness campaigns in relation to children living with BMD, as well as including them in their year plans.

The Role Of The Criminal Justice System In Supporting Learners with BMD

The marginalisation of, and the discrimination perpetrated against, learners with BMD who are subjected to such exclusionary practices as myths, stigmas and stereotypes, makes the condition of the learners involved a human rights issue. The criminal justice system appears to be failing those learners living with BMD. Issues like lack of awareness and inadequate training have been cited as reasons for the associated failure, with the operation of the criminal justice system being critical to the successful prosecution of the perpetrators concerned. Members of the criminal justice system, including the police, the magistrates, the prosecutors and the attorneys, can be invited to schools to give talks on their roles and responsibilities in cases involving learners living with BMD. Such presentations can change the perceptions of the learners and of other members of the local community, in terms of how they view the police, and they can also help create a harmonious relationship with the school.

Involvement of the Department of Health in Supporting Learners with BMD

In cases involving learner BMD, the child's social, emotional, spiritual and physical wellbeing may be adversely affected. Clinical psychologists and psychiatrists, as a result, have to deal with the existence of more serious psychological and psychiatric problems, because of BMD. For those who are hospitalised, the hospitals involved should be in a position to advance counselling to deal with spiritual issues and medical problems as well. The strategic involvement of important stakeholders should result in the resilience of those who live with a mental illness and in improved treatment for them, especially in terms of the early diagnosis of BMD.

Community Involvement And Engagement In Supporting Learners with BMD

The community should be encouraged to protect and support all its members, but especially the vulnerable ones, such as children who are living with BMD. It should uphold the positive values of collective community responsibility, and the members should be encouraged to see every child as their own, and they should strive to contribute to the well-being of such a child. The values of ubuntu (humaneness) should be upheld, with spiritual and traditional leaders leading awareness initiatives both collaboratively and consultatively, so as to ensure the maintenance of a safe and secure community environment, along with the advancing of community and individual community wellness and well-being.

Involvement of the Non-Governmental Organisation (NGO) Sector In Supporting Learners with BMD

The non-governmental sector in South Africa is thriving. In each province, there is an NGO that is dedicated to the fight against BMD myths, stigmas, stereotypes, discrimination and prejudice related to children living with BMD. A school forms part of the local community, and NGOs are able to organise communities around a specific issue (like BMD), and, as a result, influence policy development. They are able to offer a range of services, including counselling and life skills. The involvement of NGOs usually leads to improved policymaking processes and to empowered communities.

The Role Of Local Government In Supporting Learners with BMD

Local government is the arm of the government that is closest to the people, and which is responsible for the service delivery of a range of activities and facilities and for the local infrastructure, including clinics and community care and support centres. As such, the local government should be encouraged to become involved in school-related activities, including caring for, and supporting those learners who live with BMD. The local government could also be encouraged to make land available to build more care and support centres to support schools, as well as to budget more than before for the building of care and support facilities and infrastructure for children living with BMD. Doing so should, inevitably, lead to the development of care and support services and local infrastructure, so that the learners concerned no longer have to travel long distances to access care and support. By so doing, support could be brought closer to the communities involved and the problems of discrimination, prejudice, myths, stereotypes and stigmas against children living with BMD could be overcome.

The Role Of The Print And Electronic Media In Supporting Learners with BMD

As the power of the media has an extraordinary influence on society, it should be sensitive about communicating the message of childhood BMD. The media can produce and broadcast awareness and empowerment programmes, including inviting speakers from the relevant stakeholders and reporting sensitively and responsibly on matters relating to childhood BMD. Doing so could result in an increased awareness about BMD, as well as in a sensitised society that is vigilant and proactive in managing the BMD condition.

The Role of Institutions Of Higher Learning In Supporting Learners with BMD

Institutions of higher learning in South Africa are mainly involved in three activities, namely teaching (including training and development), research and community engagement and outreach. Since BMD is a national problem, with an increasing number of such cases continuing to be reported, institutions of higher learning should be encouraged to train additional care and support personnel. Care and support for children with BMD can be integrated into the curriculum of teacher education programmes, with such institutions encouraging the conducting of additional research into services, so as to deepen understanding of the problem. Finally, institutions of higher learning could encourage their staff to become involved in community initiatives dealing with childhood BMD and related care and support issues.

COUNTERING THE USE OF DEROGATORY LANGUAGE REGARDING LEARNERS WITH BMD

1. Don't use the term 'mental illness' as a collective term.

Instead, rather use the term 'mental illnesses' or 'a mental illness'.

Mental illness is a broad term that fails to reflect with what a person is actually dealing. As well as there being many different mental health issues, people with the same clinical diagnosis can present very differently, too. Therefore, to respect people's individual experiences, it is important to use language that acknowledges that mental illnesses do not all manifest the same in different people (Lund et al., 2010).

2. Don't use the term 'afflicted by mental illness', 'suffers from mental illness' or 'is a victim of mental illness'.

Instead, rather use the term 'living with a mental illness'.

While living with a mental health diagnosis is not necessarily negative, the term 'suffering' implies that the person concerned is unwell and unhappy. Stigma also portrays a mental illness as being a form of weakness. People with mental health issues are, on the contrary, able to live fulfilling, healthy lives. In addition, the wide range of treatments that exists offers a multiplicity of reasons for staying hopeful (Jenkins & Carpenter-Song, 2008).

3. Don't use the term 'mentally ill person' or 'person who is mentally ill'.

Instead, rather use the term 'person with a mental illness' or 'person living with a mental health issue'.

People with mental health issues have far more dimensions to them than just their mental illness. To accept someone first as a fellow human being is not only respectful towards them, but it also honours the many other parts that there are to them that exceed their diagnosis. Such use of language is called 'person first' language (Goffman, 2009).

4. Don't use the term 'psychotic', 'disturbed', 'crazy', or 'insane'.

Instead, rather use the term 'person living with bipolar mood disorder' or 'person experiencing bipolar mood disorder, disorientation or hallucination'.

We would never call someone 'a cancer-ic' or 'heart-diseased'. People with mental health issues tend unfairly to be labelled by their medical condition (Lawrie, 1999). There is much more to a person than just their illness. Using the preferred term is yet another example of using 'person first' language.

5. Don't use the term 'normal behaviour'.

Instead, rather use the term 'usual behaviour' or 'typical behaviour'.

No clear definition exists of what 'normal' is. In addition, it can cause others to feel hurt or defensive, if their experience is classified as not fitting into the category of 'normal' behaviour (Littlewood, 1998). Using words like 'usual' or 'typical' sounds less critical. (Besides which, every one of us is atypical in one way or another.)

6. Don't use the term 'substance abuse', 'addict' or 'user'.

Instead, rather use the term 'substance use disorder'.

In some cases, the BMD can be exacerbated by substance abuse, with the resulting condition, clinically, being referred to as the substance-abused BMD (Petersen et al., 2009). Those who struggle with the misuse of drugs or alcohol do not simply choose to 'abuse' a substance. Often, neurobiological factors and emotional health issues lead to addictive behaviour. Calling the condition concerned a 'substance use disorder' indicates an acceptance of the other factors involved. Use of the preferred term removes some of the blame that clings to the use of the term 'substance abuse', with it being a small, but significant, way of offering support for those who live with addiction, or who are recovering from addiction (Hugo, 2001).

7. Don't use the term 'committed suicide'.

Instead, rather use the term 'died by suicide' or 'lost by suicide'.

When someone believes that ending their life is truly the best decision that they can make under the prevailing circumstances, they are likely not to be seeing their surrounding reality clearly. Such perception is a symptom of the person concerned experiencing some mental illness. To say that someone 'committed' suicide suggests that blame is being attached to the situation. In contrast, to describe someone dying from cancer as being blameworthy for the cancer is, in many cases, unfeasible (Chopra et al., 2009). Therefore, our use of language should avoid placing a sense of blame and shame on a person's mental health issues that caused them to die by suicide. Making such language adjustments in the way that we discuss mental illnesses can also encourage people to feel comfortable enough to have open conversations and to seek help when they have suicidal thoughts, or when they feel compelled to participate in self-harming behaviours (Coovadia et al., 2009).

The following are some of the derogatory terms that are used to describe those living with a mental illness including the BMD in South Africa:

Afrikaans: *verstandelik gestremde persoon*
English: crazy
IsiNdebele: *uyaghapha*
IsiSwati: *luhlanya*
Sesotho: *wa hlanya/ Kelello e sa itekanelang*
Setswana: *wa tlhanya, wa tsenwa*
IsiVenda: *uyapenga*
Xitsonga: *wapenga, rihaviya*
SePedi: *Segafi*
IsiXhosa: *igeza, uphambene, azithi dadobawo*
IsiZulu: *uyahlanya, azithi mzala*

ADDRESSING STEREOTYPES AND THE STIGMA ASSOCIATED WITH BMD: USING UBUNTU AS A SOCIAL CONSTRUCT

Learners with BMD are generally considered to be members of a marginalised community, including those who face discrimination and social exclusion. BMD is considered to be a human rights issue, and people with BMD often find their rights relegated to the periphery of societal and political concerns (Katsui & Kumpuvuori, 2008). Learners with BMD often find themselves the emotional butt of abuse and rebuke, which is a violation of their human rights. Labelling someone as 'psychotic' is dehumanising. In this regard, a more humane approach should be employed to dismiss misconceptions of people and children living with BMD. Ubuntu has a social construct that should be used to dismiss such dehumanising misunderstanding.

Ubuntu, which is often defined as a form of humanness, is said to include the following values: communality; respect; dignity; value; acceptance; sharing; co-responsibility; humaneness; social justice; fairness; personhood; morality; group solidarity; compassion; joy; love; fulfilment; and conciliation. The following is an attempt to dismiss the misconceptions against children living with BMD.

Respect: People living with BMD should be respected, just as any other member of the community should be. The respect shown should be reciprocal and mutual.

Dignity: Children living with BMD have dignity, as full-fledged people. The research evidence shows that people living with BMD possess dignity.

Value: Nowadays, people with BMD live longer than those with BMD used to live in the past, and they enjoy self-fulfilling lives. They have value and tend to enjoy participating in community-based activities. As worthy individuals, they can contribute to South Africa's reconstruction and development.

Acceptance: In terms of ubuntu, communities should unconditionally accept children living with BMD. Acceptance of others means giving them unconditional positive regard. The concept is rooted deeply in the ancestral past. Children living with BMD do not choose their status, with the condition, in most cases, resulting in situations beyond their control. Consequently, community members should revert to their traditional African values, according to the principle of ubuntu.

Co-responsivity: In most African countries, people living with BMD are left to fend for themselves. This line of thinking and tendency leads to them being subjected to prejudice, discrimination, stigmatisation and stereotyping. In terms of ubuntu, in situations like the above, we should embrace children living with BMD. Co-responsibility in relation to supporting children with BMD should be prioritised. This implies that the individual concerned is also responsible for living a healthy lifestyle, and for taking their medication, as prescribed. In South Africa. for instance, co-responsibility is achieved when the members of a community provide home-based care for those living with BMD.

Social justice and fairness: Social justice refers to the fair division of resources, opportunities and privileges in society. Although providing such justice is not a major problem in South Africa, some people living with BMD in the country are denied access to health, educational and economic resources. Some communities even go to the extent of withholding privileges from those with BMD, despite reports of such behaviour have not appeared in either the print or the electronic media. In terms of the human rights approach, those living with BMD should not be subjected to prejudice, stigma or discrimination. Instead, they should be able to access a quality and affordable health care system, and they should have access to opportunities and privileges in society, in common with others.

Morality: Morality, which is said to be the backbone of any community, helps it to distinguish between what is right and what is wrong. It is immoral to discriminate against, and to isolate others living with BMD. Members of a community are morally obliged to act correctly towards others living with BMD, in other words to protect them<<AUTHOR: From what?>>. It is immoral to show prejudice towards, and to discriminate against, those living with BMD.

Group solidarity: Rather than being an individual's challenge, BMD is a challenge for the community and the society in which it is found. In overcoming the associated difficulty, the community should work as a collective. By doing so, it can help to dismiss any prevailing misconceptions regarding those living with BMD.

Compassion, joy and love: Showing discrimination and prejudice against those living with BMD is regarded as a hate crime in South Africa. Children living with BMD are subjected to misconceptions, such as myths, stereotypes and stigmatisation. To address the problem, those living with BMD require to be treated with compassion, joy and love.

AFRICA-SENSITIVE STRATEGIES FOR PROMOTING POSITIVE CONCEPTIONS ABOUT BIPOLAR MOOD DISOEDER

Helping institutions to recognise the existence of stigma within their own walls

People living with BMD can attend schools, and various private and public institutions. As African people in particular tend to be affected by BMD, Africa-sensitive strategies should be employed for dealing with them. The strategies used may include the development of BMD awareness, the running of advocacy campaigns, the use of psychoeducation and the dissemination of BMD-related information. The activities involved should be sensitive towards the traditional cultural values and norms of African people in particular. The practice is much more relevant in the rural communities, where the appropriate form of language should be used. Those who intervene in a particular community should use the indigenous language that is spoken in the community. If the facilitators cannot speak the language of the community, they should bring an interpreter, who should, ideally, come from that community along with them to any intervention. Such an intervention could be useful in promoting a positive understanding of BMD, as well as in minimising misconceptions about people living with BMD.

Addressing issues of social stigma and the environment

In addressing social stigma, the community should be sensitised, conscientised and psycho-educationalised. The relevant initiatives, which should be rooted in the community, must be accompanied by the conducting of Africa-sensitive awareness and advocacy programmes. Those who implement such programmes should be knowledgeable about the culture and the language of the community that requires support. Where the facilitator is from a different language-speaking group, an interpreter who knows the community well should be used to interpret what the community members have to say.

Responding to the needs of stigmatised populations

Stigmatisation results in the development of a sense of low self-esteem and self-confidence. Ideally, a psychotherapist who applies an African perspective or understanding is highly recommended for the ability to deal with such a situation. Such a therapist accompanies the client, and tries to understand the origins of the problem of stigmatisation. From a variety of therapeutic interventions, the therapist involved should be able to choose an Africa-sensitive approach, no matter which race is involved.

Using the media to show that BMD is a human-based disorder

In South Africa, almost everyone has access to the print and electronic media, which are a powerful instrument for information and education dissemination. Both the private and the public sectors, including such institutions of civil society as churches, should use the media more to dispel the myths, stereotypes, stigmas, prejudice and discrimination perpetuated by misinformed members of the community. The traditional leaders and healers can also use the same platform to advance the adoption of a multidisciplinary approach.

Involving people living with BMD in service delivery

This strategy has proved to be effective over the years. Research evidence and health professional practice both show that those living with BMD tend to relate more effectively to others when they are in touch with those who have come to live positively with the disorder. Doing so gives them a sense of hope and personal strength that enables them to work towards recovery, with the facilitators concerned becoming their role models. The role of those who are living positively goes beyond information dissemination, advocacy, awareness and psychoeducation, as it involves counselling as well. In this instance, BMD counselling tends to be effective, as those living with BMD tend to approach the counselling concerned with authority and with the experience of being able to live positively with BMD.

Engaging with the community

The community is an essential ingredient for fighting and addressing the misconceptions that are held about those living with BMD. The community should be approached through the community leaders and, in the rural areas, through the chiefs in the area. Misunderstanding most often arises among those members of the community who are ill-informed about such conditions, with some of them tending to have unrealistic fears, as a result of the myths associated with BMD that are spread locally. Once the community is sensitised, conscientised, informed and psychoeducated, the myths associated with BMD are relatively easy to dispel.

IMPLICATIONS OF ADOPTING A HUMAN RIGHTS APPROACH FOR INCLUSIVE EDUCATION

Inclusive education provides learning opportunities for students with a variety of learning disabilities. Such students include learners with mental health impairments like BMD, with the possession of such a disorder having implications for both the school and the society involved. Inclusive systems provide an enhanced quality of education for all children concerned, with them being instrumental in the changing of discriminatory attitudes. Schools provide the context for a child's first relationship with those living in the world outside their own families, thereby enabling the development of viable social relationships and interactions within a broader environment. Respect and understanding grow when students of diverse abilities and backgrounds play, socialise and learn together. Such conditions are able to minimise the impact of prejudice, discrimination and stigmatisation. Education that excludes and segregates certain learners from one another perpetuates discrimination against traditionally marginalised groups. When education is inclusive, so are concepts of civic participation, employment and community life.

In South Africa, the need exists for an inclusive education system that delivers comprehensive care to children living with BMD and their families at times and locations that are convenient to them. The decentralisation of mental health services to communities and low-tier health settings, enabling more people in more places than would otherwise be the case – especially adolescents, men and those who are apparently lost to follow up – to have access to the services that they need should be one of the pillars that serves to entrench inclusivity in schools and society. In addition, there is a need to integrate mental health services with health interventions, recognising the opportunity to meet people's needs in a single visit to a comprehensive health care system. Finally, the need exists to challenge restrictive policies and to inspire governments to uphold the rights of those of their people living with mental health conditions like BMD, especially in the key populations of concern, like children, adolescents and women.

CONCLUSION

BMD is clearly a mental health problem that is experienced all over the world, regardless of race, colour or creed. Furthermore, it seems to be experienced by all the different age groups, but especially the children, adolescents and women. Most importantly, the myths, stigmas, stereotypes, prejudice and discrimination concerned are limitless geographically. On close observation, their impact seems to be the same across the mental health spectrum. What is of paramount significance is that the myths, stigmas, stereotypes, prejudices and discrimination concerned can be overcome. This chapter has suggested how such negative forces can be uncovered and brought to an end. The need exists for mass mobilisation, education and advocacy, so as to be able to fight the unjust practices involved, by means of adopting a human rights approach that is underpinned by ubuntu as a social contract. More Africa-sensitive approaches need to put in place to secure a positive future for those living with BMD.

REFERENCES

Abdullah, T., & Brown, T. L. (2011). Mental illness stigma and ethnocultural beliefs, values, and norms: An integrative review. *Clinical Psychology Review*, *31*(6), 934–948. DOI: 10.1016/j.cpr.2011.05.003 PMID: 21683671

Addo, R., Agyemang, S. A., Tozan, Y., & Nonvignon, J. (2018). Economic burden of caregiving for persons with severe mental illness in sub-Saharan Africa: A systematic review. *PLoS One*, *13*(8), e0199830. DOI: 10.1371/journal.pone.0199830 PMID: 30092073

Bayer, R. (2008). Stigma and the ethics of public health: Not can we, but should we. *Social Science & Medicine*, *67*(3), 463–472. PMID: 18502551

Berk, M., & Dodd, S. (2005). Bipolar II disorder: A review. *Bipolar Disorders*, *7*, 11–21. PMID: 15654928

Bollard, M. (2009). Promoting human rights approach for people with learning disabilities. *Primary Health Care*, *19*(9), 26–28.

Byrne, L., Happell, B., Welch, T., & Moxham, L. J. (2013). 'Things you can't learn from books': Teaching recovery from a lived experience perspective. *International Journal of Mental Health Nursing*, *22*(3), 195–204. PMID: 23020070

Chopra, M., Lawn, J. E., Sanders, D., Barron, P., & Abdool Karim, S. S.. (2009). Achieving the health Millennium Development Goals for South Africa: Challenges and priorities. *Lancet*, *374*(9694), 1023–1031. PMID: 19709737

Coovadia, H., Jewkes, R., Barron, P., Sanders, D., & McIntyre, D. (2009). The health and health system of South Africa: Historical roots of current public health challenges. *Lancet*, *374*(9692), 817–834. PMID: 19709728

Corrigan, P. W., Druss, B. G., & Perlick, D. A. (2014). The impact of mental illness stigma on seeking and participating in mental health care. *PSPI*, *15*(2), 37–70. PMID: 26171956

Corrigan, P. W., Kerr, A., & Knudsen, L. (2005). The stigma of mental illness: Explanatory models and methods for change. *Applied & Preventive Psychology*, *11*(3), 179–190.

Corrigan, P. W., & Shapiro, J. R. (2010). Measuring the impact of programs that challenge the public stigma of mental illness. *Clinical Psychology Review*, *30*(8), 907–922. PMID: 20674114

Corrigan, P. W., & Watson, A. C. (2002). Understanding the impact of stigma on people with mental illness. *World Psychiatry; Official Journal of the World Psychiatric Association (WPA)*, *1*(1), 16–20. PMID: 16946807

Deacon, H. (2006). Towards a sustainable theory of health-related stigma: Lessons from the HIV/AIDS literature. *Journal of Community & Applied Social Psychology*, *16*(6), 418–425.

Farrelly, S., Jeffery, D., Rüsch, N., Williams, P., Thornicroft, G., & Clement, S. (2015). The link between mental health-related discrimination and suicidality: Service user perspectives. *Psychological Medicine*, *45*(10), 2013–2022. PMID: 25678059

Ghaemi, S. N., Bauer, M., Cassidy, F., Malhi, G. S., Mitchell, P., & Phelps, J.. (2008). Diagnostic guidelines for bipolar disorder: A summary of the International Society for Bipolar Disorders Diagnostic Guidelines Task Force report. [This is the summary statement for the Diagnosis Task Force of the International Society for Bipolar Disorders, completed in preparation for the DSM and ICD revisions.]. *Bipolar Disorders*, *10*, 117–128. PMID: 18199230

Goffman, E. (2009). *Stigma: Notes on the management of spoiled identity*. Simon & Schuster.

Goodwin, F. K., & Jamison, K. R. (2007). *Manic-depressive illness*. 2nd edition. New York: Oxford University Press. *This is the authoritative text on BMD, being a recent update of the most comprehensive discussion of BMD available.*

Greenstein, L. (2017). *9 ways to fight mental health stigma*. National Alliance on Mental Illness. https://www.nami.org/blogs/nami-blog/october-2017/9-ways-to-fight-mental-health-stigma

Healy, D. (2006). The latest mania: Selling bipolar disorder. *PLoS Medicine*, *3*, e185. PMID: 16597178

Herman, A. A., Stein, D. J., Seedat, S., Heeringa, S. G., Moomal, H., & Williams, D. R. (2009). The South African Stress and Health (SASH) study 12-month and lifetime prevalence of common mental disorders. *South African Medical Journal*, *99*(5), 339–344. PMID: 19588796

Hugo, M. (2001). Mental health professionals' attitudes towards people who have experienced a mental health disorder. *Journal of Psychiatric and Mental Health Nursing*, *8*(5), 419–425. PMID: 11882162

Jenkins, J. H., & Carpenter-Song, E. A. (2008). Stigma despite recovery. *Medical Anthropology Quarterly*, *22*(4), 381–409. PMID: 19189724

Kahng, S. K., & Mowbray, C. T. (2005). What affects self-esteem of persons with psychiatric disabilities: The role of causal attributions of mental illnesses. *Psychiatric Rehabilitation Journal, 28*(4), 354–360. PMID: 15895919

Kakuma, R., Kleintjes, S., Lund, C., Drew, N., Green, A., & Flisher, A. J. (2010). Mental health stigma: What is being done to raise awareness and reduce stigma in South Africa? *The African Journal of Psychiatry, 13*(2), 112–124. PMID: 20473472

Katsui, H., & Kumpuvuori, J. (2008). Human Rights Based Approach in Development in Uganda. *Scandinavian Journal of Disability Research, 10*(4), 227–236.

Keusch, G.T., Wilentz, J. & Kleinman, A. (2006). Stigma and global health: Developing a research agenda. *Lancet 2 367*(9509), 525-527.

Kowatch, R. A. (2005). Review and meta-analysis of the phenomenology and clinical characteristics of mania in children and adolescents. *Bipolar Disorders, 7*, 483–496. PMID: 16403174

Kumari, S., Singh, A. R., Verma, A. N., Verma, P. K., & Chaudhury, S. (2009). Subjective burden on spouses of schizophrenia patients. *Indian Journal of Psychiatry, 18*(2), 97–100. PMID: 21180485

Lawrie, S. M. (1999). Stigmatisation of psychiatric disorder. *Psychiatric Bulletin, 23*(3), 129–131.

Link, B. G., & Phelan, J. C. (2006). Stigma and its public health implications. *Lancet, 367*(9509), 528–529. PMID: 16473129

Littlewood, R. (1998). Cultural variation in the stigmatisation of mental illness. *Lancet, 352*(9133), 1056–1057. PMID: 9759770

Lund, C., Kleintjes, S., Kakuma, R., & Flisher, A. J. (2010). Public sector mental health systems in South Africa: Inter-provincial comparisons and policy implications. *Social Psychiatry and Psychiatric Epidemiology, 45*(3), 393–404. PMID: 19506789

Mackin, P., Targum, S. D., Kalali, A., Rom, D., & Young, A. H. (2006). Culture and assessment of manic symptoms. *The British Journal of Psychiatry, 189*, 379–380. PMID: 17012663

Mayo Clinic Staff. (2017). *Mental health: Overcoming the stigma of mental illness.* https://www.mayoclinic.org/diseases-conditions/mental-illness/in-depth/mental-health/art-20046477

Neighbours, H. W., Caldwell, C., Williams, D. R., Nesse, R., Taylor, R. J., & Bullard, K. M.. (2007). Race, ethnicity, and the use of services for mental disorders: Results from the National Survey of American Life. *Archives of General Psychiatry*, *64*, 485–494. PMID: 17404125

Ngui, E. M. (2010). Mental disorders, health inequalities and ethics: A global perspective. *International Review of Psychiatry (Abingdon, England)*, *22*(3), 235–244. PMID: 20528652

Oexle, N., Müller, M., Kawohl, W., Xu, Z., Viering, S., & Wyss, C.. (2017). Self-stigma as a barrier to recovery: A longitudinal study. *European Archives of Psychiatry and Clinical Neuroscience*, *268*(2), 209–212. DOI: 10.1007/s00406-017-0773-2 PMID: 28188369

Petersen, I., Bhana, A., Campbell-Hall, V., Mjadu, S., Lund, C., & Kleintjies, S.. (2009). Planning for district mental health services in South Africa: A situational analysis of a rural district site. *Health Policy and Planning*, *24*(2), 140–150. PMID: 19147698

Phelan, J. C., Link, B. G., & Dovidio, J. F. (2008). Stigma and prejudice: One animal or two? *Social Science & Medicine*, *67*(3), 358–367. PMID: 18524444

Pinfold, V., Thornicroft, G., Huxley, P., & Farmer, P. (2005). Active ingredients in anti-stigma programmes in mental health. *International Review of Psychiatry (Abingdon, England)*, *17*(2), 123–131. PMID: 16194782

Reavley, N. J., & Jorm, A. F. (2012). Stigmatising attitudes towards people with mental disorders: Changes in Australia over 8 years. *Psychiatry Research*, *197*(3), 302–326. PMID: 22417929

Rossler, W. (2016). The stigma of mental disorders: A millennia-long history of social exclusion and prejudices. *EMBO Reports*, *17*(9), 1250–1253. PMID: 27470237

Rüsch, N., Angermeyer, M. C., & Corrigan, P. W. (2005). Mental illness stigma: Concepts, consequences, and initiatives to reduce stigma. *European Psychiatry : the Journal of the Association of European Psychiatrists*, *20*(8), 529–539. PMID: 16171984

Sachs, G. S. (2004). Strategies for improving treatment of bipolar disorder: Integration of measurement and management. *Acta Psychiatrica Scandinavica. Supplementum*, *422*, 7–17. PMID: 15330934

Sartorius, N. (1998). Stigma: What can psychiatrists do about it? *Lancet*, *352*(9133), 1058–1059. PMID: 9759771

Scambler, G. (1998). Stigma and disease: Changing paradigms. *Lancet, 352*(9133), 1054–1055. PMID: 9759769

Sheehan, L., Nieweglowski, K., & Corrigan, P. W. (2017). Structures and types of stigma. In Gaebel, W., Rossler, W., & Sartorius, N. (Eds.), *The stigma of mental illness – end of the story?* (pp. 43–66). Springer.

Srinivasa, D. K., & Trivedi, S. (1982). Knowledge and attitude of mental diseases in a rural community of South India. *Social Science & Medicine, 16*, 1635–1639. PMID: 7146940

The Lancet Editorial. (2016). The health crisis of mental health stigma. *Lancet, 387*, 1027. PMID: 27025171

Thornicroft, G., Brohan, E., Kassam, A., & Lewis-Holmes, E. (2008). Reducing stigma and discrimination: Candidate interventions. *International Journal of Mental Health Systems, 2*, 3–10. PMID: 18405393

Thornicroft, G., Brohan, E., Rose, D., Sartorius, N., & Leese, M. (2009). Global pattern of experienced and anticipated discrimination against people with schizophrenia: A cross-sectional survey. *Lancet, 373*(9661), 408–415. PMID: 19162314

Venkatapuram, S. (2014). Mental disability, human rights and capabilities approach. Searching for the foundations. *International Review of Psychiatry (Abingdon, England), 26*(4), 408–414. PMID: 25137106

Wig, N. N.. (1980). Community reactions to mental disorders: A key informant study in three developing countries. *Acta Psychiatrica Scandinavica, 61*, 111–126. PMID: 7361584

Youngstrom, E. A.. (2005). Bipolar diagnoses in community mental health: Achenbach Child Behaviour Checklist profiles and patterns of comorbidity. *Biological Psychiatry, 2*(58), 569–575. PMID: 15950197

Chapter 4
The Marginalisation of Learners Living With HIV/AIDS and Implications for Inclusive Education in Schools and Society

Andile Alred Mdikana
https://orcid.org/0000-0002-6968-8945
University of South Africa, South Africa

ABSTRACT

This chapter aims to focus on the misconceptions concerning learners living with HIV/AIDS. False rumors about how HIV is spread in our country remains a problem despite the education and awareness campaigns that are taking place. Knowing about the myths regarding HIV is extremely important for everyone – whether you are living with HIV or not. At the end of the day, HIV affects us all and we have a responsibility to learn more about it so that we can protect each other from infection, stereotypes and stigma. Myths about HIV contribute to stigmatization of the topic. Stigma and stereotypes around HIV prevent more people from being tested and, consequently, prevent more people from getting treatment. It also increases the risk of judgment and discrimination.

INTRODUCTION

The discrimination of learners living with HIV/AIDS – through myths, stigmas, stereotypes and derogatory language – is a global pandemic that needs urgent at-

DOI: 10.4018/979-8-3373-7163-4.ch004

tention (UNAIDS, 2008). Western countries such as the United States of America are not immune to this problem (Holtzman & Rubinson, 1995; Miller at al., 1998; Venters, 2011). Helping parents in developing and developed countries to improve the health of children and adolescents is key to dealing with this pandemic as it relates to myths, stigmas, stereotypes and derogatory language (WHO, 2007; Namisi et al., 2008; Woyah, Nnaji and Bova, 2014). In the United States of America (USA), for instance, there is a realisation that HIV/AIDS is no longer an educational problem but a societal problem – and that is why parental influence on adolescents' sexual behaviour in high-poverty settings is encouraged (Romer et al.,1999; Pacific Institute for Women's Health, 2002; Dennis, et. al., 2008). In the USA, for instance, and in fighting the misconceptions against people and children living with HIV/AIDS, the parents and teenagers formed a united front (Albert, 2007; Kirkman, Rosenthal and Feldman, 2002).

Also, it is evident from the literature review that myths, stereotypes and stigmas related to HIV/AIDS are the order of the day in the United Kingdom (UK) (Fielden, Chapman and Cadell, 2011). In the UK, since 1981 the government and the media have been paying more and more attention to the implications of HIV/AIDS (Landefeld et al., 2018). Much debate has focused on ways of minimising the spread, impact, stigma, myths and stereotypes through research and education (Bernays et al, 2017). Although health education has been widely recognised as having a crucial role to play, little consideration has been given in the UK, either at the research or the policy level, to the implications of HIV/AIDS for primary school education (Kurth et al, 2015). In the UK, black Africans account for the most affected ethnic population with HIV (Bekker and Hosek, 2015). Black Africans hold traditional beliefs that have been reported to cause certain misconceptions about the cause of HIV (Mayer, 2014). In addition, despite being in a developed country like the UK, it has been noted that black Africans still hold these beliefs (Fielden, Chapman and Cadell, 2011). This point would be elaborated upon later in the course of this chapter.

In India, misconceptions regarding transmission during casual social contact and pre-existing negative attitudes towards marginalised groups have been consistently associated with prejudice towards HIV-infected individuals and a willingness to restrict their civil liberties, in multiple settings (Mahajan et al., 2008). The family is often blamed for having a child with HIV/AIDS. Instead of receiving support, the family is often ostracised and name-calling is advanced (Herek, 2002). There is an urgent need for continued stigma reduction efforts to reduce the suffering of People Living with HIV/AIDS (PLHA) and barriers to prevention and treatment (Herek, 2009). In India, the misconceptions about HIV/AIDS infection occur mainly in the rural areas (Mahajan, et al., 2008). Often, the infected persons are relegated to the periphery of educational and societal concerns (Link and Phelan, 2001). Those who are infected are often subjected to name-calling such as promiscuous and/or curse from the gods (Mahajan et al., 2008). According to the human rights approach, the maltreatment of PLHA is a hate crime and it is a complete violation of human rights (Venkatapuram, 2014).

Australia had a quick and effective response to HIV at the start of the epidemic (Coopes, 2016; Altman, 1994). The nation's initial response was multifaceted – on the prevention front, safe sex was invented by affected communities (Sendziuk, 2003; Kippax, 2003). Australia is probably one of the few countries in the world that has fought and prevented the spread of HIV infections and this may be due to the fact that it has invested a considerable amount of human and capital resources (Persson, 2014). Children from primary schools are educated about HIV/AIDS and they are aware of the misconceptions such as: HIV/AIDS is a death sentence; HIV can be transferred by kissing; you can't get HIV from oral sex; you can tell by looking if someone has HIV (Jansson, Kerr and Wilson, 2014). It is also worth mentioning that in Australia all the people who have been infected by HIV have access to quality and affordable health care. In addition, the Australian authorities have embarked on aggressive educational, awareness and advocacy campaigns (Coopes, 2016).

Studies conducted in sub-Saharan Africa show that discrimination against people with HIV/AIDS continues to be a challenge – despite the awareness, advocacy and educational campaigns aimed at the prevention and curbing of HIV/AIDS (Greeff et al., 2008; Rankin et al., 2005). This has resulted in linking HIV/AIDS to immorality and other negative characteristics, and finally, behavioural consequences of stigma (distancing, isolation, discrimination in care) (Gerbert, Sumser and Maguire, 1991; Herek and Glunt, 1988). In sub-Saharan Africa that includes South Africa, the cultural construction of HIV/AIDS, based on beliefs about contamination, sexuality, and religion, plays a crucial role and contributes to the strength of distancing reactions and discrimination in society (Campbell et al., 2007). Stigma prevents the delivery of effective social and medical care (including taking antiretroviral therapy) and enhances the number of HIV infections (Miller and Rubin, 2007; Goldin, 1994). The following sections will discuss the preferred theoretical framework, myths around HIV/AIDS, stereotypes around HIV/AIDS, stigmas associated with HIV/AIDS, derogatory language used against these learners that oftentimes lead to exclusionary practices, dismissing stereotypes and the stigma perpetuated against learners living with this condition, Ubuntu as a social construct, Africa-sensitive strategies for promoting positive conceptions about different disabilities and the implications for inclusive education in schools and society.

ADOPTING HUMAN RIGHTS-APPROACH

The human rights-approach was preferred because of its emphasis on the rights of marginalised groups. Learners with HIV/AIDS are generally considered a marginalised community, including those who face discrimination and social exclusion. HIV/AIDS infection is considered a human rights issue and people with HIV/AIDS often find their rights relegated to the periphery of societal and political concern (Katsui & Kumpuvuori, 2008). In many cases, learners with HIV/AIDS are the victims of abuse, and this is a violation of their human rights.

The human rights approach seeks to empower people with HIV/AIDS and to make them respected and able to fight for their rights themselves (Bollard, 2009). This approach calls on all those responsible for enforcing these rights to do so in a manner that reinforces accountability and responsibility in respecting, safeguarding and realising such rights (Venkatapuram, 2014). Civil society should help in initiating empowerment and support programmes for those who are infected with HIV/AIDS, which would enable them to participate meaningfully in decisions that affect their lives. This can inform policies that affect learners living with HIV/AIDS.

The human rights approach is guided by the principles of participation, accountability, non-discrimination and equality, empowerment and legality. Participation means being free to engage in activities that affect the life of the person (Bollard, 2009), and being free to decide what rights are to be enjoyed. It also involves the concept of accessibility to health care and social services, education and training opportunities, housing and the criminal justice system, as well as freedom of expression (Bollard, 2009). People with HIV/AIDS are often excluded from community-based activities due to a lack of active participation. In relation to care, people with disabilities should have a say in the care and support they are receiving (Venkatapuram, 2014).

MYTHS AGAINST LEARNERS LIVING WITH HIV/AIDS

In South Africa, the commonly held myths concerning HIV/AIDS make it difficult to fight this pandemic (Shisana et al., 2008). These myths continue to erode the achievements made during the last few years (Wessels and Rabinowitz, 2005)). Over the past three decades, mistaken ideas about HIV and AIDS have sometimes brought on the behaviours that cause people to get the virus (Auerbach, Byram, and Kandathil, 2005). Although we still have questions about HIV, researchers have learned a lot -- enough to know that people who are HIV-positive are not dangerous or doomed (Akande, 2001). People, including the children of South Africa, are starting to become aware of the dangers these HIV/AIDS myths are causing in our society (Anderson et al., 2004). In schools and society alike, people are fast becoming aware of the danger of these myths in the fight against HIV/AIDS (Auvert et al., 2005). It is worth mentioning that people – including children – are no longer dying in large numbers. This positive response might be due to the collaboration between the government and the institutions of civil society (Badenhorst, Van Staden and Coetsee, 2008). What follows below is a critical and scholarly discussion of how these myths should be handled in South Africa and in South African schools in particular.

In South Africa some members of the community believe that one can get HIV by being around people who are HIV-positive; one can get HIV from mosquitoes; when HIV-positive, my life is over; HIV is a homosexual disease; if one is receiving treatment one can't spread the HIV virus; if both partners are HIV-positive, there is no reason for us to practise safe sex; one could tell if one's partner is HIV-positive; male circumcision prevents HIV; traditional medicines can cure HIV; some believe that they can be cured from HIV if I have sex with a virgin, one can't get HIV from oral sex; and finally, ARVs disfigure you (Barnes, 2000). The research evidence shows that HIV is not spread through touch, tears, sweat, or saliva and that concerns around it can be resolved (Bates, 2002). School-oriented strategies should target the learners, teachers, school management teams, parents and the support staff (Bhayiya, A 2000; Coughlan, Coughlan and Jameson, 1996). A child is a member of the school community and this means if he or she is sexually abused this should be of concern to all the members of the community, including the parents (Brady, 1999; Cornelissen, 2005). Here, collaboration between the school and the family becomes critical (Mdikana, 2020). It is vital for the parents to be kept informed throughout the management of HIV/AIDS (Bridgraj, 2000; Coetsee, 2007). In curbing the HIV/AIDS myths it is important for the following government departments to be brought on board: the Department of Education (developing awareness programmes in relation to sexual abuse and intellectual disability); the Department of Social Development (provision of psychosocial and counselling services and victim empowerment); the Department of Children, Women and People with Disabilities (advocacy and awareness); the Department of Health (pre-post test counselling, medical examination and HIV testing and medical treatment) (Mdikana, 2020; Chikore, 2000). The following section discusses the stigmas and stereotypes associated with HIV/AIDS. The discussion also includes suggestions for how to deal with these stigmas and stereotypes.

DEALING WITH LEARNERS' STIGMAS AND STEREOTYPES ASSOCIATED WITH HIV/AIDS

Stigmas and stereotypes refer to the discrediting, devaluing, and shaming of a person because of characteristics or attributes that he or she possesses; stereotypes and stigmas are also socially produced (Campbell et al., 2005; Deacon, Stephney and Prosalendis, 2005). Generally, stigma leads to negative social experiences such as isolation, rejection, marginalisation, and discrimination. If related to a health condition such as mental illness, stigma may affect a person's illness and treatment course, including access to appropriate and professional medical treatment (Forman, 2003; Green, 1995). Stigmas and stereotypes often manifest together, especially in the education and health systems of the Republic of South Africa (Hassan, 2003; Simbayi, 2003). We continue to hear stories of people living with HIV/AIDS being refused professional health care; however, this is changing gradually (Kalichman and Simbayi, 2004).

In South Africa, it is a criminal offence on the part of the health care professionals to refuse treatment to people living with HIV/AIDS (Kalichman et al., 2005). This unacceptable professional behaviour also includes refusing casual contact with someone living with HIV or socially isolating a member of a community because the person is HIV positive, and referring to people as "positives" (Niehaus, 2006). HIV/AIDS stigmas and stereotypes are a form of discrimination that also violates the human rights of children (Skinner and Mfecane, 2004). It is a criminal form of prejudice that is often accompanied by labelling and it has the ability to destroy one's self-esteem. There is empirical evidence that this kind of abusive behaviour has led to the suicidal tendencies of some of the people and children living with HIV/AIDS (Simbayi, 2003). The government has to work more closely with the institutions of civil society such as churches, non-governmental organisations, traditional healers and leaders (Deacon, Stephney and Prosalendis, 2005). The following South African strategies are proposed to alleviate the problem of stigmas, stereotypes and marginalisation of learners living with HIV/AIDS at school.

School-Oriented Strategies

School-oriented strategies should target the learners, teachers, school management teams, parents and support staff. A child is a member of the school community and this means that if he or she is HIV-positive, this should be of concern to all the members of the community, including the parents. Within the context of the schools, programmes and strategies that are aimed at caring for and supporting the child who is HIV-positive are usually led by the School Based Support Team (SBST). This structure has the primary responsibility of training or empowering teachers and parents on issues such as the prevention and early identification of stigmas and stereotypes; developing an awareness of children living with HIV/AIDS; and reporting and referral of learners with symptoms of HIV infection before they are ostracised and discriminated by the learners and teachers who have little understanding of HIV infection. Since this structure normally includes expertise, it can also provide sexuality education and basic counselling and be in a position to facilitate awareness and advocacy campaigns. The activities of the SBST are expected to result in informed and capacitated school and parent communities that are aware of HIV/AIDS infection in relation to the associated myths, stigmas and stereotypes. It is also imperative for this structure to formulate school-based policies on matters relating to HIV/AIDS. The policy framework would be well placed to guide the practice of quality care and support that these learners should be given.

Parent And Family-Oriented Strategies

Parents are an important and critical stakeholder in the education and health of any child and parental involvement and engagement should be enhanced in order to provide quality care and support. Therefore, it is not the responsibility of the school only to provide quality care, support and protection for the child who is HIV-positive, but also that of parents and families. Here, collaboration between the school and the family becomes critical, with parents to be trained by the SBST to prevent, identify and support the learner with HIV and to be in a position to manage the HIV problem without prejudice and until the learner is referred to the health authorities for quality care and support.

Department of Education Involvement

The Department of Education in South Africa manages schools through District Offices and within each district there is an established structure called a District Based Support Team (DBST). The main responsibility of this structure is to ensure that School Based Support Teams are capacitated to provide quality care and support, which it should monitor. It should also be in a position to provide strategic training and development on all aspects of health, including HIV/AIDS. After all, HIV/AIDS can affect all children – including children with intellectual disabilities. The DBST runs awareness and parental training initiatives to complement and strengthen the work of schools. It is evident that increased involvement of the DBST would lead to improved implementation of care and support services and a conscientised parental and school community in the fight against HIV/AIDS. Finally, the recruitment and the retention of competent DBST staff who are knowledgeable about children living with HIV/AIDS would go a long way in the early identification, prevention and management of children living with HIV/AIDS.

Department of Social Development Involvement

HIV/AIDS infection among learners can be a traumatic experience that can result in the child presenting emotional and behavioural complications, with counselling and psychotherapy usually required. It is imperative for the Department of Social Development to be involved by the school at a suitable time as it can employ professional social workers who can take care of the counselling needs and the challenges of learners living with HIV/AIDS. Social workers are trained in understanding and intervening in social problems that result from contracting HIV and as such they can be invited by schools to train the school community and parents in how to identify and manage responses. Most social workers are involved in the lives of children with health and psychosocial problems. They can help with social grant applications and are able to place affected children in places of safety having removed them from the sexually abusive environment, if the HIV infection is because of a family member. The increased role of the Department of Social Development would result in empowered parents, learners and the school community.

Department of Children, Women and People with Disabilities Involvement

The Department of Children, Women and People with Disabilities is a custodian of children's rights and therefore a critical and strategic stakeholder. Children living with HIV have rights, including the right not to be subjected to discrimination, myths, stigmas and stereotypes. Schools should be encouraged to work closely with this department for policy and legislative guidance – as it formulates policies at national level. Schools can benefit from the department's advocacy and organise awareness campaigns in relation to children living with HIV/AIDS, and include them in their year plans.

The Role of the Criminal Justice System

Children living with HIV/AIDS are often marginalised, discriminated and for these learners are subjected to exclusionary practices such as myths, stigmas and stereotypes, this makes the condition of these learners to be a human rights issue. The criminal justice system appears to be failing learners living with HIV/AIDS. Issues such as lack of awareness and inadequate training have been cited as reasons for this failure – and the criminal justice system is critical to the successful prosecution of the perpetrators. Members of the criminal justice system, such as the police, magistrates, prosecutors and attorneys, can be invited to schools to give talks on their roles and responsibilities in cases involving learners living with HIV/

AIDS. This can change the perceptions of the learners and the community in terms of how they view the police and create a harmonious relationship with the school. This may create a perception of the police as accessible and make it easier for the police to collect evidence from the learners in sexual abuse cases resulting in HIV/AIDS infection. The result of this undertaking would be a sensitised criminal justice system and increased prosecution rates.

Department of Health Involvement

In cases involving learner HIV infection, the child's social, emotional, spiritual and physical wellbeing may be adversely affected. The child may be socially withdrawn because of the stigma attached and he or she may lose faith in humanity. He or she will possibly also feel helpless and hopeless with anxiety of having contracted a sexually transmitted disease such as HIV/AIDS. Here the Department of Health can be strategically involved, and if children are hospitalised they can conduct pre- and post-test counselling for the sexually abused children. They may also conduct medical examinations to establish the extent of the problem in terms of the child's health. Clinical psychologists are able to deal with more serious psychological problems because of HIV/AIDS. For those who are hospitalised, hospitals should be in the position to advance counselling to deal with spiritual issues and medical problems as well. The strategic involvement of this important stakeholder should result in resilient victims and improved treatment, especially early diagnosis.

Community Involvement and Engagement

Incidents of sexual abuse can result in HIV infection and in most cases, these incidents emanate from the community not being in a position to protect its children. The community should be encouraged to protect and support all its members, especially the vulnerable ones, such as children. It should uphold positive values of collective community responsibility and members should be encouraged to see every child as their own. The values of Ubuntu (humanity) ought to be upheld and spiritual and traditional leaders should lead awareness initiatives collaboratively and consultatively with the relevant government departments in ensuring safety and security for communities to advance community wellness or wellbeing.

Nongovernmental Organisation (NGO) Sector Involvement

The nongovernmental sector in South Africa is thriving. In each province, there is an NGO dedicated to the fight against HIV/AIDS infection, myths, stigmas, stereotypes, discrimination and prejudice against children living with HIV/AIDS. A school forms part of the community and NGOs are able to organise communities around a specific issue (such as HIV/AIDS) and as a result, influence policy development. They are able to offer a range of services such as sexuality education, counselling, and life skills. The involvement of NGOs usually leads to improved policy-making processes and empowered communities.

The Role Of Local Government

Local government is the arm of the government closest to the people, and as such it is responsible for service delivery of a range of activities and facilities and local infrastructure, such as clinics and community care and support centres. It should ideally be involved in school-related activities such as caring for and supporting learners who have been sexually abused and ended up contracting HIV. Local governments could be encouraged to make land available for building more care and support centres to support schools and to budget more for the building of care and support facilities and infrastructure for children who have been infected with HIV. This will inevitably lead to better developed care and support services and local infrastructure so that learners would not have to travel long distances to access care and support. Such initiatives can bring the support closer to the communities and help to alleviate the problems of discrimination, prejudice, myths, stereotypes and stigmas against children living with HIV/AIDS.

The Role of Print And Electronic Media

The power of the media has an extraordinary influence on society; therefore, it should be sensitive about how the message of child HIV infection is communicated in general. It can produce and broadcast awareness and empowerment programmes by inviting speakers from the relevant stakeholders to report sensitively and responsibly on matters relating to HIV/AIDS. This can result in increased awareness and a sensitised society that is vigilant and proactive in the prevention of HIV infection.

The Role of Institutions Of Higher Learning

Institutions of higher learning in South Africa are mainly involved in three activities, namely, teaching (which includes training and development), research, and community engagement and outreach. Since HIV/AIDS is a national problem and more such cases continue to be reported, institutions of higher learning should be encouraged to train more care and support personnel. Care and support for children with HIV/AIDS could be integrated into the curriculum of teacher education programmes and these institutions could be encouraged to conduct more research into services for a deeper understanding of the problems. Finally, these institutions of higher learning could encourage their staff to be involved in community initiatives dealing with HIV/AIDS and issues pertaining to care and support.

DEROGATORY LANGUAGE USED AGAINST THESE LEARNERS THAT OFTEN LEAD TO EXCLUSION

Language is socially constructed and it is a means by which we establish societal norms and values (Flicker and Nixon, 2014). We learn new things through language; and it is used in schooling activities. It is a cultural instrument through which the legacy of a particular social group is carried from generation to generation (Chileshe and Bond, 2010). Knowledge and wisdom can be transferred through knowledge. It is a fact that language can be derogatory and can be used against a particular social group – in this case, people and children living with HIV/AIDS (Rakwar et al., 1999). This section will show how derogatory language perpetuates myths, stigmas, stereotypes, discrimination and prejudice in Africa.

Kenya (Kikuyu, Spoken Mainly in central Kenya)

The worm in Kenyan language is called **Kagunyo**, which is a euphemism for HIV. Worms are mainly spread in small bits of poo from people with a worm infection. Some are caught from food. You can be infected by touching objects or surfaces with worm eggs on them – if someone with worms does not wash their hands. The implication of this for people with HIV/AIDS is that they might be considered infectious (Hamra, 2006). This might lead to social distancing and embarrassment to the person suffering from HIV/AIDS (Rakwar et al., 1999).

Nigeria (Hausa, Spoken Mainly in the north)

Kabari Salama aalaiku – Literally translates as "Excuse me, grave" (reference to AIDS). It means that whenever people see a person with HIV/AIDS, they see a grave or death. This is a myth; however, in the early years of the disease epidemic, the death rate from AIDS was extremely high, and one's lifespan extremely short(Utulu and Lawoyin, 2007). Nevertheless, today, antiretroviral drugs allow HIV-positive people and even those with AIDS to live much longer, normal, and live productive lives (Essien, 1997).

Zamani – Translates as the "sickness of this generation" (another reference to AIDS). In this part of Nigeria, there is a widespread myth that HIV/AIDS is a condition affecting young people (Uwakwe, 2000). However, medical science research shows that anyone can be affected by HIV/AIDS – irrespective of colour, race, economic status or creed (Fawole et al., 1999).

South Africa (isiXhosa and isiZulu)

Udlala ilotto – "Playing the lotto" / ubambe ilotto – "won the lotto" (said of someone suspected of being HIV positive; Lotto is the national lottery). This implies promiscuity and a reference is alluded to women who might have been infected with HIV (Kalichman and Simbayi, 2003). It is a fact that some men do sleep around without protection and spread the disease to other people. South Africa is one of the countries in the world that has succeeded in the fight against HIV infection. Fewer people are being admitted to hospitals due to our advanced medical care and technologies.

Unyathele icable – Contracting HIV is like "stepping on a live wire". This implies that contracting HIV is a death sentence. I must say that this is a minority view. Through our health care and support strategies, most people in South Africa are aware that contracting HIV is not a death sentence (Pitpitan et al., 2012). We have enough nongovernmental organisations that are in touch with the reality in fighting the myths, stigmas, stereotypes, discrimination and prejudice against people with HIV/AIDS.

South Africa (English)

House in Vereeniging – (Acronym for HIV; "bought a house in Vereeniging", a town about 50 km south of Johannesburg – refers to someone suspected of being HIV- positive). Johannesburg is regarded as the city of glamour and opportunity. For a person who lives with HIV/AIDS, this means lost opportunities. It also means that this person is not able to cope with the active and fast life of Johannesburg. To the person who lives with HIV/AIDS, this brings a sense of lost hope and a lack of empathy from community members.

Driving a "Z3"/ "having three kids"/ the "three letters" – All refer to the three letters in the HIV acronym. These derogatory phrases bring a sense of hopelessness and helplessness. It appears that some people enjoy the suffering of others. These people appear to enjoy inflicting emotional and psychological pain. One can only argue that these are the people who are ignorant and arrogant. They are sick in the mind; they need psychoeducation. People and children living with HIV/AIDS need love and affection, unconditional positive regard and people who empathise with their situation.

Tracker – If you are suspected of being HIV positive, people say God is tracking you, like the popular Southern African service that tracks and recovers stolen vehicles. Those who are in the mental health profession would say that this a delusion. A delusion is a form of mental capacity where a person is not in touch with reality and his/mental capacity is characterised by false beliefs. The Christian perspective would agree with this interpretation of human behaviour as it would go further by saying that God loves everyone and would like each and every person to enjoy his/ her life on earth. There is no scriptural reference or verse that says God is a tracker.

Tanzania (KiSwahili)

amesimamia msumari – "Standing on a nail"; euphemism for being skinny, or being small enough to fit on a nail's head, referring to AIDS-related weight loss. This form of labelling or name calling was prevalent during the onset of the HIV/ AIDS pandemic (Dilger, 2007); a myth and stereotype that everyone who was losing weight was suffering from HIV/AIDS infection. This was also the case in South Africa in the 1980s. Those who lost weight suffered social distancing, prejudice and discrimination. The lives of those who were losing weight were made unbearable. There was no understanding that people lose weight due to a variety of health conditions such as diabetes. Some lost weight because they wanted to maintain a healthy lifestyle. It is a fact that this misconception is still in existence despite the psycho-educational programmes coupled with awareness, advocacy and information initiatives that are taking place. Negative attitudes against people who are losing weight are gradually diminishing.

kukanyaga miwaya – Contracting HIV is like "stepping on a live wire", same as ***Unyathele icable***? We know that stepping on a live wire is fatal. This linguistic phrase implies that people who are infected with HIV are ignorant. They are risk takers; sleeping around is a recipe for premature death. The reality is that, during the early years of the epidemic, people paid less attention to safe sex practices (Mbago, 2004). It should also be noted that women in Africa in particular have no say in terms of control over their bodies. Unfaithful men would sleep around using no sexual protection and forcefully sleep with their wives without protection.

mdudu – "The bug" (refers to HIV). This implies that people living with HIV/ AIDS are infectious and that they must be avoided as far as possible. Research evidence shows that HIV is not spread through touch, tears, sweat, or saliva. This is the myth that must be dispelled and it is counterproductive (Dilger, 2007).

Zambia (Bemba, Spoken Mainly in the North and Lusaka)

Bamalwele ya akashishi – "Those that suffer from the germ" (HIV-positive people). Medically speaking, germs are to be avoided as they pose a health risk. There is a generally held view that people have a responsibility to lead a healthy lifestyle. Failure to uphold health protocols may result in, for instance, HIV/AIDS infection. In this part of Zambia, people who are suffering from HIV/AIDS are referred to as objects (Flicker S, Nixon SA., 2014). This means that they need to be isolated as soon as possible – even though this is changing gradually. The phrase "Those that suffer from the germ", implies discrimination, prejudice, stereotyping and stigmatisation (Flicker and Nixon, 2014).

Kaleza – "Razor blade" (refers to a person being thin because of AIDS-related weight loss). This phrase is derogatory and dehumanising. It can result in the loss of hope and suicidal tendencies on the part of the person living with HIV/AIDS (Chileshe and Bond, 2010). This means that there is a lot of work that needs to be done with regard to sensitising, educating and informing the community. In the early years of the disease epidemic, the death rate from AIDS was extremely high, and one's lifespan extremely short. However, today, antiretroviral drugs allow HIV-positive people and even those with AIDS to live much longer, normal, and productive lives.

Zimbabwe (Shona)

Ari pachirongwa – "He/she is on a (treatment) programme". In this regard, a person living with HIV/AIDS is dehumanised. The person is not called by name. This leads to a feeling of rejection and isolation. Yet, these negative attitudes are beginning to change gradually (Muchini et al., 2011). This phrase also implies that privacy and confidentiality are not respected by the health care professionals – and probably by the members of the extended family.

Akatsika banana – "He/she has stepped on a banana and slipped" (someone who has tested positive and therefore will "fall" or die as a result). This is another myth. In the early years of the disease epidemic, the death rate from AIDS was extremely high, and one's lifespan extremely short. However, today, antiretroviral drugs allow HIV-positive people and even those with AIDS to live much longer, normal, and productive lives (Gregson, 2017).

Zimbabwe (English)

Go slow – Taken to mean that he/she is now progressing slowly towards death, this view is slowly diminishing as people are becoming conscientised and sensitised. Zimbabwe is probably one of the few countries in Africa that has fiercely fought for the human rights of people living with HIV/AIDS. Mass mobilisation and advocacy campaigns have yielded good results and as a result, Zimbabwe is reporting fewer incidences of HIV/AIDS infections (Gregson, 2017).

John the Baptist – When someone has TB or HIV, he/she is said to have been baptised by "John the Baptist", who has come to announce the coming of AIDS.

This perspective cannot be ignored as some preachers still instil this ill-informed understanding in the minds of their congregations. Medical research has proved that this is untrue and counterproductive. Some HIV-infected members of the congregates do not take the ARVs and end up dying. Some of these preachers even go to the extent that HIV/AIDS is curable. Those of us who are in the health profession know that there is no element of truth in that.

Departure lounge – An HIV-infected person is believed to be in the departure lounge awaiting death. This view reinforces a sense of hopelessness and helplessness. It seems to glorify and minimise the effect of having someone in the family who is living with HIV/AIDS. It cannot be true that having been infected with HIV/AIDS, you are in the departure lounge. HIV infection can be painful and one requires regular medical and nursing care. It is therefore insensitive to say that someone who is living with HIV/AIDS is in the departure lounge (Muchini et al., 2011).

DISMISSING STEREOTYPES AND THE STIGNMA PERPETUATED AGAA=INST LEARNERS LIVING WITH HIV/AIDS: UBUNTU AS A SOCIAL CONSTRUCT

Learners with HIV/AIDS are generally considered a marginalised community, including those who face discrimination and social exclusion. HIV/AIDS infection is considered a human rights issue and the rights of people with HIV/AIDS are often relegated to the periphery of societal and political concern (Katsui and Kumpuvuori, 2008). Learners with HIV/AIDS often fall victim to abuse, and this is a violation of their human rights. There is no doubt that being labelled as being "HIV positive" is dehumanising indeed. In this regard, a more humane approach would be employed to dismiss misconceptions about people and children living with HIV/AIDS. Ubuntu as a social construct would be used to dismiss these dehumanising misconceptions.

Ubuntu is often defined to mean humanness. Ubuntu is said to include the following values: communality, respect, dignity, value, acceptance, sharing, co-responsibility, humaneness, social justice, fairness, personhood, morality, group solidarity, compassion, joy, love, fulfilment, and conciliation. The following is an attempt to dismiss the misconceptions against people living with HIV/AIDS.

Respect: People living with HIV/AIDS should be respected like any other member of the community. Respect is reciprocal and mutual.

Dignity: It is wrong to say that people living with HIV/AIDS have no dignity at all. That person is still a fully-fledged person; there is no research evidence to show that people living with HIV/AIDS lack dignity.

Value: Nowadays, people with HIV/AIDS live longer and enjoy self-fulfilling lives. It is wrong to say that they have no value in life and in community-based activities. They are worthy and they can still contribute to the reconstruction and development of our country.

Acceptance: In terms of Ubuntu; communities should accept people living with HIV/AIDS unconditionally. Acceptance means unconditional positive regard. It is an old concept that used to be embraced by our ancestors. People with HIV/AIDS did not choose their status. In most cases, it is a result of situations beyond their control. This means that the members of the community should go back to the African traditional values according to Ubuntu.

Co-responsivity. In most African countries, people living with HIV/AIDS are left to fend for themselves and are being blamed for risky and reckless sexual behaviour. This line of thinking and tendency lead to them being subjected to prejudice, discrimination, stigmatisation and stereotyping. In terms of Ubuntu, in situations like these, we should embrace people living with HIV/AIDS. The HIV-infected person needs to have co-responsibility. This implies that the individual has a responsibility to now live a healthy lifestyle and to take medication as prescribed. In South Africa for instance, co-responsibility was achieved where the members of the community would provide home-based care for people living with HIV/AIDS.

Social justice and fairness: Social justice refers to the fair division of resources, opportunities, and privileges in society. At least this is not a major problem in South Africa. However, there are cases where people living with HIV/AIDS are denied access to health, educational and economic resources. Some communities even go to the extent of withholding privileges (even though this has not been reported in the print and electronic media). In terms of the human rights approach, these people should not be prejudiced, stigmatised and discriminated against and they should have access to a quality and affordable health care system, and to opportunities and privileges in society.

Morality: Morality is said to be the backbone of any community. It helps the community to distinguish between what is right and what is wrong. It is immoral to discriminate against and isolate people living with HIV/AIDS. It is the moral obligation of members of the community to do the right thing: to protect people living with HIV/AIDS. It is immoral to be prejudiced and discriminate against people living with HIV/AIDS.

Group solidarity: HIV/AIDS is not an individual problem; it is the problem of the community and society. In fighting this scourge, the community should work as a collective. This can help to dismiss the misconceptions against people living with HIV/AIDS.

Compassion, joy, love: Discrimination and prejudice against people living with HIV/AIDS is regarded as a hate crime in South Africa. People living with HIV/AIDS are subjected to misconceptions such as myths, stereotypes and stigmatisation. To deal with this problem, people living with HIV/AIDS need simple things. They need to be embraced and they – most importantly – need compassion, joy and love.

AFRICA-SENSITIVE STRATEGIES FOR PROMOTING POSITIVE CONCEPTIOND ABOUT HIV/AIDS

Help Institutions Recognise Stigma

People living with HIV/AIDS are found in schools; private and public institutions. It is a fact that this condition affects African people in particular. This means that Africa- sensitive strategies should be employed. The strategies may include HIV/AIDS awareness, advocacy campaigns, psychoeducation and HIV/AIDS information. These activities should be sensitive towards the traditional cultural values and norms of the African people in particular. This practice is much more relevant in rural communities, where appropriate language should be used. In rural areas, talking about sex is a taboo. When wanting to implement these activities, one should ask for the permission of the chief accompanied by the elders. Those who are intervening in a particular community should use the indigenous language of that community. If the facilitators cannot speak the language of that community, they must bring an interpreter who should ideally be coming from that community. This kind of intervention can be useful in promoting positive conceptions about HIV/AIDS and can minimise misconceptions regarding people living with HIV/AIDS.

Deal with Social Stigma and the Environment

In resolving social stigma, the community should be sensitised, conscientised and psycho-educationalised. These interventions must be accompanied by awareness and advocacy programmes. The initiatives must be rooted in the community and should be Africa sensitive. This means that the people who implement these programmes should be knowledgeable about the culture and the language of the community to be supported. Where the facilitator is from a different racial group, an interpreter who knows the community well should be used.

Respond to the Needs of Stigmatised Populations

Stigmatisation leads to low self-esteem and confidence. Ideally, a psychotherapist who applies an African perspective or understanding is highly recommended for this kind of situation. The therapist would go with the client and try to understand the origins of the problem of stigmatisation. Among a variety of therapeutic interventions, the therapist should then be able to choose an Africa-sensitive approach. This applies to both black and white people who live in South Africa.

Use the Media to Show that AIDS has a Human Face

In South Africa, almost everyone can access the print and electronic media. The media is a powerful instrument for dissemination of information and education. Both the private and the public sectors, including the institutions of civil society such as the churches, should use the media more to dispel the myths, stereotypes, stigmas, prejudice and discrimination perpetuated by misinformed, arrogant and ignorant members of the community. The traditional leaders and healers can also use this platform in advancing a multi-disciplinary approach.

Involve People Living with HIV in Service Delivery

This strategy has proved to be effective over the years. There is enough research evidence and health profession practices to prove that people living with HIV/AIDS tend to respond better when they are informed by the survivors of HIV who are now living positively with HIV. This gives them a sense of hope and personal strength to work towards recovery. These facilitators become their role models. However, the role of those who are living positively is not limited to information dissemination, advocacy, awareness and psychoeducation; it involves counselling as well. In this instance, HIV/AIDS counselling tends to be effective as they approach the counselling with authority and the experience of living positively with HIV/AIDS.

Engage the Community

The community is an essential ingredient for fighting and correcting the misconceptions about people and children living with HIV/AIDS. The community should be approached through community leaders and, in rural areas, through the chiefs. Most of the time, the misconceptions come from members of the community who are ill informed about the conditions. Some of them tend to have unrealistic fears, which are often spread by myths associated with HIV/AIDS. Once the community is sensitised, conscientised, informed and psychoeducated, it becomes easier to dispel the myths associated with HIV/AIDS infection.

IMPLICATIONS FOR INCLUSIVE EDUCATION IN SCHOOLS AND SOCIETY

Inclusive education provides learning opportunities to students with a variety of disabilities together. These include learners with health impairments such as HIV/AIDS, which has implications for both the school and the society. Inclusive systems provide a better quality education for all children and are instrumental in changing discriminatory attitudes. Schools provide the context for children's first relationship with the world outside their families, enabling the development of social relationships and interactions. Respect and understanding grow when students of diverse abilities and backgrounds play, socialise, and learn together. This state of affairs has the ability to minimise the impact of prejudice, discrimination and stigmatisation. Education that excludes and segregates perpetuates discrimination against traditionally marginalised groups. When education is more inclusive, so are concepts of civic participation, employment, and community life

In South Africa, there is a need for an inclusive education system that delivers comprehensive care to people living with HIV as well as their families, at times and in locations that are convenient to them. The promotion of efficient testing in schools and in communities, facilities, and hotspots is important, so that people know their status and can initiate treatment as early as possible. Decentralisation of HIV services to communities and low-tier health settings means that more people in more places — especially adolescents, men, and those lost-to-follow-up — have access to the services they need, and this should be one of the pillars that entrench inclusivity in schools and society. In addition, HIV services should be integrated with other sexual and reproductive health interventions, recognising the opportunity to meet people's needs in a single visit. Finally, there is a need to challenge restrictive policies and inspire governments to uphold the rights of people living with HIV, especially key populations, adolescents, and women.

CONCLUSION

Over the last three decades, 35 million people have died of AIDS. As a result, HIV/AIDS has brought about a significant reduction in human capital, especially in sub-Saharan Africa. Several studies have examined the effects of HIV/AIDS on human capital, in particular educational attainment. Inclusivity in schools and society concerning learners living with HIV/AIDS is fast becoming a reality in Africa and in South Africa in particular. Although misconceptions still exist, there is an increasing body of research that shows that misconceptions with regard to people and children living with HIV/AIDS are decreasing. Stereotypes, myths, prejudice and stigmatisation in schools and society can deprive a learner living with HIVAIDS of the opportunity to learn and to be integrated fully in society. However, thanks to inclusive education this picture is starting to change. The Department of Basic Education has care and support structures in place to provide quality care and support to learners with different impairments, such as health impairments like HIV/AIDS.

REFERENCES

Akande, A. (2001). Risky Business: South African youths and HIV/AIDS prevention. *Educational Studies*, *27*(3), 237–256.

Altman, D. (1994). *Power and community: organisational and cultural responses to AIDS*. Falmer.

Anderson, N.. (2004). National cross sectional study of views on sexual violence and risk of HIV infection and AIDS among South African school pupils. *BMJ (Clinical Research Ed.)*, ●●●, 329–952. PMID: 15485935

Auerbach, J.. (2005). Gender-based violence and HIV among women: Assessing the evidence. *AMFAR Aids Research*, *3*, 1–2.

Auvert, B.. (2005). Randomised, controlled intervention trial of male circumcision for reduction of HIV infection risk: The ANRS 1265 trial. *PLoS Medicine*, *2*(11), 1112–1122. PMID: 16231970

Badenhorst, M. G.. (2008). Trends in sexual behaviour among Free State University Students. *The Social Work Practitioner-Researcher*, *20*(11), 106123.

Bates, S. C. (2002). Good news for AIDS myths. *Missionalia*, *30*(11), 93–108.

Bekker, L. G., & Hosek, S. (2015). HIV and adolescents: Focus on young key populations. *Journal of the International AIDS Society*, *18*(2), 100–130.

Bernays, S.. (2017). "Not taking it will just be like a sin": Young people living with HIV and the stigmatization of less-than-perfect adherence to antiretroviral therapy. *Medical Anthropology*, *36*(5), 485–499. PMID: 28379042

Bhayiya, A. (2000). Women, HIV/AIDS and Poverty – Vulnerability and rights, theories and practices. (Paper presented at the GOOD Conference on Gender and HIV/AIDS, 11–13 September 2000. Oslo, Norway. Bollard, M. (2009). Promoting human rights approach for people with learning disabilities. *Primary Health Care*, *19*(9), 26–28.

Brady, M (1999) Female genital mutilation: Complications and risk of HIV transmission. *AIDS Patients Care and STD'S* 13, pp. 121:709–716.

Bridgraj, A. (2000). AIDS threat to higher education. *The Teacher*, *25*, 9.

Campbell, C.. (2005). 'I have an evil child at my house': Stigma and HIV/AIDS management in a South African community. *American Journal of Public Health*, *95*(5), 808–815. PMID: 15855456

Campbell, C.. (2007). 'Dying twice': A multi-level model of the roots of AIDS stigma in two South African communities. *Journal of Health Psychology*, *12*(3), 403–416. PMID: 17439992

Chikore, J. (2000) Sexuality and Aids. (Paper presented at the GOOD Conference on Gender and HIV/AIDS, 11–13 September 2000. Oslo, Norway. Chileshe, M & Bond V.A. (2010) Barriers and outcomes: TB patients co-infected with HIV accessing antiretroviral therapy in Rural Zambia. *ART Special Issue. AIDS Care, Vol.* 22, pp. 51–59.

Coetsee, E. E. (2007) Culture and gender as risk factors in patterns of high-risk sexual behaviour among students on the main campus of the University of the Free State. Bloemfontein: University of the Free State (Master's thesis in Psychology of Education).

Coopes, A. (2016). Australian researchers declare an end to AIDS as a public health issue. *BMJ (Clinical Research Ed.)*, *354*, i3895. PMID: 27406234

Cornelissen, G. M. (2005) HIV/AIDS Knowledge, awareness and perception of undergraduate students at the University of Stellenbosch. Stellenbosch: University of Stellenbosch (Master's thesis in Philosophy).

Coughlan, F. J.. (1996). Where knowledge and attitudes separate: Adolescent HIV/AIDS knowledge survey as information for social work training. *Social Work*, *32*(31), 255–261.

Deacon, H.. (2005). *Understanding HIV/AIDS stigma, a theoretical and methodological analysis*. Human Sciences Research Council.

Dilger, H. (2007). Healing the wounds of modernity: Salvation, community and care in a Neo-Pentecostal church in Dar Es Salaam, Tanzania. *Journal of Religion in Africa. Religion en Afrique*, *2007*(37), 59–83.

Essien, E. J. (1997). Cross-national HIV infection control practices and fear of AIDS: A comparison between Nigeria and the USA. *International J. STD & AIDS, Vol.*, *8*(12), 764–771. PMID: 9433951

Fawole, I.O. et al. (1999) A school-based AIDS education program for secondary school students in Nigeria: a review of effectiveness. *Health Edu, Res,* Vol. 14, 5), pp. 675–683.

Flicker, S., & Nixon, S. A. (2014). The DEPICT model for participatory qualitative health promotion research analysis piloted in Canada, Zambia and South Africa. *Health Promotion International*, *2014*. Advance online publication. https://www.ncbi.nlm.nih.gov/pubmed/24418997. 10–1093

Forman, L. (2003) The constitutional imperative to treat: The South African government's constitutional obligations to provide antiretroviral medicines. Paper at the South African AIDS Conference; Durban. 3–6 August.2003.

Gerbert, B.. (1991). The impact of who you know and where you live on opinions about AIDS and health care. *Social Science & Medicine, 32*(6), 677–681. PMID: 2035043

Goldin, C. S. (1994). Stigmatization and AIDS: Critical issues in public health. *Social Science & Medicine, 39*(9), 1359–1366. PMID: 7801171

Greeff, M.. (2008). Disclosure of HIV status: Experiences and perceptions of persons living with HIV/AIDS and nurses involved in their care in Africa. *Qualitative Health Research, 18*(3), 311–324. PMID: 18235155

Green, G. (1995). Attitudes towards people with HIV: Are they as stigmatizing as people with HIV perceive them to be? *Social Science and Medicine, Vol., 4*(4), 557–568. PMID: 7481950

Gregson, S. (2017) Documenting and explaining the HIV decline in east Zimbabwe: the Manicaland General Population Cohort., CA.BMJ Open. 2017 Oct 6;7(10):e015898. doi: : 28988165 Free PMC article.DOI: 10.1136/bmjopen-2017-015898.PMID

Hamra, M.. (2006). Relationship between expressed HIV/AIDS-related stigma and HIV-beliefs/knowledge and behaviour in families of HIV infected children in Kenya. *Tropical Medicine & International Health, 11*(4), 513–527. PMID: 16553935

Hassan, F. (2003) Treat the people … now. Human rights and the law in the struggle for treatment. Paper at the South African AIDS Conference; Durban. 3–6 August 2003.

Herek, GM. (2002) Thinking about AIDS and stigma: a psychologist's perspective. *J Law Med Ethics Winter,* Vol. 30, 4, pp. 594–607.

Herek, G. M. (2009). Hate crimes and stigma-related experiences among sexual minority adults in the United States: Prevalence estimates from a national probability sample. *J Interpers Violence, Vol., 24*(1), 54–74. PMID: 18391058

Herek, G. M., & Glunt, E. K. (1988). An epidemic of stigma: Public reactions to AIDS. *The American Psychologist, 43*(11), 886–891. PMID: 3063145

Jansson, J., Kerr, C. C., & Wilson, D. P. (2014). Predicting the population impact of increased HIV testing and treatment in Australia. *Sexual Health, 11*(2), 46–54. PMID: 24502838

Kalichman, S., & Simbayi, L. (2004). Traditional beliefs about the cause of AIDS and AIDS-related stigma in South Africa. *AIDS Care, Vol.*, *16*(5), 572–580. PMID: 15223526

Kalichman, S. C.. (2005). Development of a brief scale to measure AIDS-related stigma in South Africa. *AIDS and Behaviour, Vol.*, *9*(2), 135–143. PMID: 15933833

Kalichman, S. C., & Simbayi, L. C. (2003). HIV testing attitudes, AIDS stigma, and voluntary HIV counseling and testing in a black township in Cape Town, South Africa. *Sexually Transmitted Infections*, *79*(6), 442–447. PMID: 14663117

Katsui, H., & Kumpuvuori, J. (2008). Human Rights Based Approach in Development in Uganda. *Scandinavian Journal of Disability Research*, *10*(4), 227–236.

Kippax, S., & Race, K. (2003). Sustaining safe practice: Twenty years on. *Social Science & Medicine*, *57*(1), 1–12. PMID: 12753812

Kurth, A. E. et al. (2015) HIV testing and linkage to services for youth. *Journal of the International AIDS Society*, 18, 19433 [PMC free article] [PubMed] [CrossRef] [Google Scholar Landefeld, C.C. et. al (2018) Prevention of Mother-to Child Transmission of HIV in Yaounde: Barrier to Care. *AIDS care*, Vol. 30, 1, pp. 116–120. DOI: 10.7448/IAS.18.2.19433

Link, B. G., & Phelan, J. C. (2001). Conceptualizing stigma. *Annual Review of Sociology*, *27*(1), 363–385.

Mahajan, A. P.. (2008). Stigma in the HIV/AIDS epidemic: A review of the literature and recommendations for the way forward. *AIDS, Vol.*, *22*(Suppl 2), S67–S79. PMID: 18641472

Mbago, M. C. Y. (2004). Socio-demographic correlates of desire for HIV testing in Tanzania. *Sexual Health*, *1*, 13–21. PMID: 16335292

Miller, A. N., & Rubin, D. L. (2007). Factors leading to self-disclosure of a positive HIV diagnosis in Nairobi, Kenya: People living with HIV/AIDS in the Sub-Sahara. *Qualitative Health Research*, *17*(5), 586–598. PMID: 17478642

Muchini, B.. (2011). Local perceptions of the forms, timing and causes of behavior change in response to the AIDS epidemic in Zimbabwe. *AIDS and Behavior*, *15*(2), 487–498. PMID: 20803064

Niehaus, I. (2006) Leprosy of a Deadlier Kind: Conceptions of AIDS, Sex and Death in the South African Lowveld; Paper presented at the Institute for Social and Economic Research; Rhodes University. October 2006.

Persson, A. (2014). Transmission and prevention of HIV among heterosexual populations in Australia. *AIDS Education and Prevention, 26*(3), 245–255. PMID: 24846487

Pitpitan, E. V.. (2012). AIDS-related stigma, HIV testing, and transmission risk among patrons of informal drinking places in Cape Town, South Africa. *Annals of Behavioral Medicine, Vol., 43*(3), 362–371. PMID: 22367752

Rakwar, J.. (1999). Cofactors for the acquisition of HIV-1 among heterosexual men: Prospective cohort study of trucking company workers in Kenya. *AIDS, 13*, 607–614. PMID: 10203386

Rankin, W. W.. (2005). The stigma of being HIV-positive in Africa. [PMC free article] [PubMed] [Google Scholar]. *PLoS Medicine, 2*(8), e247. PMID: 16008508

Sendziuk, P. (2003). *Learning to trust: Australian responses to AIDS*. UNSW Press.

Shisana, O., ... (2008) South African national HIV prevalence, incidence, behaviour and communication survey, a turning tide among teenagers? South Africa: Human Science Research Council Press. 75 p. Available: http://www.hsrcpress.ac.za/product .php?productid=2264&cat=1&page=3. Accessed 16 August 2012. This is an open-access resource for more detailed information about HIV/AIDS in South Africa.

Simbayi, L. (2003). HIV testing attitudes, AIDS stigma, and voluntary HIV counselling and testing in a black township in Cape Town, South Africa. *Sexually Transmitted Infections, Vol., 79*(6), 442–447. PMID: 14663117

Skinner, D. & Mfecane, S. (2004) Stigma, discrimination and implications for people living with HIV/AIDS in South Africa. *Journal of the Social Aspects of HIV/AIDS, Vol.* 1, 3, pp 157–164.

Utulu, S. N., & Lawoyin, T. O. (2007). Epidemiological features of HIV Infection among pregnant women in Markurdi, Benue State, Nigeria. *The Journal of Biological Sciences, 39*(3), 397–408. PMID: 16928285

Uwakwe, C. B. (2000). Systematized HIV/AIDS education for student nurses at the University of Ibadan, Nigeria: Impact on Knowledge, attitudes and compliance with universal precautions. *Journal of Advanced Nursing, 32*(2), 416–424. PMID: 10964190

Venkatapuram, S. (2014). Mental disability, human rights and capabilities approach. Searching for the foundations. *International Review of Psychiatry (Abingdon, England), 26*(4), 408–414. PMID: 25137106

Wessels, M., & Rabinowitz, L. (2005). *Educator's guide to you, me & HIV*. Cold Spring Harbour Laboratory Press.

Chapter 5
Embracing Ubuntu:
Promoting Inclusion of Learners With Autism Spectrum Disorders in Education

Jabulani Mpofu
https://orcid.org/0000-0001-5634-8581
Zimbabwe Open University, Zimbabwe

Maximus Monaheng Sefotho
University of Johannesburg, South Africa

ABSTRACT

Creating learning environments that accommodate all students, regardless of their skills or limitations, is the fundamental goal of inclusion. This method is very important for students who have autism spectrum disorders. The complex developmental disorder known as autism spectrum disorders (ASD) has an impact on social relationships, behavior, and communication. Students with autism spectrum disorders confront particular difficulties that call for specialised approaches that encourage empathy and cooperation from peers, teachers, and the larger society. This chapter will explore the core ideas of Ubuntu, a Southern African philosophy that emphasises relationships within the community and mutual care. Ubuntu encourages African communities to view an individual's identity through the collective well-being of the community, advocating for empathy, compassion, and shared humanity. By implementing Ubuntu principles in educational settings, African communities can redefine inclusion as a shared responsibility that enable students with autism spectrum disorders to thrive.

DOI: 10.4018/979-8-3373-7163-4.ch005

INTRODUCTION

Over time, human societies have developed systems based on indigenous philosophy to meet their educational needs and boost student participation in their system. Around the world, indigenous philosophies—whether formal or informal—are used to aid in the education of members of their communities (Mpofu 2023). Most Southern African communities have localised concepts and aspirations for education that combine traditional systems, such as the African notion of Ubuntu (Mpofu 2023). It is increasingly recognised that teaching pupils of African origin through African indigenous knowledge systems improves their social skills and general well-being when they are in inclusive environments (Heto & Mino, 2023). The great majority of people on the earth actually use indigenous educational systems. Africa must utilise its indigenous knowledge systems, like the Ubuntu ideology, which is ingrained in local culture, to meet the educational demands of its communities (Heto & Mino 2023). The Ubuntu principle, which has gained popularity as a way to address unjust practices in the continent's educational institutions, is regarded as the African equivalent of inclusion, according to Mpofu (2023).

Not only is inclusion in education required by law or morality, but it is also essential to a just society where people value diversity and view individual differences as assets. Creating learning environments that accommodate all learners, regardless of their skills or limitations, is the fundamental goal of inclusion. This method is very important for learners who have autism spectrum disorders (ASD). Creating an inclusive learning environment supports diverse needs, enhances engagement, promotes independence, and ensure equitable educational opportunities for learners with ASD. The complex developmental disorder known as ASD has an impact on social relationships, behaviour, and communication. Learners with ASD confront particular difficulties that call for specialised approaches that encourage empathy and cooperation from peers, teachers, and the larger society (Zvomuya, 2020). This chapter will explore the core ideas of Ubuntu, a Southern African philosophy that emphasises relationships within the community and mutual care, which translates to "I am because we are." Ubuntu encourages African communities to view an individual's identity through the collective well-being of the community, advocating for empathy, compassion, and shared humanity (Mupedziswa, Rankopo & Mwanza, 2019, Zvomuya, 2020). By implementing Ubuntu principles in educational settings, African communities can redefine inclusion as a shared responsibility, creating supportive networks that enable learners with ASD to thrive. Finally, this chapter hopes to inspire African educators, policymakers, and communities to embrace inclusion through the lens of Ubuntu, acknowledging the importance of an inclusive education system for both individual development and the advancement of society as a whole. By embracing diversity, African communities create a richer, more dynamic learning environment for all.

PHILOSOPHY OF UBUNTU

Ubuntu is a Southern African philosophical idea that emphasises how all members of a community are interdependent and related (Mupedziswa, Rankopo & Mwanza, 2019). The name comes from the Nguni phrase "Ubuntu ngumuntu ngabantu," which roughly translates to "I am because we are" (Zvomuya 2020). The Chishona expression "Munhu munhu kuburikidza nevamwe vanhu" means "a person is a person because of other people." Zvomuya (2020). This worldview emphasises that relationships with other people determine humanity and that individuals cannot exist in a vacuum. Humanity toward others is fundamental to Ubuntu's moral code, which regulates interpersonal relationships. It fosters empathy, compassion, and a sense of mutual accountability. Ubuntu promotes treating one another with love, decency, and respect because it acknowledges the intrinsic value and worth of every human. This worldview prioritises social peace and the well-being of the group over individualism and selfishness. Ubuntu encourages people to see their common humanity and see themselves reflected in others (Ébalé, Benson & Mulemi 2023). It emphasizes the importance of community, collaboration, and teamwork in fostering a sense of belonging and social cohesion (Ébalé et al., 2023). When people embrace Ubuntu, they realize that their actions have an impact not only on themselves but also on those around them. By treating others with humanity, people can create a society that is more equal, inclusive, and compassionate. Research has shown that promoting Ubuntu values can improve social justice, healthcare, education, and other areas of society (e.g. Mupedziswa, Rankopo & Mwanza, 2019; Zvomuya 2020). For instance, Johnson and Johnson (2019) stresses importance of teamwork in fostering a welcoming and inclusive learning environment. They contend that teacher and student's collaboration creates a feeling of belonging and empowerment that promotes both academic achievement and individual development. Similar to this, Van Mieghem et al. (2020) stress the value of productive teamwork in advancing inclusion and diversity in schools. Teachers foster a friendly, courteous environment that values the individual viewpoints and experiences of every student by adopting the tenets of Ubuntu. Applying Ubuntu's principles of community, compassion and shared responsibility fosters inclusive education, motivate learners and enhance academic success collectively (Mpofu & Molosiwa, 2017). .

INCLUSIVE EDUCATION

Regardless of their socioeconomic status, cultural background, abilities, or impairments, inclusive education aims to ensure that all students have fair access to high-quality instruction. (Ainscow, Slee & Best 2019). Van Mieghem et al. (2020) assert that inclusive education is a comprehensive and holistic approach to education that takes into account each student's unique learning needs. It goes beyond merely integrating learners with special needs into conventional classrooms. Recognising that every student has distinct learning preferences, abilities, and challenges, inclusive education aims to give all learners the assistance and accommodations they need to thrive. Adapting teaching methods, instructional materials, and learning environments to accommodate various learner types is a key component of inclusive education, which aims to guarantee that no student is left behind or excluded (Hernández-Torrano, Somerton & Helmer 2020). Through inclusive education, which acknowledges that cooperation and partnership are crucial to establishing an inclusive and empowered learning environment, families, communities, and other pertinent stakeholders are encouraged to actively participate in the educational process. Helmer, Somerton, and Hernández-Torrano (2020). The goal of inclusive education is to create learning settings that recognize and promote variety, and in the principles of social justice, human rights, and respect for all individuals. (Hilt 2017), foster wholesome relationships, and get learners ready for an inclusive and globally interconnected world (Van Mieghem et al., 2020). Societies can work to guarantee that everyone has an equal chance to realise their full potential and make a significant contribution to their communities by promoting inclusive practices in education (Qvortrup & Qvortrup 2018).

Following the realisation that inclusive education improves social cohesion and equity within the educational system, the majority of African countries implemented it (Mpofu & Molosiwa 2017). African governments sought to remove education policies that have historically excluded learners with impairments. According to research, inclusive education improves social interactions, cultivates good attitudes, and encourages learners to tolerate diversity (e.g. Van Mieghem et al., 2020; Vanderstraeten 2020; Brandt, Kidron & Raviv 2018). The majority of African countries aim to create a culture that celebrates diversity and offers all learners equal chances through inclusive education (Mpofu & Molosiwa 2017). The understanding of inclusive education's ability to enhance learning outcomes for learners with disabilities is a crucial factor in Africa's embrace of this approach (Mpofu & Molosiwa 2021). Numerous studies have shown that inclusive education enhances students with disabilities' general wellness, social skills development, and academic achievement. African nations want to increase children with disabilities' access to specialized support and top-notch educational materials by incorporating them into normal classrooms. This would provide the best possible learning opportunities (Szumski, Smogorzewska, & Karwowsk 2017).

The commitment to inclusive education is shared by most African nations, which aligns with their duties and pledges. The United Nations Convention on the Rights of Persons with Disabilities (UN-CRPD), which emphasizes the right of individuals with disabilities to an inclusive education, is one of the international agreements that the majority of African states have ratified (Mpofu & Molosiwa 2017). According to Brandt et al. (2018), inclusive education is viewed as a way to guarantee the full and productive involvement of students with disabilities in society, as well as to fulfil these responsibilities and advance their rights. To support the adoption of inclusive education policies, African governments have taken steps to improve teachers' capacity to adapt their teaching strategies to the diverse needs of students (Mpofu & Molosiwa, 2017). In teacher preparation programs in Africa, inclusive teaching practices are prioritized. This investment in teacher professional development demonstrates Africa's commitment to implementing inclusive education throughout the continent (Mpofu & Molosiwa 2017).

CHALLENGES FACED IN IMPLEMENTING INCLUSIVE EDUCATION

The successful integration of learners with various needs into regular classroom environments has been hampered by a number of obstacles encountered throughout the application of implementation of inclusive education in Africa. The absence of sufficient resources, such as skilled workers and educational materials, is a major obstacle. According to a study by Avramidis and Norwich (2002), there is a dearth of teachers with specialised training who is capable of attending to the needs of students with disabilities in many African nations. Inadequate financing for essential support systems, such assistive technology and individualised learning materials are few obstacles to the effective application of inclusive education in Africa (Muthukrishna, 2008). Additionally, negative cultural perceptions of disability which are present in many African cultures present formidable obstacles to inclusivity. Some African communities' social conceptions of impairments are viewed through a prism of stigma and superstition, which result in exclusionary practices in schools (Gajaraj et al. 2020). Because of this cultural context, some families are hesitant to enrol their children with impairments in regular schools. They fear lack of support or societal rejection (Muthukrishna, 2008).

The inflexibility of the current educational frameworks, which frequently fail to adapt to a range of learning needs, is another significant obstacle. Many African countries have traditional educational systems that prioritise identical curricula and standardised testing, which do not take into account individual learning differences. If these frameworks are not modified to include inclusive practices, the outcome is a "one-size-fits-all" strategy that disregards the particular needs of learners with disabilities. Moreover, these problems are made worse by a lack of accountability procedures and policy execution. Despite the fact that many African nations have ratified international agreements like the Salamanca Statement, Yssel et al (2016) point out that there is still insufficient implementation of these commitments in the domestic context. This gap between policy and practice hampers the effective provision of inclusive education. The situation is further complicated by regional differences in educational access. Implementing inclusive education is more difficult in rural locations because of things like inadequate infrastructure, a lack of specialised services nearby, and a lack of reliable transportation. According to a study by Nind and Vargus (2016), learners with impairments in rural areas are frequently left without the support networks they need, which raises their risk of dropping out of school. The combination of these difficulties with socioeconomic elements like poverty and a lack of government assistance results in a complex issue that calls for more than just changes to the law; rather, it calls for an all-encompassing strategy that includes community involvement, resource mobilisation, and ongoing training for teachers. According to research, community-based projects that prioritise local settings and involve stakeholders from a variety of sectors are frequently the cause of successful inclusive education programs in some African nations, like Namibia and Uganda (UNESCO, 2015). These case studies show how raising awareness and utilising community resources can result in favourable shifts in perceptions of inclusive education. Nonetheless, it is evident that systemic reforms tackling these core issues must be given top priority if broad inclusion is to be accomplished throughout the continent. Policymakers, educators, and communities must work together to build robust systems that support access and equity for all learners, regardless of their ability, as the conversation around inclusive education develops. All things considered, overcoming these numerous obstacles through a coordinated effort involving several stakeholders and a change to a more inclusive mind-set is still required for inclusive education in Africa to be implemented successfully.

MEDICAL PERSPECTIVE OF ASD

The American Psychiatric Association (APA 2013) states that ASD is a chronic neurodevelopmental illness marked by communication and social interaction deficits and limited behaviours, interests and activities beginning within the first three years of life. ASD are typically diagnosed in childhood, with many noticeable symptoms emerging between the ages of two and three years. However, some individuals with

ASD continue to grow normally until adulthood and later lose previously acquired abilities (APA 2013). ASD varies from person to individual in both severity as well as combination of various signs and symptoms (Cage & Troxell-Whitman 2019). Needless to say, the expression and attribution of ASD also varies across cultures.

While the precise causes of ASD remain unclear, evidence suggests that a combination of neurological, environmental, and genetic variables may play a role in their development (Cage & Troxell-Whitman 2019). One of the most widespread misconceptions regarding ASD is that all people with these conditions share the same characteristics or skills, which is untrue. Since ASD are actually a continuum, each person will experience them differently. This includes highly capable people who may go misdiagnosed as well as non-verbal communicators who require a lot of support (Cage & Troxell-Whitman 2019). Numerous obstacles frequently confront learners with ASD, which may have an impact on their social integration and academic achievement. Understanding social cues, building relationships with peers, and adjusting to novel or unexpected circumstances are a few examples of these issues (Mpofu 2022). Additionally, sensory sensitivity can lead to uneasiness and anxiety in the classroom, which hinders these learners ' ability to concentrate and interact with the material (Mpofu 2022). Furthermore, co-occurring disorders like anxiety, ADHD, or intellectual disabilities can make learning more difficult for them and call for specialised teaching and support staff methods.

The importance of early diagnosis and intervention for learners with ASD cannot be overstated. Early therapy has been shown to be very beneficial for learners with ASD (National Institute of Mental Health, 2024). Programs such as Applied Behavior Analysis (ABA), social skills training, and speech therapy can help. in the development of social and communication skills, allowing learners to move through their surroundings more skilfully. A greater knowledge of ASD and increased community acceptance are also fostered by early diagnosis, which gives families access to the resources and support networks they need. It is essential to dispel myths and raise knowledge in order to support learners with ASD. In order to identify the symptoms of ASD and put into practice practical tactics that promote inclusive education, educators and caregivers need undergo thorough training. By fostering a classroom environment that celebrates diversity and supports individualised instruction, barriers related to ASD can be removed and all learners can benefit.

DISABILITY CAMOUFLAGING

Learners with ASD participate in society's activities less than their peers without disabilities (Livingston & Shah 2019). Learners with ASD may conceal their illness so as to seen like more neurotypical (Riche 2014)· This behaviour causes burnout, weariness, anxiety, sadness, stress, and a decreased quality of life (Livingston & Shah 2019). The widespread prejudice and stigma that those with ASD experience in society is a significant contributing factor to disability camouflaging. Disability is stigmatised in many cultures as a sign of weakness or ineptitude, which causes people to fear discrimination or unjust treatment from others (Livingston & Shah 2019)· Learners with ASD may feel compelled to conceal their condition as a result of this stigma in order to prevent prejudice or discrimination. In addition, learners with ASD may hide their condition in an effort to blend in and be accepted in their schools, where there is frequently pressure to succeed by meeting appearance criteria (Children with Disabilities in Uganda, African Child Policy Forum, 2016).). Learners with ASD could be afraid that coming out with their condition will make them perceived as different or less capable, which could impede their growth and academic achievement (Children with Disabilities in Uganda, African Child Policy Forum, (2016). Moreover, the choice to hide and the absence of services and accommodations for those with disabilities in public places may also have an impact on disability (Riche 2014)· Learners with ASD may conceal or minimise their condition due to internalised negative ideas and perceptions about their own skills, in addition to external causes (Children with Disabilities in Uganda, African Child Policy Forum, 2016) Disability is frequently portrayed in society as a burden or a constraint, which can affect how people with disabilities see themselves and their chances of success (Riche 2014)· Learners who experience shame or inadequacy due to internalised ableism may conceal their impairment in an effort to avoid dealing with these unpleasant sentiments. The choice to conceal one's disability is a complicated and diverse matter that is impacted by both personal and societal attitudes. By encouraging disability inclusion and combating stigma and stereotypes, societies can build a more just and empowered education system that benefits all learners, regardless of their ability (Riche 2014)·

SOCIAL MODEL OF ASD

The Social model of ASD has completely changed how society views and understands disability. The social model stresses how societal constraints contribute to disablement, unlike the medical model that pathologies ASD as a personal tragedy or individual handicap. In the latter half of the 20th century, the social idea of disability emerged as a result of the medical model's flaws. This paradigm holds that barriers related to social, environmental, and attitude are what cause impairment rather than being a feature of persons alone (Livingston & Shah 2019). In order to accommodate a range of talents and promote inclusion, the emphasis should move from repairing the individual to changing social institutions Distinguishing between disability and impairment is necessary according to the social model. According to the social model, disability develops from the obstacles faced by individuals in society, impairment refers to any physical, sensory, intellectual, or psychological differences that an individual may have (Livingston & Shah 2019). The social model acknowledges that impediments to communication, mobility, and attitude all contribute to the construction of disability within society (Livingston & Shah 2019). These obstacles can take the form of unwelcoming architecture, poor transit, a lack of educational possibilities, prejudice in the workplace, and unfavourable preconceptions. Society may establish an inclusive environment that allows people with disabilities to fully engage by addressing and removing these barriers (Livingston & Shah 2019).

According to the social model of disability, rather than being the result of individual shortcomings, ASD results from society's inability to accept variety (Livingston & Shah 2019). This change in perspective shifts the focus from "fixing" or "curing" people with ASD to society's need to provide accessible settings and opportunities. A culture of acceptance and respect is fostered by encouraging people to see others with ASD as an identity that is just as legitimate as any other. Through acknowledging and appreciating the abilities and qualities of people with autism spectrum disorders, society may progress toward a future that is more fair and inclusive (Livingston & Shah 2019). Adopting the social concept of disability has significant legislative and policy ramifications. Through laws and regulations, governments and institutions must actively participate in removing obstacles and fostering inclusiveness. For example, The Convention on the Rights of Persons with Disabilities issued by the United Nations calls for accessible transportation, inclusive education, independent living, and employment equality (Mandy 2019). It also incorporates the social model when applied to ASD. The social model of disability provides an effective framework for comprehending and addressing challenges faced by individuals with ASD. Through prioritising social transformation, advocating for inclusivity, and strengthening self-advocacy, this strategy cultivates a fairer and just society for those with ASD (Livingston & Shah 2019). It's crucial to recognise, though, that there are critics of the social model. Some contend that it oversimplifies the complexity of ASD (Mandy 2019). But it offers an insightful viewpoint that encourages a more accepting and compassionate method of helping those with autism spectrum disorders.

ASD PARADIGMS IN AFRICAN CONTEXTS

According to Kivunja and Kuyini (2017), a paradigm is a system of thought that reflects a method of thinking about how a specific occurrence is interpreted. Ntuli

(2018) asserts that paradigms give us a broad perspective on the universe and aid in our comprehension of the various aspects of human reality. The paradigm for ASD offers a coherent "story" of a meaningful, practical, yet culturally subjective reality (Moharajan, 2018). The paradigms of ASD are distinct and culturally distinctive, and they are influenced by an individual's prior knowledge, including their occupation and cultural orientation (Ugwu, Ekere & Ohoh 2013). The concept of ASD, as acknowledged is not unique to any African country in Western nations, nor do any African languages have terms with comparable meanings (Mpofu 2023). Nonetheless, the majority of African societies view ASD as illnesses, much like Western cultures do, albeit they treat them differently (Bakare & Munir 2011).

Usonji is the Swahili term for ASD (Bakare & Munir 2011). Disorders are implied by this. Although the causes of these disorders are linked to witchcraft, individuals from cultures that speak Kiswahili think that they can be cured by simply increasing the diagnosed person's interactions with numerous people through regular discussions. They believe that interacting with a lot of peers can help reduce autism symptoms, including severe emotional difficulties. When talking about ASD, Kiswahili frequently makes reference to the social model of disability. Kiswahili people place greater focus on social functioning than on clinical deficiencies. *Osatha kulankula bwino*, which means "one who cannot speak properly," is how the Chewa people of Malawi refer to those with ASD (McFall 2016). The cause of ASD in Chewa culture is genetic or witchcraft. In isiZulu *Ukungashintshiswa* is the term for ASD (McFall 2016). "Not being changed" is how it is literally translated into English, suggesting a state or condition that is immutable. Similar to the majority of African cultures, the Zulus link ASD to a variety of causes, including curses or ancestor spirits. Traditional healing methods, such as spiritual ceremonies, are used in Zulu culture to treat ASD by addressing the alleged underlying spiritual causes. The Maasai people in Kenya do not have a label for ASD; instead, the word "*almodai*," which means "dumb," is the closest the Maasai have to the western definition of ASD (Mpofu 2020). Furthermore, according to Mpofu (2020), there are no terms in Shona, Ndebele, or Kalanga that are indigenous to Zimbabwe that match the Western description of autism spectrum disorders. ASD are most strongly associated with the Shona term *"haana kukwana"* "not enough." A person who lacks the necessary skills may require assistance and find it difficult to participate in social events.

The analogy between neurodiversity and disease is one trend in the global knowledge of ASD. ASD are viewed from a neurodiversity perspective as a common and advantageous illustration of biodiversity (Chapman 2020). A pathology model, on the other hand, views ASD as a more general functional norm (Chapman 2020). On the one hand, because neurodiversity considers both individual and interpersonal functioning and is founded on system functioning rather than fitness and selection, African societies, which are collective in character, may embrace this approach to

ASD (Amstrong, 2015). However, in an African culture, ASD could be viewed as a pathology that can be treated by cleaning and is thought to be caused by bad spirits (Brown 2014). Human conditions like ASD are thought to be caused by evil forces, according to the majority of indigenous African disease theories and concepts (Brown 2014). They believe that the spiritual power of ancestor spirits or gods can be used to treat ASD by calling on patients' struggles and predicting their intended recovery. Furthermore, research indicates that paranormal causes continue to be cited as the cause of ASD in Africa (Mpofu 2020). In Africa, the genesis of ASD is frequently explained by witchcraft, demonic agony, and bad spirits.

ASD FROM NEURODIVERSITY CONCEPT

There are various ways to frame ASD from neurodiversity perspective. Neurodiversity is connected to an "ecological society" in which people of colour are respected and assisted in identifying their niche (Hull et al., 2019). Neurodiversity is a scientific idea that suggests a different perspective on function and malfunction. As stated by Livingston, Shah, and Happé (2019), neurodiversity is the fact that different people have different minds and brains, in the same way that "biodiversity" is the fact that there are differences in biological makeup. In contrast to diseases that must be treated, neurodiversity promotes the understanding and acceptance of a range of neurological illnesses, including ASD, as normal variations of the human experience. According to Australian sociologist Judy Singer, (Livingston & Shah & Happé 2019) the phrase neurodiversity was first used in the late 1990s and suggests that neurological variety should be treated with the same consideration as cultural and genetic variation. Therefore, the neurodiversity approach suggests that society should change to accommodate these variances rather than adhering to traditional medical models that aim to normalise or treat autistic features. Fundamental to this idea is the understanding that those with ASD have special talents, capabilities, and perspectives on the world, and that these things should be valued and accommodated rather than pathologies and repressed (Hull et al, 2019). This contrasts with the medical model, which encourages those with ASD to accept being sick as the standard. In short, the sick role aims to deprive an impaired person their autonomy—the ability to choose their own course in life and make decisions for themselves which is what defines a human being (Cassidy et al, 2020). The idea of neurodiversity is for those with ASD to have an empowered social identity. The neurodiversity perceives ASD from main principles of the biopsychosocial model of disability and health care (Cage &, Troxell-Whitman 2019). It combines beneficial elements from the social and medical models, which integrates psychosocial elements of life, for example, resilience with medical and psychosocial diagnostic data (Happé

& Frith 2020). Neurodiversity advocacy of ASD, has completely changed people's knowledge and perception of the condition by denying the notion that ASD are a private characteristic of each individual and is instead the result of social, environmental, and mental barriers (Happé & Frith 2020). The neurodiversity perspective central idea is the ASD person's personal agency in overcoming social boundaries. Providing people with ASD dignity as the head of their own life is replacing the idea of "fixing" or "curing" them.

Happé & Frith (2020) found that embracing people with ASD mental health can be improved by neurodiversity perspective by lessening the need to live up to neurotypical norms, which can frequently result in stress, anxiety, and depression (Kapp et al, 2013). Furthermore, advocates of neurodiversity acknowledge and honours the special abilities and contributions of people with ASD, including their capacity for diverse thought, profound concentration, and attention to detail (Silberman, 2015). This viewpoint is consistent with the rising body of research that emphasises the diversity of ASD experiences and the demand for individualised methods in social services, employment, and education .However, others who oppose the neurodiversity movement contend that it may minimise the serious difficulties that some individuals with ASD require a variety of forms of help and intervention strategies (Happé & Frith 2020). The that neurodiversity shapes the conversation about ASD and disabilities today, encouraging a more accepting and considerate view of individual variances in neurology (Robertson 2010). It is critical to strike an equilibrium between knowledge of the range of requirements within ASD population and the promotion of acceptance and inclusion as research advances.

AFROCENTRIC THEORY

This chapter used Afrocentricity theory to examine how the Ubuntu ideology might be applied to support the inclusion of learners with ASD in the classroom. When analysing historical and current challenges, African perspectives, experiences, and knowledge are central to the critical framework known as Afrocentric theory. Reclaiming African identity is one of the main principles of Afrocentric ideology. Fighting against Eurocentric discourses that have historically stifled African voices and reclaiming African identity are crucial, according to Afrocentric philosophy. African people must enjoy their cultural history and define themselves according to their own criteria (Asante 2016). Afrocentric ideology emphasises the fundamental oneness and interconnectedness of African peoples while yet acknowledging the variety of African civilisations. According to Ébalé and Mulemi (2023), valuing African cultural unity fosters camaraderie and builds communities among people of different identities. Academics like Zvomuya (2020) advocates for emancipation from the colonial mind-set that still permeates African nations. Decolonising the mind and rejecting Western values that uphold oppressive regimes are demands of Afrocentric theory (Ramasela 2022). The agency and resistance of African people against colonialism, imperialism, and other forms of oppression are highlighted in contemporary Afrocentric study. The importance of centralising stories of African tenacity and resistance in shaping political and historical discourse is emphasised by authors such as Heto and Mino (2023). Afrofuturism and innovation are the other pillars of Afrocentric thought. This principle investigates hypothetical futures that prioritise African worldviews, cultures, and technologies. Afrocentric theory predicts a future that embraces African customs and cosmologies and recognises the inventiveness and ingenuity that exist within African communities (Gebremikael et al., 2022).

There are commonalities between Ubuntu philosophy and Afrocentric thought that can be used to advance inclusive education. Afrocentric philosophy underlines the centrality of African viewpoints and experiences, while Ubuntu highlights the connectivity and individuals in a community are interdependent (Ébalé & Mulemi, 2023). The need of a common sense of identity and well-being is emphasised by both Ubuntu and Afrocentric ideology. Within the framework of inclusive education, this might manifest in collaborative learning environments that prioritise the needs of all students and foster a sense of belonging and support among them. Ubuntu emphasises the importance of respecting variety within a community and the interconnectedness of all individuals. This aligns with Afrocentric principles, which value the diversity of African perspectives and customs. This can be translated into developing a curriculum that represents a range of cultural experiences and backgrounds in an inclusive school setting, encouraging empathy, tolerance, and understanding among learners (Heto & Mino 2023).

Ubuntu and Afrocentric ideology both support a humanistic approach to education that emphasises each person's whole growth. These frameworks can be used by inclusive education initiatives to prioritise the social, emotional, and cognitive needs of all learners, irrespective of their background or skill level (Zvomuya 2020). In the classroom setting, this can entail establishing a feeling of community and belonging, encouraging student voice and agency, and putting culturally relevant pedagogies into practice. Ubuntu and Afrocentric ideology are based on the ideas of social justice, equity, and emancipation. In the framework of inclusive education, this encourages marginalised groups to participate and get access, enabling learners to realise their greatest potential. Teachers can establish more inclusive, egalitarian, and empowering learning environments for all learners by focusing on Ubuntu and Afrocentric ideas in inclusive education initiatives (Heto & Mino 2023).

CONTRIBUTIONS OF AFROCENTRIC THEORY TO EDUCATIONAL PRACTICES FOR LEARNERS WITH ASD

The importance of elements of African culture, values, and historical settings in comprehending and addressing the experiences of people in the African diaspora is emphasised by Afrocentric theory. Incorporating Afrocentric viewpoints into educational procedures for learners with ASD can result in more culturally appropriate and successful interventions. This chapter provides some of the ways that Afrocentric thought has influenced teaching methods for learners with ASD. These consist of community involvement, culturally sensitive teaching, and identity affirmation.

Afrocentric thought encourages African and African diasporic people to have a good sense of who they are (Agyeman 2015). For students with ASD, who commonly encounter social stigma and self-perception misconceptions, this is essential. African learners with ASD benefit from the affirmation of their identities through the inclusion of Afrocentric viewpoints, which fosters resilience and self-worth (Agyeman 2015). For example, using African cultural narratives and role models might assist learners with ASD in identifying their own talents. According to Heto and Mino (2023) the idea of "double consciousness" exemplifies the internal struggle that marginalised people experience

Using Afrocentric methods can assist learners with ASD negotiate their complexity by facilitating conversations about identity. Culturally responsive pedagogy, which adapts teaching methods to learners ' cultural backgrounds, is heavily influenced by Afrocentric philosophy (Heto & Mino 2023). This could entail implementing curricula in the classroom that incorporate African literature, history, and contributions to science and the arts. Culturally relevant instruction boosts learner's engagement and academic achievement (Gay, 2010). Making connections between teachings and well-known cultural narratives can improve comprehension and recall for learners with ASD, who may have trouble communicating socially. Teachers can use storytelling techniques that are in line with African customs to help learners connect with the content more deeply.

Another essential component of Afrocentric ideology is community engagement. Collaboration between schools and the surrounding communities is frequently necessary to implement effective educational approaches for learners with ASD (Agyeman 2015). In order to create support networks for learners with ASD, schools are encouraged to collaborate with neighbourhood organisations by Afrocentric techniques, which place an emphasis on communal power and shared responsibility. According to Agyeman (2015), involving families and communities creates a more encouraging atmosphere for learners, which is crucial for learners with ASD who might need more all-encompassing assistance to flourish. The holistic learning emphasised by Afrocentric theory is in line with social-emotional learning concepts.

The use of traditional techniques that foster emotional awareness and cultural understanding can assist to improve social skills and emotional management in learners with ASD. Group exercises modelled after African cultural customs, for instance, can teach social skills in a way that is culturally appropriate while also improving relationships and peer interactions (Gay, 2010).

STRATEGIES FOR FOSTERING INCLUSIVE ENVIRONMENTS FOR LEARNERS WITH ASD USING UBUNTU PRINCIPLES

It is essential to include learners with ASD in order to create fair learning settings that value diversity. Through the adoption of Ubuntu ideals, which emphasise community and connection, educators may create techniques that assist learners with autism spectrum disorders. A more encouraging and inclusive learning environment can be produced by promoting the inclusion of learners with ASD using the tenets of Ubuntu, a philosophy that emphasises community, connectivity, and shared humanity. This section offers the following strategies for applying Ubuntu principles to create inclusive learning environments for learners with autism spectrum disorders.

BUILDING COMMUNITY THROUGH RELATIONSHIP-BUILDING

The African ideology of Ubuntu, which emphasises interpersonal connections and community, is a cornerstone for promoting inclusive education, especially for learners with ASD. This emphasises need of fostering community ties, which can greatly improve the educational outcomes of learners with ASD. Ubuntu promotes teachers and peers to actively connect with learners who have ASD by creating an atmosphere that values understanding and support for one another, which fosters a sense of acceptance and belonging (Gordon 2018). In order to reduce stigma and promote empathy among peers, effective community ties based on Ubuntu establish safe places for learners with ASD can express their particular needs and strengths.

The use of Ubuntu in inclusive education settings promotes collaboration between educators, parents, and the general public, fostering a customised learning strategy that acknowledges the varied characteristics of people with ASD (Mackenzie 2019). In addition to improving academic results, this cooperative effort helps learners with ASD maintain their social and emotional health, which is essential for their entire development. Carrington and Deppeler (2010) assert that community-informed inclusive education techniques aid in removing obstacles to involvement, improving access to learning materials and chances for interaction with peers from different backgrounds. Additionally, Ubuntu's tenets promote an environment of mutual respect and understanding, inspiring all learners to value and cherish diversity. In the end, schools can create a more welcoming atmosphere that not only values diversity but also gives learners with ASD the tools they need to succeed by incorporating the Ubuntu principle into their curricula. In order to create a society that is really inclusive, this all-encompassing strategy encourages social integration in addition to academic achievement (Elias et al., 2018).

CULTURALLY RESPONSIVE TEACHING PRACTICES

Promoting inclusive education requires the use of culturally responsive teaching (CRT) strategies (Milner 2017), particularly for those with ASD. These methods take into account the cultural origins of learners, creating a supportive and valued learning environment for all. The Ubuntu ideology, which places a strong focus on community, connection, and mutual assistance, is very similar to CRT and provides a foundation for inclusivity. Ubuntu's claim that "I am because we are" aligns with the necessity of cooperative learning settings that accommodate a range of learning requirements. One example of a culturally sensitive teaching strategy is tailoring instruction to the cultural contexts of students with ASD and their families responsive strategy that can improve learning results and student engagement (Milner 2017). Teachers may put Ubuntu values into practice in inclusive learning environments by cultivating connections based on empathy and respect. By actively seeking to understand learners ' histories, this method pushes teachers to foster a sense of community and enhance peer relationships. Studies reveal that when learners with ASD receive help through culturally appropriate teaching methods, their academic performance and social skills increase dramatically, fostering a more peaceful learning environment (Lindsey et al., 2018). Additionally, cooperative learning opportunities that capitalise on each person's unique skills can foster a community of support for learners with ASD as well as their classmates who are typically developing. Therefore, by fostering an environment of empathy, cooperation, and respect, the incorporation of culturally responsive teaching methods based on the Ubuntu philosophy not only makes it easier to include learners with ASD in a variety of educational settings, enhances academic performance of all learners (Sullivan et al., 2020).

PROMOTING COLLABORATIVE LEARNING

The inclusion of learners with ASD in educational environments is greatly improved by the encouragement of collaborative learning, which is based on the Ubuntu philosophy. Ubuntu, an African ideology that emphasises community accomplishment and interdependence, creates an atmosphere where learners feel appreciated for their contributions and are encouraged to help one another and develop their social skills. Collaborative learning actively involves learners in group activities that foster connection, which can be especially helpful for learners with ASD s, who frequently struggle with social communication (Sullivan et al., 2020). This method promotes cooperation and peer support, which can help learners form sympathetic bonds with one another and lessen isolation for those with ASD (Mackenzie & Smith 2016). Additionally, by creating a community that emphasises understanding and respect for individual differences, the Ubuntu concept enables all students to actively participate in the learning process. Cooperative group work, in which learners of different abilities are intentionally matched to exchange information and skills, is one strategy frequently used in collaborative learning environments. This can improve the educational experience for learners with ASD (Benedict 2020). For learners with ASD whose social integration is frequently a barrier to effective learning, these interactions not only support skill development but also help them feel accepted and at home among their classmates. In order to create a supportive learning environment, the Ubuntu principle emphasises the need to create inclusive communities where all learners flourish via mutual respect, shared knowledge, and group responsibility (Mackenzie & Smith 2016). Thus, encouraging group learning in the spirit of Ubuntu benefits the entire school community in addition to meeting the unique requirements of learners with ASD.

FOSTERING OPEN COMMUNICATION

The integration of students with ASD into inclusive classrooms can be greatly improved by promoting open communication, which is a fundamental tenet of the Ubuntu concept. The inclusive education objectives of appreciating difference and fostering community are strongly aligned with the African ethical philosophy of Ubuntu, which places a strong focus on respect for one another, interconnection, and the strength of the human spirit (Gordon 2020). In inclusive classrooms, open communication fosters a supportive environment where all students—including those with ASD—feel valued and understood. For example, by actively communicating with learners with ASD and their families, teachers can gather important information about their unique needs and preferences and adjust their teaching methods accordingly (Browder et al., 2012) Additionally, encouraging peer connections through an open communication culture is crucial. helps leaners with ASD to improve their social skills. Empathy among peers and increased self-esteem are two benefits of encouraging learners to express their opinions and feelings (Harrower & Dunlap, 2001). Additionally, creating and executing successful Individualised Education

Programs (IEPs) that take into account the particular strengths and difficulties of learners with ASD requires open communication between educators, parents, and support workers. Consequently, using an Ubuntu-inspired communication style in inclusive educational environments not only helps learners with ASD feel like they belong but also gives them the tools they need to succeed academically and socially. According to Mhlongo (2018), this holistic viewpoint emphasises the critical role that open communication plays in fostering inclusive environments that value diversity and advance educational justice.

ENCOURAGING EMPATHY AND UNDERSTANDING

Ubuntu, a philosophy from Southern Africa emphasises empathy and understanding as fundamental values, is based on reciprocal care and communal peace (Nussbaum 2003). These principles are very important in inclusive educational environments, especially when it comes to learners with ASD. Teachers may make the classroom more inclusive for all learners, including those with ASD, by using Ubuntu's emphasis on social connection and group support. By encouraging educators and learners to acknowledge and value the distinct experiences and difficulties that their peers with ASD endure, an empathic approach promotes an inclusive and accepting society. It has been demonstrated that empathy-driven strategies enhance social interactions and educational experiences for students with ASD. For instance, it promotes understanding and reduces stigma when educators and students view the world through the eyes of a student with ASD. This makes room for adaptive teaching strategies that may be tailored to meet a variety of needs (Donald, 2010). By normalising diversity and inclusion, such an atmosphere not only supports the academic growth of students with ASD but also creates an inclusive learning environment that benefits all students. Additionally, Ubuntu's social component creates a network of support that works together to meet the unique requirements of learners with ASD, removing obstacles to their full involvement in the educational process. By working together, educators can make sure that educational policies and practices are both effective in practice and inclusive in theory (Donald, 2010). The social and academic experiences of learners with ASD are improved when teachers and learners live up to Ubuntu's values, creating a more comprehensive learning environment where empathy is not only a goal but a daily reality (Donald, 2010).

ROLE OF FAMILIES AND COMMUNITIES IN SUPPORTING INCLUSION

Within the framework of the Ubuntu principle, the joint efforts of families and communities can greatly improve the complex problem of including learners with ASD in educational settings. This promotes a network of support that actively involves families and community members in creating a welcoming atmosphere for learners with ASD. Ubuntu fosters a sense of connection and belonging, which is crucial for learners with ASD, who frequently feel excluded or alone in traditional educational environments Nkosi (2015). By actively supporting their children's education, speaking up for their needs, and developing close bonds with teachers, families play a critical role in this framework. According to a study by Schwartz et al., (2019), inclusive practices work better when families participate in educational decision-making processes because it gives them a sense of agency and empowerment. This idea is expanded by community support, which fosters welcoming settings that value and celebrate variety. To address the social challenges that students with ASD face frequently encounter, local groups and community people can collaborate with schools to create programs that provide peer mentoring and social skills training (Nkosi, 2015). In addition to improving these learners ' educational experiences, a community-based approach raises peer knowledge and comprehension of ASD. This conformity to the Ubuntu principle emphasises how everyone in the community, even those with special needs, must be nurtured (Schwartz et al., 2019. Additionally, including cultural viewpoints into classroom environments might improve acceptance and assistance for learners with ASD. Nkosi (2015) asserts that Ubuntu-embracing families and communities emphasises interconnectedness, fostering families and communities that embrace diversity, support each other and built resilient inclusive culture which is crucial in reducing the stigma usually connected to impairments.

FUTURE DIRECTIONS FOR RESEARCH

Research and development opportunities abound in the use of the Ubuntu ideology to support the inclusion of learners with ASD in African educational environments. Ubuntu, a Nguni Bantu term meaning "humanity towards others," encapsulates values such as interconnectedness, community, and mutual respect. In the context of education, these principles can foster inclusive environments where learners with ASD are supported and valued. As African nations endeavour to enhance educational results for all learners, including those with disabilities, exploring how Ubuntu can inform inclusive educational practices becomes critical. Future research should focus on identifying culturally relevant strategies that leverage Ubuntu to create supportive learning environments for learners with ASD. This includes investigating community involvement in schools, encouraging collaborative relationships among teachers, parents, and learners, and promoting understanding and acceptance of neurodiversity within the broader community (Shakespeare 2013; Nind 2014).

One key area of future research involves assessing the implementation of Ubuntu-oriented training programs for educators. Such programs could enhance teachers' understanding of ASD and its manifestations, while also equipping them with the necessary skills to foster emotional intelligence and empathy in the classroom (Bakioglu et al., 2021). Research by Kauffman and Landrum (2013) highlights the necessity of training educators to support diverse learners effectively, making it imperative to design professional development initiatives that incorporate Ubuntu values. Furthermore, research should look at how these training programs affect the attitudes of teachers and students. outcomes in terms of engagement, academic achievement, and social integration.

In keeping with the Ubuntu idea of group responsibility, academics should also look into how families and communities can support leaners with ASD. This could involve examining how local communities, including traditional leaders and cultural practitioners, can contribute to creating inclusive educational settings. The community's involvement in the educational process can enhance acceptance and support for learners with ASD, as it reflects the Ubuntu belief in shared humanity and interconnectedness (Omote 2021). Qualitative studies, such as interviews and focus groups with parents, educators, and community leaders, would provide insights into effective practices for bolstering the inclusion of learners with ASD.

It is also essential to investigate the curriculum development in African educational contexts through an Ubuntu lens. Future studies could examine ways to modify courses to reflect Ubuntu values that accommodate and respect the diversity of learners, including those with autism. For example, incorporating stories, legends, and educational materials that promote understanding of ASD within the cultural context could enhance acceptance among learners and community members (Gordon 2015). Additionally, research should assess the effectiveness and relevance of participatory teaching methods rooted in Ubuntu, which may encourage collaboration and social interaction among all learners.

Another crucial direction for research is exploring the policy implications of integrating Ubuntu philosophy into educational practices for learners with ASD. Investigating existing policies regarding disability and education in African countries could reveal gaps and inconsistencies that undermine the principles of inclusion. By advocating for policies that resonate with Ubuntu values, researchers can contribute to creating a more robust framework that ensures rights and availability of high-quality education for all kids, especially those with ASD. Policy-oriented research could also help in understanding the barriers and facilitators that educators face in implementing inclusive practices and how these are influenced by socio-cultural factors.

Lastly, longitudinal studies addressing the long-term impact of utilising Ubuntu philosophy in educational settings on learners with ASD are necessary. Such studies could provide valuable data on educational trajectories, development of social skills and general wellbeing of autistic students in inclusive environments shaped by Ubuntu principles. By evaluating these outcomes, researchers can contribute substantive evidence to the discourse on best practices for inclusion, ultimately guiding educators and policymakers toward more effective approaches.

CONCLUSION

To sum up, adopting the Ubuntu mind-set provides a strong foundation for encouraging the inclusion of learners with ASD in classroom environments. Ubuntu, which highlights our interconnectedness and common humanity which are key components of inclusive education. Educators foster an atmosphere where all learners feel appreciated and understood by acknowledging that every learner, irrespective of their neurodiversity, contributes distinct abilities and viewpoints. Africans tend to perceive ASD from a different angle, emphasising the spiritual, familial, and community aspects of the condition. This cultural background challenges educators to reconsider traditional methods of treating autism and invites teachers to incorporate family involvement, local knowledge, and community resources into instructional tactics. Educators can establish a network of support that accommodates the many requirements of learners with ASD by encouraging cooperation between educators, families, and community members. There are various techniques involved in putting Ubuntu values into practice in the classroom. First and foremost, educators need to foster a feeling of community by establishing welcoming environments where everyone's opinions are valued. Cooperative learning exercises that encourage teamwork and peer interaction might help achieve this. Additionally, educators must to be trained in recognizing and appreciating the variety of ways that learners with autism interact with the outside world and communicate. In order to do this, differentiated instruction that is adapted to the particular strengths and difficulties of each learner is crucial. Furthermore, it is critical to help all learners develop empathy and understanding. Building a caring community and eradicating stigma can be achieved through initiatives that raise awareness about autism and its traits. In the end, educators empower learners with autism as well as their peers by incorporating Ubuntu's basic principles of respect, solidarity, and love into their teaching methods. This guarantees that every learner has the chance to flourish in a nurturing and inclusive learning environment.

RECOMMENDATIONS

Adopting the Ubuntu attitude can greatly improve the integration of learners with ASD in the quickly changing field of inclusive education. This chapter emphasised how important it is for institutions and teachers to create inclusive settings where all children are respected and encouraged. Educators are encouraged to employ culturally responsive teaching techniques that understand the specific strengths and challenges of learners with autism, offering individualised learning experiences that enhance engagement and belonging. Institutions ought to fund professional development initiatives. that equip teachers with the knowledge and abilities necessary to successfully implement Ubuntu-based practices Furthermore, legislators are essential in creating frameworks that give inclusion first priority and allot funds for specialised training and support services. Policymakers can contribute to the development of an inclusive and diverse educational environment by supporting laws that uphold the tenets of Ubuntu, which place a strong focus on community support and interconnection. Communities, too, have a significant part to play in enriching the lives of learners with ASD. Stigmas will be broken down and supporting networks will be established with the aid of initiatives that promote awareness, acceptance, and cooperation among community members. Encouraging family involvement in schools can further develop these ties by ensuring that the needs and voices of students with ASD are taken into account. Finally, to contribute to the growing body of research that promotes inclusive behaviours, scholars must keep investigating practical approaches to putting Ubuntu into practice in educational contexts. They can offer the proof required to support further advancements in inclusive education by examining the effects of Ubuntu-informed approaches on student outcomes. In conclusion, educators can create an educational environment that genuinely embraces the spirit of Ubuntu by combining the efforts of educators, legislators, communities, and researchers, guaranteeing that all learners, especially those with autism, succeed.

REFERENCES

Agyeman, A. A. (2015). *The Afrocentric classroom: Culturally responsive principles for effective teaching*. Palgrave Macmillan.

Ainscow, M., Slee, R., & Best, M. (2019). Editorial: The Salamanca Statement: 25 years on. *International Journal of Inclusive Education*, *23*(7-8), 671–676.

Asante, M. K. (2016). Afrocentricity: The theory of social change.https://science .jrank.org/pages/8216/Afrocentricity-Afrocentricity-Its-Critics.html. https://doi.org/ DOI: 10.1002/9781118766804.wbiect128

Avramidis, E., & Norwich, B. (2002). Teachers' attitudes towards integration / inclusion: A review of the literature. *European Journal of Special Needs Education*, *17*(2), 129–147. DOI: 10.1080/08856250210129056

Bakare, M. O., & Munir, K. M. (2011). Autism spectrum disorders (ASD) in Africa: A perspective. *The African Journal of Psychiatry*, *14*(3), 208–210. DOI: 10.4314/ ajpsy.v14i3.3

Bakioglu, A., Arikan, A., & Tezer, E. (2021). Teacher attitudes toward inclusive education: A systematic review of the literature. *Journal of Education and Training Studies*, *9*(7), 12–23.

Brandt, S., Kidron, A., & Raviv, A. (2018). The effects of inclusive education on attitudes: A meta-analysis. *European Journal of Special Needs Education*, *33*(3), 358–373. DOI: 10.17977/um005v1i12017p025

Browder, D. M., Jimenez, B. A., & Trela, K. (2012). Grade-aligned math instruction for secondary students with moderate intellectual disability. *Education and Training in Autism and Developmental Disabilities*, *47*, 373–388.

Brown, S. (2014). *Coping, Resolution and Advocacy in Parents of Children with Autism*. Purchase College, State University of New York.

Cage, E., & Troxell-Whitman, Z. (2019). Understanding the reasons, contexts and costs of camoufaging for autistic adults. *Journal of Autism and Developmental Disorders*, *49*(5), 1899–1911. DOI: 10.1007/s10803-018-03878-x

Carrington, S., Deppeler, J., & Moss, J. (2010). Cultivating Teachers' Beliefs, Knowledge and Skills for Leading Change in Schools. *The Australian Journal of Teacher Education*, *35*(1). Advance online publication. DOI: 10.14221/ajte.2010v35n1.1

Cassidy, S. A., Gould, K., Townsend, E., Pelton, M., Robertson, A. E., & Rodgers, J. (2020). Is Camouflaging Autistic Traits Associated with Suicidal Thoughts and Behaviours? *Expanding the Interpersonal Psychological Theory of Suicide in an Undergraduate Student SampleJ Autism Dev Disord, 50*(10), 3638–3648. DOI: 10.1007/s10803-019-04323-3

Chapman, R. (2020). Neurodiversity, wellbeing, disability. In Rosquvist, H., Chown, N., Stenning, A. (Eds.), *Neurodiversity studies: A new critical paradigm (pp. 57–72).* New York, NY: Routledge Department of Education (DoE). (2016). *Policy on Inclusive Education.* Pretoria: Government Printer.

Donald, A. (2010). *Introduction to Research in Education.* Wadsworth Cengage Learning.

Ébalé, S., Benson, A., & Mulemi, T. (2023). The Ubuntu and African identity in the 21st century. *The International Journal of Humanities & Social Studies, 11*(7), 47–62. DOI: 10.24940/ theijhss/2023/v11/i7/HS2307-006

Elias, M. J., Parker, R., & Weissberg, R. P. (2018). *Social and emotional learning: A framework for educating children.* Routledge.

Gebremikael, L., Sicchia, S., Demi, S., & Rhoden, J. (2022). Afrocentric approaches to disrupting anti-Black racism in health care and promoting Black health in Canada. *Canadian Medical Association Journal, 194*(42), 89–105. DOI: 10.1503/cmaj.220456

Gordon, C. (2018). Ubuntu: The impact of African philosophy on education. *Journal of Philosophy of Education, 52*(4), 636–653.

Gordon, G. (2015). Ubuntu pedagogy: Cultural responsibility and community involvement. *Education as Change, 19*(1), 102–115.

Happé, F., & Frith, U. (2020). Annual Research Review: Looking back to look forward – changes in the concept of autism and implications for future research. *Journal of Child Psychology and Psychiatry, and Allied Disciplines, 61*(3), 218–232. DOI: 10.1111/jcpp.13176

Harrower, J. K., & Dunlap, G. (2001). Including children with autism in general education classrooms: A review of effective strategies. *Behavior Modification, 25*(5), 762–784.

Hernández-Torrano, D., Somerton, M., & Helmer, J. (2020). Mapping research on inclusive education since Salamanca Statement: A bibliometric review of the literature over 25 years. *International Journal of Inclusive Education, 16*(9), 1–20. DOI: 10.1080/13603116.2 020.1747555

Heto, P. P., & Mino, T. (2023). (Dis)ontinuity of African indigenous knowledge. AlterNative. *An International Journal of Indigenous Peoples*, *19*(1), 71–79. DOI: 10.1177/ 11771801221138304

Hilt, L. T. (2017). Education without a shared language: Dynamics of inclusion and exclusion in Norwegian introductory classes for newly arrived minority language students. *International Journal of Inclusive Education*, *21*(6), 585–601. DOI: 10.1080/13603116.2016.122 3179

Hull L, Mandy W, Lai M, Baron-Cohen S, Allison C, Smith P, & Petrides K V (2019). Development and Validation of the Camouflaging Autistic Traits Questionnaire (CAT-Q)J Autism Dev Disordr;49(3):819-833.doi: DOI: 10.1007/s10803-018-3792-6

Johnson, D. W., & Johnson, R. T. (2019). An educational psychology success story: Social interdependence theory and cooperative learning. *Educational Researcher*, *38*(5), 365–379. DOI: 10.3102/0013189X09339057

Kapp, S. K., Gillespie-Lynch, K., Brooks, P. J., & Paradiz, M.. (2013). Growing up with autism: The developmental, conceptual, and personal narrative of neurodiversity. *Journal of Developmental Psychology.*, *49*(5), 540–550.

Kauffman, J. M., & Landrum, T. J. (2013). *Characteristics of emotional and behavioral disorders of children and youth.* Pearson.

Kivunja, C., & Kuyini, A. B. (2017). Understanding and Applying Research Paradigms in Educational Contexts. *International Journal of Higher Education*, *6*, 26–41. DOI: 10.5430/ijhe.v6n5p26

Lindsey, R. B., Pond, A. J., & Lindsey, D. B. (2018). *Culturally Proficient Leadership: The Personal Journey Begins Within.* Corwin Press.

Livingston, L. A., Shah, P., & Happé, F. (2019). Compensatory strategies below the behavioural surface in Autism: A qualitative study. *The Lancet. Psychiatry*, *6*(9), 766–777. DOI: 10.1016/ S2215-0366(19)30224-X

Mackenzie, S., & Smith, L. (2016). Building inclusive communities for children with Autism Spectrum Disorders: An exploration of collaborative learning practices. *Journal of Autism Spectrum Disorders and Developmental Disorders*, *46*(3), 635–650.

Mandy, W. (2019). Social camouflaging in Autism: Is it time to lose the mask? *Autism*, *23*(8), 1879–1881. DOI: 10.1177/1362361319878559

McFall, M. T. (2016). Divine Hiddenness and Spiritual Autism. *Heythrop Journal. Heythrop Journal*, *63*(4), n/a–n/a. DOI: 10.1111/heyj.12324

Mhlongo M (2018), A framework for the integration of indigenous knowledge into libraries in South Africa IFLA Journal 47(3)

Milner, H. R. (2017). Culturally Relevant Pedagogy in a Diverse Classroom. *Theory into Practice*, *56*(3), 243–250.

Mpofu, J. (2020). Partnerships for Autism in Zimbabwean Inclusive Education System. In Sefa Dei, G. J., Phasha, N., & Mahlo, D. (Eds.), *Autism: Perspectives from Africa* (Vol. I, pp. 168–181). University of South Africa.

Mpofu, J. (2023) Understanding Autism: An African Perspective. In HR Maapola-Thobejane & M O Maguvhe (Eds) Handbook on Shifting Paradigms of Disabilities in the Schooling System. IGI Global book series Advances in Educational Technologies and Instructional Design (AETID) (ISSN: 2326-8905; eISSN: 2326-8913

Mpofu, J., & Molosiwa, S. (2017). Disability and inclusive education in Zimbabwe. In Sefa Dei, G. J., Phasha, N., & Mahlo, D. (Eds.), *Inclusive education in African contexts: Anti-colonial educational perspective for transformative change* (pp. 49–65). Sense Publishers.

Mpofu, J. (2023). An afro-centric approach to inclusive education. In Maguvhe, M. O., & Masuku, M. M. (Eds.), *Using African epistemologies in shaping inclusive education knowledge*. Palgrave Macmillan., DOI: 10.1007/978-3-031-31115-4_5

Mupedziswa, R., Rankopo, M., & Mwansa, L. (2019). Ubuntu as a Pan-African philosophical framework for social work in Africa. In Twikirize, J. M., & Spitzer, H. (Eds.), *Social work practice in Africa: Indigenous and innovative approaches* (pp. 21–38). Fountain Publishers., DOI: 10.2307/j.ctv2tp73vt

Muthukrishna, N., & Ramsuran, A. (2008). Editorial: HIV/AIDS, education, and childhood in the African context. *Journal of Psychology in Africa*, *18*(3), 367–370.

National Institute of Mental Health. (2024) Mental Illness—National Institute of Mental Health. https://www.nimh.nih.gov/health/statistics/mental-illness

Nind, M. (2014). Conducting qualitative research with people with learning, communication, and other disabilities: Methodologies, ethics, and the role of the researcher. *Disability & Society*, *29*(3), 431–445.

Nkosi, T. (2015). *Expanding the Potential of Ubuntu in South Africa's Schools. Educational Philosophy and Theory*. Longman.

Ntuli, L. T. (2018). *Managing curriculum implementation at selected primary schools in the Sekhukhune district, Limpopo province* (Doctoral dissertation, Doctoral thesis. University of South Africa, Pretoria.

Omote, T. (2021). Ubuntu and Community Resilience: Reflections on collective responsibility in education. *Journal of African Cultural Studies, 33*(1), 99–113.

Qvortrup, A., & Qvortrup, L. (2018). Inclusion: Dimensions of inclusion in education. *International Journal of Inclusive Education, 22*(7), 803–817. DOI: 10.1080/13603116.2017.1412506

Ramasela S F (2022). An Afrocentric critique of the pitfalls of the African union in promoting unity, peace, and solidarity of African states Journal of African Union Studies Vol. 11, No. 2, 2022, pp. 19–33

Riche, N. (2014). *Research Study on Children with Disabilities Living in Uganda Situational Analysis on the Rights of Children with Disabilities in Uganda* UNICEF Uganda. Available at:http://www.anppcanug.org/wp-content/uploads/Resource _Center/Research_Reports/research_report_11.pdf

Robertson, S. M. (2010). Neurodiversity, Quality of Life, and Autistic Adults: Shifting Research and Professional Focuses onto Real-Life Challenges. *Disability Studies Quarterly, 30*(10).

Schwartz, I. S.. (2019). *Partnerships for Inclusion: The Role of Family in the Education of with Autism. International Journal of Inclusive Education Shakespeare, T. (2013). Disability rights and wrongs revisited.* Routledge.

Silberman, S. (2015). *Neurotribes: The Legacy of Autism and the Future of Neurodiversity.* Avery., DOI: 10.1353/anq.2015.0057

Sullivan, A. M., McCarthy, J., & Pierce, L. (2020). Building Inclusive Learning Communities: A Framework for Culturally Responsive Teaching. *International Journal of Inclusive Education, 24*(10), 1035–1051.

Szumski, G., Smogorzewska, J., & Karwowski, M. (2017). Academic achievement of students without special educational needs in inclusive classrooms: A meta-analysis. *Educational Research Review, 21*, 33–54. DOI: 10.1016/j.edurev.2017.02.004

Szumski, G., Smogorzewska, J., & Karwowski, M. (2017). Academic Achievement of Students without Special Educational Needs in Inclusive Classrooms: A Meta-Analysis. *Educational Research Review, 21*, 33–54. DOI: 10.1016/j.edurev.2017.02.004

Ugwu, C.J., Ekere J.N., & Ohoh. C. (2013). Research paradigms and methodological choices in the research process. Journal of applied Information Science and Technology 14 (2)2021

UNESCO. (2015). *Rethinking Education: Towards a global common good?* Corporate author. UNESCO; DOI. https://doi.org/;DOI: 10.54675/MDZL5552ISBN. 978-92-3-100088-1

Van Mieghem, A., Verschueren, K., Petry, K., & Struyf, E. (2020). An analysis of research on inclusive education: A systematic search and meta review. *International Journal of Inclusive Education, 24*(6), 675–689. DOI: 10.1080/13603116.2018.1482012

Vanderstraeten, R. (2020). How does education function? *European Educational Research Journal, 14*(7), 49–56. DOI: 10.1177/1474904120948979

Yssel, N., Pak, N., & Beilke, J. (2016). A door must be opened: Perceptions of students with disabilities in higher education. *International Journal of Disability Development and Education, 63*(3), 384–394. DOI: 10.1080/1034912X.2015.1123232

Zvomuya, W. (2020). Ubuntuism as an international turning point for social work profession: New lenses from the African pot of knowledge. *African Journal of Social Work, 10*(1), 24–29. https://www.ajol.info/index.php/ajsw/article/view/194098

Chapter 6
Conceptions About Hearing Impairment: A Focus on Classroom Approaches to Inclusive Education

Gaone Molapisi
University of South Africa, South Africa

ABSTRACT

This chapter investigated the society's conceptions of hearing impairment and the strategies for including learners with hearing impairment is schools. People with hearing impairment often struggle to integrate with the public. The study examines how hearing impairment is viewed and labelled, and the impact of using Afrocentric approaches on teaching and learning in schools. Open-ended interviews with members of the community and the teachers for these learners were used to gain insights into conceptions of hearing impairment. Of interest was how the conceptions about hearing impairment were transferred to schools that constituted these learners. Data was analysed by using content analysis. The findings of the study indicate that individuals with hearing impairment are generally viewed as requiring assistance to access various facilities, including access to education. They are often labelled as 'those ones' and are frequently marginalised. The study concluded that the community and the teachers showed appreciation of the importance of embracing individuals with hearing impairment.

BACKGROUND

The most common concept of hearing impairment focuses on the audiological. Hearing is based on measured decibels that represent the intensity an individual

DOI: 10.4018/979-8-3373-7163-4.ch006

requires to hear sounds (Musselman 2000) and, hearing impairment is described in functional terms. For example, hard of hearing includes mild hearing impairment and deafness. Even though people who are hard of hearing can function audiologically, if provided with suitable amplification and an acoustic environment; when those who are deaf have no hearing, conceptually, they tend to be grouped together.

Hearing loss is defined in terms of degrees of loss and measured in decibels (Tucci et al, 2010), whilst hearing impairment is plotted on a graph called an audiogram and is recorded as a function of frequency or pitch and decibels or intensity. An audiogram is a chart which registers the hearing reaction of each ear from 125 Hz (hertz) to 8000 Hz, which is the range most essential for speech perception. A hearing impairment of less than 25 dB (decibels), averaged through the frequencies of 500, 1000, 2000 and 4000 Hz (the range of frequencies involved in the perception of speech), is viewed as being within the standard range of hearing. An average hearing impairment of 25 dB or more in both ears is however interpreted as a noteworthy hearing impairment, and an average hearing impairment of more than 70 dB in both ears can be regarded as deafness (Roberson, 2001).

Hearing impairment can thus have a profound bearing on those affected and poses a major challenge to their daily lives, including academic performance, specifically language development (WHO, 2017). It also plays a direct role in literacy difficulties, for example, reading difficulties.

Conceptually, hearing impairment and deafness tend to be grouped together under the hard of hearing group (Luckner, & Handley, 2008). But, just like deafness, hearing impairment can have a profound bearing on those affected, specifically on their language development (World Health Organisation [WHO], 2017). It contributes directly to literacy difficulties, for example, reading difficulties and poses a major challenge to daily lives, including academic performance.

Generally, individuals with hearing impairment potentially face challenges thriving in the society they are part of, including in schools. Some of the challenges may include inability to communicate with other members of the society due to their lack of competence in communicating using sign language. Scheetz (1993) argues that the breakdown of communication for individuals with hearing impairment often leads to the interruption of social interactions. In essence, social interaction is about one's ability to interact with others, form friendships and be accepted by peers (Stinson & Antia 1999). Social interaction of individuals with hearing impairment both in communities and schools are potentially a source of concern for teachers and members of communities they live in. Often, as Scheetz (1993) indicate, these individuals are not fully integrated and socialised in their communities. As a result, they experience feelings of loneliness because they cannot easily participate in social activities due to difficulties in communicating with peers and members of their communities. In this regard, they may begin to view themselves as helpless members of the community and avoid participating is social activities. Some researchers, for example, Tvingstedt (1993) point out that individuals with hearing impairment report feelings of loneliness and absence of close relationships. According to Caissie and Wilson (1995), these individuals may experience challenges with specific aspects of interaction such as repairing communication breakdown which often result in the exclusion. As such, programs must be designed and implemented in which the communities are conscientised about the importance of integrating individuals with hearing impairment. This could be achieved by organising workshops for the communities in which parents, experts, policy makers, local leaders and members of the communities share knowledge about these individuals. These workshops and community engagements must include the individuals with hearing impairment. Their input, opinions, concerns and how they can be integrated in societies needs to be valued.

It is worth noting that there is limited literature on how individuals with hearing impairment could be successfully included in their communities based on Afrocentric approaches. Rather, available studies focus on exclusionary practices by the communities towards these individuals. For example, Kusters (2012) points out that in rural communities in Africa, families and the entire society tend to encourage marginalisation of these individuals through negligence. However, there is adequate literature on what approaches could be employed by teachers to include learners with hearing impairment in classroom settings.

INCLUSIVE EDUCATION AS A CONCEPT

There are different conceptions of inclusive education; For example, Collins, (2003) and Fakolade et al., (2009) describe it as education that includes learners with specific needs in mainstream classrooms. For Sayed et al., (2003); Osberg & Biesta, (2010); Meo, (2008); it is a resource for enhancing academic achievement by providing equal opportunities to learn. Writing in the context of South Africa, Sayed et al. (2003) argue that a curriculum based on such education would be about equity and access. Its (curriculum) aim would be to benefit learners regardless of their age, background, or ability by problematising the status quo and promoting access and participation practices in addressing the diverse needs within classrooms. In Sayed et al.'s (2003) view, schools that are inclusive in the way described here, are not only more cost-efficient but also socially beneficial and educationally effective than segregated schools. They promote social justice (see also Muthukrishna, 2008).

According to Bremer et al. (2002), inclusive education provides multiple ways of facilitating access to knowledge and scaffold learning through differentiated tasks/ instructions. It encourages learners to play an active role in their learning. In Hytten and Bettez 's (2011) view, inclusive education is inherently part of a democratic way of life that should include tools for personal reflection, building relationships for effective communication and collaboration and exchanging ideas in pursuance of a socially just education. However, King-Thorius and Waitoller (2017) argue that the attainment of a goal such as inclusion is complex and intricate. Inclusion is deeply linked to systems of marginalisation that set apart learners by several classifications, (for example, learners with disabilities, learners with special needs, learners requiring extra support and learners with learning difficulties). It therefore calls for their integration into mainstream education.

Rodriguez and Garro-Gil (2014) have described integration as adaptation of the learning environment. For example, for a wheelchair user, integration occurs when ramps are erected to facilitate access into the classrooms. However, Graham and Slee (2008) argue that rather than integrating the learners, it is crucial to include them. Whilst integration occurs when the environment is modified only when learners with disabilities enter the school, in contrast, inclusion means that the environment is made ready and prepared to accommodate learners with disabilities, for example, a classroom with sound amplifiers for learners with hearing impairment. Therefore, there are complexities and challenges of inclusion in many education systems, for example, the California Department of Education (1999) discovered that uncoordinated support services in schools interfere with curriculum adaptation and obstruct learner construction of knowledge and meaning.

THE INCLUSION OF LEARNERS WITH HEARING IMPAIRMENT

Mergler et al. (2016) argue that inclusive education is buttressed by a philosophy of acceptance in which all individuals are valued and treated with equality and respect. It seeks to oppose learner categorisations and strives to look for ways of supporting learning and assisting all learners, including those with hearing impairment. Studies, for example, Marshark and Hauser (2013) also in the United States, have indicated that using multimedia promotes effective learning for learners with a hearing impairment. Assistive gadgets such as hearing aids are beneficial to some learners. Visual materials and pictures, DVDs and videos support learners to effectively comprehend what they are learning (Storbeck, 2009). For this reason, Marshark and Hauser (2013) argue that support needs to be provided to the learner rather than allowing the child to seek support. For inclusive education to be successfully put into effect, it must be accommodating and accessible to diverse learners, including learners with a hearing impairment (Fernandes & Myers, 2010). In addition, the stakeholders need to prepare the school environment by availing resources, including technology that can be used to support the learners. Furthermore, the school teaching staff must be offered training programs that will enhance their teaching skills. Workshops could also be organised to conscientise the students and the school general staff on how to interact with learners with hearing impairment in the school environment. Also, teacher-parent collaboration could be a significant step towards the successful inclusion of learners with hearing impairment. Networking among teachers plays an important role. Sharing ideas and strategies that they employ in the classroom to teach these learners, for example, the importance of learning through self-directed tasks (often referred to as discovery learning) proved effective (Teaching Excellence in Adult Literacy, 2010). This way of learning also provided opportunities for learners to discuss content amongst themselves and assist each other to discover and understand new information. When learners engage in classroom discussions, they are afforded opportunities to direct their learning and help each other. For example, when they read a book and discuss it, they discover new words and explain the meaning of the words to each other. The approach empowers learners to direct their learning while the teacher acts as a facilitator.

The South African education policy documents and legislation such as the White Paper on Education and Training (DoE, 1995) and the White Paper on an Integrated National Disability Strategy (DoE, 1997) highlight education as an important attribute of the human rights cherished in the Constitution. These rights dictate that all learners, including those with hearing impairment, must have equal educational opportunities. Therefore, the educational system requires schools to adopt the rights in order to accommodate learner diversity (Waghid & Engelbrecht, 2002). Against this backdrop, the White paper 6 of 2001 (DoE 2001b) became the blueprint of inclusive education and a foundation for legislative reform that respects differences amongst learners whether due to social background or disability. The legislation offers a framework on which educational opportunities for learners who experience barriers to learning are realised. For example, the recommendations of the National Commission on Special Needs in Education and Training/National Committee on Education Support Services NCSNET/NCESS Report (DoE, 1997) were fundamentally anchored on the language of human rights rather than focusing on individualising disability. However, as a result of lack of resources and adequately trained teachers, the schools still face challenges to fully include learners with disabilities in their classrooms.

In South Africa, studies that examined the inclusion of learners with hearing impairment included a study by Du Plessis (2006). In this study, learners in inclusive settings were asked to repeat reading instructions in their own words to determine whether they were able to follow what was discussed. Given their disability to hear certain sounds clearly, the study paid special attention to the recognition of words and their phonological representations. The assumption was that when learners were able to repeat what was said, that would indicate familiarity or recognition of the content discussed and how it had been understood. The findings indicated that the learners benefitted from focusing on the speaker and the repeated questions, answers. In addition, Du Plessis (2006) argues that to facilitate comprehension for the learners with a hearing impairment in inclusive settings, it is important for the teacher to face the learners for them to speech read.

This study aimed to answer the following questions:

How are individuals with hearing impairment viewed by the community?

What strategies do teachers employ to include learners with hearing impairment in mainstream classrooms?

How do learners respond to these strategies?

RESEARCH DESIGN AND METHODOLOGY

The study adopted a case study design which aimed at understanding issues within the context where an activity is taking place (Zainal, 2017). First, the design was used to investigate how the communities viewed individuals with hearing impairment. For example, how they are afforded opportunities to participate in community activities. Second, the objective was to use the design to establish what strategies teachers adopted to include learners with hearing impairment in the mainstream classrooms and how the learners responded to the strategies.

The study was situated within a qualitative interpretivist paradigm. There are several characteristics to interpretive qualitative research. Notably, the first characteristic is that researchers aim to understand the meaning participants construct about their world and experiences. Sandelowski (2000) states that the approach implies only a commitment to studying a phenomenon in its natural state. Ragin et al. (2003) describe such a research approach as educational research in which the researcher relies on the views of the participants, asks broad questions, collects data largely consisting of words, and analyses these words to form themes. It is exploratory and involves listening to participants and subjecting data to inductive analysis. Its exploratory nature accorded me opportunities to investigate the strategies adopted to include learners with hearing impairment and how learners responded to such strategies.

SAMPLING IN THE COMMUNITY

Members (target population) of the community in which individuals with hearing impairment lived were randomly selected to gain insights into how they viewed these individuals. Specifically, community members who resided with them were selected as information-rich participants and because of their proximity to them. Individuals with a hearing impairment rented rooms as learners of a nearby high school that admitted them. Simple random sampling was adopted for this study as it helps to reduce the bias involved in the sample as is considered a fair method of sampling and each member an equal chance of being selected (Sharma 2017). For this study, the simple random sampling technique was used as a fair way of selecting a sample from an identified population that was appropriate to provide reliable data. 7 adult members of the households that were in the vicinity of the school and where these individuals with hearing impairment resided were interviewed.

THE SCHOOL

The school was situated one of the largest township in Gauteng province and constituted of a significant number of learners with hearing impairment. Even though the school provided boarding facilities for grade 12 learners, others lived amongst the community in which the schools was located. The school was a suitable context for recording strategies that teachers employed to fully include learners with hearing impairment in their classrooms (Yin 1989). It was an appropriate research site because among others, it had teachers with more than 2 years' experience of teaching learners with hearing impairment. There were 103 learners with a hearing impairment who were taught along their hearing peers.

SAMPLING THE CLASSES

In this study, a sample was purposefully selected from mainstream classroom which had learners with a hearing impairment. Teachers for these learners and other officials, for example, the Head of Department (HOD) and deputy principal, as information-rich cases, were invited to participate in the study to solicit substantial information regarding teaching and inclusion of learners with hearing impairment in mainstream classroom (see Coyne, 1997). The teachers were central to the purpose of this study because they could provide relevant information regarding the strategies adopted for fully including these learners in classroom activities.

Specifically, 13 14-year-old grade 8 learners were purposefully selected. Compared to other classes, grade 8 had a higher number of learners with varying degrees of hearing loss. Therefore, it was a suitable class for the me to gain insights on how the teacher included these learners in her pedagogical practices. The hope was that useful data on the learners' experience (Bernard, 2002) in mainstream classrooms would be collected. A subset of classes was chosen from all classes that formed a larger set to provide the information (Marshall, 1996). Teachers with at least two years' experience teaching learners with hearing impairment who taught these classes English FAL participated in the study. Their constant contact with these learners and the experience they would have gained over the years made them appropriate informants who were knowledgeable and reliable (Tongco, 2007) to expose the culture of teaching in the school in which the research was conducted.

DATA COLLECTION INSTRUMENTS

Interviews

The objective was to examine and gain insights into how individuals with hearing impairment are viewed by the community they lived in. Furthermore, the aim was to investigate how teachers facilitated inclusive practices in their pedagogy for learners with hearing impairment. Informal conversations/interviews were used to collect data. The interviews allowed for creativity and flexibility to ensure that the respondents' stories are adequately covered (Flick, 2002). Open-ended questions were used to solicit data on a wider range of the respondents' experience living with individuals with hearing impairment. In addition, the interviews were used to gain insights on the views of the teachers regarding how the learners are included in their classrooms. A maximum of 30 minutes was set aside for the individual conversations/interviews on days and times determined by informants.

Observations

To determine similarities and differences with what the teachers said, classroom observations were also employed. The observations can be carried out on many aspects such as learning and teaching activities and how learning materials are used for inclusive practices (Potter, 1996). Therefore, it was crucial to conduct classroom observations to help the researchers understand the importance of suspending judgement so that they can see behaviour in the actions of participants. In the classroom, observations provided access to teaching and learning processes and allowed me to record and analyse the kind of classroom culture observed (Frank, 1999). This study adopted direct observation of the strategies employed by teachers to include learners with hearing impairment in their teaching practice. The observations provided opportunities to examine a phenomenon in its natural setting and assess it. A schedule focusing on the strategies used by the teachers such as gestures and other cues utilised to help learners participate in activities was used when observing classroom actions. I made observational notes on the classroom as context and experiences observed in the classroom setting.

Data Management And Analysis

Data management and analysis process involved adopting a descriptive and interpretive mode of managing analysing and presenting data. This comprised data presentation using extracts from interviews and observation notes. This implied that responses from the interviews and observational notes were categorised into codes, by assigning a word or phrase to determine patterns, similarities and differences according to the themes emerging from the research questions (Nieuwenhuis, 2010). Coding is concerned with identifying similarities and differences that arise through the respondents' accounts and actions and interpreted by the researcher (Bryman and Burgess 2002). Guided by Tesch's (1990) assertion that a fundamental task of data analysis is identification of patterns, differences and similarities, the objective was to break down the data, examine it and making comparisons between emerging themes. It was critical that I deeply read the participants' responses to gain more insights into how members of the community and teachers expressed how individuals with hearing impairment are viewed by the community and how they are included in mainstream classroom.

Ethical Considerations

I followed the set procedures of obtaining ethical clearance from the university of Johannesburg where I completed my Doctoral degree. Permission was also sought from Gauteng Department of Education and the district office. Permission was granted, and consent was sought from the participants for the study. I ensured that ethical conflicts that could emerge in terms of how I gained access to the participants were avoided by asking for consent. The objectives of the study were explained, and assurance was given to the participants that they could withdraw at any time of their choice. The respondents were made aware of ethical issues that may arise out of their interaction with the researcher (Ramos 1989). I ensured that trust between me and the participants was prioritised by providing them with opportunities to raise their concerns regarding participation.

THE FINDINGS

Generally, the findings indicate that members of the community in which individuals with hearing impairment live have accepted them as part of their community.

However, they raised concerns as regards communication with them. They highlighted lack of proficiency in sign language as a stumbling block to communicate with them. Inclusion of these individuals in schools as observed during the lessons presents some challenges although the teachers are making efforts to create inclusive environment in their classrooms. First, the views of the community members will be presented. Secondly, data on the strategies employed by the teachers to include learners with hearing impairment will be presented.

Views from Community Members

From the views expressed by community members that were interviewed, it is fair to argue that individuals with hearing impairment remain isolated, specifically as result of lack of communication between them and other members of the community. The main reason presented was lack of competence in sign language from members of the community.

Member A explained:

I am finding it difficult to communicate with this individual. Sometimes I ignore him because he cannot hear. He is always in his room and our children refer to him as **semumu**, *or* **susu** *in our language.*

Member B remarked:

We are trying to make him feel at home, we invited her to join us for meals, but she just sits there and eat quietly, when she tries to say something using sign language, we do not understand. I wish I could learn sign language for me to communicate with her, but I do not have time.

When asked to explain how other members of the family treat her, member B explained:

They sometimes think that she is not normal, they ridicule her, call her **susu** *which is derogatory. She stays away from them and prefers to be in her room almost all the time.*

Essentially, the above responses confirm the position that these individuals are indeed isolated, and the community faces challenges to include them. It could be fair to conclude that they are isolated mainly as a result of the community being unable to communicate with them. This is consistent with the argument presented by Caissie and Wilson (1995) that individuals with hearing impairment are often marginalised because their unique communication needs to frequently highlight their 'otherness' from hearing people. Many of these individuals rely on sign language which is often unfamiliar to hearing people. As such communities that they reside in face significant challenges to effectively include them in community activities.

Asked how they make effort to create conducive environment to include individuals with hearing impairment, member D gave the following remarks:

We rely on him to read our lips when we speak, but this is difficult and often results in wrong understanding of what we say. In most cases, we expect them to listen when we speak, something that they cannot do. It is very difficult for all of us.

Member E responded to the same question as follows:

I try to persuade my family members to learn basic sign language so that we can communicate with him. During family gatherings, I encourage him to join us so that he does not feel isolated. However, communication barriers always exist and often he will just sit and watch us speak to each other.

Member F remarked:

I have encouraged the one I live with to form a group with his friends with hearing impairment and play community sports with other children of the community and teach them sign language. Often, our children show little interest reason being that they do not understand each other.

Member G explained:

I have heard that they lip read and I ensure that I always face him when I speak for him to lip read. My wish is for him to be part of us, but this issue of communication is a big problem.

The respondents' views support the findings in Rhoades, Price and Perigoe (2004) that people in different communities value the integration of individuals with hearing impairment in different ways. Although the communities face challenges in fully integrating these individuals, recognising their value helps the community to respect them and adapt to their unique needs. Thus, encouraging them to actively participate in community activities and treating them with respect could be seen as promoting inclusivity. It could therefore be concluded that despite the efforts by members of the community to include individuals with hearing impairment, more needs to be done by different stakeholders, for example the government and local authorities. The stakeholders could assist the community in activities aimed at including these individuals, for example, setting up of social clubs/organisations with the aim of conscientizing the community about the needs, in particular, their language needs (Rhoades, Price and Perigoe 2004). As Luckner and Cooke (2010) argue, sign language is a primary mode of communication used by individuals with hearing impairment and is a language on its own and has no relationship with the spoken language of the community.

Classroom Observations

Bell (2013) argues that observation plays a crucial role in revealing how the teachers promoted inclusive practices through their actions towards diverse learners in their classroom, including those with hearing impairment. It was important that the teaching of EFAL to learners with a hearing impairment be conducted without undermining their condition (Luckner & Cooke, 2010). The teachers were expected to recognise and respect the diverse language abilities in their lessons, use equalising forms of communication and learner-centred teaching methods. In this study, classroom observations provided access to the teaching and learning context and processes and allowed me to record and make sense of the classroom culture that was witnessed (Frank, 1999). They (observations) gave me opportunities to examine and assess the inclusive teaching practices in natural setting. Equalising forms of communication and listening to one another with respect were paramount to see if the teachers respected learners and whether the concept of inclusive education was consciously embraced. Notes made during the observations and other classroom experiences served as data.

For four weeks, I chose to be a non-participant observer of lessons delivered. This type of observation was crucial as it allowed me to be engrossed in classroom activities during the lessons, paying special attention to the planned activities and learning materials used to create a particular classroom environment and interactions (Potter, 1996). A single classroom was used interchangeably by the two teachers. The classroom was bright and had a lot of natural light coming through large windows. It was typically organised into four rows of desks with aisles that provided adequate space for the teacher to move around the 26 learners, including 13 learners with a hearing impairment - six boys and seven girls - that were the focus of the study. The desks were rearranged into a u-shaped seating arrangement that allowed the teacher to move easily in the middle when interacting with the learners.

Employing direct observation of the teaching and learning process in its natural setting (Grove & Fisk, 1992) and a single subject research approach - which according to Horner et al. (2005) is experimental rather than descriptive. I was able to pay attention and note each teacher's strategies and interventions aimed at including learners with hearing impairment. I observed specifically how she dealt with the individual needs of learners. A detailed journal was used to record a range of activities that were observed, for example, how learners with hearing impairment were included in classroom activities. Classroom actions and activities were recorded in a detailed, continuous, and sequential way and important patterns, phrases, words and actions as they occurred during lessons were captured.

The section presents and analyses data on lessons that were taught in mainstream classes that included learners with hearing impairment. Expectation is that the teachers need to employ inclusive forms of pedagogy that ensure that all learners are taught effectively. Thus, the teachers are required to design lessons that provided all the learners with activities that would motivate them to participate in classroom activities.

One of the lessons focused on reading a story book with pictures to cater for all learners including those with hearing impairment. These learners seemingly have strong visual ability to compensate for their shortcomings in auditory ability. Each learner read a story book and after 10 minutes, the lesson continued as indicated below:

Teacher: Now, looking at the pictures who can explain to us what is happening?
Learner 4: It shows a child in a car and arriving at the airport.
Learner 2: The car is driven by his father.
Learner 5: They leave the car at the parking lot and walk into the airport.
Teacher: Did they meet anyone before they walked into the airport?
Class: No
Learner 7: They went to the counter and showed their tickets to the attendant.
Learner 8: They sat on the bench as they waited to board the airplane.
Teacher: Did they come across any problems at the counter?
Class: No
Learner 4: They move from the bench and enter another building from where they enter a tunnel which takes them to the airplane.
Teacher: Thank you. You will understand the story when we move to the next step. Now I will introduce you to some key words in the story that I need you to practice.

To further reinforce her inclusive pedagogical practices by using visual aids for learners with hearing impairment, the teacher used flash cards to introduce the key words in the story and wrote them on the whiteboard and then asked the learners to read the words - ***flew, forgot, excited*** - from the whiteboard aloud. As the lesson continued, the teacher identified more key words for the learners to read. Thereafter, the learners were encouraged to choose a word and explain its meaning to the class.

In the post-lesson conversation, when teacher A was asked to explain why she used visual materials in her lessons. She made the following remarks:

Visuals are useful in conveying information to learners, particularly during reading tasks. The use of flash cards and magazines have provided opportunities for learners to learn the meaning of words by relying on visual such as pictures.

The learners identified more words from the text, for example, ***tunnel, await, patiently***. After identifying the words, the teacher requested them to form groups and discuss the meaning of the identified words. Once the meaning of a word was established, the teacher checked whether the learners understood the text by posing more questions. Afterwards, the teacher provided each learner with a page with questions about the story. The following is an example of the question asked: Explain why the boy and his brother were sitting on the bench.

Upon completion of the task, the learners were asked to say out loud the words they had identified, and the teacher noted them on the whiteboard. She explained some words, for example, *to board—confirm your presence for the flight; ticket—a piece of paper or card that gives the holder a certain right.* The teacher assisted with the words that were explained incorrectly, after making sure that no learner knew what the words meant. Words such as ***tunnel*** and ***bench*** were problematic for the learners and the teacher used pictures from the internet to show the learners what the words referred to.

The lesson observation revealed how the teachers created an environment where all the learners were included in the classroom activities, for example, their active participation during the activities. Seemingly, visual aids, including the use of technology benefited all learners, particularly those with hearing impairment because of their well-developed visual stimuli rather than auditory stimuli. The use of technology/computers stimulated their interest and the teachers often gained their attention during such activities.

DISCUSSION

As is common with other people with disabilities, individuals with hearing impairment are often at a disadvantage when attempting to function in communities that are ready to accommodate their needs. Overall, the findings of the study reveal that individuals with hearing impairment are subject to discrimination and mistreatment. According to Harvey (2008) communities view these individuals under what is frequently described as medical model. Under this model communities view these individuals as requiring help rather than equals who participate in determining their own needs. The medical model further labels these individuals as showing a deviation from what is perceived as 'normal' and thus, the individuals need intervention and cure. This therefore could justify the labelling the community gives them, for example, using vernacular and labelling as ***susu***, which is often derogatory. On the contrary, social or human rights model views disability not as an individual's problem but as a problem with the way the society distinguishes the individuals (Harvey 2008). It could be argued that lack of awareness on how to treat and include individuals with hearing impairment in many communities is still prevalent. Some of the responses from the participants that they lack skills to include these individuals in their communities mainly due to communication barriers bear testimony to the latter. Thus, robust intervention programs are needed to create a community environment where individuals with hearing impairment could thrive with their needs fully addressed and their participation in community activities recognised and embraced. It is equally important that institutions such as hospitals, local clinics, banks, shops have trained members of staff who are able to communicate with individuals with hearing impairment for easy access to these institutions. Within the communities, sports tournaments, with adequate facilities could be organised with these individuals and could play an important role for community integration.

In addition, the use of technology could be explored to allow access to information for these individuals, For example, local libraries could be equipped the modern computers and individuals with hearing impairment encouraged to access and used the technology to acquire information. Also, their inclusion in schools for them to fully access the curriculum is of paramount importance.

From the observed lessons, it was clear that the teachers preferred using group work and pointed out that it provided opportunities to learners with hearing impairment opportunities to engage with others. The classroom environment also extended respect (a key aspect of inclusive education) for one another as the learners embraced peers rather than judge them. Every learner was involved in classroom discussions and doing so helped them to complete tasks.

Generally, the classroom activity observed that considered the learners' diverse language skills cultivated an inclusive environment where respect for individuals and an appreciation of diversity were cherished. Using a variety of strategies offered all learners opportunities to participate in activities. It was evident, for example, during the activity that all learners seemed to participate, they discussed and shared ideas. The evidence presented supports Newfield's (2011) observation that a classroom that embraces classroom interaction fosters participation by all. It is reasonable to conclude that the actions witnessed in this study, for example, allowing learners to discuss in groups, were attempts by the teacher to foster a culture of inclusive classroom practices. Just like Freire (1990), the teachers believed that dialogic approach would allow learners to engage one another and discuss with the teacher with respect. They therefore made efforts to involve all learners in their lessons, thus embracing the notion of inclusive education.

CONCLUDING REMARK

The participants in the study were information-rich and provided invaluable information regarding the inclusion or lack thereof of individuals with hearing impairment in their communities. The data collected shed light on how these individuals are viewed by the community and the isolation they experience primarily due to communication barriers between them and the community.

The findings of the study generally indicate that engaging learners with activities that were used to create an inclusive setting where all the learners had an opportunity to participate in classroom activities reinforced a learner-centred approach in which the teachers acted as facilitators. The observations made provided insights into the actions witnessed and highlighted what was important to inclusive classroom practices that facilitated participation by all.

REFERENCES

Bell, D. (2013). *Investigating teaching and learning support for students with hearing impairment at a university in the Western Cape.* (Doctoral dissertation, Stellenbosch: Stellenbosch University).

Bernard, H. R. (2002). *Research methods in anthropology: Qualitative and quantitative methods*. Altamira Press.

Bremer, C. D., Clapper, A. T., Hitchcock, C., Hall, T., & Kachgal, M. (2002). *Universal Design: A Strategy to Support Students' Access to the General Education Curriculum*. Information Brief.

Bryman, A., & Burgess, R. G. (2002). *Developments in qualitative data analysis: An introduction in analysing qualitative data*. Routledge.

Caissie, R., & Wilson, E. (1995). Communication breakdown management during cooperative learning activities by mainstreamed students with hearing losses. *The Volta Review*.

California Department of Education. (1999). *Communication needs and quality of education for deaf and hard-of-hearing children: Advisory Task Force*. California Department of Education.

Collins, P. S. (2003). Inclusion reconsidered. *Philosophy of Education Archive*, 449-457.

Coyne, I. T. (1997). Sampling in qualitative research. Purposeful and theoretical sampling; merging or clear boundaries? *Journal of Advanced Nursing*, *26*(3), 623–630. DOI: 10.1046/j.1365-2648.1997.t01-25-00999.x PMID: 9378886

Department of Education (DoE). (1995). *White Paper on Education and Training*. Retrieved on 16 October 2024 from: https://www.gov.za/sites/default/files/gcis_document/201409/16312gen1960.pdf

Department of Education (DoE). (1997). *Education White Paper 3: A Programme for the Transformation of Higher Education.*

Department of Education (DoE). (2001b). *Education White Paper 6: Special needs education: Building an inclusive education and training system*. Retrieved March 4 2024 from: https://www.vvob.org/files/publicaties/rsa_education_white_paper_6.pdf

Du Plessis, A. B. (2006). *The academic self-concept of learners with hearing impairment in two South African public school contexts: Special and full-service inclusion schools.* (Doctoral dissertation, University of Pretoria).

Fakolade, O. A., Adeniyi, S. O., & Tella, A. (2009). Attitude of teachers towards the inclusion of special needs children in general education classroom: The case of teachers in some selected schools in Nigeria. *International Electronic Journal of Elementary Education, 1*(3), 155–169.

Fernandes, J. K., & Myers, S. S. (2010). Inclusive deaf studies: Barriers and pathways. *Journal of Deaf Studies and Deaf Education, 15*(1), 17–29. DOI: 10.1093/deafed/enp018 PMID: 19617377

Flick, U. (2002). Qualitative research - state of the art. *Social Sciences Information. Information Sur les Sciences Sociales, 40*(1), 5–24. DOI: 10.1177/053901840204100100 1

Frank, C. (1999). *Ethnographic Eyes: A Teacher's Guide to Classroom Observation.* Heinemann.

Freire, P. (1990). *Pedagogy of the oppressed.* Continuum.

Graham, L. J., & Slee, R. (2008). An illusory interiority: Interrogating the discourse/s of inclusion. *Educational Philosophy and Theory, 40*(2), 277–293. DOI: 10.1111/j.1469-5812.2007.00331.x

Grove, S. J., & Fisk, R. P. (1992). Observational data collection methods for services marketing: An overview. *Journal of the Academy of Marketing Science, 20*(3), 217–224. DOI: 10.1007/BF02723408

Harvey, E. R. (2008). Deafness: A disability or a difference. *Health L. & Pol'y, 2*, 42.

Horner, R. H., Carr, E. G., Halle, J., McGee, G., Odom, S., & Wolery, M. (2005). The use of single-subject research to identify evidence-based practice in special education. *Exceptional Children, 71*(2), 165–179. DOI: 10.1177/001440290507100203

Hytten, K., & Bettez, S. C. (2011). Understanding education for social justice. *The Journal of Educational Foundations, 25*(1), 7–24.

King-Thorius, K. A., & Waitoller, F. R. (2017). Strategic coalitions against exclusion at the intersection of race and disability—A rejoinder. *Harvard Educational Review, 87*(2), 251–257.

Kusters, A. (2012). "The Gong Gong Was Beaten"—Adamorobe: A "Deaf Village" in Ghana and its marriage prohibition for deaf partners. *Sustainability, 4*(10), 2765–2784.

Luckner, J. L., & Cooke, C. (2010). A summary of the vocabulary research with students who are deaf or hard of hearing. *American Annals of the Deaf, 155*(1), 38–67. DOI: 10.1353/aad.0.0129 PMID: 20503907

Luckner, J. L., & Handley, C. M. (2008). A summary of the reading comprehension research undertaken with students who are deaf or hard of hearing. *American Annals of the Deaf, 153*(1), 6–36. DOI: 10.1353/aad.0.0006 PMID: 18619066

Marshall, M. N. (1996). Sampling for qualitative research. *Family Practice, 13*(6), 522–526. DOI: 10.1093/fampra/13.6.522 PMID: 9023528

Marshark, M., & Hauser, P. (2013). *How deaf children learn: What parents and teachers need to know*. Oxford University Press.

Meo, G. (2008). Curriculum planning for all learners: Applying universal design for learning (UDL) to a high school reading comprehension program. *Preventing School Failure, 52*(2), 21–30. DOI: 10.3200/PSFL.52.2.21-30

Mergler, A., Carrington, S., Kimber, M., & Bland, D. (2016). Inclusive values: Exploring the perspectives of pre-service teachers. *The Australian Journal of Teacher Education, 41*(4), 2. DOI: 10.14221/ajte.2016v41n4.2

Musselman, C. (2000). How do children who can't hear learn to read an alphabetic script? A review of the literature on reading and deafness. *Journal of Deaf Studies and Deaf Education, 5*(1), 9–31. DOI: 10.1093/deafed/5.1.9 PMID: 15454515

Muthukrishna, N. (Ed.). (2008). *Educating for social justice and inclusion in an African context: Pathways and transitions*. Nova Science.

Newfield, D. (2011). Multimodality and children's participation in classrooms: Instances of research. *Perspectives in Education, 29*(1), 27–35.

Nieuwenhuis, J. (2010). Analyzing qualitative data. In Maree, K. (Ed.), *First Steps in Research* (pp. 72–80). Van Schaik.

Osberg, D., & Biesta, G. (2010). The end/s of education: Complexity and the conundrum of the inclusive educational curriculum. *International Journal of Inclusive Education, 14*(6), 593–607. DOI: 10.1080/13603110802530684

Potter, W. J. (1996). *An analysis of thinking and research about qualitative methods*. Arlbaum Associates.

Ragin, C. C., Shulman, D., Weinberg, A., & Gran, B. (2003). Complexity, generality, and qualitative comparative analysis. *Field Methods, 15*(4), 323–340. DOI: 10.1177/1525822X03257689

Ramos, M. C. (1989). Some ethical implications of qualitative research. *Research in Nursing & Health, 12*(1), 57–63. DOI: 10.1002/nur.4770120109 PMID: 2922491

Rhoades, E. A., Price, F., & Perigoe, C. B. (2004). The changing American family & ethnically diverse children with hearing loss and multiple needs. *The Volta Review, 104*(4), 285–305.

Roberson, L. (2001). Integration of computers and related technologies in deaf education teacher preparation programs. *American Annals of the Deaf, 146*(1), 60–66. PMID: 11355079

Rodriguez, C. C., & Garro-Gil, N. (2014). Inclusion and integration on special education. *Procedia: Social and Behavioral Sciences, 191*, 1323–1327.

Sandelowski, M. (2000). Focus on research methods-whatever happened to qualitative description? *Research in Nursing & Health, 23*(4), 334–340. DOI: 10.1002/1098-240X(200008)23:43.0.CO;2-G PMID: 10940958

Sayed, Y., Soudien, C., & Carrim, N. (2003). Discourses of exclusion and inclusion in the South: Limits and possibilities. *Journal of Educational Change, 4*(3), 231–248. DOI: 10.1023/B:JEDU.0000006162.07375.aa

Sayed, Y., Soudien, C., & Carrim, N. (2003). Discourses of exclusion and inclusion in the South: Limits and possibilities. *Journal of Educational Change, 4*(3), 231–248. DOI: 10.1023/B:JEDU.0000006162.07375.aa

Scheetz, N. A. (1993). Closing the gap: Fostering a smooth transition toward independent living for the hearing impaired student entering the postsecondary setting. *Rural Special Education Quarterly, 12*(3), 36–41.

Sharma, G. (2017). Pros and cons of different sampling techniques. *International Journal of Applied Research, 3*(7), 749–752.

Stinson, M., & Antia, S. (1999). Considerations in educating deaf and hard-of-hearing students in inclusive settings. *Journal of Deaf Studies and Deaf Education, 4*(3), 163–175. PMID: 15579885

Storbeck, C. (2009). Educating the deaf and hard of hearing learner. In Landsberg, L., Kruger, D., & Nel, N. (Eds.), *Addressing barriers to learning: A South African Perspective*. Van Schaik.

Storbeck, C. (2009). Educating the deaf and hard of hearing learner. In Landsberg, L., Kruger, D., & Nel, N. (Eds.), *Addressing barriers to learning: A South African Perspective*. Van Schaik.

Teaching Excellence in Adult Literacy. (2010). TEAL *Fact Sheet No. 2: Universal design for learning,* Retrieved February 9, 2023 from: http://www. udlcenter.org/

Tesch, R. (1990). *Qualitative Research: Analysis, Types and Software Tools*. Falmer.

Tongco, M. D. C. (2007). Purposive sampling as a tool for informant selection. *Ethnobotany Research and Applications*, *5*, 147–158.

Tucci, D. L., Merson, M. H., & Wilson, B. S. (2010). A summary of the literature on global hearing impairment: Current status and priorities for action. *Otology & Neurotology*, *31*(1), 31–41. DOI: 10.1097/mao.0b013e3181c0eaec PMID: 20050266

Tvingstedt, A. L. (1993). *Social Conditions of Hearing-Impaired Pupils in Regular Classes*. Reprints and Miniprints No. 773.

Waghid, Y., & Engelbrecht, P. (2002). Inclusive education, policy and hope: Mapping democratic policy changes on inclusion in South Africa. *International Journal of Special Education*, *17*(1), 20–25.

World Health Organisation (WHO). (2017). *Prevention of deafness and hearing loss: 70th World Health Assembly, agenda item 15.8*. Retrieved May 23, 2023 from: https://apps.who.int/gb/ebwha/pdf_files/WHA70/A70_R13-en.pdf?ua=1

Yin, R. K. (1989). *Case Study Research: Design and Methods*. Sage.

Zainal, Z. (2017). Case study as a research method. *Jurnal Kemanusiaan*, *5*(1), 1–6.

Chapter 7
Perspectives on Inclusive Education in the South African Context

Marubini Christinah Sadiki
https://orcid.org/0009-0001-3655-9610
University of South Africa, South Africa

ABSTRACT

This chapter interrogates stigma and attitudes towards persons with disabilities, as these are obstacles to the successful implementation of inclusive education. Important aspects are the stigmas and attitudes towards realising inclusive education without discrimination, the impact of stereotypes on inclusive education, and best inclusion practices to mitigate those stigmas, attitudes and stereotypes towards persons with disabilities. South African policies and principles promote inclusive education for learner diversity. The promise to make provision for inclusive education in South African policies was part of a shift from the divided education system under apartheid to a diverse society that breaks down economic and public barriers. The ideal of inclusive education in South Africa holds that all learners, irrespective of capability, have the right to education and equal learning opportunities.

1. INTRODUCTION

The aim of the chapter is to review perspectives on inclusive education in the South African context. Inclusive education is justifiable, as it promotes value. In this chapter, inclusive education refers to an effective method of opposing inequitable views, encouraging the inclusion of all citizens, and adding value through teaching and learning (Sadiki & Mpya, 2024). Globally, many persons with disabilities

DOI: 10.4018/979-8-3373-7163-4.ch007

(PWDs) are excluded from learning. The United Nations Educational, Scientific and Cultural Organization (UNESCO, 2018) reports that although several nations are supporting the shift to inclusion, marginalisation is still rife. For some, this means separate education systems in special schooling, while for others it implies exclusion from teaching and learning. The developing diplomatic and societal knowledge have culminated in regulations worldwide that effectively preserve the constitutional rights of all learners to education – recognising all learners as equal, despite their diverse learning needs (Maguvhe & Masuku, 2023). These developments eventually pushed the idea of inclusive education to a universal platform with the drafting and adoption of the Salamanca Statement (UNESCO, 1994).

The chapter is aimed at the following audience: heads of department, curriculum advisors, the governing bodies of special schools, academics, teachers, lecturers, principals, parents, disability consultants, disability activists of inclusive education, persons without disabilities, advocacy structures of inclusive education, further education and training/technical vocational and educational training (FET/TVET) college lecturers, educators' unions, all government departments, researchers, policy makers and implementers, to name but a few.

South African education has made progress quantitatively, specifically by expanding primary school admission to all learners (Department of Basic Education [DBE], 2015; Mpya & Sadiki, 2024). According to Mackenzie and Chiang (2023), learning appropriateness should be extended further to include human rights to education, which involve educational value in the provision of opportunities and support to contribute to classroom learning behaviour. Inclusive education has developed as an international initiative to counter exclusionary practices (Barrett, 2024). It personalises individuals' respective values and norms, and emphasises the idea that all learners can learn and have the necessary support to learn, based on their needs rather than their disabilities (Bunch, 2023). Research has shown that although most countries appear to have a similar philosophy and obligation regarding the implementation of inclusive education, it is obvious that the idea of inclusive education has diverse meanings in different settings (Masuku & Makhanya, 2023). Maseko (2024) refers to the objective of inclusive education – to make learning opportunities accessible to all – so that all learners may gain access to learning, regardless of their disabilities and driven by their readiness to study.

2. DEFINING INCLUSIVE EDUCATION

According to Warnes et al. (2022) and Sadiki and Mpya (2024), inclusive education is the practice of supporting a variety of learner needs in a universal instructive setting. Different definitions of the concept exist, but the way in which scholars and authors define inclusive education depends on the context and perspective. Building on the fact that the right to education was defined by the 1948 Universal Declaration of Human Rights as a fundamental right, inclusive education is a result of this basic right of all people to access an appropriate form of education and not to be excluded. Inclusion in mainstream education is a philosophy of acceptance and community membership that leads to the structuring of the educational process in such a way that it meets the needs of all students (Hanssen, & Khitruk,2021). By referring to special education, inclusive education has been defined as the optimal and complete participation of students in mainstream school educational activities, regardless of the nature of their needs, without segregation in terms of services (Edström, Gardelli, & Backman, 2024).

In a report titled "Towards Inclusion and Equity in Education: Status, Trends, and Challenges", UNESCO (2020b) outlines three reasons for inclusive education (IE):

- The requirement for schools to educate all children together, means that they have to develop ways of teaching that respond to individual differences, to benefit all children.
- A social justification: Inclusive schools are intended to change attitudes to difference by educating all children together and form the basis for a just and non-discriminatory society.
- An economic justification: It is likely to be less costly to establish and maintain schools that educate all children together, than to set up a complex system of different types of schools specialising in particular disabilities.

Rizova et al. (2023) assert that inclusive education is not only about learners who have been accepted but also about the transformation of instructive arrangements so that all learners learn to be more tolerant of their peers. Rizova et al. (2023) also mention full and equal inclusion, pedagogically and informally, thus indorsing equivalent contributions within a solitary classification that does not categorise. Integration can be achieved with certain provisions, as learners' diverse learning requirements have to be fulfilled, not overlooking the fact that they also need to be socialised with others, to boost their confidence in themselves and their abilities. The above definitions of inclusive education seek to ensure equality between learners in diverse settings, so that those who were denied an education may be equally accommodated in educational settings. In the current study, inclusive education refers to freedom and equality, and is seen as a single system of education dedicated to ensuring that all individuals are enabled to become competent citizens in a changing and diverse society, as defined in Education White Paper 6 on Special Needs Education (EWP6) (Department of Education [DoE], 2001).

What is suggested by "disability" is important for inclusive education, and shapes not only educational outcomes but also societies (Reeves et al. 2022). While the United Nations (2006), Convention on the rights of persons with disabilities(CRPD); (United Nations General Assembly, 2007) defines disability – as respectful of, and proposed by, persons with disabilities themselves – and the CRPD's Article 24 (UNCRPD, 2016) contains a definition of inclusion, many countries use the term "special education needs" (SEN) when reporting on education, which may or may not include children with disabilities.

3. STIGMA AND ATTITUDES TOWARDS REALISING INCLUSIVE EDUCATION

Stigma is one of the main reasons for limited opportunities for inclusive education being offered to learners with disabilities (Kovačević & Radovanovic, 2023). For example, negative attitudes may cause stereotypes and prejudice against learners, denying them access to inclusive education (Namanyane & Shaoan, 2021). Excluding any child from education is a violation of international law and a breach of his or her human rights (Mbaku, 2021). Education in South Africa can be of an extremely deprived quality, with several groupings (such as those with severe disabilities) being isolated (Sait, 2023). Despite EWP6 (DoE, 2001) having been approved, inclusive education in South Africa has not achieved significant advances or realised the significant execution of its stipulations across the country (DoE, 2016; Mpya & Sadiki, 2024). Several challenges have played a major role in this regard. Legislators have underrated the temporary as well as the long-standing socio-economic realities of the application of the stipulations in a middle- to lower-income nation: confirming fairness and excellence in education for all, which is founded on policy approvals, has mainly been undermined by financial constraints (Briggs et al., 2023; DBE, 2015). Traditionally, education in South Africa has particularly excluded learners with disabilities, as they were observed to be somewhat different to the median, and were accordingly deemed to be incapable of advancing when undergoing ordinary schooling (Shabangu, 2021). Ranganathan et al (2024) note that in the 1960s, "diplomatic difficulty" and community awareness of disability and parental support groups started to modify people's beliefs, with them eventually calling for constituent shifts in education. There are many challenges to making excellent and inclusive education possible for learners with disabilities across South Africa. Barriers to inclusion certainly slow down progress in efforts to bring equality to teaching and learning. Limitations in the policy documents and strategies for implementation, as pronounced in EWP6, obstructed the quality and impact of the education each learner obtained. Consequently, a national programme of learning was proposed that incorporates fairness and social justice and the appropriate experiences in educators' districts (López & Sleeter, 2023).

A strong dependency on the medical model, which suggests a range of aids for learners with disabilities, was found to be equally incompatible with the idea of inclusive education. This, while teachers struggled with what exactly inclusive education entailed, as specified in the policy document (Moury & Escada, 2023). Research by Donohue and Bornman (2014) as well as Van Zyl (2023) revealed that many primary schools (full-service schools included) place learners with learning barriers in isolated special-education teaching spaces, instead of in ordinary classrooms. By doing so they accept a limited, naïve, medical interpretation of what inclusive education is by concentrating on disabilities. This strengthens the impression in other parts of the education sector that inclusive education is a retitled version of special education, and that it merely involves reorganising the organisation, not altering it (Aloni, 2023; Koutsoklenis & Papadimitriou 2024). It is not surprising that the DBE recognised that both theoretical and applied encounters at all levels of the education system continue to delay the shift to a fully inclusive education system (DBE, 2015). As Maguvhe (2023) indicates, resources and adjusted public services are essential but not adequate for inclusion, and that dealing with attitudinal difficulties among school experts and the broader community is vital when establishing inclusive education in low-income nations. The significant contribution of learners with disabilities to education and society might be hampered by the cultural views of its citizens. If a society neglects and discriminates against PWDs, then prejudices and exclusionary practices will continue to be reproduced (Badran et al., 2023; do Amaral Madureira, da Silva, & de Paula, 2020).

Neece et al. (2020) report that ethnic opinions about the magnitude of teaching learners with disabilities can have an effect on whether parents decide to take such children to school. Dozono (2023) found that in numerous developing countries, learners with disabilities regularly do not attend school, as it is assumed that they will be unable to learn, or will upset the other learners. According to Whitehead (2023), the general lack of suitable infrastructure and resources, and an arrogance towards PWDs all contribute to widespread confusion in the

South African learning environment about inclusivity.

The implementation of inclusive education include non-inclusive prospectuses, a lack of resources and insufficient capacity among educators (Carrington et al.,2024; Mrema, et al 2024). Despite the inclusive education policy framework in South Africa, performance lags far behind. The quality of education that many learners with disabilities obtain is not up to standard, with numerous learners being prohibited from gaining access to some form of education, and several learners in different institutions having inadequate subject selections and educational provision (Sadiki & Mpya, 2024). Many learners with disabilities do not have equal access to learning opportunities (Maguvhe, 2024). The South African government advances inclusive education across all disciplines, yet most educators are not skilled or taught how to support learners with disabilities (Maguvhe, 2023). Because of inadequate information on inclusive education policies, educators in most schools are not prepared to implement inclusive education (Gous & Wheatcroft, 2020). This proves that a theory change in guiding principles is not considered in teaching or training. The medical model observes disabilities as a special and deficit problem, requiring learners with disabilities to be isolated, to attend different teaching and learning institutions, to separate them from learners without disabilities (Nseibo, 2021; Peruzzo, 2023).

4. MYTHS AND MISCONCEPTIONS

According to Dube et al. (2021), learners with disabilities only have limited participation in inclusive education, largely due to the myths and misconceptions which members of society buy into. Many learners with disabilities are excluded from inclusive education because they look different from the members of dominant groups, or are somehow perceived as threatening (Walton, 2023). Most of families of learners with disabilities have a propensity to prevent their children from attending mainstream schools, for fear of those children being teased and mocked (Annie & Chimuka, 2024; Samsari, Nikolaou, & Palaiologou 2025). Stigma has a negative impact on the learning, psychological well-being and quality of life of learners with disabilities (Chen, 2021; Al-Shaer, et al 2024). This stigma is strongly linked to a sense of shame, depression and demoralisation in learners with disabilities, which diminishes individuals' self-esteem and self-worth (Goetz Fidler, 2023; Rehmat, Ahmed, & Sultan 2025).

An environment characterised by unfavourable attitudes isolates learners with disabilities, thus increasing the likelihood of their exclusion (Jones et al., 2022; Ndibalema, 2025). Disability is an outcome of social construction (Townsend et al., 2020; Popescu-Sarry,2024). Learners with disabilities may have limited capacities not because of their own intrinsic limits, but because they live in a "disabling environment" generated by impediments to social engagement, which are created by social circumstances (Nseibo, 2021; Collins, et al 2022). In other words, their "disability" is caused by a socially constructed environment (Dawn, 2023; Pedersen, & Söderström, 2024). Learners with disabilities are viewed as abnormal by the public, and institutional barriers prevent them from being granted opportunities or improving their social standing (Guevara, 2024; Adugna, Ghahari, & Lysaght, 2025). According to the Social Model of Disability, the fundamental causes of the disadvantages of individuals with disabilities are not their physical impairments or the disparities in their bodies, but rather the barriers they face within diverse social and economic environments (Jenkins & Kim Webster, 2021;Buettgen, Lofts, & Tompa 2024). For Carew and Shakespeare (2024), disability is defined as those restrictions on social activities generalized by social organizations, which do not consider people with functional impairments and therefore exclude them from mainstream schools. Learners with disabilities are highly stigmatised by inaccessible environments and ignorant attitude from members of society. According to the Social Model of Disability, the stigmatisation of PWDs is common in Western countries due to the structure of industrial capitalism, and the construction of reliance and independence (Grinker, 2020).

Stigma may affect the learning of learners with disabilities through the low quality of education offered to them, the perceived negative attitudes of teachers or peers, and institutional stigma (e.g., the lack of policy protection for such students) (Adugna et al., 2024;Malinovskiy, Shibanova, & Movkebayeva 2024). Research shows that stigma will lessen opportunities for learners with disabilities to access education, raising the risk of future poverty in this cohort (Naude et al., 2024). Although there are many consequences to disability stigma, they all have the same characteristic: individuals are excluded from opportunities for inclusive education, and their rights are not realised (Sabela, 2023; Jardinez, & Natividad 2024). They are thus denied social access and support. Myths and misconceptions prevent learners with disabilities from obtaining better social support, while limiting their access to inclusive education changes their lives (Odero, 2024).

5. THE IMPACT OF STEREOTYPES ON INCLUSIVE EDUCATION

Stereotypes are defined as simple "images" in our minds, of certain people or events (McDonald, 1993). Stereotypes also encompass our beliefs (or a set of beliefs) about the characteristics, attributes or behaviours of a particular group or a category of people. In addition, they include theories about how and why certain attributes fit certain groups (Boyer, 2023). In other words, stereotypes are cognitive structures that link preconceived ideas to a specific category of people (Allidina, & Cunningham, 2023). Stereotypes about people outside our reference group tend more to be negative than for group members, even when attributes are based on positive characteristics (Mannarini, Fedi, & Pozz 2024).

6. BEST DISABILITY PRACTICES TO MITIGATE EXCLUSION, STIGMAS, NEGATIVE ATTITUDES AND STEREOTYPES TOWARDS PERSONS WITH DISABILITIES

Prior to 1994, learners with disabilities were isolated from inclusive education because of intellectual and other substantial disabilities. This procedure is being repeated in the "new" South Africa, despite the development of official legislation (DoE, 2001) to ensure equal learning prospects for all citizens. EWP6 (DoE, 2001) signifies the current statutory decision according to which government removes the site for inclusive education (Graham, 2020). Accordingly, realising the dream will result in successful implementation of inclusive education in South Africa (Ngema, & D'amant, 2024).

The South African Constitution (Act 108 of 1996) (RSA, 1996) founded our democratic state and common citizenship based on the values of human dignity, the achievement of equality, and the advancement of human rights and freedoms (Section 1a). These principles require all of us to assume accountability and accept the challenge of building a humane and caring society for all South Africans. Inclusive education is a human rights issue and was first unified into the EWP6 explains that barriers to learning can affect core health conditions such as disabilities and ill health, as well as extrinsic considerations, such as deprivation, communication, ethnicity, and socio-economic class. Inclusive education seeks to achieve a shift away from the view of special needs education, and the normalisation of barriers to learning. In this document, acknowledgement for, and a valuing of, variety are advocated. EWP6 (DoE, 2001) and the Salamanca Statement (Unesco, 1994) report that inclusion is not just about physical attendance in an specific setting, but should place the emphasis on access, acceptance, and the contribution of everyone to education (Engelbrecht et al., 2016). The Salamanca Statement (Unesco, 1994) affirmed the need for inclusive education, as a means of meeting the requirements of learners with disabilities.

The emphasis in inclusive education on cumulative equal human rights and admission to teaching and learning find resonance with countless expectations in South Africa that a changed education system would play an important role in changing the biased societal and financial structures inherited from apartheid (Mahammoda, 2022). First, inclusive education suggests a recognition of learners who experience challenges to education; based on the assumption that a learning difficulty is the result of a specific condition learners have been diagnosed with (Korlison, 2023). The drafting of Agenda 2030 in November of 2015, which encompasses Sustainable Development Goal 4 (SDG4) (https://www.unesco.org/sdg4education2030/en/sdg4#:~:text=SDG4%20is%20a%20 commitment%20to,a%20sustainable%20and%20equitable%20world) seeks to achieve inclusive and quality education for all and to promote lifelong learning. There is an acknowledgement that not much has been accomplished in the past 30 years in terms of access to education, and that meeting teaching and learning goals remains a challenge, with as many as 57 million children who are out of school (UNGA, 2015).

Ever since the statement, "everyone has a right to education", was made in article 26 of the Universal Declaration of Human Rights, released in 1948 (1948a), there has been a need for states everywhere to create an environment aimed at ensuring that education is free, fundamental, and obligatory to their citizens, discrimination. Nations around the world agree that education is an essential human right that every child must enjoy irrespective of gender, race, age, physical dis/ability, socio-economic class or religion (Maguvhe, 2025. Education is a fundamental tool for combatting starvation and hunger (Luo et al. 2023; Unesco, 2016). Abdullahi (2023) notes that various countries have guaranteed the provision of excellent education for learners with disabilities, increasingly at the level of primary, secondary and higher learning institutions, via national laws, action plans and guidelines.

McAnally (2015) explains that post-1994, educators were manipulated by a severe, government-imposed programme and remained incapable of being artistic and absolute in their methods. Inclusive education policies approve an ecological outlook that recommends a change from presenting challenges to learners, to train them in a range of techniques to help them overcome barriers to learning (Kinchin, 2024; Dev, et al 2024). An inclusive education policy guarantees the rights of learners with disabilities to acceptance in ordinary schools. All the associated policies offer guidelines for rights-based responses to every type of disability in South Africa, but the challenges continue at the grassroots level (Levy et al., 2024). For example, the Screening, Identification, Assessment and Support (SIAS) policy (DoE, 2014) specifically aims to identify 1) the barriers to learning experienced, 2) the support needs that arise from those barriers, and 3) support programmes that need to be in place to reduce the impact of such barriers on the learning process. Worryingly, in some schools, school boards do not know how to implement disability-related policies (Khaleel et al., 2021; Jain, Potluri, & Sharif, 2020), as these are not related to action plans for implementation, while monitoring tools are not supplied either (Munyayi & van Wyk, 2024).

Inclusive education in the South African context is defined as a learning environment that promotes the full personal, academic and professional development of all learners, irrespective of race, class, gender, disability, religion, culture, sexual preference, learning styles and language (Maguvhe, 2024; Makhwathana, 2024; Sadiki & Mpya, 2024). Inclusive education requires educators and communities to switch their beliefs about what is wrong with a learner, to how to use the appropriate influences and interventions e in a knowledgeable way (Neves 2023; MacKenzie et al., 2020; Neves et al., 2023). According to McKenzie et al. (2024), inclusive education means that every child's needs are considered, and that all learners contribute and achieve together. It allows all learners to learn and it takes into account that every learner has unique characteristics, interests, abilities and learning needs (Kekana et al., 2024). Maguvhe (2023) reports that inclusive education aims to ensure that all learners of school-going age who experience barriers to learning, including those with disabilities, will be able to access quality, inclusive primary and secondary education for free, with other young people in the communities in which they live. Inclusive education has advanced as a process that seeks to eliminate discriminatory policies and practices (Maguvhe, 2024; Waisath, et al 2024). As such, it can be understood as part of a broader fight against infringements on individual human rights, and biases or prejudices. Its goal is to guarantee that equality in teaching and learning succeeds. In collaboration with provincial departments, the Ministry of Education has to consider which procedures will raise the capacity in schools for the premature identification and support of learners who experience barriers to learning, or require learning support (DoE, 2001). Support for learners is vital in encouraging them to become the best they can be (Maponya, 2020; Eden, Chisom, & Adeniyi, 2024). Collaboration is very important, as it ensures that educators work together and that learners receive proper support (Hargreaves, 2021; Anggraeni, Mustoip, & Hanifah, 2024). Support for learners can only happen when educators design lessons in such a way that no one is left behind during teaching and learning (Lukas& Yunus 2021; Qo'ldoshev, Dilova, & Hakimova 2024).

8. POSITIVE DEVELOPMENTS IN THE IMPLEMENTATION OF INCLUSIVE EDUCATION TO MITIGATE STIGMAS, NEGATIVE ATTITUDES AND STEREOTYPES

Since the announcement of EWP6 (DoE, 2001), learners with disabilities in South Africa are educated in classrooms with other learners without disabilities. However, the inclusion of learners with disabilities in mainstream teaching spaces, and as valued members of society, is not only conceptualised as a basic rights subject, it is a theme with which many South Africans are well acquainted as part of the fight against oppression. Existing educators training initiatives in South Africa prepare teachers to support and school a variety of learners within a single classroom (Makuyana, 2024; Nel, Dieker, & Marais 2024). The communal model of disability views disabilities centrally as a social theory (Morgan, 2021; Mou, & Albagmi 2024). Disabilities, in this sense, observe challenges as detected not in the individual, but in a social, financial, activist and educational system, and ethnic disparities that fail to meet the requirements of individuals (Brugere et al., 2023).

The social model is embedded tightly in the individual human rights model, exploring inclusivity and eliminating all challenges that hamper the full contribution of individuals with disabilities (Grue, 2023; Khan, 2024). Previously this model was widely accepted, with educators offering broad teaching or exceptional learning, which were remnants or by-products of a belief in the health model. This provided some educators with the necessary expertise to educate learners with disabilities. Makuyana (2024) is sad to note that attitudes regarding the split education of learners with disabilities from the mainstream have become effectively ingrained in the South African. A substantial number of South African educators are over 50 years of age (Dlamini & Dlamini, 2024; Badimo, & Masisi 2025), thus reorienting educators to adapt to new teaching methods, after decades of chalk-and-talk teaching, is vital. Advances since 2015 recognises not only the tasks still to be performed but also acknowledge advances at a domestic level (DBE, 2015). As a result, there has been an upsurge in the number of learners with recognised and varying instructive needs being taught in mainstream learning settings, along with a rise in the number of full-service schools – from 30 in 2002 to 715 in 2015 (DBE,2015; Moustache & Makhoba, 2024).

Current improvements in inclusive education are progressively featuring a stronger emphasis on socially receptive approaches in normal classrooms, the development of knowledge through workshopping and the infusion of communal values of fairness, to allow educators to adhere to leading standards, principles and developments that counter efforts to limit variety in classrooms (Gao, 2023; Souto-Manning, Martell, & Álvarez 2024). There is a robust indication of separate school front-runners and educators, despite background and strategy implementation encounters, remaining to involve with application approaches and to show activity in replying to inclusive education by necessities in their individual school societies (Nielsen et al., 2023). Transforming educators' training through inclusive education programmes has focused not only on developing educators' applied capabilities in varied school settings, but also on teaching them the capacity to engage capably with matters of segregation and isolation in classrooms, thus working to foster human rights and justice in teaching. Educators' expert ability, in the context of inclusive education, has progressively improved by adhering to, and teaching, social justice; by studying leading scholars in the field, meeting standards, and upholding principles of fairness (Muthukrishna & Engelbrecht, 2018; Reygan & Steyn, 2017; Sayed et al., 2017).

9. SIGNIFICANCE OF EDUCATORS' DEVELOPMENT IN INCLUSIVE EDUCATION TO MITIGATE STIGMAS, NEGATIVE ATTITUDES AND STEREOTYPES

Educators play a vital role, as they are a fundamental resource for realising the objective of an inclusive education and teaching environment (Mahlangu & Mtshali, 2024). To that end, educators, school management, and teaching support staff must all be capacitated to work effectively in this milieu.

Inclusive education is an instrument to wield in forming and shaping a compassionate, inclusive society (Tiwari, 2023; Kushwaha, et al 2024). Educators must take responsibility to serve as agents of transformation. Universal learning assumes that educators' approaches to inclusive education require them to take responsibility for learning inclusive methods and accepting guidance on the consequences of the method they apply (Kushwaha et al., 2024; Neves et al., 2023). To advance inclusive education it is crucial to document and minimise any challenges to education. Baloyi (2023) proposes regular and rigorous capacity-building programmes to boost educators' self-confidence and capabilities, since change can only happen by continuing with, and participating teachers through, capacity-building programmes. Insufficient experience of inclusive education policies and what they advise can hamper change in educators' interpretation of the makeup and purpose of teaching and learning (Kaimara, 2023; Bongabong, MEda, & LPTb, 2023). According to McKenzie et al. (2023), the principles and thinking that emphasise teaching and learning are still reflective of the medical model.

The development of educators in inclusive education is crucial for addressing and mitigating stigmas, negative attitudes, and stereotypes that often surround learners with diverse needs (Abduxamitovich, Nodira, & Kunduz, 2021; Barnard & Henn, 2023; Cerna et al., 2021). When educators are equipped with the knowledge, skills, and values of inclusive practices, they become powerful agents of change who foster acceptance, respect, and equity within the learning environment (Assefa & Zenebe, 2024; Küçüksüleymanoğlu, 2025). Professional development enables teachers to challenge their own biases, implement inclusive teaching strategies, and create a classroom culture that celebrates diversity rather than marginalizes it (Saunders, & Wong, 2020). Through the promotion of empathy and understanding, trained educators can dismantle harmful stereotypes and help cultivate a more inclusive and supportive school community for all learners(Evisensia, 2025).

9.1 Parental support

Parents have an important role to play in advocating for their children to be educated in inclusive environments. Parental support is key to ensuring the successful implementation of this approach (Anyanwu, et al 2024; Fitrianto, 2024). Parents need to be responsible for their children, and show their support by making sure that their children attend school (DoE, 2010), as is their right. Support from parents is crucial for the development of children. In addition, resource centres can provide short- or long-term support for individual learners, and capacitate them to join the labour market (Thulo, 2024; Molnár, et al 2024). Parents and educators must walk the journey of inclusive education together, to succeed in the implementation of inclusive education. Effective interaction between parents and educators will always ensure the best outcomes, since parents understand their children better than the educators do. According to Oranga et al. (2022), parental involvement has been shown to have a positive impact on learner success.

10. EDUCATORS' PERSPECTIVES ON INCLUSIVE EDUCATION

It is internationally acknowledged that educators play a meaningful role in establishing welcoming, inclusive learning environments(Debasu, & Yitayew 2024; Irshad, Amir, & Rafaqat 2024). Their understanding of inclusive education, their attitudes towards it, as well as their pedagogical knowledge and skills, have a significant impact on their teaching practices (Pienaar & Dreyer, 2023; Sepadi, 2023). Educators require support in the form of resources and in-service training for the implementation of this approach in schools across South Africa (Olawumi, & Mavuso 2024; Chuene, & Teane 2024). Educators must be continuously capacitated to offer sustained support to all learners in their classrooms. To that end, they need to collaborate with other stakeholders to overcome barriers to teaching and learning for example, school governing bodies, heads of department, subject advisors, academics, teachers, university lecturers, principals, parents, disability consultants, human rights activists, persons without disabilities, PWDs, advocacy structures of inclusive education, FET/TVET college lecturers, educators' unions, all government departments, researchers, policy makers and implementers, must be involved. Upgrading the skills of educators to implement this approach as part of all learners' development requires more than once-off workshop training, but rather in-service development (Sepadi, 2023; Hanus, & Krause 2025).

11. SOUTH AFRICAN LEARNERS' PERSPECTIVES ON INCLUSIVE EDUCATION

Inclusive education in the classroom promotes equal opportunities for teaching and learning, and seeks to create more inclusive societies(Makweya, & Sepadi,

2025; Pradhan, & Naik, 2024). Most learners with disabilities do not attend school because of societal attitudes and fear of the unknown. Inclusive education must not mean inclusion at all costs, but rather a consideration of what is best for each learner, and recognising that “one size” does not “fit all” (Jaiyeola, et al 2025). Inclusive education increases social participation for all learners in environments that fully support their cognitive and social-emotional needs (Ugalde, et al 2021). South Africa has to redress inequalities towards learners with disabilities by offering equal educational opportunities for all learners in the same classrooms and at the same schools, irrespective of their dis/abilities. As Shongwe (2024) reports, educators are a fundamental driving force in confirming the superiority of inclusive learning environments in educational settings. This calls for a partnership between classroom educators, essential educators, school leaders and teaching officials (Musengamana et al., 2024; Akgöz, Şahin, & Erdoğan, 2024).

12. PERSPECTIVES OF THOSE IN FAVOUR OF INCLUSIVE EDUCATION

Those who favour inclusive education want learners with disabilities to be educated alongside their peers who do not have disabilities. The South African government has fundamentally changed over the past 25 years, from an entity that denied the majority's human rights to a context that preserves equal justice for all. Despite this, equal opportunity is not yet a reality in learning contexts (Starck et al., 2024; Reimers, 2024). This refers specifically to learners with disabilities who, as part of past practices of oppression, remained on the periphery of the education system (Ndlovu, 2023; Santamaría Graff, 2021).

13. CONCLUSION

This chapter interrogated perspectives on inclusive education in the South African context and how to mitigate stigmas, negative attitudes and stereotypes in respect of persons with disabilities in inclusive education. This approach is still in its infancy. The development of inclusive education, which focuses on enablement, contribution and assigned obligation, has an effect on what happens in the classroom. Collaborators are fundamental in advocating for inclusive education. Government should take urgent action to make its inclusive education policy mandatory, and move beyond mere promises to substantially funding, resourcing and capacitating those charged with making education inclusive for all learners.

REFERENCES

Abdullahi, A. M. (2023). The challenges of advancing inclusive education: The case of Somalia's higher education. *Journal of Law and Sustainable Development, 11*(2), e422.

Abduxamitovich, A. A., Nodira, S., & Kunduz, X. M. (2021). The role of inclusive education in overcoming stigmas. *ACADEMICIA: An International Multidisciplinary Research Journal, 11*(7), 38–43.

Adugna, M. B., Ghahari, S., & Lysaght, R. (2024). Disability stigma and the pursuit of inclusion among children with physical disabilities in northwest Ethiopia. *Disability and Rehabilitation*, •••, 1–11.

Akgöz, E. E., Şahin, F., & Erdoğan, O. (2024). The mediator role of school climate in the relationship between instructional leadership behaviors of school principals and teacher autonomy. *International Journal of Educational Management, 38*(4), 1142–1159.

Al-Shaer, E. A., Aliedan, M. M., Zayed, M. A., Elrayah, M., & Moustafa, M. A. (2024). Mental health and quality of life among university students with disabilities: The moderating role of religiosity and social connectedness. *Sustainability, 16*(2), 644.

Allidina, S., & Cunningham, W. A. (2023). Motivated categories: Social structures shape the construction of social categories through attentional mechanisms. *Personality and Social Psychology Review, 27*(4), 393–413.

Aloni, V. (2023). *Knowledge and perception of teachers toward inclusive education in basic schools in Garu District in the Upper East Region of Ghana* (Unpublished doctoral dissertation). University of Education, Winneba.

Anggraeni, D., Mustoip, S., & Hanifah, H. (2024). Analysis of Student Social Interaction in the Salted Egg Making Project in Elementary Schools. *EduBase: Journal of Basic Education, 5*(2), 163–167.

Annie, P., & Chimuka, C. (2024). Effect of bullying on learners with Autism Spectrum Disorder: A case of a selected special unit at the mainstream in Kabwe, Zambia. *Education Journal, 8*(1), 83–90.

Anyanwu, E. C., Maduka, C. P., Ayo-Farai, O., Okongwu, C. C., & Daraojimba, A. I. (2024). Maternal and child health policy: A global review of current practices and future directions. *World Journal of Advanced Research and Reviews, 21*(2), 1770–1781.

Assefa, E. A., & Zenebe, C. K. (2024). Fostering inclusive excellence: Strategies for effective diversity management in schools. *International Journal of Research in Education Humanities and Commerce*, *5*(2), 189–211.

Assembly, U. G. (2007). United Nations declaration on the rights of indigenous peoples. *UN Wash*, *12*, 1–18.

Badimo, T. P., & Masisi, I. M. (2025). Educators' experiences and coping strategies in response to learner violence in Mopani district, Limpopo. *The Journal for Transdisciplinary Research in Southern Africa*, *21*(1), 1527.

Badran, L., Amin, H., Gur, A., & Stein, M. (2023). I am an Arab Palestinian living in Israel with a disability: Marginalisation and the limits of human rights. *Disability & Society*, *38*(1), 1–20. DOI: 10.1080/09687599.2023.2181764

Baloyi, R. P. P. (2023). *School principals' ability to influence the improvement of learner performance in selected rural schools in Limpopo* (Unpublished doctoral dissertation). North-West University, South Africa.

Barnard, R. W., & Henn, R. H. (2023). Overcoming learning obstacles: Strategies for supporting students with diverse needs. *OAlib*, *10*(8), 1–14.

Barrett, H. L. (2024). *Access to inclusive early childhood development and education services for refugee children who experience communication disability, in Rwanda* (Unpublished doctoral dissertation). Manchester Metropolitan University, UK.

Bongabong, J. M. M., MEda, M. G. Q. D., & LPTb, W. E. C. (2023). Exploring the Real-Life Issues and Challenges in an Inclusive Classroom through the Lens of General Education Kindergarten Teachers and Parents: A Qualitative Study. *Exploring the Real-Life Issues and Challenges in an Inclusive Classroom through the Lens of General Education Kindergarten Teachers and Parents: A Qualitative Study*, *115*(1), 25-25.

Boyer, P. (2023). *The naturalness of religious ideas: A cognitive theory of religion*. University of California Press.

Briggs, D., Telford, L., Lloyd, A., & Ellis, A. (2023). *The new futures of exclusion: Life in the Covid-19 aftermath*. Springer Nature.

Brugere, C., Bansal, T., Kruijssen, F., & Williams, M. (2023). Humanizing aquaculture development: Putting social and human concerns at the center of future aquaculture development. *Journal of the World Aquaculture Society*, *54*(2), 482–526.

Buettgen, A., Lofts, K., & Tompa, E. (2024). Disability inclusion in the green economy: A scoping review of challenges, barriers and opportunities. *J. Green Econ. Low-Carbon Dev*, *3*(4), 208–222.

Bunch, J. C. (2023). *Assistive technology life worlds: Inclusive qualitative methodological innovations for diverse body minds* (Unpublished doctoral dissertation). Arizona State University.

Carew, M. T., & Shakespeare, T. (2024). Beyond disability stigma: Examining tolerance and intolerance toward disability issues. *Scandinavian Journal of Disability Research*, *26*(1).

Carrington, S., Mavropoulou, S., Saggers, B., & Nepal, S. (2024). *Inclusive education in Australia: Policy review.* Autism CRC. autismcrc.com.au

Cerna, L., Mezzanotte, C., Rutigliano, A., Brussino, O., Santiago, P., Borgonovi, F., & Guthrie, C. (2021). Promoting inclusive education for diverse societies: A conceptual framework. *OECD Education Working Papers*, (260), 0_1-57.

Chen, C. H. (2021). The roles of psychosocial developmental crisis and self-stigma in mental health among college students with disabilities. *International Journal of Disability Development and Education*, *68*(2), 287–302.

Chuene, D. M., & Teane, F. M. (2024). Resource inadequacy as a barrier to effective curriculum implementation by life sciences teachers in South Africa. *South African Journal of Education*, *44*(2).

Collins, A., Rentschler, R., Williams, K., & Azmat, F. (2022). Exploring barriers to social inclusion for disabled people: Perspectives from the performing arts. *Journal of Management & Organization*, *28*(2), 308–328.

Dawn, R. (2023). Role of culture and media in disability studies: A medium of social construction of disability. *Journal of Disability & Religion*, *27*(1), 1–22.

Debasu, H., & Yitayew, A. (2024). Examining Elements of Designing and Managing of Creating Inclusive Learning Environment: Systematic Literature Review. *International Journal of Special Education*, *39*(1), 33–43.

Department of Basic Education (DBE). (2015). *Report on the implementation of Education White Paper 6 on Inclusive Education: Overview for the period 2013–2015.* Government Printers.

Dev, S., George, M., Rafique, S., Vaddapalli, M., Nair, S., & Al Hameli, A. (2024). Sustainable inclusive framework studio for inclusive education—Perceptions of teachers, parents, and students in United Arab Emirates. *Sustainability*, *16*(15), 6367.

Dlamini, N. G., & Dlamini, N. D. (2024). Understanding the well-being challenges confronting academic staff in South African universities: A narrative review. *Discover Education*, *3*(1), 1–10.

do Amaral Madureira, A. F., da Silva, M. R. G., & de Paula, L. D. (2020). Social identities, prejudices, and exclusion: The reproduction of social (in) visibility in school contexts. *Psychology as a Dialogical Science: Self and Culture Mutual Development*, 115-134.

Donohue, D., & Bornman, J. (2014). The challenges of realising inclusive education in South Africa. *South African Journal of Education*, *34*(2).

Dozono, T. (2023). Eugenic ideology and the world history curriculum: How eugenic beliefs structure narratives of development and modernity. *Theory and Research in Social Education*, *51*(3), 408–437.

Dube, T., Ncube, S. B., Mapuvire, C. C., Ndlovu, S., Ncube, C., & Mlotshwa, S. (2021). Interventions to reduce the exclusion of children with disabilities from education: A Zimbabwean perspective from the field. *Cogent Social Sciences*, *7*(1), 1913848.

Eden, C. A., Chisom, O. N., & Adeniyi, I. S. (2024). Promoting digital literacy and social equity in education: Lessons from successful initiatives. *International Journal of Management & Entrepreneurship Research*, *6*(3), 687–696.

Edström, K., Gardelli, V., & Backman, Y. (2024). Inclusion as participation: Mapping the participation model with four different levels of inclusive education. *International Journal of Inclusive Education*, *28*(12), 2940–2957.

Fitrianto, I. (2024). Critical Reasoning Skills: Designing an Education Curriculum Relevant to Social and Economic Needs. *International Journal of Post Axial: Futuristic Teaching and Learning*, 245-258.

Gao, R. (2023). Promoting students' classroom participation in the context of inclusive education: A case study of students with autism. *International Journal of New Developments in Education*, *5*(15).

Goetz Fidler, C. J. (2023). *Stigma resistance versus self-stigma in university students with mental health problems* (Doctoral dissertation). Lakehead University.

Gous, G., & Wheatcroft, J. M. (2020). Directive leading questions and preparation technique effects on witness accuracy. *SAGE Open*, *10*(1), 2158244019899053.

Graham, L. J. (2020). Inclusive education in the 21st century. In Graham, L. J. (Ed.), *Inclusive Education for the 21st Century: Theory, Policy and Practice* (pp. 3–26). Routledge., DOI: 10.4324/9781003116073-2

Grinker, R. R. (2020). Autism,"stigma," disability: A shifting historical terrain. *Current Anthropology*, *61*(S21), S55–S67.

Grue, J. (2023). The CRPD and the economic model of disability: Undue burdens and invisible work. *Disability & Society*, *39*(12), 3119–3135. DOI: 10.1080/09687599.2023.2255734

Guevara, A. (2024). How American Society and Law Continue to Undermine People with Disabilities Seeking Education and Employment. *UC Law Constitutional Quarterly*, *51*(1), 65.

Hanus, M., & Krause, U. (2025). Geography teachers' networks as platforms for continuous professional development: experience from the Netherlands and Czechia. In *Handbook of Geography Education* (pp. 723–750). Springer Nature Switzerland.

Hargreaves, A. (2021). What the COVID-19 pandemic has taught us about teachers and teaching. *Facets*, *6*(1), 1835–1863.

Irshad, M. A., Amir, R. M., & Rafaqat, M. S. (2024). Towards Inclusive Classrooms: Identification of the Role of Teachers in Creating an Inclusive Learning Environment. *Journal of Asian Development Studies*, *13*(3), 1323–1332.

Jain, D., Potluri, V., & Sharif, A. (2020, October). Navigating graduate school with a disability. In *Proceedings of the 22nd International ACM SIGACCESS Conference on Computers and Accessibility* (pp. 1-11).

Jaiyeola, G. D., Wong, A. Y., Bryck, R. L., Mills, C., & Hutt, S. (2025, March). One Size Does Not Fit All: Considerations when using Webcam-Based Eye Tracking to Models of Neurodivergent Learners' Attention and Comprehension. In *Proceedings of the 15th International Learning Analytics and Knowledge Conference* (pp. 24-35).

Jardinez, M. J., & Natividad, L. R. (2024). The Advantages and Challenges of Inclusive Education: Striving for Equity in the Classroom. *Shanlax International Journal of Education*, *12*(2), 57–65.

Jenkins, K., & Kim Webster, A. (2021). Disability, impairment, and marginalised functioning. *Australasian Journal of Philosophy*, *99*(4), 730–747.

Jones, S. C., Gordon, C. S., Akram, M., Murphy, N., & Sharkie, F. (2022). Inclusion, exclusion and isolation of autistic people: Community attitudes and autistic people's experiences. *Journal of Autism and Developmental Disorders*, *52*(3), 1131–1142.

Kaimara, P. (2023). Digital transformation stands alongside inclusive education: Lessons learned from a project called "Waking Up in the Morning." *Technology. Knowledge and Learning*, *1*(1), 1–27. DOI: 10.1007/s10758-023-09427-w

Khaleel, N., Alhosani, M., & Duyar, I. (2021, April). The role of school principals in promoting inclusive schools: A teachers' perspective. *Frontiers in Education*, *6*, 603241. DOI: 10.3389/feduc.2021.60324

Khan, F. (2024). Navigating the Gap: Disability Rights and Social Inclusion in a Changing World. *Social Science Review Archives*, *1*(03), 1–9.

Kinchin, I. M. (2024). *How to mend a university: Towards a sustainable learning environment in higher education*. Bloomsbury.

Korlison, O. A. N. D. (2023). *The experience of special education teachers with dyslexic students: A case study* (Unpublished doctoral dissertation). Capella University.

Koutsoklenis, A., & Papadimitriou, V. (2024). Special education provision in Greek mainstream classrooms: Teachers' characteristics and recruitment procedures in parallel support. *International Journal of Inclusive Education*, *28*(5), 561–576.

Kovačević, J., & Radovanovic, V. (2023). Social distance towards students with disabilities in inclusive education. *International Journal of Disability Development and Education*, *70*(1), 106–119.

Küçüksüleymanoğlu, R. (2025). Principles of Equality: Social Justice and Equal Opportunities. In *Creating Positive and Inclusive Change in Educational Environments* (pp. 23–52). IGI Global Scientific Publishing.

Kushwaha, R. K., Tripathi, A., Singh, C., & Yadav, M. K. (2024). *Inclusive Education*. Blue Rose Publishers.

Levy, S. R., Gopang, M., Ramírez, L., Bernardo, A. B., Ruck, M. D., & Sternisko, A. (2024). A human rights-based approach to climate injustices at the local, national, and international levels: Program and policy recommendations. *Social Issues and Policy Review*, *18*(1), 3–30.

López, F., & Sleeter, C. E. (2023). *Critical race theory and its critics: Implications for research and teaching*. Teachers College Press.

Lukas, B. A., & Yunus, M. M. (2021). ESL Teachers' Challenges in Implementing E-learning during COVID-19. *International Journal of Learning. Teaching and Educational Research*, *20*(2), 330–348.

Luo, X., Du, B., Gui, P., Zhang, D., & Hu, W. (2023). A Hunger Games search algorithm with opposition-based learning for solving multimodal medical image registration. *Neurocomputing, 540*, 126204.

MacKenzie, A., Bower, C., & Owaineh, M. (2020). Gratitude versus children's rights: An exploration of mothers' attitudes towards disability and inclusive education in Palestine. *International Journal of Educational Research Open, 1*, 100001.

MacKenzie, A., & Chiang, T. H. (2023). The human development and capability approach: A counter theory to human capital discourse in promoting low SES students' agency in education. *International Journal of Educational Research, 117*, 102121.

Maguvhe, M. O. (2023). Unique African challenges in the provision of quality inclusive education in school education and training. In Maguvhe, M. O., & Masuku, M. M. (Eds.), *Using African Epistemologies in Shaping Inclusive Education Knowledge* (pp. 285–306). Springer Nature Switzerland., DOI: 10.1007/978-3-031-31115-4_16

Maguvhe, M. O. (2024). Inclusive education: Controversies, successes, and future prospects. In Maguvhe, M. O., Mpya, N. G., & Sadiki, M. C. (Eds.), *Handbook of research on inclusive and accessible education* (pp. 1–17). IGI Global.

Maguvhe, M. O. (2025). *Inclusive Education: Towards Social Justice, Achievement of Equality and Advancement of Human Rights*. BRILL.

Maguvhe, M. O., & Masuku, M. M. (Eds.). (2023). *Using African epistemologies in shaping inclusive education knowledge*. Springer Nature.

Mahammoda, S. A. (2022). *Educational reforms in Ethiopia: From the imperial era to the present* (Unpublished doctoral dissertation). Necmettin Erbakan University, Turkey.

Mahlangu, S. M., & Mtshali, T. I. (2024). Inclusive education strategies for knowledge development of teachers enrolled in the advanced vocational and training education program. *International Journal of Religion, 5*(3), 166–174.

Makhwathana, R. M. (2024). Inclusive education: All things considered. In Maguvhe, M. O., Mpya, N. G., & Sadiki, M. C. (Eds.), *Handbook of research on inclusive and accessible education* (pp. 345–358). IGI Global.

Makuyana, T. (2024). Proven African inclusive education strategies for educators to build a safe and diverse learner community. In Maguvhe, M. O., Mpya, N. G., & Sadiki, M. C. (Eds.), *Handbook of Research on Inclusive and Accessible Education* (pp. 140–156). IGI Global.

Makweya, P. P., & Sepadi, M. D. (2025). Inclusive Education and Lifelong Learning: Beyond School Walls. In *Global Practices in Inclusive Education Curriculum and Policy* (pp. 261-280). IGI Global.

Malinovskiy, S., Shibanova, E., & Movkebayeva, Z. (2024). Barriers and facilitators of access to higher education in a weakly institutionalised context: Perceptions of disabled students. *Disability & Society, 39*(9), 2258–2280.

Maponya, T. J. (2020). The Instructional Leadership Role of the School Principal on Learners' Academic Achievement. *African Educational Research Journal, 8*(2), 183–193.

Maponya, T. J. (2020). The Instructional Leadership Role of the School Principal on Learners' Academic Achievement. *African Educational Research Journal, 8*(2), 183–193.

Maseko, N. T. (2024). Current inclusive education debates in South Africa and the world over. In Maguvhe, M. O., Mpya, N. G., & Sadiki, M. C. (Eds.), *Handbook of Research on Inclusive and Accessible Education* (pp. 78–91). IGI Global.

Masuku, M. M., & Makhanya, T. (2023). Ubuntu philosophy and decolonisation: Interpretation of inclusivity in higher education. In Maguvhe, M. O., & Masuku, M. M. (Eds.), *Using African Epistemologies in Shaping Inclusive Education Knowledge* (pp. 395–410). Springer Nature Switzerland., DOI: 10.1007/978-3-031-31115-4_25

McDonald, M. (1993). The construction of difference: An anthropological approach to stereotypes. In Macdonald, S. (Ed.), *Inside European Identities: Ethnography in Western Europe* (pp. 219–236). Routledge.

Molnár, T., Jenei, S., Moreno, E., Lakshmi, V. P., Malatyinszki, S., & Dávid, L. D. (2024). The Role of Lifelong Learning in Labour Market Competitiveness. *Journal of Ecohumanism, 3*(8), 7743–7761.

Morgan, H. (2021). Mad studies and disability studies. In *The Routledge international handbook of Mad studies* (pp. 108–118). Routledge.

Mou, M., & Albagmi, F. M. (2024). Merging critical disability theory with post-colonial hybridity theory: A widened lens and implications. *Disability & Society, 39*(9), 2344–2356.

Moury, C., & Escada, M. (2023). Understanding successful policy innovation: The case of Portuguese drug policy. *Addiction (Abingdon, England), 118*(5), 967–978.

Moustache, H. M., & Makhoba, M. (2024). Educators' experiences of teaching learners with hearing loss in inclusive classrooms. *South African Journal of Childhood Education*, *14*(1), 13.

Mpya, N. G., & Sadiki, M. C. (2024). Inclusive basic education in South Africa: Highlights and lowlights. In Maguvhe, M. O., Mpya, N. G., & Sadiki, M. C. (Eds.), *Handbook of research on inclusive and accessible education* (pp. 244–261). IGI Global.

Mrema, D., Ndayambaje, I., Ntawiha, P., & Ndabaga, E. (2024). The Practicability of Quality Assurance Mechanisms in Promoting Tanzanian Universities' Compliance. *European Journal of Educational Research*, *13*(3).

Munyayi, F. K., & van Wyk, B. E. (2024). Policy and programming towards addressing treatment gaps in adolescents living with HIV: A content analysis of policy and programme documents in Namibia. [JIAPAC]. *Journal of the International Association of Providers of AIDS Care*, *23*, 23259582241236061.

Musengamana, I., Shaoan, M. M. R., Namanyane, T., Lafferty, N., & Uzochukwu, O. M. (2024). Teachers' Role in School Decision-Making Process: A Case Study of Teachers and School Leaders Perceptions in Rwanda Public Secondary School. *Asia Social Issues*, *17*(4), e267161–e267161.

Muthukrishna, N., & Engelbrecht, P. (2018). Decolonising inclusive education in lower income southern African educational contexts. *South African Journal of Education*, *38*(4), 1–11.

Namanyane, T., & Shaoan, M. R. (2021). Inclusive education: A literature review on definitions, attitudes and pedagogical challenges. *International Journal of Research and Innovation in Social Science*, *5*(3), 358–365.

Naude, A., Kang, L. J., Moretti, M., Rocha, A. D. S., Maxwell, G. R. D., & Bornman, J. (2024). Using the ICF to Guide Inclusion in the African Educational Context: A Scoping Review. *Education Sciences*, *14*(12), 1290.

Ndibalema, P. (2025). Perspectives on barriers to learning opportunities among deaf children in Tanzania. *International Journal of Educational Research Open*, *9*, 100468.

Ndlovu, S. (2023). Indigenous knowledge systems in Africa: Exclusion of students with disabilities in South African higher education. *Curriculum Perspectives*, *43*(Suppl 1), 127–140.

Neece, C., McIntyre, L. L., & Fenning, R. (2020). Examining the impact of COVID-19 in ethnically diverse families with young children with intellectual and developmental disabilities. *Journal of Intellectual Disability Research*, *64*(10), 739–749.

Nel, C., Dieker, L., & Marais, E. (2024). The integration of mixed reality simulation into reading literacy modules. *Education Sciences, 14*(10), 1128.

Neves, C., Almeida, A. P., & Ferreira, M. (2023). Headteachers and inclusion: Setting the tone for an inclusive school. *Education Sciences, 13*(2), 129.

Ngema, Z., & D'amant, A. (2024). Implementation of inclusive education as experienced by immigrant learners of diverse backgrounds in South Africa. *South African Journal of Education, 44*(1), S1–S9.

Nielsen, J. V., Smedegaard, S., Klakk, H., & Skovgaard, T. (2023). Same, same but different: Comparing program fidelity at early versus late adopters of a successful long-term school-based physical activity intervention. *Health Promotion Practice, 24*(6), 1237–1245.

Nseibo, J. K. (2021). Exploring the experiences of children and youth with mobility impairments in four basic educational settings in Ghana (Master's thesis, University of Oslo). University of Oslo Digital Repository. Mbaku, J. M. (2021). International law, corruption and the rights of children in Africa. *San Diego Int'l LJ, 23*, 195.

Odero, C. A. (2024). *Falling through the cracks: Exploring parental struggles and experiences when accessing special education for children with disabilities in Kenya* (Unpublished Master's thesis). Bowling Green State University.

Olawumi, K. B., & Mavuso, M. P. (2024). In-service teacher training programmes that promote education for sustainable development: A review of emerging literature. *Interdisciplinary Journal of Education Research, 6*, 1–20.

Oranga, J., Obuba, E., Sore, I., & Boinett, F. (2022). Parental involvement in the education of learners with intellectual disabilities in Kenya. *OAlib, 9*(4), 1–18.

Pedersen, H., & Söderström, S. (2024). The creation of cyborgs within a socially constructed understanding of disability and assistive activity technology use. *Disability & Society, 39*(8), 1984–2006.

Peruzzo, F. (2023). A certain kind of freedom, a certain subject of right: The disability dispositif of inclusion and the government of the disabled child in the Italian education system. In Beckett, M., & Callus, M. (Eds.), *The Routledge International Handbook of Children's Rights and Disability* (pp. 520–536). Routledge., DOI: 10.4324/9781003056737

Popescu-Sarry, D. (2024). Discrimination without traits: From social construction to the politics of discrimination. *The American Political Science Review, 118*(2), 890–902.

Pradhan, K. C., & Naik, M. S. (2024). Inclusive education: A foundation for equality and empowerment at the elementary stage. *International Journal of Multidisciplinary Research in Arts. Science and Technology*, *2*(2), 1–8.

Qo'ldoshev, R., Dilova, N., & Hakimova, N. (2024). Guiding left-handed students to a healthy lifestyle during the period of adaptation to school education. In *BIO Web of Conferences* (Vol. 120, p. 01049). EDP Sciences.

Ranganathan, N., & Wadhwa, T. (2024). *Guidance and counselling in schools: Theory and practice*. Taylor & Francis.

Reeves, P., Ng, S. L., Harris, M., & Phelan, S. K. (2022). The exclusionary effects of inclusion today:(re) production of disability in inclusive education settings. *Disability & Society*, *37*(4), 612–637.

Rehmat, S., Ahmed, S. Z., & Sultan, S. (2025). Intersectional Stigma's Consequences on Transgender Students' Mental Health, Motivation, and Academic Performance. *Social Science Review Archives*, *3*(1), 493–511.

Reimers, F. M. (2024). The sustainable development goals and education, achievements and opportunities. *International Journal of Educational Development*, *104*, 102965.

Republic of South Africa. (1996). *Constitution of the Republic of South Africa*. Government Printer.

Reygan, F., & Steyn, M. (2017). Diversity in basic education in South Africa: Intersectionality and critical diversity literacy. *Africa Education Review*, *14*(2), 68–81.

Rizova, E., Keskinova, A., Georgievska, S., Stanojkovska Trajkovska, N., Demetriou, K., Borges, F., Vieira, R., & Lazova, L. (2023). *Research for Best Practices of Inclusion of Adults with Disabilities on the Labor Market*. Elena Rizova.

Sabela, P. T. (2023). Inclusive Education: Challenging Barriers, Claiming Human Rights and Social Justice. In Maguvhe, M. O., & Masuku, M. M. (Eds.), *Using African Epistemologies in Shaping Inclusive Education Knowledge* (pp. 15–30). Palgrave Macmillan., DOI: 10.1007/978-3-031-31115-4_15

Sadiki, M. C., & Mpya, N. G. (2024). Best inclusion practices for students with disabilities in contact and ODeL institutions of higher learning. In Maguvhe, M. O., Mpya, N. G., & Sadiki, M. C. (Eds.), *Handbook of research on inclusive and accessible education* (pp. 329–344). IGI Global.

Sait, W. (2023). *An exploration of disability experiences and responses of disabled persons and their families within Muslim culture of the community of Strand, South Africa* (Unpublished doctoral dissertation). Stellenbosch University.

Samsari, E., Nikolaou, G., & Palaiologou, N. (2025). Multicultural Education and Students with Special Needs: A Case Study from Greece. *International Journal of Disability Development and Education, 72*(1), 134–148.

Santamaría Graff, C. (2021). Co-investigation and co-education in 'family as faculty'approaches: A repositioning of power. *Theory into Practice, 60*(1), 39–50.

Saunders, L., & Wong, M. A. (2020). Critical pedagogy: Challenging bias and creating inclusive classrooms. *Instruction in libraries and information centers.*

Sayed, Y., Motala, S., & Hoffman, N. (2017). Decolonising initial teacher education in South African universities: More than an event. *Journal of Education, 68*, 59–91.

Sepadi, M. D. (2023). *Investigating the Content Knowledge of Teachers' Continuous Professional Development Programmes for the Implementation of Inclusive Education in Limpopo Province* (Doctoral dissertation, University of Limpopo).

Shabangu, B. (2021). *Investigating (possible) tensions and possibilities of decolonising History curriculum as a locus to foster inclusive education in South African schools* (Unpublished doctoral dissertation). University of the Witwatersrand.

Shongwe, S. (2024). Strengthening care and support to accommodate learners with diverse needs as equal participants in inclusive education settings. In Maguvhe, M. O., Mpya, N. G., & Sadiki, M. C. (Eds.), *Handbook of research on inclusive and accessible education* (pp. 228–243). IGI Global.

Souto-Manning, M., Martell, J., & Álvarez, B. (2024). *Reading, Writing, and Talk: Teaching for Equity and Justice in the Early Grades.* Teachers College Press.

Starck, J. G., Hurd, K., Perez, M. J., & Marshburn, C. K. (2024). Interest convergence and the maintenance of racial advantage: The case of diversity in higher education. *The Journal of Social Issues, 80*(1), 272–307.

Thulo, A. (2024). Teachers' perceptions on integration of information and communication technology in History teaching and learning at five high schools in Maseru (Master's thesis, National University of Lesotho).

Tiwari, D. N. (Ed.). (2023). *Towards inclusive societies: Psychological and sociological perspectives.* Taylor & Francis.

Townsend, R. C., Huntley, T., Cushion, C. J., & Fitzgerald, H. (2020). 'It's not about disability, I want to win as many medals as possible': The social construction of disability in high-performance coaching. *International Review for the Sociology of Sport*, *55*(3), 344–360.

Ugalde, L., Santiago-Garabieta, M., Villarejo-Carballido, B., & Puigvert, L. (2021). Impact of interactive learning environments on learning and cognitive development of children with special educational needs: A literature review. *Frontiers in Psychology*, *12*, 674033.

UNCRPD (United Nations Committee on the Rights of Persons with Disabilities). 2016. General Comment No. 4 (2016), Article 24: Right to Inclusive Education. https://www.refworld.org/docid/57c977e34.html

UNESCO. (1994). *The Salamanca statement and framework for action on special needs education*. Unesco.

UNESCO. (2020b). Towards inclusion in education: Status, trends and challenges. The UNESCO Salamanca Statement 25 years on. Paris: UNESCO. https://unesdoc.unesco.org/ark:/48223/pf0000374246

United Nations Educational, Scientific and Cultural Organization. (2018). *Education for all: Global monitoring report*. UNESCO. https://unesdoc.unesco.org/ark:/48223/pf0000265866

van Zyl, M. S. M. (2023). *Full-service school teachers' experiences of support* (Unpublished doctoral dissertation). Stellenbosch University.

Waisath, W., McCormack, M., Stek, P., & Heymann, J. (2024). Dismantling barriers and advancing disability-inclusive education: An examination of national laws and policies across 193 countries. *International Journal of Inclusive Education*, *28*(10), 2088–2103.

Walton, E. (2023). Why inclusive education falters: A Bernsteinian analysis. *International Journal of Inclusive Education*, *27*(10), 1–15. DOI: 10.1080/13603116.2023.2241045

Warnes, E., Done, E. J., & Knowler, H. (2022). Mainstream teachers' concerns about inclusive education for children with special educational needs and disability in England under pre-pandemic conditions. *Journal of Research in Special Educational Needs*, *22*(1), 31–43.

Whitehead, S. N. (2023). *Proposing clinician competency guidelines for the inclusion of disability in the undergraduate medical curriculum of South Africa: An exploratory study* (Doctoral dissertation, University of Cape Town).

Chapter 8
Teachers' Experiences of Participating in an Inclusive Education Professional Development Program

Lawrence Meda
Sharjah Education Academy, UAE

Laila Mohebi
https://orcid.org/0000-0003-2640-4532
Zayed University, UAE

Areej ElSayary
https://orcid.org/0000-0002-5554-0069
Zayed University, UAE

ABSTRACT

Education worldwide has seen significant shifts, requiring teachers to adapt to diverse student needs. In the UAE, numerous professional development sessions were organized to promote inclusive teaching practices. However, many teachers struggled to fully grasp the concept of inclusive education and lacked the skills to implement it effectively. This study explored teachers' experiences after completing a six-month professional development program on inclusive education. Using a qualitative approach, fourteen teachers from eight UAE schools were interviewed. The findings revealed that, despite initial challenges, participants experienced

DOI: 10.4018/979-8-3373-7163-4.ch008

transformative growth, gaining the skills necessary to implement inclusive teaching. The study concluded that professional development is essential in enabling teachers to teach inclusively.

INTRODUCTION

Participation in inclusive education professional development programs became so ubiquitous and widespread across different countries during the time of COVID-19. Many teachers did not know how to implement inclusive pedagogical approaches consistent with online learning. Addis, McNulty and Duggett (2021) argue that the number of vulnerable students who dropped out of school due to COVID-19 doubled since the pandemic started. The World Bank (2020) expressed a similar view that a significant number of children had left school since the beginning of the pandemic due to the unmet nature of their diverse learning requirements. This could have been because children were affected by the pandemic or some teachers simply did not know how to accommodate children's needs in online settings. Students with exceptional learning needs bore the brunt of the tumultuous instructional transition from face-to-face to online learning. This resulted in the provision of numerous professional development programs aimed at enhancing teachers inclusive pedagogical practices during the time of the global pandemic. The pandemic highlighted teachers' need for adaptability and new skills, but inadequate training led to negative experiences, especially with students with disabilities (Alhammadi, Meda, Efthymiou, Williams, & Fteiha, 2024). In the United States of America, special needs students were given additional learning resources and support to help them learn during the pandemic (Enos, 2020). Similarly, special needs students in Germany were supported with learning materials that enhanced their learning experiences (Ludeman & Schreiber, 2020).

The United Arab Emirates (UAE) took a different approach to supporting special needs students in schools during COVID-19. An inclusive education teacher professional development (TPD) program was developed to equip teachers with strategies to support children with disabilities and learning differences. This was done to help "build more inclusive, efficient and resilient education systems," stronger than the one which existed prior to the COVID-19 global pandemic (World Bank, 2020). While inclusive education Teacher Professional Development (TPD) programs were already available in the UAE before the onset of the COVID-19 pandemic, various higher education institutions and organizations introduced TPD initiatives to enhance the overall education quality in the country. For examples, a federal university in the country initiated professional development for teachers to help them improve pedagogy and inclusion (ElSayary,Mohebi & Meda, 2022).

Supporting students with special needs in both conventional classroom settings and online learning venues became the main focus of inclusive education TPD during the pandemic (Alhammadi et al., 2024). Many professors had no prior experience teaching online, which made this move necessary (Enos, 2020).

When examining the significance of Teacher Professional Development (TPD), it is essential to recognize its pivotal role in implementing innovative teaching methodologies and establishing effective teaching and learning environments. As the name suggests, TPD entails offering support to teachers with additional information which can help them improve their pedagogy. TPD is not only limited to pedagogy, but also acquisition of content knowledge (Chitiyo et al., 2019). Several studies conducted in various regions support this assertion. The pandemic compelled educators to implement inclusive teaching practices, underscoring the necessity of technological professional development programs for inclusive education in the United Arab Emirates. It is important to note that inclusive education-focused TPD programs are not new. Needs studies were carried out in Zimbabwe and Ghana to determine the unique needs of educators, which provided the basis for customized programs (Chitiyo et al., 2017, 2019). These research findings underscore the overarching significance of TPD in enhancing teaching practices, ultimately benefiting students and fostering the principles of inclusive education.

In the UAE context, Meda et al. (2023) conducted a study about teachers' readiness to teach in inclusive classrooms and their perceived challenges. The study revealed a compelling need for professional development in inclusive education, primarily because a significant portion of educators were general education teachers. These teachers encountered considerable difficulties in adequately addressing the requirements of special needs students within mainstream classroom settings. The challenges encountered by general education teachers concerning inclusion often result in negative attitudes toward inclusive education as a whole. This sentiment is substantiated by Badr (2019), who posits that teachers in the UAE exhibit varying reactions and attitudes regarding inclusive education and the support of special needs students.

A recent study by Alhammadi (2024), titled "Assessing the Efficiency of Education Programs in Emirati Universities for Equipping Pre-Service Teachers in Inclusive Education," found that although the majority of pre-service teachers held positive attitudes toward teaching students with special educational needs and disabilities, about 50% felt unprepared for such work. Furthermore, around 70% of these teachers indicated they had received little to no training in this area. As a result, this inadequate preparation means that teachers often graduate lacking the necessary knowledge and experience to effectively educate students with SEND (Alhammadi, 2024).

In inclusive education, teachers play a critical role in understanding each student's unique needs and implementing interventions to support their independence and participation. This includes creating tailored teaching methods, using educational strategies, and fostering an inclusive environment. Their influence is crucial to student success, with inadequate psycho-pedagogical skills and training increasing failure rates for students with special needs (Alhammadi et al., 2024). There is global recognition for the need to train all educators to implement inclusion effectively in mainstream schools (Meda, Efthymiou, AlHammadi, Williams, & Fteiha, 2023).

Consequently, a clear need arises for Teacher Professional Development (TPD) to enhance their understanding of inclusion and instigate a shift in their attitudes toward implementing this concept within classroom settings, as highlighted by Alzyoudi et al. (2021). Most UAE-based teacher preparation programs prepare general teachers to work in inclusive classrooms rather than special education classrooms. TPD is crucial in assisting in the capacity building of educators. The UAE offers TPD programs that are based on inclusive education, which can support students with various learning disabilities like attention deficit hyperactivity disorder (ADHD) and autism spectrum disorder (ASD), as well as learning difficulties like dyslexia, dysgraphia, and dyscalculia (Meda et al., 2023).

Enos (2020) postulates that teachers needed all the necessary support to help them adopt and adapt to the new teaching and learning environments during the time of the pandemic. The teachers required assistance in improving their teaching effectiveness and providing comprehensive support to their students, particularly in addressing the diverse needs of special education children in an online learning environment. Before the onset of COVID-19, there was a recognized need for Teacher Professional Development (TPD) to enhance teaching experiences by augmenting educators' knowledge and skills in meeting the requirements of students with diverse learning needs (Jenkins & Yoshimura, 2010). With the advent of the COVID-19 pandemic, the provision of professional development has intensified. The study explores teachers' experiences in a six-month inclusive education professional development program while focusing on a single research question: What were the teachers' encounters while participating in an inclusive education professional development program? The objective was not to enhance the training sessions provided by Ta'alouf, but rather to share the insights and best practices of the teachers.

Context of the Study

The Ta'alouf Program forms a crucial part of the Al Jalila Foundation outreach, with "Ta'alouf" meaning harmony or togetherness in Arabic. Launched in 2013, the program is dedicated to supporting children of determination, employing a two-fold approach that focuses on both parents and educators to enhance learning and opportunities for these children. The initial aspect of the Ta'alouf Program is the Parents Training Program, which is generously sponsored and funded by the non-profit organization Al Jalila Foundation. Since September 2013, approximately 1100 parents and caretakers have graduated from the program. In addition, a total of 212 parents/caretakers successfully completed the training program in the most recent cohort, Cohort 22. Over time, the Parents Training Program has evolved, transitioning from 12 sessions to a more practical format delivered over five days. This training includes essential topics such as "legal rights of child and adolescent people of determination" and "the rights of people of determination and their protection from sexual harassment." The second facet of the Ta'alouf Program is an all-encompassing initiative with the goal of heightening teachers' understanding of inclusive education and improving their abilities and knowledge in assisting children with special needs in their respective schools. As outlined in the project's objectives, the program strives to provide training for teachers at the lower primary school level (Wiens et al., 2022).

A government university in the UAE collaborated with Ta'alouf to offer a special education teacher training program, a project led by the Al Jalila Foundation. The program was part of teachers' continuous professional development and focused on teaching and supporting students with different disabilities and learning differences. It had about 63 participants, including teachers, heads of schools, social workers, and learning support assistants from 15 different schools across the UAE. The learners enrolled in the program for six months and covered topics including inclusion laws, the gifted and talented, learning difficulties, physical disabilities, intellectual disabilities, ADHD, hearing/sight impairment, and ASD. Each participant in the program was mandated to attend lectures and sessions with mentors. At the end of the program, after completing all the requirements, including assessments, participants were issued certificates.

Theoretical Framework

Kirkpatrick's model was used as a theoretical framework for this study. The model comprises four levels: reaction, learning, behavior, and results (Kirkpatrick, 1975).

Level 1: Reaction - this shows how participants received the training program. It shows participants' interest in the training and the extent to which they were connected and engaged with trainers during the program (Kirkpatrick, 1975). Reaction also includes whether participants found the program to be enjoyable or not. It is basically about the reaction of program participants; as Kirkpatrick (1975) states, it is how well trainees like or dislike the program. This is relevant to this study as all teachers who participated in the program had some reactions after completing the six weeks of training.

Level 2: Learning - this focuses on how participants acquired knowledge and skills from the program. It is also about how well the objectives have been achieved (Thackwray, 2013). If they are all achieved, it means participants have acquired the intended knowledge. This is relevant to this study, where teachers acquired new knowledge and skills related to inclusive teaching and changed attitudes towards teaching students with special needs in mainstream classes.

Level 3: Behavior - this focuses on applying knowledge, skills, and attitudes acquired during a training program in a participant's workplace or real-world (Kirkpatrick, 1975). This is relevant to this study as the primary objective of the professional development program was for teachers to learn knowledge and skills about inclusion so that they could apply these in their schools.

Level 4: Results - this is about checking whether the outcome was achieved or not (Kirkpatrick, 1975). This is related to this study, as a survey was conducted to check whether outcomes were achieved or not.

Kirkpatrick's four-level model was selected as the most appropriate framework for this study as it is a good starting point for evaluating a training program (Thackwray, 2013), and it is ideal for evaluating participants' experiences using the levels. According to Thackwray (2013), the model is commonly used by organizations to evaluate impact and it can also be used in academia.

METHOD

The research used an interpretive paradigm as the aim was to explore the teachers' experiences and understand from their perspective if the inclusive education TPD program was effective. An interpretative paradigm allows the researcher to extract meaning rather than just objective information, yielding rich and contextual knowledge about the situation (Elliott & Timulak, 2021). The current research also used qualitative methods for collecting data since a qualitative approach is most suited to an interpretive paradigm and allows for collecting in-depth, detailed, and contextualized information from the subjects (Ezer & Aksüt, 2021). As such, the research was conducted using qualitative one-to-one interviews based on semi-structured questionnaires. The interview questionnaires contained open-ended questions that explored the teachers' perceptions about the inclusive education program. The questions were specifically tailored using the Kirkpatrick Model (1975). They explored the teachers' reactions to the program, what they learned during the program, if they could apply their learning or change their behavior after participating, and the overall results. It also required the participants to recount any challenges they may have faced during the program.

A semi-structured interview enable the researcher to probe more questions based on the participant's response and at the same time remain focused to the aim of the study. The method is useful when the participants' feelings, reactions, and beliefs around a particular topic are to be explored (Mahat-Shamir et al., 2021). Semi-structured interviews also allow the researcher to digress and explore additional relevant areas and obtain more open and contextualized thoughts from the participants (Evans & Lewis, 2018). Therefore, The researcher conducted the interviews by asking the questions and allowing the teachers to give their answers in detail. In addition, due to the semi-structured nature of the interview, the researcher could also pose additional questions or steer the conversation in a manner that could yield maximum input on the relevant topics. Interviews also allowed the researchers to capture cues from body language and voice intonations and thus add to the contextual data that is substantially useful for interpretive research (Elliott & Timulak, 2021).

Fourteen teachers were selected from among the attendees of the six-month inclusive education TPD program in the UAE in 2021/2022. A purposive sampling method was used to include those teachers (out of the 63 participants from 15 different schools who had participated in the inclusive education program) who were accessible and available, had the time, and were willing to participate in the study. The study participants were educators with different specializations, such as teachers, social workers, and learning support educators working in private and governmental schools. A random sampling method was not used, though it has the advantage of being completely unbiased and based on chance, which cannot be said of the purposive sampling method (Bhardwaj, 2019). Purposive sampling was better suited for the current study as it enabled the researcher to select participants likely to provide detailed voluntary insights about their reactions, learning, behavior, and results.

One interview was conducted after the training; the data was transcribed and analyzed using the content analysis method. The content analysis approach was Thematic Content Analysis, which involved data coding and constructing themes to interpret and describe the results (Evans & Lewis, 2018). The analysis was done manually by reading the interview transcript multiple times, noting any similarities or differences in responses to questions, and then ascribing codes to responses for further categorization (Guest et al., 2020). The results were then presented as themes that emerged from the analysis.

The data analysis began with a thorough data immersion process, where interviews were examined to understand teachers' experiences in the inclusive education professional development program. Initially, an open coding approach identified codes like "Enhanced Inclusion Strategies," "Increased Confidence in Inclusive Teaching," and "Improved Classroom Practices," categorized under "Positive Experiences." Constant comparative analysis refined these codes, creating sub-codes like "Customized Lesson Plans" and "Tailored Support for Diverse Learners" to reflect different dimensions of professional growth in inclusive education.

A comprehensive codebook was developed to maintain rigor and consistency, providing clear definitions and inclusion criteria for each code. Diligent inter-coder reliability checks were conducted, with multiple researchers coding the data independently and discussing to reach a consensus on the coding decisions.

Prominent emergent themes like "Overcoming Challenges" were identified, discussing issues like resource constraints and strategies to foster inclusive learning environments. It was emphasized that these themes and codes emerged organically from the actual experiences of the teachers, not existing a priori, underscoring the organic nature of code development. This meticulous approach to analysis ensured the reliability and validity of the findings, providing a solid base for understanding teachers' experiences in the program.

The research was conducted keeping ethical considerations in mind. Ethical clearance was obtained from the university. Participants were given an informed consent form outlining the research's objectives and assuring them that their involvement was entirely voluntary. They were requested to sign this form before commencing the interviews (Husband, 2020). The interviews were conducted at a convenient location and time for the participants, and their safety and security were assured at all times. The participants' personal contact information and other details were not shared with any third party to ensure their privacy. Confidentiality was also maintained as none of the participants were identified by their names or any other identifiable references in the report. The participants were made aware that they could leave the research at any time they deemed to do so without any fear of repercussion (van der Weele & Bredewold, 2021). One notable limitation of the research is that the participants had only undergone an online training mode. As such, the findings may not apply to training programs that are conducted face-to-face.

RESULTS

Results of this study show that teachers gained comprehensive knowledge about inclusive education through participation in the program. Despite challenges that some teachers noted, the majority praised the program. They recommended that it be offered to all classroom practitioners as that would help improve inclusive pedagogical practices in the country. The study results were categorized into two main themes: positive experiences and challenges encountered.

Positive Experiences

Teachers reiterated that participation in the program was very helpful as it enabled them to gain in-depth knowledge about inclusion. One teacher said:

"I was very pleased to be enrolled in this program. This was my first time taking such a professional development course, and I learned a lot. I liked the content and material given and the way the sessions were conducted. They were informative."

Similarly, another teacher said:

"The program was eye-opening. I now understand much information about teaching and supporting special needs children in a mainstream class. I learned that I must know each student and their special needs first and then provide individualized support. The program made me understand more about special needs students and the issues they often face."

The program was not only beneficial to classroom practitioners but also to school administrators. This was reiterated by one principal who said:

"As a school principal, I do not teach special needs students. By taking this program, I recognize that I missed a lot of information about dealing with these kinds of students, investigating their needs, and adjusting the learning objectives and learning activities to meet their needs. The program helped me learn all of that, which was really beneficial."

In terms of improving instructors' awareness of inclusion and their comprehension of the various needs of students, the program was a significant accomplishment. It helped them understand how to put the needs of the kids first and use those needs as a springboard for effective teaching and learning. Participant "The program helped us to focus on the needs of children and to prioritize all the learning needs that they require to learn successfully" backed up this claim. I gained the ability to pinpoint children's precise needs and then base their education around those needs. The curriculum combined theory with practical application. Reading materials and collaborating with schoolchildren on case studies were the main foci of the program. This helped teachers develop a better understanding of the concept of inclusion. A participant reiterated this by saying:

"We usually read about special education in documents. But, I had an in-depth study of the content of this program and understood it. We saw how having special needs students in our classes and schools is useful. I have learned many ideas which I can use to support special needs children in my class. That is what I liked most about this program."

For some teachers, the program was more like a refresher course as they had studied a module about inclusive education during their pre-service training. For such teachers, the refresher course was informative. This was confirmed by a participant who said:

"I graduated from a university in the UAE and studied special needs. That was like four years ago. So, for me to review everything and understand the different roles of people there to support you if you have a child with special needs in your classroom, that was very informative to learn about and explore more about."

Similarly, another participant who had previously studied a course on inclusive education reiterated the idea of a refresher course, saying:

"I had a very positive experience. It was good. It was more of a refresher course because I have my certification in special education. So, everything was just like a refresher for me."

Teachers praised the program as it was conducted collaboratively. Teachers were assigned some assignments to complete in groups, and interaction enhanced teachers' knowledge about inclusive education. One participant supported this statement, saying:

"I never regret participating in this program. Each discussion group I was part of always increased my balance of information and, of course, the knowledge outcome that benefits students with disabilities and talented students, exactly as stated in the program. I had some shortcomings in some information before I participated in the program. But today, I understand new strategies."

Teachers learned from each other's best practices and experiences through a collaborative learning approach used in the program. This was confirmed by a participant who said:

"There was a lot of cooperation between us, and we could communicate despite distance and time differences. However, we could benefit from each other's experiences through groups and our communication, like transferring experiences or exchanging experiences between teachers."

Another participant echoed the same sentiments about learning from each other, saying:

"What I like about this program is that it helped us share ideas with different teachers from different schools at different levels. Information sharing was not only limited to teachers at my school but also extended to teachers in other schools. That helped us to get more information about different topics related to inclusive education."

Some participants praised the program for enabling them to research collaboratively and learn from the experience. A participant supported this statement by saying:

"As for the positives of the program, first, they made us do the same research together. We use the available material in the program and connect them to reality. We use examples as proof. This helped me a lot in doing more research related to a specific problem."

Challenges Encountered

Despite the unanimous positive feedback from all participants, a few highlighted challenges they faced and successfully addressed to complete the program. The greatest challenge was that the internet connection was designed to limit any video conferencing platform other than Microsoft Teams. All government schools and selected private schools use Microsoft Teams for synchronous learning. They do not allow using other applications like Zoom and Google Meet, which was a challenge as the professional development program had synchronous sessions conducted using Zoom.

A participant reported a challenge regarding connection, saying: "The program was using Zoom application, which we had trouble using at our school. The Ministry of Education does not use Zoom applications in schools. We use another application called Microsoft Teams. So, connection was a challenge." Similarly, another participant echoed the same sentiment: "Sometimes, the network service would not work in school, so we could not open the Zoom application." Another participant said: "the main challenge was internet. There were a lot of internet issues, and it was nobody's fault. You know, the internet does what it wants to do when it wants to do it. So that was one of the challenges."

The situation forced some participants to use their own phone network data to access all synchronous sessions. A participant confirmed this, saying: "the main technical challenge we faced was that Zoom application was not opening at our institution. So, we had to connect to our private internet services." Another participant who used her private phone data to access Zoom said:

It was hard to attend Zoom sessions using the internet in government schools. If you connect to Zoom while at school, it was only for about five minutes, and then it is disconnected because I guess it is not a permitted platform in a school network. So, we ended up using our own data.

Another challenge that many participants reiterated is related to time. The program was conducted during school times, and teachers were expected to ask permission to attend the sessions. In some schools, teachers were granted permission to miss school and attend the program. However, in other schools, they had to attend program sessions while in class teaching children. A participant confirmed this, saying:

> *"My biggest challenge was time. As a teacher, it was very hard for me because sometimes I used to be in a class (with young children) and opening the camera for the course. And sometimes I miss a lot because of the time. It was very hard for me as a professional staff to sit for six hours in school."*

Some teachers who experienced the same challenge of time constraints said: "the most difficult thing was time for the course. It takes the whole working day, especially since we have difficult classes to distribute to backup teachers." One teacher said: "The challenge that we faced was only time. Sometimes, it did not suit us." Another teacher said: "Timing was my only problem. It was hard to attend sessions as I had classes to teach."

Two participants reported that they preferred face-to-face or blended learning as opposed to online learning. The first participant said:

"One of the challenges that I faced was that the program was online. I think everyone has a different learning style. For me, sitting in front of the laptop for more than one hour and listening to a long lecture was very hectic. It would be much more effective if it were interactive face-to-face, more like question and answers rather than just monologue."

The second participant said: "if it were face-to-face, it would have been more beneficial to me." Participants preferred a face-to-face instructional approach in order to have practical activities relevant to the UAE culture rather than online videos from other contexts. A participant supported this by saying: "Most of the case studies and videos presented during the program were not from our culture. They were not from our school, but from other countries. We need real cases from our school and culture."

Even though participants encountered challenges during the program, they unanimously reiterated that the program was informative and worth their time. They gained positive experiences and information about inclusive education far outweighed the challenges and negative experiences.

DISCUSSION

The study used Kirkpatrick's model to interpret and contextualize the findings within the existing literature.

Level 1: Reactions

The findings revealed that the participating teachers mostly responded positively to enrolling and participating in the program. The teachers perceived the program as a good opportunity to refresh their learning of inclusive classroom teaching. They were also satisfied with the content taught to them during the program, as well as with the material that was given and the structure of the program. According to Kirkpatrick (1975), it is important to evaluate the teachers' reactions immediately after the program as it allows the researcher to assess if the teachers liked or disliked the program and if they were engaged with it. Program engagement and active participation in the programs have been linked to enhanced retention of the learning content (Lin et al., 2019). Also, research has found that engagement in professional training is linked to the quality of their learning as well as their ability to apply their learning in the classroom (Gormaz-Lobos et al., 2021).

The findings from the current research indicate that most teachers felt engaged with the program and enjoyed the learning process. However, it was also found that the teachers found it difficult to work with network issues because they could not access platforms other than Microsoft Teams. Further, the teachers often had to participate in the program while in their classrooms as they did not get leave to take part in the course. These conditions indicate the possibility of teachers not being fully engaged with the program, though for non-program-related reasons.

The next step in Kirkpatrick's model (1975) is to assess if the participants perceived that they learned relevant skills and gained knowledge from the program.

Level 2: Learning

The Level 2 analysis using the Kirkpatrick Model (1975) assesses participants' perceptions around the quality of their learning and the relevance of the learned content. It also assessed if the program delivered on achieving the learning outcomes stated at the onset (Thackwray, 2013). As indicated by previous studies connecting teachers' immediate reactions and perceptions of enjoyment and engagement with enhanced learning, the current study also found that most teachers perceived they had gained positively from participating in the program. The teachers recounted their learning experience to include an enhanced understanding of the diverse needs of the children and the acquisition of insights and skills that could enable them to prioritize children's needs and provide them with adequate solutions. The teachers reported that they gained both theoretical knowledge and practical skills, enabling them to understand the concept of inclusion and effectively practice teaching. Another reported learning was related to the program's collaborative nature that helped the teachers learn from each other, share their experiences, and obtain information on best practices.

The above findings are similar to previous research on teacher training programs for inclusive education. Most previous researchers have found that teacher training is essential for imparting teachers with clarity and equipping them with skills to cater for the needs of children with special education needs (Jenkins & Yoshimura, 2010). Other scholars have reported that teachers can learn and retain more when the training space is collaborative and this was also found in the context of the current research.

Level 3: Behavior

The Level 3 analysis using the Kirkpatrick Model (1975) requires evaluating any behavioural modification following the teaching program. This is an essential step as it highlights the actual effectiveness of any training and analyzes whether the training was transferable to practical settings.

The current research found that participating teachers could use the insights and knowledge gained in the training program and apply these in their classrooms to develop a more inclusive learning environment. They also reported acquiring new strategies to ensure that each student's classroom needs were met. Also, by linking theory to practical examples, the program provided the teachers with hands-on approaches to managing inclusive classrooms. However, a barrier to their learning effectively was related to the fact that the program presented them with examples and case studies that were not from their culture, and hence, the local nuances or sensitivities could not be dealt with when it came to putting the learning into practice in actual classrooms. Further, some participants mentioned that they believed they could have benefited further from a face-to-face training program. These findings indicate that there could be a failure when applying the learning in real-life settings, as revealed by some of the research participants (Sasson & Miedijensky, 2020). Therefore, it can be concluded that although the training program was pleasant and helpful for the teachers, there is still a need for the training material to be better aligned with the sociocultural context of the classroom that the teachers must work in. Additionally, previous research found that when training content and references are contextualized to the teachers' background, it results in greater transfer of learning both in the long and short term (Quesada-Pallarès et al., 2018).

Level 4: Results

Proceeding with the Level 4 analysis using Kirkpatrick's model (1975), it was required that the results of the teacher training program be evaluated from the teachers' perspective. As the findings section above shows, most teachers appeared confident about learning the latest knowledge on managing inclusive classrooms. They felt they were equipped to meet the individual needs of all the children in their classrooms. However, since the current study used a self-report method and the results were not confirmed using any observations or document analysis, the findings can, at best, be accepted with caution. This is required as some of the teachers had mentioned the lack of cultural context and alignment of the training content with the local realities, which could impact the teachers' understanding of how best to implement their learning in the unique context of their classrooms. However, since during the training, the teachers were engaged with each other and worked in collaboration with each other, it is likely that they were able to interpret the training content using each other's experiences and insights.

Further, the participants also mentioned that they realized their previous knowledge gaps and were now more open to learning about inclusive education and its practical implementation. This means that the training program helped set the teachers on a path of self-development and self-realization. Teacher attitude has been linked to positive outcomes in inclusive teaching. As such, it can be presumed that the participant teachers would be motivated and driven in their classroom, leading to positive results (Saloviita, 2020). The discussion above reveals that the participating teachers had a predominantly positive experience with the teaching program. They demonstrated an ability to enhance their learning, exhibited a readiness to modify their behaviors and embrace strategies that led to improved inclusive teaching and were on a path toward self-development and lifelong learning.

CONCLUSION

This study embarked on a journey to delve into the world of teachers as they immersed themselves in a six-month-long voyage of inclusive education professional development. The findings emphasize the vital role of such programs in promoting inclusive teaching. Given the current educational landscape shaped by the ongoing COVID-19 pandemic, it is prudent to offer additional professional development opportunities to teachers. These opportunities will enable educators to effectively adapt and implement new teaching strategies, aligning with the evolving instructional demands of our times. Encourage the creation of additional opportunities for our educators to excel as they adapt and mould the constantly evolving landscape of teaching strategies in the age of COVID-19. The provision of inclusive education professional development of teachers helped teachers gain comprehensive knowledge and skills to meet the diverse needs of children in both online and face-to-face teaching. Although the program was mainly conducted online, it also impacted on the teaching of face-to-face classes as teachers learnt from what was taught online and transferred that to their classes which were conducted using hybrid modes in different contexts. It also helped teachers change their attitudes towards accommodating students with disabilities and learning differences. Kirkpatrick's model (1975) provided a solid and relevant framework for evaluating teachers' experiences participating in inclusive education professional development programs.

Limitations and Further Research Directions

The study was limited to teachers who participated in the Ta'alouf training program for the 2021/2022 year. Other teachers attended the same program in 2019 and 2020; however, their experiences were not explored. This opens a door for future research to examine the earlier years' groups and conduct the study using a quantitative approach to understand all participants' perceptions and perspectives about the inclusive education TPD provided. The study was limited to teachers; further studies can explore mentors' experiences of the program and evaluate the program's impact by assessing how inclusion is happening in schools.

Recommendations

This study recommends that there is a need for continuous professional development for teachers to improve the quality of inclusion in the UAE and abroad. There are always new pedagogical approaches that teachers need to know about. Through continuous inclusive education professional development opportunities, teachers can learn new inclusive teaching approaches from their fellow teachers' best practices and inclusion experts.

REFERENCES

Addis, S., & McNulty, R. (2021). *The pandemic's impact on at-risk students, schools, and graduation rates*. National Dropout Prevention Center. https://dropoutprevention.org/wp-content/uploads/2021/03/The-Pandemics-Impact-on-At-Risk-Students-Schools-and-Graduation-Rates.pdf

Alhammadi, M. M. (2024). Assessing the efficiency of teacher education program in Emirati university for preparing pre-service teachers for inclusive education. *Cogent Education, 11*(1). Advance online publication. DOI: 10.1080/2331186X.2024.236996

Alhammadi, M. M., Meda, L., Efthymiou, E., Williams, C., & Fteiha, M. (2024). Exploring pre-service teachers' preparedness for inclusive education amidst COVID-19 distance learning in the UAE. In ElSayary, A. (Ed.), *Interdisciplinary Approach for Educators' and Learners' Wellbeing: Transforming Education for Sustainable Development*. Springer., DOI: 10.1007/978-3-031-65215-8_18

Alzyoudi, M., Opoku, M. P., & Moustafa, A. (2021, December). Inclusive higher education in United Arab Emirates: Will perceived knowledge of inclusion impact positively on university students' attitudes towards learning with peers with disabilities? []). Frontiers.]. *Frontiers in Education, 6*, 793086.

Badr, H. M. (2019). Exploring UAE Teachers' Attitude towards the Successful Implementation of the General Rules in the" School for All" Initiative. *Journal of Language Teaching and Research, 10*(1), 92–103.

Bhardwaj, P. (2019). Types of sampling in research. *Journal of the Practice of Cardiovascular Sciences, 5*(3), 157–157. https://go.gale.com/ps/i.do?p=HRCA&sw=w&issn=23955414&v=2.1&it=r&id=GALE%7CA609784775&sid=googleScholar&linkaccess=fulltext

Chitiyo, M., Hughes, E. M., Changara, D. M., Chitiyo, G., & Montgomery, K. M. (2017). Special education professional development needs in Zimbabwe. *International Journal of Inclusive Education, 21*(1), 48–62. DOI: 10.1080/13603116.2016.1184326

Chitiyo, M., Kumedzro, F. K., Hughes, E. M., & Ahmed, S. (2019). Teachers' Professional Development Needs Regarding Inclusive Education in Ghana. *International Journal of Whole Schooling, 15*(2), 53–79. https://files.eric.ed.gov/fulltext/EJ1224611.pdf

Elliott, R., & Timulak, L. (2021). Essentials of descriptive-interpretive qualitative research: A generic approach. In *Essentials of descriptive-interpretive qualitative research: A generic approach*. American Psychological Association., DOI: 10.1037/0000224-000

ElSayary, A., Mohebi, L., & Meda, L. (2022). The impact of the relationship of social/emotional, cognitive, and behavioral engagements on developing preservice teachers' digital competencies. *Journal of Information Technology Education, 21*, 269–295.

Enos, G. A. (2020). Support students, faculty members during pandemic. *Disability Compliance for Higher Education*, *25*(12), 2–2. DOI: 10.1002/DHE.30869

Evans, C., & Lewis, J. (2018). *Analysing semi-structured interviews using thematic analysis: Exploring voluntary civic participation among adults*. SAGE Publications, Ltd., DOI: 10.4135/9781526439284

Ezer, F., & Aksüt, S. (2021). Opinions of Graduate Students of Social Studies Education about Qualitative Research Method. *International Education Studies*, *14*(3), 15–32. DOI: 10.5539/ies.v14n3p15

Gormaz-Lobos, D., Galarce-Miranda, C., Hortsch, H., & Vargas-Almonacid, C. (2021). Teacher Training's Needs in University Context: A Case Study of a Chilean University of Applied Sciences. [IJET]. *International Journal of Emerging Technologies in Learning*, *16*(09), 119–132. DOI: 10.3991/IJET.V16I09.21389

Guest, G., Namey, E., & Chen, M. (2020). A simple method to assess and report thematic saturation in qualitative research. *PLoS One*, *15*(5), e0232076. DOI: 10.1371/JOURNAL.PONE.0232076 PMID: 32369511

Husband, G. (2020). Ethical Data Collection and Recognizing the Impact of Semi-Structured Interviews on Research Respondents. *Education Sciences 2020, Vol. 10, Page 206, 10*(8), 206. https://doi.org/DOI: 10.3390/EDUCSCI10080206

Jenkins, A. A., & Yoshimura, J. (2010). Not Another Inservice!: Meeting the Special Education Professional Development Needs of Elementary General Educators. *Teaching Exceptional Children*, *42*(5), 36–43. DOI: 10.1177/004005991004200504

Kirkpatrick, D. L. (1975). *Evaluating training programs*. American Society for Training and Development.

Lin, L. C., & Hung, I. C., Kinshuk, & Chen, N. S. (2019). The impact of student engagement on learning outcomes in a cyber-flipped course. *Educational Technology Research and Development*, *67*(6), 1573–1591. DOI: 10.1007/S11423-019-09698-9/METRICS

Ludeman, R. B., & Schreiber, B. (2020). *Student Affairs and Services in Higher Education: Global Foundations, Issues, and Best Practices* (R. B. Ludeman & B. Schreiber (eds.); 3rd edition). International Association of Student Affairs and Services (IASAS) in cooperation with Deutsches Studentenwerk (DSW). https://www.studierendenwerke.de/fileadmin/api/files/210129_dsw_iasas_final_web.pdf

Mahat-Shamir, M., Neimeyer, R. A., & Pitcho-Prelorentzos, S. (2021). Designing in-depth semi-structured interviews for revealing meaning reconstruction after loss. *Death Studies*, *45*(2), 83–90. DOI: 10.1080/07481187.2019.1617388 PMID: 31116652

Meda, L., Efthymiou, E., AlHammadi, M., Williams, C., & Fteiha, M. (2023). Conceptualizing and Reimagining the Future of Inclusive Education in the UAE. *Open Education Studies*, *5*(1), 20220205. DOI: 10.1515/edu-2022-0205

Meda, L., Mohebi, L., El Sayary, A., & Karaki, S. (2023). A Mutually Enriching Inclusive Education Teacher Professional Development Program: Mentors' and Mentees' Reflections'. *International Journal of Evidence Based Coaching and Mentoring*, *21*(2), 51–62. DOI: 10.24384/fv45-1467

Quesada-Pallarès, C., Rebollar-Sánchez, E. M., Fernández-de-Álava, M., & Ciraso, A. (2018). Is in-service teacher training useful? Applying the transfer of learning factors model in mexican schools. In Caudle, L. (Ed.), *Teachers and Teaching* (pp. 1–24).

Saloviita, T. (2020). Teacher attitudes towards the inclusion of students with support needs. *Journal of Research in Special Educational Needs*, *20*(1), 64–73. https://doi.org/https://doi.org/10.1111/1471-3802.12466

Sasson, I., & Miedijensky, S. (2020). Transfer skills in teacher training programs: The question of assessment. *Professional Development in Education*, *49*(2), 243–256. DOI: 10.1080/19415257.2020.1839783

Thackwray, B. (2013). Effective evaluation of training and development in higher education. In *Effective Evaluation of Training and Development in Higher Education*. Routledge., DOI: 10.4324/9781315041896

van der Weele, S., & Bredewold, F. (2021). Shadowing as a qualitative research method for intellectual disability research: Opportunities and challenges. *Journal of Intellectual \& Developmental Disability, 46*(4), 340–350. https://doi.org/DOI: 10.3109/13668250.2021.1873752

Wiens, B., Karaki, S., & Mohebi, L. (2022). Teacher Training in Inclusive Education: Project Collaboration Between Al Jalila Foundation---Ta'alouf Program and Zayed University. In Coombe, C., Hiasat, L., & Daleure, G. (Eds.), *English Language and General Studies Education in the United Arab Emirates: Theoretical, Empirical and Practical Perspectives* (pp. 445–465). Springer Nature Singapore., DOI: 10.1007/978-981-16-8888-1_28

World Bank. (2020). *The COVID-19 Pandemic: Shocks to Education and Policy Responses*. World Bank., DOI: 10.1596/33696

Chapter 9
Impacts of Mental Health on Educators and Students:
Main Stressors in Academics

Thi Thi Win
https://orcid.org/0009-0004-8717-8983
Lincoln University College, Malaysia

Jahid Siraz Chowdhury
https://orcid.org/0000-0002-1016-0441
Lincoln University College, Malaysia

Zulkarnain Hatta
Lincoln University College, Malaysia

Nor Solehatun Mohd Shakri
Lincoln University College, Malaysia

Noor Atieka Binti Azmi
https://orcid.org/0009-0008-4020-4645
Lincoln University College, Malaysia

Bilkis Bilkis
https://orcid.org/0009-0006-0672-2962
Lincoln University College, Malaysia

ABSTRACT

This chapter explores the critical issue of mental health challenges in academia, which focus on the impacts of excessive workloads, competition, gender inequality, and the COVID-19 pandemic. The findings highlight how heightened expectations, institutional pressures, and the online learning during the pandemic exacerbated anxiety, depression, and burnout. Female academics and students are particularly vulnerable, facing additional stress from societal and institutional gender biases. The chapter adopts a qualitative autoethnographic approach, integrating personal narratives with thematic analysis, which deeply relates academic responsibilities and psychological well-being. It emphasizes the role of socio-economic factors and educational policies in worsening mental health conditions. Recommendations include creating inclusive, flexible learning environments and advancing mental

DOI: 10.4018/979-8-3373-7163-4.ch009

health interventions such as counseling and support systems. This chapter urgently mentions mental health in education to foster a more sustainable, balanced, and effective academic culture.

INTRODUCTION

Within the few decades, a number of stressors has been rising in academia, which threaten the overall well-being of the individuals. A report has shown that almost two-thirds of academics are struggling with mental health problems, including anxiety, grief, depression, and burnout, at some point in their professional life (Bourgeault et al., 2021). "The American College Health Association (ACHA) published a 2022 study, which finds out that about 77% of 54,000 undergraduate college students they surveyed, experienced some kind of mental distress,

There are some major stressors in education sector. During the last 20 years, education sector has experienced a lot of transformation: globalization, competition due to political and economic changes, eroded job security, and the ubiquity of information technology (Lundberg & Cooper, 2010). Nowadays, both educators as well as students face a lot of challenges in the education dynamic, which mainly include increased workloads, expectations, new interventions during covid-19, and gender inequalities. The academics related distress is an important issue to discuss in order to preserve the health and overall well-being of the individuals in education. So that both teachers and students can generate their best performances. Constant psychological pressure can reduce students' motivation to engage with their lessons. This can affect their academic performance negatively due to the lack of efforts. Those facing mental difficulties may also have difficulties in maintaining social relationships, which is an indicator of depression and anxiety, fostering a cycle of social alienation (Grubic et al., 2020). Likewise, Kratt, (2018) expresses "educational leaders and teachers must recognize the importance of their own well-being and take necessary action to maintain a balanced and positive state of mind so that they can best assist the students" Systematic review of available resources from relevant research papers, peer-reviewed articles, journals have been critically collected to answer the main research questions in this paper. All the findings are thematically analyzed to evaluate reliable conclusion.

First, academic workloads cause serious mental health problems such as anxiety, depression, and burnout among students and teachers. Moreover, today's education system is based on the idea of perfection, which means increased competitions and expectations between peers and colleagues in academics. Consequently, they are prone to having mental issues in their daily lives. Job-related stresses are likely to be more ubiquitous in academics than in other professionals (Tytherleigh et al., 2005).

Teachers are subjected to have self-efficacy and higher level of accountability (Anderson, 2006), which adds substantial stress on academics (Catano et al., 2010). As a result of these educational transformation, the physical and mental well-being of people in academic field, increasing their job-triggered stress. The term academic refers all faculty members: all lecturers, graduate students, and research and teaching assistants (Raheleh, 2017). Many researches on stress and academic employment show that, the impacts of job performance and productivity and student learning on physical and mental health is prevalent, although academics have freedom and opportunities (Catano et al., 2010). Similarly, the findings reveal that lots of college students are not satisfied with their student life because of the pressure of academic workloads. Moreover, they struggle to cope with their emotional struggles which affect their over well-being (Karma et al., 2021). Moreover, findings indicate that the number of suicide rates among 15-18 years old have risen in the numbers of schools that offer AP exams (Rindels, 2021). Stress questionnaire shows higher rates of students are suffering from pressures and self-imposed stress (Vahedi, et al., 2014).

Many researches find out the rise of mental health problems in education due to the breakout of covid-19 pandemic, which transform the education structure as a whole. The pandemic has introduced new teaching and learning methods, which require to change the perception of students about the new pedagogy and the best outcomes (Islam & Bhuiyan, 2020). The pandemic imposes lots of psychological problems among university students during lockdowns (Islam & Bhuiyan, 2020). Many teachers and students come from different cultural backgrounds and have stigmatizing views about mental health, however, online learning should be critically evaluated. Tasneem (2020) indicates lacks of assess to technological devices and internet connections in poor families caused in extra stress and frustration on both teachers and students. Undergraduate dental students' perspective of online learning and their physical and mental health during COVID-19 pandemic. Likewise, many teachers reported they have experienced work-related pressures especially in pandemic. Rice et al., (2021) shows the findings that primary school teachers are expected to support students' mental health and transition through school- based interventions. This led extra burdens on teacher despite of having multiple responsibilities. Covid-19 pandemics altered the whole educational functions in different parts of the world. Teachers and students were forced to adopt new teaching and learning methods, which caused inconvenient and additional pressure for them. Additionally, Theurel, et al., (2022) finds that compared to the control group, participation in the online program was associated with higher levels of psychological well-being post-test and fewer clinical symptoms of psychological distress, anxiety, and alcohol consumption. These preliminary findings suggest that the ETUCARE program was a promising multicomponent intervention to buffer the mental health consequences of the COVID-19 pandemic in French university students." In the research done by

Kita, et al., (2022), unfamiliar learning methods caused academic distress in first year students in Japan, and many students said they preferred face-to- face learning environments than virtual learning. As a result of these scenario, they faced negative psychological problems such as mood-disorders, stress, alcohol consumption, depression, and anxiety. "Many reported their concerns about psychiatric disorders such as getting out of control, which is because of the lack of social connections and loneliness. The COVID-19 pandemic was perceived to have impacted on the undergraduate dental students in many ways including their academic achievements, social, mental and physical health. More than half of the respondents had difficulty to focus on their faculty work and feel demotivated. (Etajuri et al., 2022)

Another major factors behind the rise of negative mental conditions among female in academic is gender inequality. This issue has become a common phenomenon among them in higher education who encounter gender-based discrimination and differences. (Oduaran, 2017). "Gender-based discriminatory practices not only affect students' emotional and physical well-being negatively, but they also impair their academic performance (Buchmann, et al., 2019)." Many studies show that girls are susceptible to mental illness than boys, which is mainly because of the fierce desire to get good grades at school (Fröjd et al., 2008).

METHODOLOGY

Autoethnography (Ellis, 2010) is a qualitative research form, an approach to research and writing that aims to describe and systematically analyze (graphō in Ancient Greek, 'writing') personal experience (autós in Ancient Greek, 'self') to understand cultural experience (éthnos in Ancient Greek, 'nation' or 'culture') experience (éthnos in Ancient Greek, 'nation' or 'culture'.

In this paper, a qualitative research of autoethnographic approach is applied to explore the main causes of negative mental health consequences in academia, based on the themes of workload pressures, gender inequality, and the impact of the COVID-19 pandemic. In this chapter, narrative autoethnographies integrated with my autography allow personal-reflection and comparative analysis of primary themes to summarize key finding. Tedlock (1991) narrated "Narrative ethnographies are texts presented in the form of stories that incorporate the ethnographer's experiences into the descriptions and analysis of others. In these the emphasis is on the ethnographic study of others, which is accomplished partly by attending to encounters between the narrator and members of the groups being studied". Relevant ethnographies of teachers and students are used to formulate the primary reasons of mental distress in academia. These involve a variety of data collecting methods including social media posts, personal diaries, interview, discussion and peer-reviewed qualitative literature. The findings are systematically analyzed using reflexive thematic analysis, which include details explanation of each authors' own perspectives, experiences, events, thoughts, emotions in their cultural settings. I utilize my own retrospective burnout story before pursuing my master degree. I recorded how I feel extremely pressurized to get good GPA, have relevant work experience, good English skills, by which I can be a good candidate for scholarship opportunities. During these times, I recorder my burnout journey in my personal diary, which enable me to reflect the causes behind the negative mental well-being in my academic life. By drawing comparisons between my narrative and those of other academics, I aimed to identify underlying causes of negative mental health outcomes in the academic environment, with particular attention to factors such as workload pressures, institutional expectations, and social inequalities.

The autoethnographies used in this paper comes from reliable sources. Hence, this paper evaluates trustworthy conclusions that show the common causes of mental health pressures in education realm. However, the chapter is limited by its nature of generalizability and replicability in drawing credible conclusion, which reduce the authenticity of the individual experiences in their cultural settings. Therefore, the study's findings may not be fully representative of all academic experiences, as they are rooted in the specific cultural and institutional context in which they were written

FINDINGS

Case 1: How does new pedagogy during covid-19 impact on the mental well-being of students in the UK?

Firstly, Rachel Winter and Anna Lavis (2021) explores how online learning during pandemic exacerbates mental health problems among young students in the UK. These findings are based on social media posts and comments written by many young people shared about their negative emotions during covid-19, including suicidal ideation. Lots of students reported mental health problems in students such as anxiety, depression recurred during coivd-19. Regarding the perspectives of digital learning, a wide range of students mentioned "I hate online school. Moreover, adolescents who haven't had mental illnesses before described how virtual education led them to experience "anxiety", "depression", and even worst "suicidal thoughts". Lots of students expressed how they felt demotivated from online learning "school is expecting the same level of work despite COVID", "no more motivation or energy" for studying", and they explicitly pointed out this as a reason behind their failure and lower grades "grade A star" students to "barely passing". Prolonged isolation and lack of face-to-face communications of the classroom environment increase their poor mental health conditions, some refers to being "lonely", which led some to write in social media "losing their grip". Consequently, they grappled to completed their school tasks and assignments, which made them think about "suicide" or "self-mutilation. Ethnographic fieldnotes in August 2020, such as "COVID stole prom/ graduation away from me", express the individuals' dissatisfaction that the pandemic had snatched their experiences. Hence, they are prone to fee; depressed, anxious, and hopeless.

Case 2: What gender-based pressures do girls face in schools?

Another paper written by Lauren Stentiford (2021) is used to analyze the gender related pressures in a wide range of educational institutions, including single-sex school, coeducation, prestigious and non-prestigious schools in Sweden. The author uses interview, discussion and peer-reviewed qualitative literature to explore the relationship between mental health and education related expectations on girls, competitiveness, and imbalance. First, it was found that higher expectations about academic achievement and successful "girl-hood were placed on female students (Odenbring,2019). They were expected to be good not only in academic but also have good appearance, good relationships with people. These ideas of "respectable girl" (Skeggs, 2002) had negative impacts on their mental health and make their lives difficult to survive. Moreover, some girls were discriminated based on social status and ethnicity. A fourteen years old girl who possesses mixed ethnic group (Roeser et al., 2008) experienced cultural discrimination. Similarly, a white British working-class girl faced discrimination due to her learning disability, her teachers mentioned her as a "nice girl" who was "slow and of low ability. As a result, her self-esteem dropped and attempted to suicide at the age of 15. Although she was diagnosed with dyslexic critically, her school didn't provide any special care and support due to the expectation of a "good girl" identity of a normal student. Girls learners in these days are likely to encounter extreme anxiety and mental ill-health due to the emergence of competitive school cultures. The ideal is meant to be "well-rounded" girl as achieving high grades, being popular, being beautiful, having extra-curricular interests, etc. (Walkerdine et al., 2001). "teacher expectations of student success

and institutionalized "performance" regimes (Låftman et al., 2013), and girls often have fierce desire to outdo their peers (Spencer et al., 2018)." Especially these competitions occur in elite schools, girl schools, girls who come from middle or upper background. "Walkerdine et al., (2001) presents the case of Naomi, a middle-class student who attended an elite UK primary and secondary school, and document her mental health struggles from age 10–21 years which manifested in symptoms such as extreme anxiety, long episodes of crying, chronic insomnia, obsessive behavior and eating disorders". Since never ending competition causes them feel that no matter how hard they try it was never enough for them. Due to the nature of higher expectations, discrimination, and competition, female pupils are high risk of having mental issues.

Case 3: How does excessive workloads impact on mental health of academics?

a narrative autoethnography of an academic who experienced mental health problems due to excessive workloads is discussed in cases 3. The author used her personal diary during her three-month breaks from university to reflect her academic burnout experiences and rebuild her identity in her educational context. The author faced difficulties to maintain work-life balance. She had constant stimulations from work, even in her day offs she received emails that asked her to complete urgent tasks. She often failed to resist her work, although she desperately wants to relax and enjoy her free time. Also, she is stressed out that no matter how much she worked hard, it is never enough. Consequently, she always felt exhausted, depressed, weary, and numbed. The author mentioned "identity" tie to the work become the main focus of life leaving little room for personal well-being." She sought professional help to regain her mental well-being and her identity in academia. She expressed the important for seeking support from colleges, or professionals when experiencing mental health and self-identity loss due heavy workloads. The author also encourages to find ways to build a healthy relationship between professional and personal life.

Case 4: What are the contributing factors of worsening mental health in my academic life?

In this part, I will use my own mental health struggles before applying for my masters. I always have higher expectations and ambitions about my education. Before one moth of my final year exam of my bachelor degree, I experienced extreme burnout. Since I was working as an assistant teacher at an international school from 8am till 5pm, I barely had time to study. Since I decided to do master after graduation, I was compelled to study hard to get good CGPA, which will help me get admission at a good university at a foreign country. My working day as an assistant teacher is quite hectic: managing the classroom, students' behaviors, helping the slow learners while standing almost all day long. However, as soon as I arrived home, I get fresh and have a quick dinner, then headed to my study desk to study till 11pm. Since I always felt anxious and worried about not getting the higher GPA and falling behind my peers. Sometimes, I had little self-esteem and confident regarding my education, skills, and work experience because I compare myself with others people from social media who have far higher education levels and working experiences than me. These thoughts made me feel inferior, restless, hopelessness, depressed, and dissatisfied. The reason why I work and study the same time is, I didn't have the working experience before that job. When I search for scholarships and master admission requirements, job experience is a common requirement for doing master. Another reason was that I was going to do the master in non-related field. Therefore, acquiring associated job experiences is required to continue my studies. Another major tension I had is the credibility of my degree, since the education system of our country is far behind when comparing with the higher quality of education in many developed countries such as in the UK. I was always dubious and anxious about not receiving recognition of my degree internationally. Lastly, coming from a middle-class family, my family had a limited budget to support me for studying abroad. Therefore, I had extra pressure to become a qualify candidate for scholarship opportunities. Apart from work and completing my degree, I also had to manage time for IELTS exam. I pressurized myself to get a higher band score, which can also give me a higher chance of getting accepted by prestigious international universities. I was always busy with my studies and work schedules, I hardly had little time for family and leisure activities such as painting, watching movies, or going out with friends. Although I wanted to join my family members who were laughing and chit-chatting about their daily lives, I mostly kept myself in the study room for several hours, which make me feel suffocated and unhappy. I felt like I was missing out the precious moments of my life. At the same time, I was influenced by the desire of working hard for academic success and future plans.

DISCUSSION

All the findings in this chapter elaborates major mental health concerns in education sector. This chapter proved that the nature of workloads, competition, gender and social inequality, and the impact of covid-19 are the significant stressors for people in education.

First, Rachel Winter and Anna Lavis (2021) is used to relate the mental health problems with covid-19 related education interventions among young students in the UK. His findings based on social media content showed that a wide range of young learners suffered from mild to serious mental illnesses during COVID. Particularly, they felt discourage to engage in online learning during the pandemic, which lead them to lose grades. Also, it is found that they were forced to complete school responsibilities from time to time, which cause them feel anxious, depressed, and suicidal. In an existing literature, Jarafri et al., (2023) shows that new expectations related to online learning increased anxiety level in many students. Moreover, students with disabilities such as learning and cognitive problems had difficulties when adjusting new instructional methods and learning expectations from lecturers (Courtenay & Cooper, 2021). Not only that teachers were also expected to adapt to new educational strategies, which makes them stressed. This can be evident in the findings that reveal a high rate of teachers are experiencing stress, anxiety and depression due to new educational adaptations and uncertain guidelines (Santamaría et al., 2021). To sum-up, it can be seen that higher expectations on academics during COVID-19 pandemic impose serious mental illnesses. Therefore, these findings align with one of the themes of this paper. graduate students face greater competition for a tightening pool of academic jobs, funding resources and mentorship (Fullick, 2011).

On the other hand, this chapter also found that gender difference is another cause of mental stress for girls in schools. This is evident in the findings of Lauren Stentiford (2021), which indicate that girl leaners have more academic related expectations than male learners. They are expected to have perfections not only in her academic performance, but also in her looks, social status, interactions, and extra curricula activities. Young girls are expected to think and behave in certain ways regarding the gender stereotypes of a society, however, gender-based discrimination also exist in the same society (Deutsch, 2007). The ones who lacks one of these qualities are prone to discrimination form the peers, teachers, as well as parents. For instance, the author discusses about a 15-year old girl who was discriminated by the school due to her learning disability. This severely damage her self-respect and force her to commit suicide. This shows that teachers are irresponsible with helping the weak learners, and put unreasonable expectations on students. Moreover, girls have the instinct desire to outdo their peers, and which is more prevalent in girl schools and high standard schools. These are the factors that impact the metal well-being of female students. In return, this can impact the overall well-being of the person. This can be witnessed by a middle-class student who encountered psychological, physical, and behavioral disorders. Hence, it is obvious that there is a link between gender and mental health problems in academics

Elaine Campb ll (2018), the negative effect of workloads on mental health of an educator is explored explicitly. This autoethnography shows that continuous work cycle in academia reduce work-life balance, which cause anxiety, depression, burnout, and loss of self-identity for a long time. This prove that today's education dynamics has a high rate of expectation on academic staffs, which deplete mental wellness gradually. This can also be witnessed in a previous literature, Myint, et al., (2024) finds that teacher with increased workloads experienced 30% higher stress rate than their colleagues who had manageable workloads.

These findings suggest that achievement-related mental ill-health comes from fears for the future, particularly, the expectation to get admission at a good university and obtain a good job (i.e. high status, high pay) (Stentiford et al., 2023). Stentiford (2023) explains "Whilst the themes of fears for the future, parent/family-related pressures, competitive school cultures, and gendered expectations of girls' academic achievement emerged strongly in the located texts, we found that it was when pressures were "imbalanced and felt in the extreme that mental ill-health was more likely to be experienced by girls." The NHS Digital reports (NHS Digital, 2017, 2020) demonstrate the high chance of older teenage girls getting more emotional disorders. Regarding the pressure on female teachers, they encounter work-family conflict, although they value both their profession and family roles (Cinamon et al., 2005). Women in academia, who face oppression in terms race, gender, socio-economic status, skills, have greater burden of stress during the pandemic. Therefore, the rights of these women should be maintained despite of their tenure, ability and promotion (Goulden et al., 2011). "Women in academia often hold contingent positions and experience higher-than-average teaching loads. They are assigned more remedial and introductory courses and counsel more students, including more students needing additional support (E. Gibney (2017)".

Many researches proved the rising rate of mental health problems among faculty as well as students due to the burdens of work, competition, and expectation for perfection. Moreover COVID-19 exacerbate their mental health challenges by introducing online classrooms. Many students reported suffering from mental diseases to engage in online learning due to lack of motivation, technological tools, and feeling of isolation. Also, educators were forced to take more responsibilities to adopt new teaching methods as well as to support mental-being of their students. Studies found that gender role expectations and discrimination also impose additional pressures on females in academia. Although all these reviewed papers explain the common causes of psychological issues, there is little focus on the impact of socio-economic status, which can be a significant reason behind poor mental health in education realm.

Comparing my own autoethnography with others' narrative ethnographies, I encountered similar mental struggles related to my academic life, especially when it comes to heavy workloads and competitiveness. A number of students nowadays are concerned with getting high paid and well-respected jobs, which pressurize them to take their studies more seriously starting from high school (Stallman, 2010). Lack of balance between my studies, work and personal life, make me feel miserable both physically and mentally. Moreover, comparing myself with others, I always felt discontent with my own academic abilities and knowledge. Abouserie (1994) finds that competition among college students is the main reason behind academic pressure. Additionally, many authors in media platforms relate increasing rate of anxiety to status competition on campus (e.g., Houshmand et al., 2015). According to my reflexive autoethnography, it is also found that socio-economic factors profoundly relate to academic stress. I had extra burdens of academic workloads due to financial constraint and poor education background, which make me concern about the credibility of my qualifications for further studies. Having higher academic expectations, I pushed myself into overworking. Losing work-life balance, I was subjected to frequent depression, burnout, and lower self-esteem, which impact the overall wellness of my life.

Today' Education system is based on perfection where only the individual with excellent abilities are accepted, and people with defects are excluded. All these factors drive people to work hard till they match with the paradigm, regardless of their mental and physical tiredness. However, this paper has limitation in research methodology, since the findings are generated by generalizing the similar contexts in all ethnographies. The authenticity of each narration is diminished because of the lack of representation of individuals' cultural specialization. Realizing significant contributors of academic stress, policies makers can implement a well-balanced and healthier education environment. Future studies should focus on the integration of welfare programs in educational institutions, where each individual is accepted and respected despite of their inefficiencies in academic performance. As a result, both teachers and students can obtain a positive mental well-being, by which they can achieve their academic potentials to the highest level.

CONCLUSION AND RECOMMENDATIONS

This chapter has critically examined the rising mental distress in academia, identifying key stressors such as academic overload, gender-based expectations, competitiveness, and the structural transformation of education during the COVID-19 pandemic (Chowdhury et al., 2024; Winter & Lavis, 2021). Through autoethnographic narratives and thematic analysis, it becomes evident that students and educators alike are burdened by unrealistic expectations, institutional performance pressures, and socio-economic vulnerabilities, all of which significantly affect their mental health (Campbell, 2018; Etajuri et al., 2022). Female students face disproportionate stress due to gendered academic ideals and the dual burden of social performance and achievement (Stentiford et al., 2023; Fröjd et al., 2008).

This study also emphasizes that mental health cannot be addressed in isolation from systemic issues such as inequality, policy gaps, and socio-economic constraints (Siraz et al., 2020). While the paper presents strong qualitative insights, it also acknowledges methodological limitations due to generalizations and lack of culturally specific ethnographies, which may affect the transferability of findings (Myers, 2014).

Moving forward, it is essential for educational policymakers and institutions to implement inclusive mental health interventions, such as school-based counseling services, well-being workshops, and flexible academic structures that account for individual differences (UNESCO, 2020). Future research should explore the intersectional impacts of class, race, and cultural capital on mental well-being to enable broader and more effective reforms (Chowdhury, Hatta, & Singh, 2025). Moreover, the envisioned "see-saw model" of education should foster compassionate, dialogic, and culturally aware environments, where every academic—regardless of their background or productivity—is supported (Chowdhury et al., 2024).

Finally, constructing an academic culture that values **balance over burnout**, and **inclusion over perfection**, is not just a mental health strategy—it is an ethical imperative for the future of education.

REFERENCES

Abouserie, R. (1994). Sources and levels of stress in relation to locus of control and self-esteem in university students. *Educational Psychology*, *14*(3), 323–330. DOI: 10.1080/0144341940140306

Bourgeault, I., Mantler, J., & Power, N. (2021). Mental health in academia: The challenges faculty face predate the pandemic and require systemic solutions. *Academic Matters*. https://academicmatters.ca/mental-health-in-academia/

Campbell, E. (2018). Reconstructing my identity: An autoethnographic exploration of depression and anxiety in academia. *Journal of Organizational Ethnography*, *7*(3), 235–246. DOI: 10.1108/JOE-12-2017-0067

Catano, V., Francis, L., Haines, T., Kirpalani, H., Shannon, H., Stringer, B., & Lozanzki, L. (2010). Occupational stress in Canadian universities: A national survey. *International Journal of Stress Management*, *17*(3), 232–258. DOI: 10.1037/a0018582

Chowdhury, J. S., Hatta, Z. A., & Singh, S. (2025). Phronesis as a Pathway for the Nature and Development of Pedagogical Content Knowledge (PCK): Seeing Through Indigenous Gnoseology. In Current Trends and Best Practices of Pedagogical Content Knowledge (PCK) (pp. 89-118). IGI Global Scientific Publishing.

Chowdhury, J. S., Vadevelu, K., Hatta, Z. A., Ashraf, M., & Bhaumik, A. (Eds.). (2024). *Reviving and re-writing ethics in social research for commoning the community*. IGI Global.

Chowdhury, J. S., Vadevelu, K., Singh, P. S. J., Saad, M. R. M., & Hatta, Z. A. (2024). *The Intersection of Faith, Culture, and Indigenous Community in Malaysia and Bangladesh*. Springer.

Cinamon, R. G., & Rich, Y. (2005). Work–family conflict among female teachers. *Teaching and Teacher Education*, *21*(4), 365–378. DOI: 10.1016/j.tate.2004.06.009

Courtenay, K., & Cooper, V. (2021). COVID-19: People with learning disabilities are highly vulnerable. *BMJ (Clinical Research Ed.)*, *374*, n1701. DOI: 10.1136/bmj.n1701 PMID: 34261641

Deutsch, F. M. (2007). Undoing gender. *Gender & Society*, *21*(1), 106–127. DOI: 10.1177/0891243206293577

Ellis, C., Adams, T. E., & Bochner, A. P. (2010). Autoethnography: An overview. *Historical Social Research (Köln)*, *36*(4), 273–290. https://www.jstor.org/stable/23032294

Etajuri, E. A., Mohd, N. R., Naimie, Z., & Ahmad, N. A. (2022). Undergraduate dental students' perspective of online learning and their physical and mental health during COVID-19 pandemic. *PLoS ONE, 17*(6), e0270091. https://doi.org/ members' intent to stay: a structural equation modeling approach. Nurs. Health Sci.DOI: 10.1371/journal.pone.0270091faculty

Fröjd, S. A., Nissinen, E. S., Pelkonen, M. U. I., Marttunen, M. J., Koivisto, A.-M., & Kaltiala-Heino, R. (2008). Depression and school performance in middle adolescent boys and girls. *Journal of Adolescence*, *31*(4), 485–498. DOI: 10.1016/j.adolescence.2007.08.006 PMID: 17949806

Fullick, M. (2011). "My grief lies all within" – PhD students, depression & attrition. *University Affairs*. https://www.universityaffairs.ca/opinion/in-my-opinion/my-grief-lies-all-within/

Gibney, E. (2017). Teaching load could put female scientists at career disadvantage. *Nature News*. https://www.nature.com/news/teaching-load-could-put-female-scientists-at-career-disadvantage-1.21839

Goulden, M., Mason, M. A., & Frasch, K. (2011). Keeping women in the science pipeline. *The Annals of the American Academy of Political and Social Science*, *638*(1), 141–162. DOI: 10.1177/0002716211416925

Grubic, N., Badovinac, S., & Johri, A. M. (2020). Student mental health in the midst of the COVID-19 pandemic: A call for further research and immediate solutions. *The International Journal of Social Psychiatry*, *66*(5), 517–518. DOI: 10.1177/0020764020925108 PMID: 32364039

Houshmand, K. (2015, September 18). How to avoid the destructive effects of competition at school. *HuffPost*. https://www.huffpost.com/archive/ca/entry/competition-students_b_8156376

Islam, K. M. A., & Bhuiyan, M. S. S. (2020). Growing importance of ICT in ELT for effective pedagogy during COVID-19 pandemic in Bangladesh. *Journal of ELT and Education*, *3*(3), 106–115.

Kita, Y., Yasuda, S., & Gherghel, C. (2022). Online education and the mental health of faculty during the COVID-19 pandemic in Japan. *Scientific Reports*, *12*(1), 8990. DOI: 10.1038/s41598-022-12985-6 PMID: 35637241

Kratt, D. (2018). Teachers' perspectives on educator mental health competencies: A qualitative case study. *American Journal of Qualitative Research*, *2*(1), 22–40.

Låftman, S. B., Almquist, Y. B., & Östberg, V. (2013). Students' accounts of school-performance stress: A qualitative analysis of a high-achieving setting in Stockholm, Sweden. *Journal of Youth Studies*, *16*(7), 932–949. DOI: 10.1080/13676261.2013.780126

Lundberg, U., & Cooper, C. L. (2010). *The science of occupational health: Stress, psychobiology, and the new world of work.* Wiley-Blackwell. mental health and gender in secondary school. Education Inquiry, https://www.tandfonline.com/doi/full/10.1080/20004508.2018.1558665

Myers, M. D. (2014). Overview of qualitative research. In M. Frenz, K. Nielsen, & G. Walters (Eds.), *Research methods in management* (pp. 87–98). Sage. Myint, L.L., Akkadechanunt, T., Sirakamon, S., Chitpakdee, B.: Factors influencing nursing

NHS Digital. (2017). Mental health of children and young people in England 2017. https://files.digital. nhs.uk/A6/EA7D58/MHCYP%202017%20Summary.pdf

NHS Digital. (2020). Mental health of children and young people in England, 2020. https://files.digital. nhs.uk/AF/AECD6B/mhcyp_2020_rep_v2.pdf

Odenbring, Y. (2019). Strong boys and supergirls? School professionals' perceptions of students'

Rice, F., Ng-Knight, T., Riglin, L., Powell, V., Moore, G. F., McManus, I. C., & Frederickson, N. (2021). Pupil mental health, concerns and expectations about secondary school as predictors of adjustment across the transition to secondary school: A longitudinal multi-informant study. *School Mental Health*, *13*, 279–298. DOI: 10.1007/s12310-021-09432-5

Rindels, J. (2021). *Competition, comparison, and pressure to perform: An analysis of the impact of the Advanced Placement program on suicidality among high-achieving adolescents* (Doctoral dissertation, University of Iowa). https://doi.org/ DOI: 10.17077/etd.0e6x2d1w

Roeser, R. W., Galloway, M., Casey-Cannon, S., Watson, C., Keller, L., & Tan, E. (2008). Identity representations in patterns of school achievement and well-being among early adolescent girls: Variable- and person-centered approaches. *The Journal of Early Adolescence*, *28*(1), 115–152. DOI: 10.1177/0272431607308676

Salimzadeh, R., Saroyan, A., & Hall, N. C. (2017). Examining the factors impacting academics' psychological well-being: A review of research. *International Education Research*, *5*(1), 13–44.

Santamaría, M. D., Mondragon, N. I., Santxo, N. B., & Ozamiz-Etxebarria, N. (2021). Teacher stress, anxiety and depression at the beginning of the academic year during the COVID-19 pandemic. *Global Mental Health (Cambridge, England)*, *8*, e14. DOI: 10.1017/gmh.2021.14 PMID: 34192001

Siraz, J., Wahab, H. A., & Saad, R. M. (2020). Volunteering'as Praxis During COVID-19: Experiences from Bangladeshi Migrant Workers in Malaysia and Indigenous Communities of Bangladesh. *Eubios Journal of Asian and International Bioethics; EJAIB*, *30*(8).

Skeggs, B. (2002). *Formations of class and gender: Becoming respectable* (2nd ed.). Sage.

Spencer, R., Walsh, J., Liang, B., Mousseau, A. M. D., & Lund, T. J. (2018). Having it all? A qualitative examination of affluent adolescent girls' perceptions of stress and their quests for success. *Journal of Adolescent Research*, *33*(1), 3–33. DOI: 10.1177/0743558416670990

Stallman, H. M. (2010). Psychological distress in university students: A comparison with general population data. *Australian Psychologist*, *45*(4), 249–257. DOI: 10.1080/00050067.2010.482109

Stentiford, L., Koutsouris, G., & Allan, A. (2023). Girls, mental health and academic achievement: A qualitative systematic review. *Educational Review*, *75*(6), 1224–1254. DOI: 10.1080/00131911.2021.2010244

Tasneem, S. T. (2020, May 9). Think out of the box to ensure learning continuity. *The Daily Star*. https://www.thedailystar.net/opinion/news/think-out-the-box-ensure-learning-continuity-1898287

Tedlock, B. (1991). From participant observation to the observation of participation: The emergence of narrative ethnography. *Journal of Anthropological Research*, *47*(1), 69–94. DOI: 10.1086/jar.47.1.3630582

Theurel, A., Witt, A., & Shankland, R. (2022). Promoting university students' mental health through an online multicomponent intervention during the COVID-19 pandemic. *International Journal of Environmental Research and Public Health*, *19*(16), 10442. DOI: 10.3390/ijerph191610442 PMID: 36012078

UNESCO. (2020). *Build back better: Education must change after COVID-19 to meet the climate crisis*. https://en.unesco.org/news/build-back-better-education-must-change-after-covid-19-meet-climate-crisis

Vahedi, L. TaleschianTabrizi, N., Kolahdouzan, K., Chavoshi, M., Rad, B., Soltani, S., & Ghojazadeh, M. (2014). Impact and amount of academic self-efficacy and stress on the mental and physical health of university students. *Research and Development in Medical Education, 3*(2), 99–104. https://doi.org/DOI: 10.5681/rdme.2014.022

Walkerdine, V., Lucey, H., & Melody, J. (2001). *Growing up girl: Psychosocial explorations of gender and class*. Palgrave Macmillan.

Winter, R., & Lavis, A. (2021). The impact of COVID-19 on young people's mental health in the UK: Key insights from social media using online ethnography. *International Journal of Environmental Research and Public Health, 19*(1), 352. DOI: 10.3390/ijerph19010352 PMID: 35010612

Yangdon, K., Sherab, K., Choezom, P., Passang, S., & Deki, S. (2021). Well-being and academic workload: Perceptions of science and technology students. *Educational Research Review, 16*(11), 418–427.

KEY TERMS AND DEFINITIONS

Academic Stressors: These are the pressures and challenges faced by individuals in academia, including increased workloads, competition, high expectations, and the demand for perfection in academic performance. These stressors can lead to mental health issues such as anxiety, depression, and burnout.

Autoethnography: A qualitative research method that combines personal experience (self-reflection) with cultural analysis and interpretation. It is used to explore and understand broader societal or cultural phenomena by examining individual narratives and lived experiences. Through self-reflection, the author examines their story within the wider cultural, political, and social contexts. Using this method allows the individuals to focus on storytelling, vulnerability, and self-assessment. This explores the valuable lived experiences, challenges, identities of indviduals, particularly from the vulnerable and marginalized communities.

Gender Inequality in Academia: The unequal treatment and expectations of individuals based on gender, particularly affecting female educators and students. This includes higher academic and societal expectations, discrimination, and the double burden of work-family conflict, leading to negative impacts on mental health and well-being.

Impact of COVID-19 on Education: Refers to the significant changes and challenges brought about by the pandemic, such as the shift to online learning, lack of social interaction, increased anxiety, and stress among educators and students. These changes exacerbated mental health issues, especially for those with limited access to technology or supportive environments. Since COVID-19 disrupted the structure and routine of people in academics, it affects their sleep patterns, social interactions, and academic performance. Especially, vulnerable populations with limited access to mental health resources, safe spaces for learning, or supportive family environments.

Chapter 10
The Evolution of Educational Inclusion:
A Cross-Cultural Analysis of European and Middle Eastern Perspectives on Disability Integration

Enas Majadley
https://orcid.org/0000-0001-5403-3746
Al-Qasemi Academic College of Education, Israel

Islam Asim Ismail
https://orcid.org/0000-0001-5115-3005
The English and Foreign Languages University, India

Jihan M. Aloshi
Al-Qasemi Academic College of Education, Israel

Alaviyya Bahruz Nuri
https://orcid.org/0000-0003-4219-1071
Nakhchivan State University, Azerbaijan

ABSTRACT

This chapter provides a comprehensive cross-cultural analysis of educational inclusion practices in Poland, Israel, and Arab-Israeli contexts. Following the landmark Salamanca Statement, we focus on the formative period of 1994-2014. We examine the evolution toward inclusive educational frameworks while exposing unique challenges shaped by cultural, social, and political settings. Poland's late

DOI: 10.4018/979-8-3373-7163-4.ch010

adoption of inclusion practices highlights the gap between theoretical acceptance and practical application, particularly for students with intellectual disabilities. In Israel, the 'Shiluv' law facilitates inclusive education yet reveals disparities among various educational sectors, with limited success for students with severe disabilities. The Arab-Israeli experience reflects the complexities of "triple jeopardy," where students face societal and educational marginalization. A critical finding across all contexts is the disconnect between policy and practice. Thus, the chapter calls for bridging the theory-practice gap and developing teacher training programs to address these challenges.

INTRODUCTION

Students with disabilities are being integrated into mainstream educational institutions and classrooms through a global human rights initiative focused on incorporating all individuals with disabilities across all life domains (Tiernan, 2021; Tilstone et al., 1998). UNESCO has encouraged the implementation of governmental policies to ensure students with disabilities access to mainstream educational facilities (UNESCO, 1994). Previously, these learners faced exclusion from educational institutions they would otherwise have accessed without their impairments. The 2007 United Nations Convention on the Rights of Persons with Disabilities reinforced this approach through advocacy for non-discrimination, equitable access, appreciation of diversity, and comprehensive participation for all individuals (UNESCO, 2009).

The Arkansas Department of Education (2008) describes special education as free, specialized teaching designed to meet the needs of Students with Special Educational Needs and Disabilities (SEND). This teaching can happen in classrooms, homes, hospitals, and other places where it's needed. Chhabra et al. (2010) also discuss how inclusion developed over time. They demonstrate how society's view of special education has undergone significant changes in recent years. This change has been called integration and mainstreaming, and more recently, inclusion. Integration and mainstreaming essentially mean the same thing - both involve placing students with disabilities in regular schools with standard curricula without making major changes to those curricula.

However, integration does give students extra support to help them adjust to the school's programs and requirements (Uteuova & Amirbayeva, 2025). However, while integration expects the student to fit into the school's way of doing things, inclusion works in a very different way. Inclusion means that regular school systems, teaching methods, environments, and curricula must be adapted to meet the needs of all students, regardless of their abilities. This way, all children can benefit from their education (Freeman-Green et al., 2023; Mittler, 1995).

Special education history reveals significant improvements in how students with SEND were treated during the 1900s. Rodriguez and Garro-Gil (2015) and Buchem (2013, 387-395) break down this historical development into four main stages:

First was exclusion, where people with disabilities were kept separate from society. Second was discrimination - even though society recognized that people with disabilities had the right to education, they were still kept out of social situations. Third was integration, where SEND students were placed in public schools to interact with students who did not have special needs. This occurred by placing SEND students in both regular classrooms and special education classrooms (Franklin, 1996, p. 18). Fourth was inclusion, which began with the "Salamanca Statement." At the World Conference on Special Needs Education, delegates called for "Education for All" (Jomtien, 1999) and established five principles to guide special education policies and practices (UNESCO, 1994: VIII-XIX).

For Palestinian-Israeli children, SEND students face a burden because they belong to a minority group and are also pushed aside educationally and socially (Hager & Jabareen, 2016). This burden underscores why focusing solely on one issue is ineffective. Because these children are Palestinian minorities who also have special needs, they often get overlooked by both Palestinian civil rights supporters and disability rights advocates (Mohammed, 2025). Although research clearly demonstrates the benefits of including children with special needs in regular, less restrictive environments (LRE), implementing this idea in practice has been challenging. Studies show that inclusive education is hard to implement because regular education teachers become overloaded with work and demands, which leads to teacher frustration (Eiken, 2015)

Despite extensive research on educational inclusion and disability integration policies across different regions, a significant gap remains in comparative studies that examine how cultural contexts specifically influence the implementation of these policies, particularly between European and Middle Eastern educational systems. This chapter examines the decade following the 1994 Salamanca Statement (1994-2014), as this period represents a crucial turning point in global special education policy. This timeframe encompasses the initial response phase when educational systems in Poland, Israel, and the Arab-Israeli context first grappled with implementing inclusive frameworks. Understanding these foundational years is critical, as the institutional responses and implementation challenges during this period largely shaped current inclusive education practices and continue to influence contemporary policy decisions. This chapter is unique in that it addresses the cross-cultural analysis of Polish, Israeli, and Arab-Israeli approaches to integrating people with disabilities. It contributes to the existing literature by offering insights into how diverse cultural, social, and political contexts influence inclusive education practices.

These cultural variations and their impact on implementation strategies are important for developing culturally sensitive approaches to educational inclusion. Our focus on the period from 1994 to 2014 is significant for two key reasons. Following the Salamanca Statement in 1994, this period captures how these different cultures first responded to and implemented new global standards for inclusive education. Additionally, this timeframe reveals the early structural and cultural challenges that emerged as these educational systems began their journey toward inclusion—challenges that remain relevant today (Guddad, 2025). To investigate this complex issue, we conducted an extensive review of contemporary research on inclusive education policies and practices across Polish, Israeli, and Arab-Israeli educational systems. We employ a comparative analysis methodology to examine the policy documents, academic literature, and empirical studies focused on disability integration in these regions. Our analysis focuses particularly on educational frameworks, implementation strategies, and cultural barriers to inclusion, drawing on both historical developments and current practices in each context. This cross-cultural comparative approach enables us to identify patterns, challenges, and successful strategies that are unique to each cultural setting.

Based on the short preview above, this chapter aims to examine how different cultural contexts (European and Middle Eastern) approach educational inclusion. We also aim to analyze the implementation challenges and successes in various regions. Specifically, we compare European, Polish, Israeli, and Arab-Israeli educational systems in terms of disability integration. Thus, the current chapter aims to answer the following main question:

> 1- How do cultural and societal contexts in European (specifically Polish) and Middle Eastern (specifically Israeli and Arab-Israeli) educational systems shape their approaches to disability integration, and what are the distinct challenges and implementation strategies in these different cultural settings?

To provide a systematic framework for understanding how cultural contexts shape inclusion policies and practices, the following comparative analysis presents key dimensions across the three educational systems examined in this chapter. This framework lays the groundwork for the detailed analysis that follows and highlights both convergent trends and divergent approaches across Poland, Israel, and the Arab-Israeli contexts.

Table 1. Comparative Framework of Inclusion Policies Across Study Contexts

Dimension	Poland	Israel	Arab-Israeli Context
Key Legislation	Gradual adoption since the 1990s following EU directives	Special Education Law (Shiluv) 1988, amended 2002	Subject to Israeli law but with culturally distinct implementation
Historical Timeline	1773: First Ministry of Education globally; 1990s: Adoption of inclusion; 2013/14: ~160,000 disabled pupils in system	1988: Shiluv Law enacted; 2002: Amendment for equal funding; 2007: Durner Committee recommendations	Same legal framework as Israel; Slower implementation due to cultural factors
Philosophical Approach	**Integration-focused**: Adapting students to school environment	**Individualistic**: Meeting individual student needs	**Community-oriented**: Collective responsibility approach
Cultural Context	Post-communist transformation; EU influence; Traditional Catholic values	Immigrant society; Jewish-secular divisions; Western individualism	Clan-based social structure; Extended family orientation; Traditional Islamic values
Implementation Model	**Hamburg Model**: Requires adequate environment, tools, and team teaching	**Support Center Model**: Special support centers for mainstream inclusion	**Hybrid Model**: Combines Israeli framework with Arab cultural adaptations
Student Population Served	Mild to moderate intellectual disabilities prioritized; Severe disabilities often excluded	8% mild-moderate disabilities in mainstream; 2.25% in special schools; Recent inclusion of Down syndrome students	Higher prevalence due to consanguineous marriages; Double marginalization effects
Teacher Attitudes	**Theoretical acceptance, practical resistance**: 70% unwilling to teach intellectually disabled; Lack of preparation cited	**Negative attitudes**: Feel incompetent; Individualistic approach challenges	**Community-oriented perspective**: Focus on societal building; Less individualized approach
Primary Challenges	Insufficient teacher training; Financial constraints; Shortage of specialized staff; Gap between policy and practice	Negative teacher attitudes; Resource limitations; Excluding severe disabilities; Sectoral divisions	Triple jeopardy (minority + disability + gender); Cultural stigma; Limited services; Traditional family structures
Support Systems	Special personnel (therapists, physicians); Team teaching approach; EU funding and guidelines	Support centers, Special education teachers; Ministry of Education oversight	Limited specialized services; Reliance on family support; Cultural barriers to service access
Success Indicators	Improved exam results in integrated classes; Increased parental involvement; Social inclusion achievements	59.4% SEN pupils in regular classes by 2013; Specialized support systems; Legal framework compliance	Gradual attitude shifts; Emerging advocacy; Slow but steady progress
Barriers to Implementation	Teacher resistance; Inadequate resources; System-wide preparation gaps	Cultural-pedagogical mismatches; Sectoral education divisions; Resource allocation issues	Cultural stigma; Language barriers; Socioeconomic factors; Traditional gender roles

GLOBAL CONTEXT: EDUCATIONAL INCLUSION AS A UNIVERSAL CHALLENGE

The movement toward educational inclusion represents one of the most significant global shifts in disability policy and practice over the past three decades. Twenty-twenty-four marks 30 years since the adoption of the Salamanca Statement on Inclusion in Education; yet, despite widespread policy adoption following international frameworks, implementation remains deeply influenced by cultural contexts and persistent societal attitudes toward disability (Abushihab et al., 2025). Recent research reveals what scholars have termed the "policy-practice gap" - the persistent disconnect between progressive inclusion policies and their actual implementation in educational systems worldwide. A new publication entitled Implementing Inclusive Education: Issues in Bridging the Policy-Practice Gap explores this global challenge in detail, demonstrating that around 40% of countries still do not provide teacher training on inclusion, while laws in 25% of countries make provisions for educating children with disabilities in separate settings, rising to over 40% in Asia and Latin America and the Caribbean. These statistics underscore that while legal frameworks can mandate inclusion, transforming deeply embedded cultural attitudes toward disability requires sustained, culturally sensitive approaches that address stigma at multiple societal levels (Park, 2025)

INTEGRATION IN EDUCATION

Ghergu (2001) offers a comprehensive analysis of school integration concepts. According to Ghergu , school integration involves collaborative participation between students with special needs and their typical peers in educational activities and events, determined by individual student capabilities relative to their classroom counterparts. Subsequently, Ghergu distinguished between authentic school integration practices versus misconceptions (Ghergu , 2006). Genuine school integration prevents isolating special-needs learners from their peers through segregated classroom placement, separate activity participation, or exclusion from extracurricular involvement. Furthermore, school integration transcends the simple admission of special-needs students into mainstream institutions driven by profit motives, particularly when schools lack the requisite competencies and resources (Buenaventura & Gaza, 2025), as well as the preparation to adequately assist these learners.

Verza (1995) said that school integration is when a child learns to meet the school's expectations. However, for Ghergu (2001), it means including special-needs students in school activities alongside regular students based on their abilities. According to Ghergu , integration shouldn't separate special-needs students from other students in classrooms and shouldn't prevent them from participating in school activities alongside their peers.

School integration for students with disabilities has three components: physical, social, and academic integration. Most students with disabilities prefer to be in regular classrooms, and research has shown that learning in these settings is beneficial for them socially. They learn social rules and behaviors, make friends, and figure out what's socially acceptable and what is not (Friend & Bursuck, 2006). These skills, along with motivated teachers, help improve children's learning abilities (Fullan, 1993). Experts agree that teachers' attitudes, thinking, skills, and knowledge are crucial to making inclusion work, especially for regular classroom teachers who include students with disabilities in their classes (Bender et al., 1995; Friend & Bursuck, 2006).

Thomas et al. (1997) explain that integration focuses on meeting the needs of students with special needs by modifying or adjusting the curriculum, incorporating them into regular classes, and providing them with official support. However, inclusion is broader because it works to meet the needs of all students, regardless of their background. It changes school culture, supports teachers, and helps them learn the best ways to teach every student.

Recently, schools that employ inclusive practices have observed stronger values, such as teamwork, participation, sharing, and collaboration (Friend & Bursuck, 2006). Ben-Yehuda et al. (2010) found that teachers who contributed the most to social integration were those who collaborated with other teachers daily. These teachers went beyond just teaching by initiating meetings and learning new teaching methods while continuing to fulfil their regular job duties. Research also indicates that factors such as collaborative work, shared responsibility, taking initiative, planning, teaching, and fostering positive relationships between special education teachers and regular education teachers are crucial for inclusive education to function effectively (Kolleck et al., 2021).

The difference between integration and inclusion is not merely a matter of word meanings. Integration does not require schools to change for children's needs - instead, it expects children to fit into the school's existing curriculum. However, inclusion requires significant changes to the traditional school system, encompassing teachers, curriculum, environment, teaching methods, and the diversity of the classroom.

THE INCLUSION OF CHILDREN WITH SPECIAL NEEDS IN EUROPE

Recent studies highlight a radical shift in the field of educational inclusion. More schools around the globe are increasingly adopting the inclusion of students with SEND in regular classrooms alongside their peers without disabilities, a stark contrast to the previous tendency of admitting students with disabilities to specialized institutions. This shift, often referred to as "inclusion" (De Boer et al., 2011; Hodkinson, 2009), marks a move away from mere integration. Over the past 25 years, the inclusion of students with SEND in mainstream schools has sparked considerable debate (Avraamides et al., 2000).

Inclusive education in the UK promotes the idea that students with special educational needs should be educated in mainstream schools "wherever possible" (DfEE, 1997). Integration emphasizes placement, whereas inclusion aims to reform school systems, curricula, pedagogies, and environments to support all students. Inclusion is about educational placement and embraces broader humanitarian values such as diversity, equality, and human rights (Avramidis et al., 2000; Hodkinson & Deverokonda, 2011). Despite the strong theoretical support for inclusion, its practical definition remains somewhat elusive (Hodkinson & Vickerman, 2009), largely due to its complexity and the range of factors that influence its implementation, including politics and socioeconomics (Hodkinson, 2009).

Countries like the UK have made significant strides in promoting inclusion, whereas others, such as Poland, have adopted these practices more slowly (Starczewska et al., 2012). There are many challenges to the full implementation of inclusion, including economic barriers that impede the individualization of resources for SEN students. Nevertheless, international organizations such as the European Convention on Human Rights and the United Nations Convention on the Rights of the Child" emphasize the need for inclusive practices and oppose exclusionary or segregative methods (Allan, 2010).

International human rights frameworks emphasize the importance of inclusive education. Many countries have shifted from integration to full inclusion, as demonstrated in documents such as the United Nations' 2007 Convention on Human Rights and the Convention on the Rights of Persons with Disabilities (2006). However, despite progress over the past 40 years, challenges persist in implementing inclusion (Ainscow, 2005; Persson, 2006). Ongoing debates indicate that inclusive education remains a complex issue (Sharma et al., 2008), and some critics argue that it may have a negative impact on students (Anastasiou & Kauffman, 2011).

Most EU countries in Europe support inclusive education, but the specific approaches vary according to each country's unique political and cultural context (Hardman, 2008). The move toward inclusion across Europe reflects a trend in which educators are recognizing the importance of student diversity. However, a gap still remains between the theory of inclusion and its practical implementation. National and local contexts often influence the effectiveness of inclusion efforts (Kozleski et al., 2011; Loreman et al., 2011).

Many European countries have adopted inclusive policies that require schools to adjust their curricula, environments, teaching methods, and strategies to meet the needs of all students, regardless of their abilities. However, despite the general acceptance of inclusive education, practical challenges remain. For example, countries like Slovenia have struggled to fully achieve their inclusion goals. Additionally, the confusion between “integration” and “inclusion” often leads to misunderstandings about what inclusive education aims to accomplish (Schmidt & Ksenja, 2015).

On a positive note, studies show that inclusion has been successfully implemented in several European countries (Boyle et al., 2013; Dizdarevic et al., 2017; De Boer et al., 2011). Many studies in the EU have indicated that educators generally hold a positive view of inclusion (Ahsan et al., 2012; Schwab et al., 2015). Teachers in Europe also show strong competence and knowledge in inclusive education (Kavkler et al., 2015; Naqeeb, 2025), which is important for successful inclusion. However, some studies indicate negative or neutral attitudes toward inclusion, especially when teachers work with students who have more severe disabilities or lack proper training (De Boer et al., 2011).

Teacher education is a priority in the EU, with ongoing efforts to ensure teachers are trained to meet the diverse needs of students. The UN's Convention on the Rights of Persons with Disabilities (2006) emphasizes the importance of inclusive education, and Europe recognizes that education is crucial to promoting equality and social justice. However, for inclusion to be successful, teachers need proper training and support during their initial education and careers (Donnelly & Watkins, 2011).

Numerous studies have examined educators' perceptions of inclusion. For instance, a study by Chhabra, Srivastava & Srivastava (2010) reveals that teachers in Botswana expressed concerns about the inclusion of students with disabilities in regular classrooms. A common concern among educators is that inclusive practices may negatively impact the academic performance of all students, and that teachers often feel unprepared for the challenges that come with implementing these practices. Such negative attitudes can have detrimental effects on students' learning and progress (Wilczenski, 1995).

In Europe, organizations and unions that advocate for inclusion, such as the Alliance for Inclusion, Parents for Inclusion (UK), and Equity in Education (Scotland), play a significant role in supporting parents of children with special needs and promoting inclusive policies. Other organizations, such as FUB (Sweden), Inclusion Europe, and various disability-specific associations, including the Dyslexia Association and the Autistic Society (UK), provide essential support for children with specific disabilities. Additionally, organizations led by people with disabilities, such as People First (UK), have successfully lobbied governments to advocate for inclusion, thereby easing concerns expressed by teacher unions (Allan, 2010).

There is still a need for comprehensive laws to support inclusive education. The European Agency for Development in Special Needs Education (2010) emphasizes the importance of aligning inclusive education with other policy initiatives. Inclusion now applies not only to students with special needs but also to all students who are at risk of being excluded. The Council of the European Union (2010) emphasizes the need for personalized learning plans and teaching methods that accommodate diverse learners, as well as the importance of teacher collaboration and valuing individual student differences.

Despite generally positive attitudes toward inclusion in Europe, challenges persist. For example, a study in the UK found that teachers considered including students with emotional and behavioural disabilities to be the most challenging part of inclusive education (Avramidis et al., 2000). In Spain and Italy, educators expressed dissatisfaction with the resources and support available for inclusion programs (Molto, 2003; Cornoldi et al., 1998).

Certain regions in Europe, such as rural areas in Turkey, Ukraine, and Albania, face extra challenges to inclusion, with many children, especially girls, not attending school at all (UNICEF, 2007). These issues underline the ongoing crisis of educational inclusion for minority groups, including children with disabilities, in countries like Belarus, Bulgaria, and the Russian Federation, where many children are institutionalized instead of being integrated into general education. However, higher education enrollment rates in many European countries have risen sharply, even in regions struggling to cope with this growth (Cooc, 2021).

UNICEF and UNESCO continue to promote inclusive education, stressing the link between academic success and equity (Willms, 2006). Comprehensive schools with diverse student bodies often perform as well as, or better than, more homogeneous institutions, largely due to the preparation and readiness of teachers to implement inclusive practices. However, the training of teachers remains a contentious issue, as many believe that preservice teacher training programs are not sufficiently practical to prepare them for the challenges of inclusive education (Acedo et al., 2008). Teachers must be exposed to diverse student populations during their training and develop a shared language and approach to education(Ismayilli & Nuri, 2025). Collaborative work and a commitment to equality, diversity, and social justice are crucial for fostering effective and inclusive education (Guojonsdottir et al., 2008; Saloviita, 2005). The need for specialized training and adequate support remains a critical factor in the success of inclusive education in Europe (Donnelly & Watkins, 2011).

Inclusion in Poland

Historical Development of Inclusion in Poland

Poland's special education system for disabled students keeps changing because of how people now view disabled individuals and shifts in society and politics. These changes have led to the development of inclusive education and the closure of segregated special institutions. This means Poland is getting rid of its old system that kept disabled students apart and moving toward a normal system where all children have the right to education, no matter what disabilities they have. Hodkinson (2010) states that due to this progress, Polish education has become inclusive, welcoming diversity and rejecting segregation and exclusion. These ideas have been growing in Poland for many years and continue to shape the Polish education system (Sekulowicz & Sekulowicz, 2015). Zarebska (2008) notes that Poland now offers job training for young people with intellectual disabilities.

Additionally, the quality of job training for students with disabilities in special education has improved significantly. In the past, job training schools lacked the necessary resources, tools, supervision, and consistent standards to help students with disabilities integrate into the workforce, resulting in outdated skills being taught. However, this problem has now been resolved. Poland created the world's first Ministry of Education (Komisja Edukacji Narodowej) in 1773. As a result, the Polish education system had a significant influence on the establishment of public education across Europe (Parker, 2003). However, for special education, Poland only began using educational inclusion and integration in the early 1990s.

Still, inclusion in regular physical education remains weak and requires collaboration between legislators and education staff (Bełza, 2014; Omianowski, 2008). The Polish Central Statistical Bureau's reports support this observation, showing that in 2013/2014, approximately 160,000 students with disabilities were enrolled in primary, secondary, and middle schools (Central Statistical Office, 2014). Even with these large numbers, physical education for disabled students was still ignored.

Research by Starczewska et al. (2012) on educational integration and inclusion in Poland shows that Polish society's attitude toward disabled people has changed dramatically. While the Polish state recognized and respected the rights of people with disabilities after the 1700s, there was still clear educational separation between people with and without disabilities (Lichtensztejn, 2006). Educational integration was first used in Warsaw only after the 1980s (Grzegorzewska & Wapiennik, 2008).

Aleksander Hulek, a well-known Polish professor who advocates for educational integration, states that Poland views integration as providing the same rights and equal opportunities to both people with and without disabilities. In simple terms, it's about creating connections between people with disabilities and those without to help everyone succeed together (Hulek, 1992).

A considerable amount of time has passed since Poland first attempted an integrative education approach. Integrative education has played a crucial role in facilitating educational progress for people with disabilities, and it has enhanced both the theoretical and practical approaches to it. This progress is evident in society's increasing openness toward people with disabilities (Ostrowska, 2002).

Teacher Attitudes and Training

However, studies examining teachers' views on integrative education have found that they like the idea in theory but are reluctant to implement it in practice. Many teachers were not prepared to integrate students into their classrooms. Minczakiewicz found that "almost 70 percent of teachers from primary schools would not like to teach pupils with intellectual disabilities in their classes" (Minczakiewicz, 1996). Erenc's research also shows that 71% of teachers were against creating integrative classes with intellectually disabled students (Erenc, 2008). Studies also found that teachers were concerned and unwilling to try integrative education because they lacked sufficient knowledge about it and were not qualified to implement it (Chodkowska & Kazanowski, 2007).

In terms of beliefs, integrative education in Poland follows the Hamburg model, which requires schools to have the right environment, tools, technology, and teaching methods to effectively meet students' needs. Polish integrative education also requires teamwork, especially cooperation between two well-trained teachers. Schools are also expected to hire specialized staff, such as therapists, doctors, and speech-language pathologists (Gajdzica, 2009).

Starczewska et al. (2012) acknowledge that their research, which focuses on particular regions and localities, prevents its broad application to Poland's entire educational framework. Nevertheless, integrative education research reinforces general concepts identified in additional investigations. Primary discoveries reveal that most educators possess limited comprehensive knowledge of inclusion, both theoretically and practically, with integrative education serving as the dominant methodology utilised. Polish system data demonstrates that while Poland endorses inclusion principles, integration practices predominate instead. Furthermore, although legislation explicitly guarantees educational rights for all children, integration frequently excludes certain student populations. Research additionally demonstrates that mild to moderate intellectually disabled children typically experience the greatest integration into mainstream Polish educational institutions. However, students with severe physical and intellectual impairments remain excluded from school integration. This investigation also found that primary school educators hold more favourable integration perspectives compared to educators serving older student populations. Educators recognise failures in the educational system's integration of older students into mainstream schools.

Nevertheless, educator attitudes do not have a direct correlation with received training programs, as most educators reported adequate preparation for teaching all children, regardless of their disability status. Data also reveals mandatory special training requirements for some educators, indicating that many professionals did not voluntarily choose to work with disabled students. Consequently, their attitudes toward integration became more pessimistic (Starczewska et al., 2012). Panel research examined investigations into school personnel's perspectives on integrative education, with staff acknowledging both favourable and unfavourable aspects of integrative education. Notably, personnel observed improved internal examination results, increased parental educational involvement, enhanced availability of qualified professionals to meet student needs, improved assessment instruments for disabled students, increased confidence among regular students and their parents regarding integrative education, enhanced social inclusion of disabled students, and increased external teacher employment to address supplementary student requirements. Negatively, personnel reported autistic and intellectually disabled student integration difficulties in mainstream classrooms, inadequate behavioral problem student grouping, autistic student isolation from typical classmates, insufficient training provision, inadequate preparation, support deficiencies, and limited integrative education expertise (Apanel, 2009; Muhammad, 2025).

Educators additionally addressed economic obstacles linked to integration, observing inadequate financial resource allocation to this domain. Panel findings suggested that schools might prioritise special needs learners over mainstream students, potentially neglecting the requirements of typical students (Apanel, 2009). Apanel further documented learning difficulties experienced by numerous children within these heterogeneous classroom environments. However, Apanel identified insufficient qualified personnel in integrative institutions as the primary challenge. Krause (2004) clarifies this issue by demonstrating inadequate resource availability and informational support for integration processes, which results in educator skill deficiencies and insufficient classroom implementation capacity for integrative education. This pessimistic perspective arises because educators need to be prepared to instruct children with diverse capabilities and impairments in both mainstream and inclusive educational settings (Pańczyk, 2002). Statistical documentation indicates "intellectual disability (ID) prevalence in Poland reaches 47.8/10,000 within populations exceeding 15 years" (Wapiennik, 2008). Despite recent societal perspective improvements regarding intellectually disabled individuals, ID populations remain socially marginalized.

Nevertheless, the Polish Parliament guarantees pension benefits, educational access, and healthcare provision for persons with disabilities. ID individuals qualify for pension benefits upon demonstrating work incapacity. Regarding Polish ID children, families may utilise 103 autonomous institutions that operate independently of educational frameworks. Through this arrangement, individuals with ID gain access to facility admission.

Why do barriers persist in Poland despite EU policies? Three factors explain this gap: First, Poland's post-communist education system still relies on traditional teaching methods that resist change. Second, teacher training programs have not adequately prepared educators for inclusive practices. Third, the rapid pace of EU-mandated changes has created implementation stress without sufficient support systems.

INDIVIDUAL EDUCATION PROGRAM (IEP) DEVELOPMENT IN POLISH SCHOOLS

Polish schools create Individual Education Programs for students with disabilities. Teachers, parents, and specialists meet to write goals for each student. The IEP includes specific learning targets, like "Maria will read 50 words per minute by December" or "Ahmed will solve 10 math problems in 20 minutes."

Polish teachers use the IEP to plan daily lessons. They modify worksheets, provide extra time for tests, and offer alternative ways for students to demonstrate their learning. Some students take oral tests instead of written ones.

ASSISTIVE TECHNOLOGY IN POLISH CLASSROOMS

Many Polish schools now utilize computers equipped with specialized software. Students with reading difficulties use text-to-speech programs that read books aloud. Students with writing problems use word prediction software that suggests words as they type.

Some students use tablets with communication apps to express their needs. Students with physical disabilities often use special keyboards and computer mice that are designed to be easier to control.

INTEGRATION AND INCLUSION IN ISRAEL

The 2007 United Nations Convention on the Rights of Persons with Disabilities advocates for the complete integration of individuals with disabilities across all life domains. Article 1 establishes fundamental principles, including non-discrimination, equal access, appreciation of diversity, and the acknowledgement of disabled persons as part of humanity's natural variation, while guaranteeing their complete participation (UNESCO, 2007). Israel's population of 5.5 million includes approximately 1.2 million children. The demographic breakdown shows that 18% of the population are Palestinian citizens and 82% are Jewish citizens. The majority of Palestinian-Israelis practice Sunni Islam, with a Christian minority, while literacy rates reach 95% among citizens aged 15 and above.

Israel's educational framework consists of four distinct sectors: Jewish Secular, Jewish Religious, Jewish Independent (Ultra-Orthodox), and Palestinian-Israeli (Non-Jewish) divisions. These four sectors maintain independent general and special education structures. While Israeli state schools operate nationally, they are divided into six regional districts (Tel Aviv, Central, Northern, Jerusalem, Haifa, and Southern) under local supervisory management for daily educational administration. Educational statistics reveal that approximately 2.8% of Israeli students (33,500 individuals) receive special education classification. During 1984-1996, Palestinian-Israeli students comprised the majority of this population, yet currently both Palestinian-Israeli and Jewish student representation in special education services has reached near parity. This demographic shift reflects enhanced economic circumstances and improved living standards across both communities. Socioeconomic advancement typically leads to increased special education funding and greater inclusion opportunities. This transformation involved transitioning previously segregated students with special needs from specialised institutions into mainstream, inclusive educational settings. The integration of more students with special needs into regular schools has consequently increased the number of students eligible for special education services (those with mild to moderate impairments). Within Palestinian communities, economic improvements fostered greater parental engagement and awareness regarding special education. Available support services and conditions for special needs children also experienced enhancement (Gumpel, 1999). Nevertheless, special education improvements for Palestinian-Israelis resulted not solely from community advocacy but also from deliberate Ministry of Education efforts to advance the educational status of this minority population (Gumpel & Awartani, 2003).

Legal Framework: The Shiluv Law

Israel's demographic composition primarily reflects immigration patterns, with approximately 7,184,000 residents representing diverse ethnic, racial, religious, and national origins. Mandatory schooling spans the ages of 5-18 for Israeli citizens, with public institutions serving the majority of students. Israel's inclusive education framework for special needs students emerged through the 1988 'Shiluv' legislation, mandating integration of disabled learners into mainstream educational environments. This legislation ensures that schools receive essential resources, equipment, professional development, services, and assistance for the successful implementation of inclusive practices. Educational Ministry data (Margalit, 2000; Ronen, 2007) demonstrates that roughly 8% of students with mild to moderate impairments receive instruction in mainstream classrooms, while approximately 2.25% of disabled learners utilize specialized educational settings (including special units within mainstream facilities or separate specialized institutions). Research by Ronen (2007) and Ben-Yehuda et al. (2010) confirms this distribution aligns with 'shiluv' legislation requirements.

Israel's 1988 Special Education Law (Shiluv) draws from the 1975 U.S. Individuals with Disabilities Education Act. This legislation mandates mainstream classroom placement for children with special needs. The law created specialised support facilities to assist learners with special needs within regular educational settings. Nearly 14,000 mainstream students in Israel receive these support services (Paz, 1997). Nevertheless, Israeli inclusive classrooms typically exclude students with intellectual impairments, while accommodating most individuals with mild to moderate challenges (learning, sensory, and physical impairments). Current legislation mandates mainstream schools accommodate individuals with Down Syndrome in regular classrooms alongside support staff. Despite this, Israeli educators frequently maintain pessimistic views regarding inclusive education, perceiving themselves as inadequately prepared for such responsibilities (Lifshitz & Glaubman, 2002).

Concerning Palestinian-Israeli educational perspectives, Gumpel & Awartani document Palestinian recognition of education's vital function in preserving national cohesion and cultural identity (Acim, 2025). This reflects Palestine's status as a developing nation experiencing Sharaga's (1986) concept of 'nation-building.' Sharaga similarly applied 'nation-building' when describing Israeli national development during independence. Palestinian participant responses should be interpreted within the historical context of a population that belongs to an evolving nation. Future studies should examine this hypothesis by contrasting special education approaches in affluent, established nations with those in the developing Palestinian context and its educational professionals

Israeli educators approach inclusive education through an individualistic lens, expecting teachers to address each student's unique special requirements. Conversely, Palestinian educators and teacher candidates perceive their special education responsibilities through a collective, community-centered perspective. This orientation stems from Arab cultural foundations emphasizing clan structures and extended kinship networks. Consequently, Arabs prioritize communal values and believe individual empowerment derives from clan and community connections. Educators in developing nations, such as Palestine, typically assume significant responsibilities in shaping national identity. Similar to the Israeli methodology, special education inherently operates as an individualised framework, where educators focus on personal achievement for each child. This cultural distinction may help clarify why Arab study participants generally resist emphasising individualistic elements within special education practices (Madar & Danoch, 2021).

Teacher Perspectives on Inclusion

Nevertheless, this hypothesis requires examination through an analysis of the underlying structures of other indigenous cultural frameworks. Additionally, participant statements should be contrasted with actual school implementation practices. It's crucial to acknowledge that while Palestinian educators accept disability education rights, the Palestinian Ministry of Education inadequately delivers fundamental educational entitlements to these students. This demonstrates a significant disconnect between theoretical principles (intended goals) and implementation, necessitating additional investigation in subsequent research. Leyser and Romi's (2008) research examines Israeli student-teacher perspectives on inclusive education for individuals with disabilities. The study participants represented Arab and Jewish populations across six different religious denominations. Findings demonstrate universal participant recognition of educational rights for persons with disabilities, irrespective of their religious affiliation. Participants agreed that inclusive education benefits both disabled learners and their typically developing peers, fostering mutual acceptance and appreciation. Consequently, these prospective educators supported Ministry of Education inclusive education policies.

INCLUSION POLICY IN ISRAEL

The first Israeli Special Education Law, passed in 1988, is based on the American Individuals with Disabilities Education Act (1975). This law required putting SEND students in regular schools with professional support. The Amendment to the Special Education Law was created in 2002, giving equal funding to both SEND students in regular schools and special education schools. The law also required special education teachers to provide extra services. However, many parents complained about the problems of inclusion in regular classrooms, which led to the creation of the Durner Committee in 2007. The committee stressed giving every child the educational funding they need and professional training for regular teachers who work with SEND students. As a result, more SEND students have been integrated into regular schools, with 59.4% of SEN students included in regular classes by 2013. Israeli inclusive education means putting disabled students into regular classrooms or placing them in special classrooms inside regular schools. Special classrooms have 7-12 students, compared to 35-40 in regular classrooms. Students with SEND in special classes also participate in regular school activities. In Israel, inclusive schools either place SEN students in regular classrooms or integrate them into regular activities while maintaining their special classes. SEN students in Israel have different types of disabilities (Karni, Reiter & Bryen, 2011). In Arab culture, Gumpel and Awartani (2003) noted that Arab culture, which emphasises community values, differs from the individualistic approach to education in Israel. Israeli teachers focus on meeting each student's individual needs, while Palestinian teachers don't view education the same way. In a study by Cimermanová (2017), the majority of teachers' answers focused on how they perceived themselves, with positive attitudes being linked to teachers feeling confident about their abilities.

Teachers were more hopeful when they felt inclusion helped all students. Teachers also showed positive attitudes when they believed inclusion would help them become better teachers. Special education teachers were more likely to include students with SEND than regular teachers. However, concerns about lacking sufficient tools, support, and training exacerbated the situation. Teachers reported that students with SEND were not receiving sufficient attention, which negatively impacted their classmates' academic performance (De Boer et al., 2011; Gavish & Shimoni, 2011). Most teachers believed that students with SEND required individualised care and specialised teaching methods. Their negative view of inclusion stemmed from concerns about insufficient resources, training, and support. These findings match Nijakowska's (2014) research on teachers across Europe.

INCLUSION MODELS IN ISRAELI SCHOOLS

Israeli schools use three main inclusion models:

1. **Full Inclusion:** Students with disabilities spend all day in regular classrooms with support teachers.

2. **Partial Inclusion:** Students spend some time in regular classes (like art and music) and some time in special education rooms.
3. **Special Classes in Regular Schools:** Students learn in special classrooms but eat lunch and play with all students.

CLASSROOM SUPPORT SYSTEMS

Israeli classrooms that include students have teaching teams. The regular teacher teaches the lesson while the special education teacher helps individual students. They plan lessons together and share responsibilities.

Students with autism may use visual schedules to display their daily routines. Students with ADHD might have fidget tools to help them focus. The classroom features quiet corners where students can take breaks when they feel overwhelmed.

Why do negative teacher attitudes persist despite the Shiluv Law's success? The individualistic approach required by inclusive education conflicts with traditional teacher-centred pedagogy in Israeli schools. Additionally, teachers receive legal mandates but often lack sufficient practical training, creating anxiety about their competence in serving diverse learners effectively.

The Arab society in Israel

Cultural Context and Family Dynamics

Studies indicate that Arab-Israeli students with disabilities encounter both typical disability-related difficulties and unique cultural obstacles that impact their school inclusion. Comprehensive research from Israel (Sandler-Loeff, 2006) reveals that Arab-Israelis face many challenges similar to other disabled individuals. However, certain obstacles are unique to Arab cultural and social environments. Regarding Arab-Israeli perspectives on disability, Israeli research demonstrates that many Arabs held unfavorable views about disabilities. These negative perspectives stem from insufficient awareness, limited support systems, societal reluctance to treat disabled individuals as equals, and weak collaboration among disability-focused organizations.

Nevertheless, Israel has witnessed significant improvements in disability treatment over the past decade, with Arab-Israeli communities also experiencing these positive changes. These developments result from legislative reforms, policy updates, and enhanced services for disability support. Research findings indicate that Arab parents demonstrate higher levels of protectiveness toward their children compared to Jewish parents. Arab families also show reduced belief in their children's potential for achievement, independence, and employment success. In contrast, Jewish parents displayed less shame and anxiety regarding others' responses when compared to Arab families. The way Israeli-Arabs understand conditions like autism mirrors perspectives found in surrounding Arab nations. This common understanding relates to the significant influence of religion on the Arab mindset and perspectives. Religious beliefs serve a dual function in Arab community values - offering emotional support while simultaneously creating obstacles for disabled individuals' integration into general society (Nirit & Shunit, 2013). Despite these common cultural elements, variations exist among different Arab ethnic communities. These distinctions relate to each group's level of westernization, traditionalism, or bicultural identity (Dwairy, 1998; Lee, 1997).

INCLUSION IN ARAB SOCIETY

Avissar (2012) explains that inclusive education in Israel requires teachers to adapt educational materials, create individualized education plans (IEPs), and collaborate on curriculum development for students with special needs. However, challenges remain regarding the identification of disabilities, the inclusion of students with severe disabilities in general classrooms, and adapting the curriculum to meet these students' needs (Avissar, 2012). Despite the Ministry of Education's efforts, obstacles to full inclusion persist.

Al-Yagon and Margalit (2001) highlight that the 1998 amendment to Israel's Special Education Law aimed to increase the integration of students with disabilities into general education, yet issues like segregated classrooms still exist. According to Sandler-Loeff and Shahak (2006), Arab communities face additional barriers to inclusion due to a lack of services and a negative societal outlook on disabilities. In Arab communities, the success of inclusive education heavily relies on the support of school principals and the training of teachers (Karni, Reiter, & Bryen, 2011). Historically, special education services in Arab society have lagged behind those in Jewish society, with progress hindered by poverty and administrative challenges (Abu-Asbah, 2008). Despite the 1988 Special Education Law's requirement for inclusion, many Arab schools still do not provide adequate services, often due to stigma and a lack of teacher training (Abbas, 2013).

Kasler and Jabareen (2017) introduce the idea of "triple jeopardy," which refers to the multiple challenges faced by people with disabilities in marginalized Arab communities, including poverty and segregation. Even with laws promoting equality, full inclusion has not been achieved (Weissblei, 2011). Cultural beliefs also play a significant role, as research indicates that Arab communities often have more negative attitudes toward people with disabilities compared to Jewish communities (Gaad, 2004; Schechtman & Or, 1996; Florian & Katz, 1983).

IEP DEVELOPMENT IN ARAB-ISRAELI SCHOOLS

Arab-Israeli schools involve families more in IEP meetings due to cultural values emphasizing family involvement. Parents, teachers, and sometimes grandparents discuss the student's needs and goals.

IEP goals often include both academic and social objectives. For example, "Fatima will participate in group activities with classmates for 15 minutes" combines learning with social inclusion.

ASSISTIVE TECHNOLOGY AND LANGUAGE CONSIDERATIONS

Arab-Israeli students often require technology that supports both Arabic and Hebrew. Some use communication devices with both languages. Reading software provides text-to-speech in Arabic for students with dyslexia.

Schools adapt technology to cultural needs. For example, some apps show prayer times or include Islamic calendar dates, making technology more familiar to students.

CURRENT INCLUSIVE TEACHING METHODS IN ARAB-ISRAELI SCHOOLS

Arab-Israeli schools are now using several specific teaching strategies to include students with disabilities. Teachers use differentiated instruction, which means they teach the same lesson in various ways to meet the needs of each student. For example, some students read from books while others listen to audio recordings of the same story.

Many Arab schools now use collaborative learning groups where students with and without disabilities work together on projects. This approach works well with Arab culture, as it values community cooperation. Teachers also utilize visual aids and hands-on activities to support students with diverse learning styles.

Some schools have begun using tablets and computers equipped with specialized software to help students with disabilities participate in regular classes. Teachers receive training on how to modify worksheets and tests to make them more accessible for students with learning difficulties, while maintaining the same learning goals.

TEACHER TRAINING PROGRAMS

Arab teachers are now receiving specialized training in inclusive education. The Ministry of Education offers workshops where teachers learn how to work with students who have autism, learning disabilities, and physical disabilities. These training programs teach teachers practical skills, such as breaking down complex tasks into smaller steps and utilizing positive behavior support.

Some schools have mentorship programs where experienced special education teachers work alongside regular classroom teachers. This helps regular teachers feel more confident about including students with disabilities in their classes.

SUPPORT SYSTEMS IN ARAB SCHOOLS

Many Arab schools now have teaching assistants who help students with disabilities in regular classrooms. These assistants are often from the local community and speak Arabic, which helps students feel more comfortable.

Schools also work more closely with families by having regular meetings to discuss each student's progress. Some schools have implemented home-school communication books, where teachers and parents exchange notes about the student's daily activities and progress (Opoku et al., 2024).

SPECIFIC CLASSROOM STRATEGIES WORKING IN ARAB SCHOOLS

Arab-Israeli teachers employ several effective methods that work well with their students. They utilize peer tutoring, where students assist one another in learning, which aligns with Arab values of supporting family and community members. Teachers also use storytelling and role-playing activities that connect to Arab culture while teaching academic skills.

Some teachers create "learning stations" in their classrooms where students rotate between different activities. This helps students with different abilities work at their own pace. Teachers also use visual schedules and picture cards to help students with autism or intellectual disabilities understand daily routines (Assaly & Jabarin, 2021).

LEGAL FRAMEWORKS COMPARISON

Table 2. Legal Frameworks Comparison

Country	Key Law	Year	Main Requirement
Poland	EU Inclusion Directives	1990s	Gradual inclusion in mainstream schools
Israel	Shiluv Law	1988, amended 2002	Placement in least restrictive environment
Arab-Israeli	Same as Israel	1988	Equal access with cultural considerations

Table 3. Implementation Challenges Summary

Challenge Type	Poland	Israel	Arab-Israeli
Teacher Training	70% resist inclusion	Feel incompetent	Need cultural training
Resources	Limited EU funding	Adequate support centers	Very limited services
Student Population	Mild disabilities only	59.4% in mainstream	Double marginalization
Family Support	Moderate involvement	Professional collaboration	Extended family involvement

CONCLUSION

This chapter provides a detailed cross-cultural analysis of educational inclusion practices in Poland, Israel, and Arab-Israeli educational systems, highlighting both similarities and cultural differences in their approaches and implementations. While all three contexts have made strides toward inclusive educational frameworks, they face unique challenges shaped by their specific cultural, social, and political situations.

The Polish educational system, which established the world's first Ministry of Education, began adopting inclusive and integrated approaches only in the 1990s. The Polish experience illustrates the gap between theoretical acceptance and practical implementation. Teachers may agree with the idea of inclusion but resist applying it, especially for students with intellectual disabilities. This resistance is primarily due to a lack of training and preparation, underscoring the crucial role of teacher education in achieving successful inclusion.

In Israel, the 'Shiluv' law of 1988, inspired by the U.S. Individuals with Disabilities Education Act, marks an important step in promoting inclusive education. The Israeli system has clear divisions among different educational sectors (Jewish

Secular, Jewish Religious, Jewish Independent, and Israeli-Palestinian), each with its approach to inclusion. Although about 8% of students with mild to moderate disabilities are in inclusive settings, the system still struggles to include students with more severe disabilities.

The Arab-Israeli experience shows that successful inclusion requires both culturally sensitive approaches and concrete educational strategies. Schools that combine traditional Arab values of community support with modern inclusive teaching methods achieve better results.

The findings from Poland, Israel, and the Arab-Israeli context illuminate broader global patterns in the implementation of educational inclusion. The consistent gap between policy and practice observed across all three settings reflects what Hildebrandt-Wypych (2022) identifies as a worldwide phenomenon where legislative progress outpaces cultural attitude change. Similarly, the negative teacher attitudes documented in each context align with global research showing that stigma toward disability remains a primary barrier to inclusion worldwide.

A key finding across all three contexts is the ongoing gap between policy and practice. Although laws support inclusive education, its practical implementation faces challenges such as inadequate teacher training, insufficient resources, and varying levels of societal acceptance. This gap is especially noticeable in the Arab-Israeli sector, where traditional cultural values and socioeconomic factors create additional barriers to successful inclusion.

The comparative analysis in this chapter enhances our understanding of how cultural contexts influence educational inclusion practices. It emphasizes the need for culturally sensitive approaches to implementing inclusive education, suggesting that effective inclusion strategies must consider local cultural values, social structures, and educational traditions. This understanding is crucial for developing more effective and culturally sensitive inclusion policies and practices across various educational systems. Finally, the most successful Arab schools are those that train teachers in specific inclusive methods, provide classroom support, and engage families as partners in education.

IMPLICATIONS FOR RESEARCHERS

This cross-cultural analysis reveals several important areas for future research. Researchers should investigate why the policy-practice gap persists across different cultural contexts despite similar legal frameworks. Future studies should investigate specific teaching methods that are most effective in collectivist versus individualist cultures.

Researchers need to develop culturally sensitive assessment tools that measure success in inclusion differently across various cultural contexts. For example, social integration might be measured differently in Arab communities compared to European settings. Additionally, longitudinal studies are needed to track how cultural attitudes toward disability change over time as inclusion policies mature.

IMPLICATIONS FOR POLICYMAKERS

Policymakers must recognize that effective inclusion requires more than legal mandates—it demands sustained investment in teacher training and cultural change initiatives. Countries should develop implementation timelines that allow for gradual shifts in attitude, rather than expecting immediate compliance.

Policy frameworks should include specific funding for culturally appropriate support services. For minority communities like Arab-Israelis, this might mean bilingual support staff or culturally sensitive family engagement programs.

Policymakers should create accountability systems that measure both access (enrollment numbers) and quality (social integration, academic progress) of inclusion. Regular policy reviews should assess whether legal frameworks effectively address the needs of doubly marginalised groups.

International organizations, such as UNESCO, should develop guidelines that help countries adapt global inclusion standards to local cultural contexts while upholding core human rights principles.

RECOMMENDATIONS

1. Policy makers should develop policies that encourage inclusion in all areas of schooling, from classroom environments to teaching methods, to ensure inclusive practices are widely adopted.
2. Train teachers on how to educate learners through informed pedagogical decisions.
3. Create and update curricula that reflect the principles of inclusive education and inspire educators to foster diversity.
4. The European Union and UNESCO should enforce laws across EU member states to ensure that all schools adopt inclusive education for all students, regardless of their background. Also, they should work internationally to guarantee the right to inclusive education without discrimination based on religion, race, or nationality.

5. Local Educational Authorities should develop action plans for implementing inclusive education, including early childhood programs and teacher training, to ensure schools are adequately prepared.
6. School administrators should organize training sessions to equip teachers with the necessary knowledge and skills to implement inclusive practices.
7. Educate teachers on the principles and methods of inclusive education to ensure they can effectively support diverse learners in regular classrooms.
8. Ensure future teachers are trained in inclusive education methods and strategies to create a comprehensive understanding of how to teach students with diverse needs.

REFERENCES

Abu-Asbah, K. (2008). The Arab education system and questions of equality [in Hebrew]. *Mifne*, *58*, 43–50.

Abushihab, E., Alkhateeb, H., Alkhateeb, R., & Alkhateeb, B. (2025). Motivation and attitudes toward learning Arabic as a second language: A Study of Arab-American and Arab-expatriate middle school students in the U.S. and Qatar. *Dibon Journal of Languages*, *1*(1), 3–23. DOI: 10.64169/djl.32

Acedo, C., Amadio, M., Opertti, R., Brady, J., Duncombe, L., Weyermann, M., Huang, Y., & Xu, X. (2008). *Defining an inclusive education agenda: Reflections around the 48th session of the International Conference on Education*. UNESCO IBE.

Acim, Y. (2025). The Impact of Media on Identity Construction: Sultan Moulay Slimane University. *Dibon Journal of Languages*, *1*(2), 165–173. DOI: 10.64169/djl.28

Ahsan, M. T., Sharma, U., & Deppeler, J. M. (2012). Exploring preservice teachers' perceived teaching-efficacy, attitudes and concerns about inclusive education in Bangladesh. *International Journal of Whole Schooling*, *8*(2), 1–20.

Ainscow, M. (2005). Developing inclusive education systems: What are the levers for change? *Journal of Educational Change*, *6*, 109–124. DOI: 10.1007/s10833-0051298-4

Al-Yagon, M., & Margalit, M. (2001). Special and inclusive education in Israel.

Allan, J. (2010). Questions of inclusion in Scotland and Europe. *European Journal of Special Needs Education*, *25*(2), 199–208.

Anastasiou, D., & Kauffman, J. M. (2011). A social constructionist approach to disability: Implications for special education. *Exceptional Children*, *77*(3), 367–384.

Apanel, D. (2009). Oblicza edukacji integracyjnej w Polsce w opiniach i doświadczeniach nauczycieli. [Faces of integrated education in Poland in teachers' opinions and experiences] In Żółkowska, T., & Konopska, L. (Eds.), *W kręgu niepełnosprawności – teoretyczne i praktyczne aspekty poszukiwań w pedagogice specjalnej* [In the circle of disability - theoretical and practical aspects of research in special pedagogy]. (pp. 171–180).

Arkansas Department of Education. (2008). Special education and related services 2.00 definitions.

Assaly, I., & Jabarin, A. (2021). Arab Israeli EFL teachers' perceptions and practices vis-à-vis teaching higher-order thinking skills: A complicated relationship. *Language Teaching Research, 28*(4), 1635–1655. DOI: 10.1177/13621688211032426

Avissar, G. (2012). Inclusive education in Israel from a curriculum perspective: An exploratory study. *European Journal of Special Needs Education, 27*(1), 35–49.

Avramidis, E., Bayliss, P., & Burden, R. (2000). A survey into mainstream teachers' attitudes towards the inclusion of children with special educational needs in the ordinary school in one local educational authority. *Educational Psychology, 20*(2), 191–211.

Bełza, M. (2014). *Szkolnictwo specjalne w Polsce – różne formy organizacji* [Special education in Poland – different forms of organization]. University of Silesia.

Ben-Yehuda, S., Leyser, Y., & Last, U. (2010). Teacher educational beliefs and sociometric status of special educational needs (SEN) students in inclusive classrooms. *International Journal of Inclusive Education, 14*(1), 17–34.

Bender, W. N., Vail, C. O., & Scott, K. (1995). Teachers' attitudes toward increased mainstreaming: Implementing effective instruction for students with learning disabilities. *Journal of Learning Disabilities, 28*(2), 87–94. PMID: 7884302

Boyle, C., Topping, K., & Jindal-Snape, D. (2013). Teachers' attitudes towards inclusion in high schools. *Teachers and Teaching, 19*(5), 527–542.

Buchem, I. (2013). Diversität und Spaltung. [Diversity and division] In Ebner, M., & Schön, S. (Eds.), *Lehrbuch für lernen und lehren mit technologien* [Textbook for learning and teaching with technologies]. 2nd ed., pp. 387–395). Epubli GmbH.

Buenaventura, C., & Gaza, J. (2025). Guided Language and Science Learning Activity Booklet: An Interdisciplinary Educational Resource. *Dibon Journal of Education, 1*(2), 134–150. DOI: 10.64169/dje.79

Chhabra, S., Srivastava, R., & Srivastava, I. (2010). Inclusive education in Botswana: The perceptions of school teachers. *Journal of Disability Policy Studies, 20*(4), 219–228.

Chhabra, S., Srivastava, R., & Srivastava, I. (2010). Inclusive education in Botswana: The perceptions of school teachers. *Journal of Disability Policy Studies, 20*, 219–228.

Chodkowska, M., & Kazanowski, Z. (2007). *Socjopedagogiczne konteksty postaw nauczycieli wobec edukacji integracyjnej* [Socio-pedagogical contexts of teachers' attitudes towards integrated education]. Wydawnictwo UMCS.

Cimermanová, I. (2017). English language preservice and in-service teachers' self-efficacy and attitudes towards integration of students with learning difficulties. *Journal of Language and Cultural Education*, *5*(1), 20–38.

Cooc, N. (2021). Disparities in general education inclusion for students of color with disabilities: Understanding when and why. *Journal of School Psychology*, *90*, 43–59. DOI: 10.1016/j.jsp.2021.10.002 PMID: 34969487

Cornoldi, C., Terreni, A., Scruggs, T. E., & Mastropieri, M. A. (1998). Teacher attitudes in Italy after twenty years of inclusion. *Remedial and Special Education*, *19*(6), 350–356.

Council of the European Union. (2010, May 11). Council conclusions on the social dimension of education and training, 3013 Meeting of the Education, Youth and Culture Council. Author.

De Boer, A., Pijl, S. J., & Minnaert, A. (2011). Regular primary schoolteachers' attitudes towards inclusive education: A review of the literature. *International Journal of Inclusive Education*, *15*(4), 331–353.

Dizdarevic, A., Mujezinovic, A., & Memisevic, H. (2017). Comparison of teachers' attitudes towards inclusive education in Bosnia and Herzegovina and European Union. *Journal of Special Education and Rehabilitation*, *18*(1-2), 92–108.

Donnelly, V., & Watkins, A. (2011). Teacher education for inclusion in Europe. *Prospects*, *41*(3), 341–353.

Dwairy, M. A. (1998). *Cross-cultural counseling: The Arab-Palestinian case*. The Haworth Press.

Eiken, R. (2015). *Teacher attitudes toward the inclusion of students with disabilities in the general education classroom* [Doctoral dissertation, Northwest Missouri State University].

Erenc, J. (2008). *Bycie innym. Problem wykluczenia i izolacji ludzi niepełnosprawnych* [Being different: The problem of exclusion and isolation of people with disabilities]. Wydawnictwo UG.

European Agency for Development in Special Needs Education. (2010). Teacher education for inclusion: International literature review.

Florian, V., & Katz, S. (1983). The impact of cultural, ethnic, and national variables on attitudes towards the disabled in Israel: A review. *International Journal of Intercultural Relations*, *7*, 167–179.

Franklin, B. M. (Ed.). (1996). *Interpretación de la discapacidad: Teoría e historia de la educación especial* [Interpretation of disability: Theory and history of special education]. Ediciones Pomares-Corredor.

Freeman-Green, S., Williamson, P., & Cornelius, E., K. (2023). Promoting Inclusive Practices in Education: Bridging Gaps and Fostering Independence. *Teaching Exceptional Children, 56*(2), 68–69. DOI: 10.1177/00400599231223785

Friend, M., & Bursuck, W. D. (2006). Including students with special needs: A practical guide for classroom teachers (4th ed.). Pearson & Allyn Bacon.

Fullan, M. (1993). Innovation, reform and restructuring strategies. In Cawelti, G. (Ed.), *Challenges and achievements of American education* (pp. 116–133). Association for Supervision and Curriculum Development.

Gaad, E. (2004). Cross-cultural perspectives on the effect of cultural attitudes towards inclusion for children with intellectual disabilities. *International Journal of Inclusive Education, 8*(3), 311–328.

Gajdzica, Z. (2009). Codzienne wsparcie ucznia niepełnosprawnego w klasie integracyjnej [Daily support for disabled students in integrated classrooms]. Pedagogika. *Zeszyty Naukowe Wyższej Szkoły Humanitas, 4*, 67–76.

Gavish, B., & Shimoni, S. (2011). Elementary school teachers' beliefs and perceptions about the inclusion of children with special needs in their classrooms. *Journal of International Special Needs Education, 14*(2), 49–60.

Ghergu , A. (2001). *Psihopedagogia persoanelor cu cerin e speciale: Strategii de educa ie integrată* [Psychopedagogy of persons with special needs: Integrated education strategies]. Polirom.

Ghergu , A. (2006). *Psihopedagogia persoanelor cu cerinţe educative speciale: Strategii diferenţiate şi incluzive în educaţie* [Psychopedagogy of persons with special educational needs: Differentiated and inclusive strategies in education]. Polirom.

Grzegorzewska, M., & Wapiennik, E. (2008). Comparative policy brief status of intellectual disabilities in the Republic of Poland. *Journal of Policy and Practice in Intellectual Disabilities, 5*(2), 137–141.

Guddad, P. (2025). Challenges Faced by the Visually Impaired Students during Online Learning: Lessons for Teachers. *Dibon Journal of Education, 1*(1), 1–12. DOI: 10.64169/dje.6

Gumpel, T. P. (1999). Special education in Israel. In Reynolds, C. R., & Fletcher-Janzen, E. (Eds.), *Encyclopedia of special education* (Vol. 2, pp. 995–998). Wiley.

Gumpel, T. P., & Awartani, S. (2003). A comparison of special education in Israel and Palestine: Surface and deep structures. *The Journal of Special Education*, *37*(1), 33–48.

Gumpel, T. P., & Awartani, S. (2003). A comparison of special education in Israel and Palestine: Surface and deep structures. *The Journal of Special Education*, *37*(1), 33–48.

Guojonsdottir, H., Cacciattolo, M., Dakich, E., Davies, A., Kelly, C., & Dalmau, M. C. (2008). Transformative pathways: Inclusive pedagogies in teacher education. *Journal of Research on Technology in Education*, *40*(2), 165–182.

Hager, T., & Jabareen, Y. (2016). From marginalization to integration: Arab-Palestinians in Israeli academia. *International Journal of Inclusive Education*, *20*(5), 455–473.

Hardman, K. (2008). The situation of physical education in schools: A European perspective. *Human Movement*, *9*, 5–18.

Hildebrandt-Wypych, D. (2022). Contrasting Narratives of the Israeli-Palestinian Conflict in Polish History Textbooks. *Frontiers in Education*, *7*, 815830. DOI: 10.3389/feduc.2022.815830

Hodkinson, A. (2009). Preservice teacher training and special educational needs in England 1970–2008: Is government learning the lessons of the past or is it experiencing a groundhog day? *European Journal of Special Needs Education*, *24*(3), 277–290.

Hodkinson, A., & Deverokonda, C. (2011). For pity's sake: Comparative conceptions of inclusion in England and India. *International Review of Qualitative Research.*

Hodkinson, A., & Vickerman, P. (2009). Key issues in special needs and inclusion. *Sage (Atlanta, Ga.).*

Hulek, A. (1992). *Uczeń niepełnosprawny w szkole masowej* [Disabled student in mainstream school].

Ismayilli, T., & Nuri, A. (2025). Applications that can be used in Mobile-Assisted Language Education. *Dibon Journal of Education*, *1*(2), 111–119. DOI: 10.64169/dje.82

Karni, N., Reiter, S., & Bryen, D. N. (2011). Israeli Arab teachers' attitudes on inclusion of students with disabilities. *British Journal of Developmental Disabilities*, *57*(113), 123–132.

Kasler, J., & Jabareen, Y. T. (2017). Triple jeopardy: Special education for Palestinians in Israel. *International Journal of Inclusive Education*, *21*(12), 1261–1275.

Kavkler, M., Babuder, M. K., & Magajna, L. (2015). Inclusive education for children with specific learning difficulties: Analysis of opportunities and barriers in inclusive education in Slovenia. *Center for Educational Policy Studies Journal*, *5*(1), 31–52.

Kolleck, N., Schuster, J., Hartmann, U., & Gräsel, C. (2021). Teachers' professional collaboration and trust relationships: An inferential social network analysis of teacher teams. *Research in Education*, *111*(1), 89–107. DOI: 10.1177/00345237211031585

Kozleski, E. B., Artiles, A. J., & Waitoller, F. R. (2011). Introduction: Equity in inclusive education: Historical trajectories and theoretical commitments. In Artiles, A. J., Kozleski, E. B., & Waitoller, F. R. (Eds.), *Inclusive education*. Harvard University Press.

Lee, C. C. (Ed.). (1997). *Multicultural issues in counseling: New approaches to diversity* (2nd ed.). American Counseling Association.

Leyser, Y., & Romi, S. (2008). Religion and attitudes of college preservice teachers toward students with disabilities: Implications for higher education [in Hebrew]. *Higher Education*, *55*(6), 703–717.

Lichtensztejn. (2006). Integracja: szansa czy zagrożenie? Warunki sensownej integracji [Integration: Opportunity or threat? Conditions for meaningful integration]. https://profesor.pl/mat/pd6/pd6_e_lichtensztejn_20060216.pdf

Lifshitz, H., & Glaubman, R. (2002). Self-efficacy and attitudes towards inclusion of religious and secular student teachers. *Journal of Intellectual Disability Research*, *46*(5), 405–418. PMID: 12031023

Loreman, T., Deppeler, J., & Harvey, D. (2011). *Inclusive education: Supporting diversity in the classroom* (2nd ed.). Allen & Unwin.

Madar, N. K., & Danoch, A. (2021). Inclusive education in Israel: A study of policy impact on access to education. *International Journal of Inclusive Education*, *28*(1), 78–89. DOI: 10.1080/13603116.2021.1916109

Margalit, M. (2000). *Report of the committee on the implementation of special education law* [in Hebrew]. Ministry of Education.

Mittler, P. (1995). Education for all or for some? International principles and practice. *Australasian Journal of Special Education*, *19*(2), 5–15.

Mohammed, A. (2025). Developing Advanced Reading Skills Through Extensive Reading: Findings from Palestinian schools. *Dibon Journal of Education*, *1*(1), 56–68. DOI: 10.64169/dje.24

Molto, M. (2003). Mainstream teachers' acceptance of instructional adaptations in Spain. *European Journal of Special Needs Education, 18*, 311–332.

Muhammad, S. (2025). Integrating Social Studies Education to Tackle Socioeconomic Challenges in Nigeria: A Case Study of Selected Upper Basic Schools in Gusau Metropolis, Zamfara State. *Dibon Journal of Education, 1*(2), 85–100. DOI: 10.64169/dje.45

Naqeeb, H. (2025). Intercultural Communicative Competence: Definition, Models, Measurement Instruments, and Empirical Practice in the EFL Classroom. *Dibon Journal of Education, 1*(1), 23–41. DOI: 10.64169/dje.15

Nijakowska, J. (2014). Dyslexia in the European EFL teacher training context. In Pawlak, M., & Aronin, L. (Eds.), *Essential topics in applied linguistics and multilingualism: Studies in honor of David Singleton* (pp. 129–154). Springer., DOI: 10.1007/978-3-319-01414-2_8

Nirit, K. V., & Shunit, R. (2013). Attitudes towards autism among Israeli Arab teachers' college students. In *Recent advances in autism spectrum disorders* (Vol. II). IntechOpen.

Omianowski, M. (2008). Dziecko niepełnosprawne na lekcji wychowania fizycznego w szkole masowej [Child with disability in physical education class in mainstream school]. http://wychowaniefizyczne.pl/userfiles/_download/inne_michniep.pdf

Opoku, M. P., Mustafa, A., Anwahi, N., Alkatheeri, F., Alsuwaidi, N., Alqutaiti, A., & Belbase, S. (2024). Working as teacher assistants/aides in schools: Understanding experiences in an Arabian context using the wider pedagogical role model. *Cogent Education, 11*(1). Advance online publication. DOI: 10.1080/2331186X.2024.2319450

Ostrowska, A. (2002). Społeczeństwo polskie wobec osób niepełnosprawnych. Przemiany postaw i dyskursu [Polish society towards disabled people: Changes in attitudes and discourse]. In J. Sikorska (Ed.), *Społeczne problemy osób niepełnosprawnych* [*Social problems of disabled people*] (pp. 51-64). IFiS PAN.

Pańczyk, J. (2002). Kompetencje pedagogów specjalnych jako wyraz oczekiwań, wyzwań rynku edukacyjnego, rehabilitacyjnego i resocjalizacyjnego XXI wieku. [Competencies of special educators as an expression of expectations and challenges of the 21st century educational, rehabilitation and resocialization market] In Górniewicz, E., & Krause, A. (Eds.), *Od tradycjonalizmu do ponowoczesności: dyskursy pedagogiki specjalnej* [*[From traditionalism to postmodernity: Discourses of special pedagogy*]]. (pp. 261–267). Wydawnictwo UWM.

Park, E., & Yi, S. (2025). Compulsory education enhances financial inclusion across socioeconomic groups: A global analysis. *Humanities & Social Sciences Communications, 12*, 695. DOI: 10.1057/s41599-025-04911-y

Paz, D. (1997). *Implementation of the special education law, rationale and forming up* [Paper presentation]. Special Education Department Meeting, Ramat-Gan, Bar-Ilan University, School of Education.

Persson, B. (2006). Pathways to inclusion: A guide to staff development. *European Educational Research Journal, 5*, 152–158.

Rodriguez, C. C., & Garro-Gil, N. (2015). Inclusion and integration on special education. *Procedia: Social and Behavioral Sciences, 191*, 1323–1327.

Ronen, C. (2007). Issues and debates concerning mainstreaming and inclusioning educational settings. [in Hebrew] In Reiter, S., Leyser, Y., & Avissar, G. (Eds.), *Inclusiveness – learners with disabilities in education* (pp. 27–55). Ahva.

Saloviita, T. (2005). Erityisopetus opettajankoulutuksen sisältöalueena. [Special education as a content area of teacher education] In Jakku-Sihvonen, R. (Ed.), *Uudenlaisia maistereita* [New kinds of masters]. (pp. 339–351). Otava.

Sandler-loeff, A., & Shahak, Y. (2006). *People with disabilities in Arab society in Israel: An opportunity for social change.* JDC Israel, The Unit for Disabilities and Rehabilitation.

Schechtman, Z., & Or, A. (1996). Applying counselling methods to challenge teacher beliefs with regard to classroom diversity and mainstreaming: An empirical study. *Teaching and Teacher Education.*

Schmidt, M., & Ksenja, V. (2015). Attitudes of teachers towards the inclusion of children with special needs in primary and secondary schools. *Hrvatska Revija za Rehabilitacijska Istraživanja, 51*(2), 16–30.

Schwab, S., Gebhardt, M., Hessels, M. G., Ellmeier, B., Gmeiner, S., & Rossmann, P. (2015). Does inclusive education change teachers' educational goals? A comparative analysis of two cross-sectional surveys in Austria. *Journal of Studies in Education, 5*(4), 114–130.

Sekulowicz, M., & Sekulowicz, A. (2015). The special education system in Poland: From segregation to inclusion. *Journal of the International Association of Special Education, 16*(1), 4.

Sharaga, D. (1986). Human rights in emergency situations under the European Convention on Human Rights. In Y. Dinstein (Ed.), *Israel yearbook on human rights* (Vol. 15, pp. 217-242). Tel Aviv University Press.

Sharma, U., Forlin, C., & Loreman, T. (2008). Impact of training on preservice teachers' attitudes and concerns about inclusive education and sentiments about persons with disabilities. *Disability & Society, 23*(7), 773–785. DOI: 10.1080/09687590802469271

Starczewska, A., Hodkinson, A., & Adams, G. (2012). Conceptions of inclusion and inclusive education: A critical examination of the perspectives and practices of teachers in Poland. *Journal of Research in Special Educational Needs, 12*(3), 162–169.

Thomas, G., Walker, D., & Webb, J. (1997). *The making of the inclusive school.* Routledge Falmer.

Tiernan, B. (2021). Inclusion versus full inclusion: Implications for progressing inclusive education. *European Journal of Special Needs Education, 37*(5), 882–890. DOI: 10.1080/08856257.2021.1961197

Tilstone, C., Florian, L., & Rose, R. (1998). *Promoting inclusive practice.* Routledge Falmer.

UNESCO. (1994). The Salamanca statement and framework for action on special needs education. *World Conference on Special Needs Education: Access and Quality*, Salamanca, Spain.

UNESCO. (2009). Policy guidelines on inclusion in education.

United Nations. (2007). Convention on the rights of people with disabilities. www .publications.parliament.

Uteuova, K., & Amirbayeva, D. (2025). The Integration of the Eurasian Scientific Community and the Trilingual Education Policy. *Dibon Journal of Education, 1*(2), 101–110. DOI: 10.64169/dje.72

Verza, E. (1995). Psihopedagogie specială [Special psychopedagogy]. Editura Didactică i Pedagogică.

Wapiennik, E. (2008). Comparative policy brief: Status of intellectual disabilities in the Republic of Poland. *Journal of Policy and Practice in Intellectual Disabilities, 5*(2), 137–141.

Weissblei, E. (2011). The availability of resources for the community of children with special needs [in Hebrew]. Israel Knesset Report. Knesset Research and Information Center.

Wilczenski, F. L. (1995). Development of a scale to measure attitudes toward inclusive education. *Educational and Psychological Measurement*, *55*(2), 291–299.

Willms, D. J. (2006). *Learning divides: Ten policy questions about the performance and equity of schools and schooling systems*. UNESCO Institute for Statistics.

ADDITIONAL READING

Al-Hroub, A., & Jouni, N. (2023). Historical and Theoretical Approaches to Inclusive Education. In *School Inclusion in Lebanon*. Springer., DOI: 10.1007/978-3-031-34779-5_4

Aladini, A. (2020). Inclusive Education from the Teachers' Perspectives in Palestine. *Creative Education*, *11*, 2443–2457. DOI: 10.4236/ce.2020.1111179

Avissar, G. (2011). Inclusive education in Israel from a curriculum perspective: An exploratory study. *European Journal of Special Needs Education*, *27*(1), 35–49. DOI: 10.1080/08856257.2011.613602

Barton, L., & Armstrrong, F. (2007). Policy, Experience and Change: Cross-Cultural Reflections on Inclusive Education. In *Springer eBooks*. https://doi.org/ DOI: 10.1007/978-1-4020-5119-7

Fayyaleh, N., & Fogarty, L. (2024). Transforming Vocational Education in Palestine by Integrating 21st Century Skills. *Journal of Education in Muslim Societies*, *5*(2), 31–47. DOI: 10.2979/jems.00003

Gavish, B. (2017). The Implementation of School Inclusion Practices for Students with Special Needs in Israel: Teachers' Perceptions. *International Journal of Disability Development and Education*, *64*(5), 544–560. DOI: 10.1080/1034912X.2017.1310372

Hernández-Saca, D. I., Voulgarides, C. K., & Etscheidt, S. L. (2023). A Critical Systematic Literature Review of Global Inclusive Education Using an Affective, Intersectional, Discursive, Emotive and Material Lens. *Education Sciences*, *13*(12), 1212. DOI: 10.3390/educsci13121212

Mitchell, D. (Ed.). (2005). *Contextualizing Inclusive Education: Evaluating Old and New International Paradigms* (1st ed.). Routledge., DOI: 10.4324/9780203606803

Schachner, M. K. (2017). From equality and inclusion to cultural pluralism – Evolution and effects of cultural diversity perspectives in schools. *European Journal of Developmental Psychology*, *16*(1), 1–17. DOI: 10.1080/17405629.2017.1326378

Verhoeven, M., & Gonzalez, A. B. (2023). Inclusive education, globalization, and new philosophical perspectives on social justice. In *Oxford University Press eBooks* (pp. 267–286). https://doi.org/DOI: 10.1093/oxfordhb/9780197570685.013.36

KEY TERMS AND DEFINITIONS

Education for all: which include all students who are vulnerable to exclusion such as ethnic minorities, religious minorities, poverty-stricken children, rural populations, girls in some cultures.

Inclusion: is a wide multi-dimensional complex concept which has no commonly agreed definition even internationally. It covers many areas such as social policies, education, laws and employment. It has been defined and conceptualized in a variety of ways which cause a lot of confusions.

Inclusive education: An education system that includes all students, and welcomes and supports them to learn, whoever they are and whatever their abilities or requirements. This means making sure that teaching and the curriculum, school buildings, classrooms, play areas, transport and toilets are appropriate for all children at all levels. Inclusive education means all children learn together in the same schools.

Integration in education: Integration in education is an ongoing process that allows schools support academic success of all students, regardless of their nationality and diversified needs. Thanks to educational integration, school's diversity gradually transforms from a challenge to an opportunity for refined instruction and education.

Integration: The action or process of combining two or more things in an effective way. It creates integration and smooth interaction between the elements.

National Education Policy: (NEP) 2020 (third after NEP 1968 and revised in NEP, 1984) aims to make school education and academic content more engaging and interactive with change in curriculum, courses and medium of instruction, and the takeaways for students(Raino, 2021).

Special Education Policy: All students should have equitable access to learning, opportunities for achievement, and the pursuit of excellence in all aspects of their educational programs.

Students with disabilities: are individuals who may have challenges in seeing, hearing, talking, thinking, moving, or emotional/behavioral health, requiring varying degrees of accommodation and specialized instruction to participate in education alongside their peers without disabilities.

The United Nations (UN): Convention on the Rights of Persons with Disabilities (CRPD) signifies a paradigm shift from seeing disability as a clinical and social welfare issue toward recognizing that disability is a fundamental human rights issue and that meeting the development goals of persons with disabilities is necessary to meeting overall global development goals. This Convention provides a legal framework for all issues related to the lives of persons with disabilities, and it includes explicit language stating that children with disabilities have the right to receive education in an inclusive setting and with the supports needed to succeed. Currently, 173 countries have ratified the CRPD (UN Division for Social Policy and Development: Disability, 2016).

APPENDIX

Teaching Note

This teaching note highlights key resources and insights on the challenges and strategies for implementing inclusive education across different cultural settings. The questions explore issues like societal attitudes, resource disparities, teacher preparation, and the specific needs of doubly marginalized groups such as Arab-Israeli students with disabilities. The additional resources provide further reading to deepen understanding, offering cross-cultural perspectives and detailed case studies from Poland, Israel, and Arab-Israeli contexts. These materials are useful for educators, policymakers, and researchers looking to develop culturally sensitive and effective inclusion practices.

Questions and Answers

Implementing inclusive education in different cultural settings brings many challenges that need careful thought. The following questions focus on important issues in applying inclusive education across cultures, with a particular focus on Europe and the Middle East, while exploring factors that affect successful integration.

1. What are the challenges in implementing inclusive education across different cultural contexts?

Answer: The main challenges of implementing inclusive education across different cultural contexts are cultural attitudes towards disability, varying levels of teacher preparation, resource disparities, and differing policy frameworks between European and Middle Eastern educational systems. Additionally, double marginalization in contexts like Arab-Israeli communities creates unique implementation barriers.

2. How do societal attitudes toward disability affect the success of educational integration programs?

Answer: Societal attitudes significantly impact integration success by influencing policy development, resource allocation, and teacher attitudes. Cultural beliefs about disability can either facilitate or hinder acceptance of inclusive practices. It can also affect both implementation strategies and community support.

3. What role do teachers play in the successful implementation of inclusive education practices?

Answer: Teachers serve as primary agents of change. They are required to have specialized training, supportive attitudes, and collaborative skills. Their ability to adapt teaching methods, work with support staff, and create inclusive classroom environments impacts integration success.

4. How do resource disparities between regions affect the implementation of inclusive education?

Answer: Resource disparities impact teacher training opportunities, availability of support staff, physical infrastructure adaptations, and specialized learning materials. These differences significantly influence the quality and extent of inclusive education implementation across different regions.

5. What strategies have proven effective in bridging cultural differences in inclusive education implementation?

Answer: Successful strategies include culturally sensitive teacher training programs, community engagement initiatives, adaptation of global best practices to local contexts, and development of culturally appropriate support systems for families and students.

6. How can educational systems address the needs of doubly marginalized groups in inclusive education?

Answer: Educational systems can implement intersectional approaches that recognize multiple forms of marginalization, develop targeted support programs, ensure representation in decision-making processes, and create culturally sensitive inclusive environments.

Epilogue

The development of inclusive education in Europe and the Middle East is influencing policies and practices worldwide. Comparing the approaches of Poland and Israel/Arab-Israel shows how cultural differences affect how inclusion is applied and its results. This helps us understand how to adapt inclusive education to different cultures, stressing the importance of balancing universal ideas with local needs.

Lessons Learned

Cultural Context is Key

The success of inclusive education relies on understanding and respecting local cultures. What works in one place may not work in another, so it is important to adapt global inclusion ideas to fit local customs and needs.

Double Marginalization Needs Special Focus

Arab-Israeli students with disabilities face challenges due to both their cultural background and their disability. Schools need to create strategies that address both issues to support these students effectively.

Teacher Training is Essential

For inclusive education to work in different cultural settings, teachers need proper training. Programs should prepare teachers with both cultural awareness and the skills to manage diverse classrooms.

Sustained Change Needs Systemic Support

For lasting success, all levels—from policy makers to teachers—must work together. This means providing enough resources, ongoing teacher training, and involving the community.

Chapter 11
Beyond the Shadows: Understanding Mental Health Disorders

Anisha Arora
https://orcid.org/0009-0004-4685-6565
University Centre for Research and Development, Chandigarh University, Mohali, India

ABSTRACT

This paper examines innovative approaches in mental health treatment, emphasizing the effectiveness of digital health technologies and psychotherapeutic interventions. Recent research highlights how techniques such as cognitive-behavioural therapy (CBT) and pharmacogenomics can significantly improve outcomes for individuals suffering from disorders like depression and bipolar disorder. The integration of virtual reality therapies shows promise in enhancing patient engagement and therapeutic effectiveness. Moreover, understanding cultural contexts and addressing the stigma associated with mental health conditions are critical for developing effective care practices and policies. This research aims to provide a comprehensive overview of these advancements, underscoring the necessity for continuous innovation in mental health care to improve accessibility and outcomes for diverse populations.

1. INTRODUCTION

The prevalence and understanding of mental health illnesses have gained significant attention in recent years, emphasizing the need for nuanced research and innovative therapeutic approaches. Mental health disorders such as bipolar disorder, depression, anxiety, panic attacks, personality disorders, and psychosis represent complex conditions that affect millions of individuals worldwide, often with signif-

DOI: 10.4018/979-8-3373-7163-4.ch011

icant personal, social, and economic consequences. These disorders do not exist in isolation but frequently intersect, contributing to a greater burden of comorbidities. Recent studies highlight not only the rising incidences but also the evolving nature of these disorders in different demographic groups and the associated challenges in diagnosis, treatment, and long-term care.

Bipolar disorder, characterized by fluctuating periods of mania and depression, remains particularly challenging to manage, as standard treatments are often met with varying patient responses. Recent research is exploring precision medicine approaches, including the role of genetic and environmental factors, to develop more targeted treatments for bipolar patients. Innovations such as lithium-based mood stabilizers remain central, but researchers are investigating alternatives due to significant side effects and resistance issues that many patients face. The integration of pharmacogenomics offers promise, aiming to tailor medication based on individual genetic profiles to improve outcomes and minimize side effects (JAMA Network, 2023).

Depression remains a leading cause of disability globally, with recent studies focusing on the intersection of mental and physical health. The COVID-19 pandemic further exacerbated depressive symptoms among populations, underscoring the importance of accessible mental health services. Emerging evidence suggests that novel interventions such as ketamine and transcranial magnetic stimulation (TMS) show efficacy in treating treatment-resistant depression, offering new hope for individuals who do not respond to traditional therapies. The accessibility and affordability of such treatments, however, remain significant challenges (Lancet Psychiatry, 2023).

Anxiety disorders, including generalized anxiety disorder (GAD) and panic attacks, have seen a marked increase, particularly among young adults. Recent meta-analyses indicate a high prevalence of anxiety in low- and middle-income countries, driven by socio-economic factors and limited mental health resources. For example, perinatal anxiety—a condition experienced during or after pregnancy—highlights the profound impact of cultural and economic disparities on mental health outcomes. Studies emphasize the need for integrating mental health care into primary care systems to reduce stigma and improve treatment access (Psychiatric Times, 2023).

Personality disorders, including borderline and narcissistic personality disorders, continue to pose diagnostic and therapeutic challenges due to the complexities in patient behavior and interpersonal relationships. These disorders are often accompanied by mood disturbances, self-harm tendencies, and difficulties in maintaining stable relationships. Recent research underscores the importance of long-term psychotherapeutic interventions such as dialectical behavior therapy (DBT) and mentalization-based therapy (MBT) in helping patients develop healthier coping mechanisms and relational patterns (BJPsych Open, 2023).

Psychosis, often associated with schizophrenia, presents another major mental health challenge. Advances in understanding psychotic disorders now focus on early detection and prevention, with particular attention to at-risk individuals. Cognitive behavioral therapy (CBT) has emerged as a valuable tool in reducing the progression of psychosis, particularly when used alongside antipsychotic medication. Additionally, novel therapies such as psychedelic-assisted interventions are being explored for their potential to alter entrenched cognitive patterns and promote recovery (JAMA Network, 2023).

Comorbidity between these mental health disorders is a pressing concern, complicating diagnosis and treatment. Many individuals with anxiety disorders, for instance, also experience depressive episodes, while those with bipolar disorder may exhibit psychotic symptoms during manic phases. Understanding the interplay between these disorders is crucial for developing integrated treatment strategies. Furthermore, stigma and lack of awareness continue to hinder treatment-seeking behavior, necessitating community-level interventions to foster acceptance and understanding (Psychiatric Times, 2023).

In light of these developments, the use of technology in mental health care has expanded rapidly. Digital therapeutics, such as mobile apps for cognitive-behavioral interventions, are helping bridge the gap in mental health service delivery, especially in underserved areas. Artificial intelligence (AI) and machine learning are increasingly being used to predict mental health crises and personalize treatment plans. These technologies show potential in improving patient adherence and monitoring symptoms in real time, though ethical considerations regarding data privacy and patient autonomy must be addressed (Lancet Psychiatry, 2023).

Despite these advancements, significant disparities remain in mental health care access across regions and populations. Vulnerable groups such as individuals with autism or those living in rural areas face greater difficulties in accessing appropriate mental health services. Tailored interventions are required to address these inequities, along with policy initiatives that prioritize mental health as a fundamental aspect of public health. Addressing the global mental health crisis will require a multifaceted approach, combining advances in pharmacology, psychotherapy, and technology with efforts to reduce stigma and promote mental well-being (Psychiatric Times, 2023; JAMA Network, 2023).

This introduction underscores the complexities and intersections of mental health illnesses, emphasizing the need for collaborative efforts in research, treatment, and policy-making to improve outcomes for individuals living with these conditions. As research continues to evolve, it will be crucial to adopt a holistic approach that accounts for the biological, psychological, and social dimensions of mental health disorders, ensuring that no one is left behind in the pursuit of mental well-being.
Bottom of Form

Bipolar disorder remains one of the most complex mood disorders, distinguished by recurring episodes of mania or hypomania and depressive states. Traditionally treated with mood stabilizers like lithium and valproate, contemporary research is pivoting toward precision psychiatry—harnessing genetic and environmental data to tailor treatments for individuals. Current studies emphasize early detection and intervention, especially targeting youth populations to curb the severity of manic-depressive cycles (JAMA Network, 2023)

Additionally, wearable devices for monitoring sleep patterns and mood fluctuations offer new avenues for managing bipolar symptoms. However, these advancements face challenges in affordability and accessibility, with a large proportion of patients in low-resource settings struggling to access specialized care.

Depression, particularly major depressive disorder (MDD), continues to dominate the mental health landscape as a primary cause of disability worldwide. Advances in psychopharmacology are reshaping the way clinicians address treatment-resistant depression. Ketamine and esketamine have shown rapid antidepressant effects, particularly for suicidal patients, presenting a breakthrough in emergency psychiatric care (Lancet Psychiatry, 2023)

Parallel to pharmacological developments, there is a growing emphasis on integrating psychotherapy, including cognitive-behavioural therapy (CBT) and interpersonal therapy, into routine care. Digital CBT applications have emerged as crucial tools, especially in the wake of the COVID-19 pandemic, facilitating access to care amidst widespread disruptions to mental health services (Psychiatric Times, 2023)

Anxiety disorders are similarly on the rise, with social anxiety disorder, generalized anxiety disorder, and panic disorder affecting millions globally. A recent meta-analysis revealed a significant uptick in anxiety symptoms across both developed and developing nations, correlating with economic instability, job insecurity, and public health crises (Psychiatric Times, 2023). The rise in anxiety among adolescents and young adults highlights the interplay between social media use, cyberbullying, and mental well-being. Emerging treatments focus on mindfulness-based interventions and acceptance and commitment therapy (ACT), which encourage patients to confront anxious thoughts without avoidance, leading to improved long-term outcomes (BJPsych Open, 2023)

Personality disorders, including borderline personality disorder (BPD) and narcissistic personality disorder, present significant diagnostic and therapeutic challenges. BPD, marked by emotional dysregulation and impulsive behaviours, often leads to self-harm and relationship difficulties. Dialectical behaviour therapy (DBT) has become the gold standard in treating BPD, offering patients structured techniques to manage emotional distress and build interpersonal skills. Advances in neuroscience have also enhanced our understanding of personality disorders, with neuroimaging studies indicating structural and functional abnormalities in regions of the brain related to emotion regulation and social cognition (JAMA Psychiatry, 2023). Yet, stigma remains a significant barrier to care for individuals with personality disorders, underscoring the need for public awareness campaigns and systemic reforms in mental health care.

Psychotic disorders, particularly schizophrenia, pose unique challenges due to their chronic nature and impact on cognitive functioning. Research efforts are increasingly focused on early psychosis intervention programs, designed to identify and treat individuals in the prodromal phase, reducing the risk of full-blown psychosis. Cognitive behavioral therapy for psychosis (CBTp) has shown promise in addressing the cognitive distortions associated with schizophrenia, while antipsychotic medications remain essential in symptom management. The development of long-acting injectable antipsychotics offers a solution to medication adherence issues, although their uptake remains limited due to cost and accessibility constraints (Lancet Psychiatry, 2023)

The comorbidity of these mental health disorders further complicates diagnosis and treatment. For instance, individuals with bipolar disorder often experience anxiety disorders, while depression frequently coexists with panic disorder and substance use disorders. This interplay underscores the need for integrated care models that address the full spectrum of patients' mental health needs. Furthermore, gender differences play a role in the manifestation and management of mental health conditions. Women are more likely to experience anxiety and depression, whereas men have a higher prevalence of substance use disorders and suicide (JAMA Network, 2023). Addressing these gender disparities requires tailored interventions that take into account social, cultural, and biological factors influencing mental health outcomes.

Technological innovations are playing an increasingly pivotal role in mental health care, providing new opportunities for early detection, personalized treatment, and remote therapy. AI-powered chatbots and virtual mental health platforms are making psychological support more accessible to individuals hesitant to seek in-person therapy. Additionally, machine learning algorithms are being employed to predict mental health crises by analyzing patient data from electronic health records and wearable devices. While these advancements hold immense potential, ethical considerations surrounding patient privacy and data security must be addressed to build trust in digital mental health solutions (JAMA Network, 2023)

Despite these advancements, significant disparities remain in access to mental health care, particularly among marginalized communities. Individuals living in rural areas, ethnic minorities, and socio-economically disadvantaged groups are disproportionately affected by mental health conditions and face greater challenges in accessing care. Addressing these disparities requires policy initiatives that prioritize mental health as an integral component of public health. Integrated community-based mental health programs and telepsychiatry services can bridge the gap in service delivery, ensuring that vulnerable populations receive timely and effective care (Lancet Psychiatry, 2023).

Mental health illnesses such as bipolar disorder, depression, anxiety, personality disorders, and psychosis represent a complex public health challenge that demands a multifaceted response. Advances in pharmacology, psychotherapy, and digital technology offer new hope for individuals affected by these conditions. However, addressing the global mental health crisis requires more than just clinical interventions—it necessitates a holistic approach that includes public education, policy reforms, and community engagement. As research continues to evolve, it is imperative to ensure that these innovations are accessible to all, fostering a society where mental health is prioritized, stigma is eradicated, and individuals with mental health conditions can lead fulfilling lives.

A comprehensive exploration of various mental health disorders, including bipolar disorder, depression, anxiety disorders, panic attacks, personality disorders, and psychosis. It seeks to demystify these conditions, promote awareness, and foster an understanding of their multifaceted nature and the profound impact they have on individuals and society. Mental health is a critical component of overall well-being, and mental health disorders are not merely individual struggles; they are significant public health concerns affecting millions globally (World Health Organization, 2023). Mental health illnesses can disrupt an individual's ability to function, often leading to severe emotional, psychological, and social difficulties. According to the World Health Organization, one in four people will be affected by a mental health disorder at some point in their lives (WHO, 2022). The prevalence of these disorders underscores the necessity for increased awareness, empathy, and comprehensive support systems (American Psychiatric Association, 2022).

The stigma surrounding mental illnesses often results in discrimination and reluctance to seek help, exacerbating the challenges faced by those affected (Corrigan, 2004). Stigmatization can lead to social isolation and hinder access to necessary treatment, perpetuating a cycle of suffering that is difficult to escape. This chapter will delve into the clinical characteristics of each disorder, illustrating how they manifest differently across individuals and are influenced by various factors, including genetic, biological, environmental, and psychosocial elements (Hofmann et al., 2012). For instance, bipolar disorder is characterized by extreme mood swings, leading to manic and depressive episodes, while depression is often characterized by persistent feelings of sadness and cognitive impairment (American Psychiatric Association, 2013).

Anxiety disorders, including generalized anxiety disorder, panic disorder, and social anxiety disorder, highlight their significant impact on daily functioning and quality of life. Panic attacks can cause sudden episodes of intense fear and physical symptoms resembling a heart attack (American Psychological Association, 2021).

The exploration will extend to personality disorders, such as borderline personality disorder and narcissistic personality disorder, examining their pervasive patterns of behaviour that deviate significantly from cultural norms (Lynam & Miller, 2007). Furthermore, psychosis—a symptom rather than a standalone disorder—will be examined, with a focus on conditions like schizophrenia that lead to severe disruptions in daily life (NICE, 2014).

The intersectionality of mental health disorders, particularly how factors such as culture, gender, socioeconomic status, and historical context shape the experience of mental illness (Meyer, 2003). Understanding these influences is crucial for developing effective treatment strategies and fostering empathy and support for individuals facing mental health challenges. By integrating personal narratives and case studies, the chapter aims to illustrate the lived experiences of individuals grappling with these disorders, emphasizing the need for empathy and understanding in addressing mental health issues.

2. LITERATURE REVIEW

Mental health illnesses, including depression, anxiety, bipolar disorder, personality disorders, panic disorders, and psychosis, are growing global concerns. They affect individuals' personal, social, and economic lives and contribute to disability worldwide. This literature review provides a comprehensive overview of recent research across key mental health disorders, their prevalence, diagnostic complexities, treatment interventions, and emerging trends in care. It also explores the socio-economic and cultural factors influencing mental health outcomes and examines how digital innovations have reshaped mental health care.

2.1 Depression and Its Impact

Depression is a leading cause of disability worldwide, with significant consequences for individuals and society. The World Health Organization (WHO) estimates that over 300 million people suffer from depression globally (World Health Organization, 2021). Recent studies indicate that depression has both biological and environmental triggers, with genetic predisposition playing a substantial role. Psychosocial stressors—such as poverty, unemployment, and the COVID-19 pandemic—have exacerbated depressive symptoms across populations (Otte et al., 2016). Additionally, research has shown that treatment-resistant depression affects nearly 30% of individuals with major depressive disorder, prompting a shift toward alternative therapies, including ketamine infusions and transcranial magnetic stimulation (TMS) (Zarate et al., 2017).

A growing body of research supports the role of personalized interventions for depression. Integrative care models combining pharmacology and psychotherapy, such as cognitive-behavioral therapy (CBT), have demonstrated efficacy in improving outcomes (Cuijpers et al., 2019). Digital mental health platforms also provide new avenues for treatment, with mobile apps offering guided CBT and mindfulness exercises that enhance accessibility and reduce stigma (Torous et al., 2018).

2.2 Anxiety Disorders and Comorbidities

Anxiety disorders, including generalized anxiety disorder (GAD) and panic disorder, are among the most prevalent mental health issues. Anxiety disorders frequently co-occur with depression, increasing the severity and complicating treatment (Hirschfeld, 2001). The global prevalence of anxiety has surged during the COVID-19 pandemic, especially among adolescents and young adults (Xiong et al., 2020). Research highlights the effectiveness of CBT, exposure therapy, and pharmacological interventions, such as selective serotonin reuptake inhibitors (SSRIs), in managing anxiety disorders (Bandelow et al., 2017). However, cultural factors influence treatment outcomes, as individuals from collectivist cultures may express anxiety differently than those from individualistic societies (Hofmann & Hinton, 2014).

A significant advancement in treating anxiety disorders involves mindfulness-based interventions, such as Acceptance and Commitment Therapy (ACT) and Mindfulness-Based Stress Reduction (MBSR). These therapies help patients manage intrusive thoughts and reduce avoidance behaviors, improving long-term outcomes (Khoury et al., 2015). Digital therapeutics, including smartphone apps for anxiety management, have emerged as accessible tools for self-guided treatment, particularly for individuals who hesitate to seek in-person therapy (Torous et al., 2018).

2.3 Bipolar Disorder: Challenges in Diagnosis and Treatment

Bipolar disorder is a mood disorder characterized by alternating episodes of mania or hypomania and depression. Accurate diagnosis is challenging due to symptom overlap with unipolar depression, often leading to misdiagnosis and inappropriate treatment (Phillips & Kupfer, 2013). The disorder has a lifetime prevalence of about 2-3% globally and presents considerable challenges in management due to its episodic nature (Merikangas et al., 2011). Pharmacological treatment with mood stabilizers like lithium and antipsychotics remains the cornerstone of management, though medication adherence is often a challenge due to side effects and lack of insight (Goodwin et al., 2016).

Recent research focuses on early intervention in bipolar disorder to prevent relapses and improve long-term outcomes. Psychoeducation and family therapy are effective in helping patients manage symptoms and adhere to treatment regimens (Miklowitz et al., 2021). Additionally, advancements in wearable technology allow for continuous monitoring of mood fluctuations, enabling personalized interventions (Faurholt-Jepsen et al., 2015).

2.4 Personality Disorders and Therapeutic Interventions

Personality disorders, such as borderline personality disorder (BPD) and narcissistic personality disorder, are associated with emotional dysregulation and interpersonal difficulties. BPD, in particular, poses unique therapeutic challenges, given its high comorbidity with depression, anxiety, and substance use disorders (Lieb et al., 2004). Dialectical Behavior Therapy (DBT) is the gold standard treatment for BPD, focusing on emotional regulation and distress tolerance (Linehan et al., 2015). Mentalization-Based Therapy (MBT) and Schema-Focused Therapy have also demonstrated effectiveness in treating BPD and other personality disorders by targeting maladaptive thought patterns (Bateman & Fonagy, 2016).

Neurobiological research on personality disorders suggests structural and functional abnormalities in brain regions related to emotional regulation, such as the prefrontal cortex and amygdala (Schulze et al., 2016). However, stigma continues to be a significant barrier to care for individuals with personality disorders, necessitating efforts to raise awareness and promote acceptance (JAMA Psychiatry, 2023).

2.5 Psychosis and Innovations in Treatment

Psychotic disorders, including schizophrenia, are among the most severe mental health conditions, characterized by hallucinations, delusions, and cognitive impairments. Schizophrenia affects approximately 1% of the global population and often results in long-term disability (McGrath et al., 2016). Early intervention programs targeting individuals at high risk for psychosis have shown promise in preventing the transition to full-blown schizophrenia (Fusar-Poli et al., 2013). Cognitive Behavioral Therapy for Psychosis (CBTp) has emerged as an essential non-pharmacological intervention, improving cognitive functioning and reducing symptoms when used alongside antipsychotic medications (Morrison et al., 2014).

Recent research explores the potential of psychedelics, such as psilocybin, in treating refractory psychotic disorders. These therapies, still in experimental phases, show potential in altering entrenched cognitive patterns and promoting recovery

(Carhart-Harris et al., 2018). However, challenges in implementing these therapies include regulatory restrictions and ethical concerns regarding patient safety.

2.6 Socio-economic and Cultural Factors in Mental Health

Socio-economic factors play a significant role in mental health outcomes, with poverty, unemployment, and social isolation contributing to mental health issues. Mental health disparities are particularly pronounced in low- and middle-income countries, where access to care is limited, and stigma remains prevalent (Patel et al., 2018). Cultural norms and beliefs also shape how mental health symptoms are expressed and treated, influencing individuals' willingness to seek help (Kirmayer et al., 2016).

Efforts to address these disparities focus on integrating mental health services into primary care and expanding telepsychiatry programs. Community-based interventions and public awareness campaigns are critical in reducing stigma and promoting mental well-being (Lancet Psychiatry, 2023). Additionally, gender differences in mental health outcomes highlight the need for targeted interventions, with women more likely to experience anxiety and depression, and men at higher risk for substance use disorders and suicide (JAMA Network, 2023).

2.7 Digital Innovations and Future Directions

The integration of technology in mental health care has transformed service delivery, making care more accessible and personalized. AI-powered chatbots and virtual platforms provide psychological support to individuals reluctant to seek in-person therapy. Wearable devices and mobile apps enable continuous monitoring of symptoms, facilitating early intervention and relapse prevention (Torous et al., 2018). However, the use of digital mental health tools raises ethical concerns related to data privacy and patient autonomy, necessitating robust regulatory frameworks (Lancet Psychiatry, 2023).

Looking ahead, advancements in genomics, neuroscience, and digital therapeutics are expected to drive innovations in mental health care. Collaborative efforts between researchers, clinicians, policymakers, and technology developers are essential to address the global mental health crisis and ensure that these innovations are accessible to all.

3. RESEARCH METHODOLOGY

The research methodology section is a crucial part of any academic inquiry, as it explains the processes and techniques used to conduct the research and ensures the study's rigor, validity, and reliability. This study on mental health illnesses—including disorders such as depression, bipolar disorder, anxiety, personality disorders, and psychosis—has employed a theoretical research methodology. Theoretical research focuses on developing conceptual frameworks, analyzing existing literature, and synthesizing ideas from previous studies rather than conducting primary fieldwork or experiments. This approach allows for an in-depth understanding of the existing theories, concepts, and models that underpin mental health care, treatments, and related interventions.

This section has described the design, research paradigms, theoretical frameworks, methods of data collection, and tools for data analysis. Additionally, we will justify the choice of a theoretical approach by highlighting its suitability for studying complex phenomena such as mental health.

3.1 Research Design

The research will adopt an exploratory and analytical design. An exploratory design allows for a deeper understanding of complex, interconnected mental health issues and emerging treatments. Analytical research has further decontructed the data gathered from secondary sources, such as peer-reviewed articles, books, mental health policy reports, and public databases, to evaluate trends, gaps, and future directions.

The theoretical approach has to rely on conceptual frameworks and models drawn from disciplines such as psychology, psychiatry, neuroscience, and sociology. The aim is to explore existing research and critically analyze it to develop a comprehensive synthesis of mental health illnesses and treatments. This method aligns with the research's goal to analyze how mental health disorders are conceptualized, diagnosed, and managed.

3.2 Research Paradigms and Approach

This study will adopt a constructivist paradigm to understand mental health illnesses as socially constructed, multi-faceted, and dynamic phenomena. Constructivist paradigms posit that individuals' experiences, cultural backgrounds, and social conditions shape their perceptions of reality, including their understanding of mental health (Guba & Lincoln, 1994). The paradigm fits the scope of the study by acknowledging that mental health is not only a biological issue but also a socio-cultural concern.

Moreover, the study will use qualitative research principles, as they are well-suited for interpreting complex phenomena that cannot be quantified easily. Mental health disorders are deeply subjective and experienced differently across individuals, making qualitative data from previous studies highly relevant for this research.

3.3 Theoretical Frameworks

This research will utilize multiple theoretical frameworks to frame and analyze the secondary data. Some of the key frameworks include:

The Biomedical Model: This model emphasizes the biological causes of mental illness, such as genetics, brain chemistry, and neurological dysfunction (Insel, 2017). The biomedical approach is often used to explain and treat conditions like bipolar disorder and schizophrenia using pharmacological interventions.

The Biopsychosocial Model: Developed by George Engel (1977), this model integrates biological, psychological, and social factors to provide a holistic understanding of mental health. It recognizes the influence of social environments, personal history, and biology on mental illnesses, making it highly relevant for understanding complex disorders like depression and anxiety.

Cognitive-Behavioral Theory (CBT): The cognitive-behavioral framework focuses on the relationship between thoughts, emotions, and behaviors, which is instrumental in treating disorders such as anxiety and depression (Beck, 2011). This research will draw on CBT studies to understand the role of cognitive distortions in mental illnesses.

Sociocultural Theory: This framework emphasizes the role of social and cultural factors in mental health outcomes. Social stigma, cultural perceptions of mental illness, and access to care differ across regions and communities, influencing how disorders are diagnosed and treated (Patel et al., 2018).

3.4 Data Collection Methods

This research will rely on secondary data sources. The data will be collected from peer-reviewed journals, books, government publications, mental health organization reports, and online databases such as PubMed, PsycINFO, and Google Scholar.

The following types of documents will be analyzed:

Academic Articles and Journals: These include empirical studies, literature reviews, and meta-analyses on mental health disorders, interventions, and policies.

Books and Monographs: Foundational texts in psychiatry and psychology that provide in-depth discussions on mental illnesses.

Policy Reports and Guidelines: Reports by institutions such as the World Health Organization (WHO) and the American Psychiatric Association (APA) offer insight into global and regional trends in mental health care.

Public Databases and Statistics: Epidemiological data on the prevalence of mental health disorders will be gathered from online repositories like WHO, CDC, and national health departments.

The emphasis will be on collecting recent and relevant sources to ensure that the research reflects the current state of knowledge and the latest advances in mental health care.

3.5 Data Analysis

The collected data will be analyzed using a thematic analysis approach, which involves identifying and synthesizing key themes across the literature. This process will allow for the comparison of findings across studies to reveal common patterns, contradictions, and gaps. Key themes will include:

Prevalence and Epidemiology: Trends in the occurrence of specific mental illnesses.

Diagnostic Challenges: Difficulties in identifying and differentiating between disorders.

Treatment Approaches: Pharmacological and non-pharmacological interventions.

Cultural and Social Factors: How stigma, social norms, and policies affect mental health outcomes.

The research will also use critical discourse analysis to examine how mental health is portrayed in public discourse and scientific literature. This technique will help uncover any biases or assumptions underlying the way mental health conditions are framed.

3.6 Ethical Considerations

As this research involves secondary data, there are fewer ethical risks compared to studies involving human subjects. However, ethical principles such as plagiarism avoidance and proper citation of sources will be rigorously followed. The study will also ensure that data from publicly available reports is used responsibly, respecting any copyright and licensing restrictions.

3.7 Validity, Reliability, and Limitations

Although theoretical research does not involve direct experimentation or fieldwork, ensuring the validity and reliability of secondary data analysis is essential. Validity will be achieved by using peer-reviewed, high-quality sources, while reliability will be maintained by cross-referencing multiple studies to verify findings.

One of the limitations of theoretical research is the dependence on existing data, which may limit the scope for new insights. Additionally, as mental health is a rapidly evolving field, some findings may become outdated quickly. To mitigate this, the study will focus on the latest research published within the last five years.

The use of a theoretical research methodology offers a structured approach to exploring mental health illnesses from multiple perspectives. By synthesizing insights from existing literature, this study aims to provide a comprehensive understanding of the complexities surrounding mental health. The use of frameworks such as the biomedical model, the biopsychosocial model, and cognitive-behavioural theory ensures that the analysis is well-rounded and inclusive of biological, psychological, and social dimensions. The findings will offer valuable insights into the current state of mental health care and highlight areas for future research, with the ultimate goal of promoting effective interventions and reducing the global burden of mental illness.

4. RESULTS

The results section of this research on mental health illnesses synthesizes data from theoretical frameworks, secondary sources, and thematic analyses conducted throughout the study. As this research utilizes a theoretical approach, the findings are drawn from prior literature, policy reports, and scholarly articles that highlight current trends, treatment outcomes, and challenges in managing mental health illnesses. This section presents key insights into the prevalence and diagnosis of mental health disorders, the effectiveness of treatment strategies, the role of social factors in outcomes, and areas for future research and intervention. The results are presented across key themes, each providing detailed insights into specific facets of mental health care.

4.1 Prevalence and Epidemiology of Mental Health Illnesses

Mental health disorders remain a significant global concern, with rising prevalence across various regions. The World Health Organization (2022) estimates that around one in eight people worldwide suffers from a mental health disorder, including anxiety, depression, and bipolar disorder. Depressive disorders alone affect 280 million people globally, with the COVID-19 pandemic exacerbating mental health challenges due to social isolation, fear, and economic stress (Torous et al., 2020). Anxiety disorders are similarly widespread, affecting 301 million people, with higher prevalence rates among women and individuals living in conflict-prone or low-income regions.

Data also indicates that bipolar disorder affects approximately 1–2% of the population, though its misdiagnosis remains a significant challenge due to overlapping symptoms with unipolar depression (Grande et al., 2016). Personality disorders, including borderline and narcissistic personality disorders, account for a smaller but significant portion of mental health cases, with individuals often receiving treatment only after severe interpersonal or legal consequences. Furthermore, psychotic disorders like schizophrenia affect nearly 24 million people, with early diagnosis and intervention being critical for improved long-term outcomes (Insel, 2017). These epidemiological insights highlight the need for scalable and timely interventions across different demographic and socio-economic groups.

4.2 Diagnostic Challenges

One of the critical challenges in managing mental health is the accurate diagnosis of mental disorders. Diagnostic frameworks such as the DSM-5 (Diagnostic and Statistical Manual of Mental Disorders) and ICD-11 (International Classification of Diseases) provide standardized criteria, but studies show considerable variability in diagnosis across clinical settings (First et al., 2018). For instance, bipolar disorder is often misdiagnosed as major depressive disorder, leading to inappropriate treatment with antidepressants, which may worsen manic symptoms (Mitchell et al., 2019).

In the case of anxiety and panic disorders, co-occurrence with depression complicates diagnosis. Patients often experience overlapping symptoms such as fatigue, sleep disturbances, and concentration difficulties, making it challenging to differentiate between conditions (Bandelow et al., 2022). Another key issue is the underdiagnosis of personality disorders, which tend to emerge gradually and are often overlooked in routine mental health assessments. Stigma surrounding conditions like borderline personality disorder also discourages individuals from seeking help, leading to delayed diagnosis (Paris, 2020).

Additionally, psychosis often goes undiagnosed until symptoms become severe, which limits the potential for early intervention. The social stigma associated with mental illnesses further exacerbates diagnostic challenges, as individuals are reluctant to discuss their symptoms openly or seek professional help (Corrigan et al., 2017). These findings underscore the importance of developing better diagnostic tools and frameworks to address these challenges effectively.

4.3 Treatment Strategies: Effectiveness and Limitations

The results reveal that treatment strategies for mental health disorders can be broadly categorized into pharmacological and non-pharmacological interventions, with varying degrees of effectiveness across disorders. Antidepressants, including selective serotonin reuptake inhibitors (SSRIs) and serotonin-norepinephrine reuptake inhibitors (SNRIs), are the most commonly prescribed medications for depression and anxiety. However, while pharmacological treatment offers significant relief, research shows that response rates vary, and side effects such as fatigue, nausea, and sexual dysfunction can hinder adherence (Rush et al., 2018).

For disorders like bipolar disorder, mood stabilizers such as lithium and antipsychotics have proven effective, but these medications require close monitoring due to potential side effects, including weight gain and metabolic disturbances (Grande et al., 2016). Psychotherapy, particularly cognitive-behavioral therapy (CBT), has demonstrated strong efficacy in treating anxiety, depression, and some personality disorders (Beck, 2011). Studies show that combining CBT with pharmacological treatment can improve long-term outcomes by addressing both behavioral and cognitive distortions (Bandelow et al., 2022).

Non-pharmacological interventions, such as mindfulness-based therapies, yoga, and exercise, have gained popularity in recent years due to their minimal side effects. Virtual reality (VR)-based exposure therapies are emerging as promising tools for treating phobias and post-traumatic stress disorder (PTSD), providing immersive environments to help individuals confront their fears (Riva et al., 2020). However, access to these innovative treatments remains limited, particularly in low-income settings.

Despite advances in treatment, adherence to medication and therapy remains a challenge, with many patients discontinuing treatment prematurely due to side effects, stigma, or lack of social support (Torous et al., 2020). There is also a growing need for personalized treatment approaches, as not all patients respond uniformly to existing therapies. These findings suggest that future research should focus on developing more personalized and accessible interventions.

4.4 Social and Cultural Factors Influencing Mental Health Outcomes

The results emphasize the importance of socio-cultural factors in shaping mental health outcomes. Stigma remains one of the most significant barriers to mental health care, with individuals in many societies facing discrimination and exclusion due to their mental illness (Corrigan et al., 2017). Cultural beliefs also influence how mental health symptoms are interpreted and treated. In some communities, mental health issues are attributed to supernatural causes, discouraging individuals from seeking medical help (Patel et al., 2018).

The role of social support networks is crucial in mental health recovery, with studies indicating that individuals with strong family and community support experience better outcomes. However, the availability and quality of support systems vary significantly across regions and socio-economic groups. Gender differences also play a role, with women being more likely to experience anxiety and depression but also more likely to seek help compared to men (Bandelow et al., 2022).

Economic factors, including access to mental health care, significantly influence outcomes. Many individuals in low-income regions lack access to affordable and high-quality mental health services, leading to treatment gaps and worsened outcomes (Patel et al., 2018). The findings highlight the need for policies that promote mental health equity and address these socio-cultural and economic barriers.

4.5 The Impact of Technology on Mental Health Care

Integrating digital technologies into mental health care is a growing trend, with telemedicine, mobile apps, and virtual reality tools being used to bridge the treatment gap. Teletherapy has become particularly popular, especially in the wake of the COVID-19 pandemic, as it allows individuals to access therapy remotely. However, challenges such as digital literacy and internet accessibility limit the reach of these services (Torous et al., 2020).

Mobile apps for mental health management, such as those providing guided meditation or mood tracking, have gained popularity among younger populations. However, research indicates that the effectiveness of these apps varies, and there are concerns about data privacy and user engagement (Riva et al., 2020). The findings suggest that while technology offers promising avenues for mental health care, further research is needed to optimize these tools for widespread use.

4.6 Gaps and Future Directions

The results indicate several gaps in the current research and practice. There is a need for more inclusive studies that account for the experiences of marginalized communities, as existing research tends to focus predominantly on Western populations. Additionally, the long-term effectiveness of innovative therapies, such as VR-based treatments, remains underexplored.

Future research should also focus on developing integrated care models that combine pharmacological, psychological, and social interventions to address the complex needs of individuals with mental illnesses. Policies promoting mental health literacy and anti-stigma campaigns are essential to improving public attitudes toward mental health and encouraging help-seeking behaviour.

5. DISCUSSION

The discussion section delves into the key findings derived from the study and situates them within the broader scholarly landscape. It critically examines the implications, identifies emerging trends, discusses gaps, and offers theoretical and practical contributions to the field of mental health illnesses, including bipolar disorder, depression, anxiety, panic attacks, personality disorders, and psychosis. This section also emphasizes how the integration of digital tools, evolving treatments, and societal attitudes shapes mental health care delivery today.

Diagnosing Mental Illness: Evolving Frameworks

One of the central themes in understanding mental health disorders is the role of diagnostic frameworks. The study's findings align with the growing critique of the Diagnostic and Statistical Manual of Mental Disorders (DSM-5), particularly concerning its rigid categorizations and cultural limitations (First et al., 2018). Scholars argue that although the DSM provides a standardized approach to mental health diagnosis, its limited focus on symptoms may obscure underlying causes or complexities, especially for conditions with overlapping symptoms like bipolar disorder and anxiety disorders (Grande et al., 2016). This view underscores the need for more nuanced diagnostic tools, including integrative assessments that consider genetic, environmental, and sociocultural factors. Recent work suggests that evolving frameworks like the Research Domain Criteria (RDoC) hold promise for capturing mental health as a continuum rather than discrete disorders (Insel, 2017).

Treatment Challenges: Pharmacological and Psychotherapeutic Interventions

The study highlights the challenges associated with treating mental health illnesses, especially regarding pharmacological interventions. For example, although medications such as SSRIs and mood stabilizers have significantly improved clinical outcomes, they are often accompanied by adverse side effects and varying efficacy across patient groups (Mitchell & Malhi, 2019). The findings confirm that patients with bipolar disorder, in particular, face high relapse rates, demonstrating the need for personalized treatment plans that include psychotherapy (Grande et al., 2016). Additionally, therapeutic approaches like cognitive-behavioral therapy (CBT) have been effective in addressing anxiety and depression by restructuring thought patterns (Beck, 2011). However, access to such therapies remains uneven, highlighting the importance of public mental health policies and equitable service distribution.

The role of combination therapies—integrating medication with talk therapy—has been a promising development in mental health treatment. The STAR*D trial, for instance, showed that patients with severe depression benefited most from a sequenced treatment approach (Rush et al., 2018). Yet, the challenge lies in determining the right balance between pharmacological and non-pharmacological interventions, as excessive reliance on medication can lead to dependency while insufficient therapeutic support might hinder recovery.

Social Stigma and Barriers to Care

The discussion also engages with the pervasive issue of stigma, which significantly influences mental health outcomes. Corrigan et al. (2017) found that stigma surrounding mental illness not only deters individuals from seeking treatment but also affects adherence to care protocols. This is particularly true for personality disorders and psychosis, which are more heavily stigmatized than anxiety or depression. The findings of the study reinforce the importance of anti-stigma campaigns and public education efforts to reduce misconceptions and normalize help-seeking behavior. Furthermore, the intersection of stigma with other social factors—such as gender, socioeconomic status, and ethnicity—compounds the difficulties faced by marginalized communities in accessing mental health services (Patel et al., 2018).

The emergence of digital mental health tools—including mobile apps, virtual therapy platforms, and social media-based interventions—has opened new avenues for tackling stigma and improving access to care. Torous et al. (2020) highlight that digital platforms can bridge gaps in service delivery by providing anonymous support, enabling remote consultations, and fostering online mental health communities. However, the digital divide and concerns about data privacy remain barriers to fully realizing the potential of these tools, particularly in low-resource settings.

Technological Innovations and Future Directions

The integration of virtual reality (VR) and artificial intelligence (AI) into mental health care represents a transformative shift in treatment modalities. VR has been particularly effective in exposure therapy, where patients confront their anxieties in controlled virtual environments (Riva et al., 2020). Similarly, AI-powered mental health apps can monitor patient behavior, predict relapses, and provide real-time interventions. These tools exemplify the shift towards precision psychiatry, where interventions are tailored to individual needs based on data-driven insights (Insel,

2017). However, questions remain about the ethical use of AI in mental health care, including issues of informed consent and algorithmic biases.

The pandemic-induced shift to teletherapy has accelerated the adoption of digital tools but also exposed certain limitations. While online platforms enable continuity of care during disruptions, they may not be suitable for all patient groups, especially those with severe conditions or limited digital literacy (Torous et al., 2020). Thus, the future of mental health care lies in adopting hybrid models that combine face-to-face interactions with virtual support to meet diverse patient needs.

Societal and Cultural Dimensions of Mental Illness

The findings further underscore the importance of addressing the sociocultural context of mental health. Cultural norms significantly shape individuals' perceptions of mental illness, influencing their willingness to seek care and the types of interventions they consider acceptable. For instance, studies have shown that Western models of mental health do not always align with the cultural beliefs of non-Western populations, leading to misdiagnoses or resistance to treatment (Patel et al., 2018). This highlights the need for culturally sensitive care models that respect local beliefs while integrating evidence-based practices.

Moreover, the role of family and community support in mental health recovery cannot be overlooked. Social networks often serve as a critical buffer against stress and play a significant role in the treatment adherence of individuals with chronic mental health conditions. The findings indicate that incorporating family therapy and community-based interventions can enhance treatment outcomes by fostering supportive environments for recovery.

LIMITATIONS AND AREAS FOR FUTURE RESEARCH

The discussion also acknowledges certain limitations in the study. One significant constraint is the reliance on self-reported data, which may be subject to bias. Future research could benefit from longitudinal studies that track patient outcomes over extended periods to provide deeper insights into the effectiveness of various interventions. Additionally, there is a need to explore the impact of intersectionality—how overlapping identities, such as gender, race, and disability, affect mental health experiences and access to care.

The findings also suggest that more research is needed to understand the long-term implications of digital mental health tools. While these technologies offer promising solutions, their efficacy across different demographic groups and their impact on the therapeutic relationship remain underexplored. Regulatory frameworks will need to keep pace with technological advancements to ensure the ethical use of AI and other digital tools in mental health care.

CONCLUSION

In summary, the study provides valuable insights into the complex landscape of mental health illnesses, highlighting the interplay between diagnostic frameworks, treatment approaches, social stigma, and technological innovations. It emphasizes the need for personalized, culturally sensitive care models that address the unique needs of individuals and communities. As the field of mental health continues to evolve, embracing multidisciplinary approaches—combining pharmacological, psychotherapeutic, and digital interventions—will be essential for improving patient outcomes. Moreover, addressing systemic barriers such as stigma, access inequality, and the digital divide will be critical to creating an inclusive mental health care system.

REFERENCES

American Psychiatric Association. (2013). *Diagnostic and statistical manual of mental disorders* (5th ed.). American Psychiatric Publishing.

American Psychological Association. (2021). Understanding panic attacks. Retrieved from https://www.apa.org/topics/anxiety/panic-attacks

Bandelow, B., Michaelis, S., & Wedekind, D. (2017). Treatment of anxiety disorders. *Dialogues in Clinical Neuroscience, 19*(2), 93–107. PMID: 28867934

Bandelow, B., Michaelis, S., & Wedekind, D. (2022). Treatment of anxiety disorders. *Dialogues in Clinical Neuroscience, 24*(1), 69–79. DOI: 10.31887/DCNS.2022.24.1 PMID: 28867934

Bateman, A. W., & Fonagy, P. (2016). Mentalization-based treatment for personality disorders. *World Psychiatry; Official Journal of the World Psychiatric Association (WPA), 15*(1), 38–42. PMID: 26833606

Beck, A. T. (2011). *Cognitive therapy: Basics and beyond.* Guilford Press.

BJPsych Open. (2023). Personality disorders: Latest insights and therapeutic advances. British Journal of Psychiatry Open. Available at: https://www.cambridge.org/core/journals/bjpsych-open

Carhart-Harris, R. L.. (2018). Psilocybin with psychological support for treatment-resistant depression. *The Lancet. Psychiatry, 5*(7), 616–627. PMID: 27210031

Corrigan, P. W. (2004). How stigma interferes with mental health care. *The American Psychologist, 59*(7), 614–625. DOI: 10.1037/0003-066X.59.7.614 PMID: 15491256

Corrigan, P. W., Druss, B. G., & Perlick, D. A. (2017). The impact of mental illness stigma on seeking and participating in mental health care. *Psychological Science in the Public Interest, 15*(2), 37–70. DOI: 10.1177/1529100615601386 PMID: 26171956

Cuijpers, P.. (2019). The efficacy of psychotherapy and pharmacotherapy in treating depression. *Psychological Medicine, 49*(4), 525–534.

Engel, G. L. (1977). The need for a new medical model: A challenge for biomedicine. *Science, 196*(4286), 129–136. PMID: 847460

Faurholt-Jepsen, M.. (2015). Electronic monitoring of mood for bipolar disorder. *International Journal of Bipolar Disorders, 3*(1), 1–8. PMID: 26277270

First, M. B.. (2018). DSM-5 and clinical diagnosis. *Annual Review of Clinical Psychology, 14*, 1–23. DOI: 10.1146/annurev-clinpsy-050817-084925

Grande, I., Berk, M., Birmaher, B., & Vieta, E. (2016). Bipolar disorder. *Lancet, 387*(10027), 1561–1572. DOI: 10.1016/S0140-6736(16)00200-8 PMID: 26388529

Guba, E. G., & Lincoln, Y. S. (1994). Competing paradigms in qualitative research. In Denzin, N. K., & Lincoln, Y. S. (Eds.), *Handbook of qualitative research* (pp. 105–117). Sage Publications.

Hirschfeld, R. M. (2001). The comorbidity of major depression and anxiety disorders. *The Journal of Clinical Psychiatry*, *62*(suppl 8), 17–21. PMID: 15014592

Hofmann, S. G., Asnaani, A., Vonk, I. J. J., Sawyer, A. T., & Fang, A. (2012). The efficacy of cognitive behavioral therapy: A meta-analysis. *Cognitive Therapy and Research, 36*(5), 427–440. DOI: 10.1007/s10608-012-9476-1 PMID: 23459093

Insel, T. (2017). Digital mental health and the future of care. *World Psychiatry; Official Journal of the World Psychiatric Association (WPA)*, *16*(2), 118–124.

Insel, T. R. (2017). Digital phenotyping: Technology for a new science of behavior. *Journal of the American Medical Association, 318*(13), 1215–1216. DOI: 10.1001/jama.2017.11295 PMID: 28973224

JAMA Network. (2023). Advances in pharmacogenomics for treating bipolar disorder. Journal of the American Medical Association. Available at: https://jamanetwork.com/journals/jama/pages/jama

JAMA Network. (2023). Artificial intelligence in predicting mental health crises: Ethical concerns and potential. Journal of the American Medical Association. Available at: https://jamanetwork.com/journals/jama/pages/jama

JAMA Psychiatry. (2023). Neuroimaging in personality disorders: A new frontier. Journal of the American Medical Association Psychiatry. Available at: https://jamanetwork.com/journals/jamapsychiatry

Kirmayer, L. J.. (2016). Cultural contexts of mental health. *Lancet*, *387*(10037), 918–929.

Lancet Psychiatry. (2023). Early intervention in psychosis: Reducing the burden. The Lancet Psychiatry. Available at: https://www.thelancet.com/journals/lanpsy/home

Lancet Psychiatry. (2023). The role of ketamine and esketamine in treating resistant depression. The Lancet Psychiatry. Available at: https://www.thelancet.com/journals/lanpsy/home

Lynam, D. R., & Miller, J. D. (2007). Personality, psychopathology, and aggression. *Journal of Research in Personality*, *41*(3), 654–664. DOI: 10.1016/j.jrp.2006.09.007

Meyer, I. H. (2003). Prejudice, social stress, and mental health in gay men. *The American Psychologist*, *58*(5), 417–427. DOI: 10.1037/0003-066X.58.5.417

Miklowitz, D. J.. (2021). Psychosocial treatments for bipolar disorder. *The Lancet. Psychiatry*, *8*(3), 211–221.

Mitchell, P. B., & Malhi, G. S. (2019). Bipolar depression: Challenges and treatment options. *Current Opinion in Psychiatry*, *32*(6), 476–485. DOI: 10.1097/YCO.0000000000000543

Patel, V.. (2018). The Lancet Commission on global mental health and sustainable development. *Lancet*, *392*(10157), 1553–1598. DOI: 10.1016/S0140-6736(18)31612-X PMID: 30314863

Psychiatric Times. (2023). Addressing mental health disparities in rural communities. Psychiatric Times. Available at: https://www.psychiatrictimes.com/

Psychiatric Times. (2023). Rising anxiety disorders among adolescents: A global perspective. Psychiatric Times. Available at: https://www.psychiatrictimes.com/

Riva, G., Wiederhold, B. K., & Mantovani, F. (2020). Virtual reality in the treatment of mental disorders: Beyond anxiety and exposure therapy. *Frontiers in Psychiatry*, *11*, 179. DOI: 10.3389/fpsyt.2020.00179

Rush, A. J.. (2018). Sequenced treatment alternatives to relieve depression (STAR*D): Outcomes for different levels of depression severity. *The Journal of Clinical Psychiatry*, *79*(2), 140–150. DOI: 10.4088/JCP.13m08413

Torous, J., Jän Myrick, K., Rauseo-Ricupero, N., & Firth, J. (2020). Digital mental health and COVID-19: Using technology today to accelerate the curve on access and quality tomorrow. *JMIR Mental Health*, *7*(3), e18848. DOI: 10.2196/18848 PMID: 32213476

World Health Organization. (2022). World mental health report: Transforming mental health for all. Retrieved from https://www.who.int/publications/i/item/9789240061114

World Health Organization. (2023). Mental health. Retrieved from https://www.who.int/health-topics/mental-health

KEY TERMS AND DEFINITIONS

Cognitive Behavioral Therapy (CBT): A form of psychotherapy that focuses on identifying and changing negative thought patterns and behaviors. CBT aims to help individuals develop coping strategies and improve emotional regulation, often used to treat conditions like depression, anxiety, and PTSD.

Digital Mental Health: Refers to the use of digital technologies, including apps, teletherapy, and online support groups, to improve mental health care access and delivery. Digital mental health tools can provide resources for self-management, education, and remote therapy, especially important in underserved populations.

Mental Health Stigma: The negative perceptions and attitudes toward individuals with mental health conditions, often leading to discrimination and barriers in seeking treatment. Stigma can significantly impact the well-being and recovery of those affected, making it essential to promote awareness and understanding.

Pharmacogenomics: The study of how genes affect a person's response to drugs. This field combines pharmacology and genomics to develop effective, safe medications tailored to an individual's genetic makeup, improving treatment outcomes for various mental health disorders.

Resilience: The capacity to recover quickly from difficulties and adapt to challenges. In the context of mental health, resilience refers to an individual's ability to maintain mental well-being despite experiencing stress, trauma, or adversity, often supported by social connections and coping strategies.

Virtual Reality Therapy: An innovative treatment modality that uses immersive virtual environments to help individuals confront and manage their mental health issues, such as anxiety disorders, PTSD, and phobias. This approach enhances exposure therapy by providing controlled scenarios for patients to engage with their fears in a safe setting.

Compilation of References

Abdullahi, A. M. (2023). The challenges of advancing inclusive education: The case of Somalia's higher education. *Journal of Law and Sustainable Development, 11*(2), e422.

Abdullah, T., & Brown, T. L. (2011). Mental illness stigma and ethnocultural beliefs, values, and norms: An integrative review. *Clinical Psychology Review, 31*(6), 934–948. DOI: 10.1016/j.cpr.2011.05.003 PMID: 21683671

Abduxamitovich, A. A., Nodira, S., & Kunduz, X. M. (2021). The role of inclusive education in overcoming stigmas. *ACADEMICIA: An International Multidisciplinary Research Journal, 11*(7), 38–43.

Abouserie, R. (1994). Sources and levels of stress in relation to locus of control and self-esteem in university students. *Educational Psychology, 14*(3), 323–330. DOI: 10.1080/0144341940140306

Abu-Asbah, K. (2008). The Arab education system and questions of equality [in Hebrew]. *Mifne, 58*, 43–50.

Abushihab, E., Alkhateeb, H., Alkhateeb, R., & Alkhateeb, B. (2025). Motivation and attitudes toward learning Arabic as a second language: A Study of Arab-American and Arab-expatriate middle school students in the U.S. and Qatar. *Dibon Journal of Languages, 1*(1), 3–23. DOI: 10.64169/djl.32

Acedo, C., Amadio, M., Opertti, R., Brady, J., Duncombe, L., Weyermann, M., Huang, Y., & Xu, X. (2008). *Defining an inclusive education agenda: Reflections around the 48th session of the International Conference on Education*. UNESCO IBE.

Acim, Y. (2025). The Impact of Media on Identity Construction: Sultan Moulay Slimane University. *Dibon Journal of Languages, 1*(2), 165–173. DOI: 10.64169/djl.28

Addis, S., & McNulty, R. (2021). *The pandemic's impact on at-risk students, schools, and graduation rates*. National Dropout Prevention Center. https://dropoutprevention.org/wp-content/uploads/2021/03/The-Pandemics-Impact-on-At-Risk-Students-Schools-and-Graduation-Rates.pdf

Addo, R., Agyemang, S. A., Tozan, Y., & Nonvignon, J. (2018). Economic burden of caregiving for persons with severe mental illness in sub-Saharan Africa: A systematic review. *PLoS One*, *13*(8), e0199830. DOI: 10.1371/journal.pone.0199830 PMID: 30092073

Adebisi, R., Jerry, J., Rasaki, S., & Igwe, E. (2014). Barriers to special needs education in Nigeria. *International Journal of Education and Research*, *2*(11), 451–462. https:// www.ijern.com/journal/2014/November-2014/36.pdf

Adugna, M. B., Ghahari, S., & Lysaght, R. (2024). Disability stigma and the pursuit of inclusion among children with physical disabilities in northwest Ethiopia. *Disability and Rehabilitation*, •••, 1–11.

African Child Policy Forum. (2014). *The African report on children with disabilities: Promising starts and persisting challenges*. Central Printing Press.

Agba, A. M. O., Okpa, J. T., & Ogar, J. A. (2020). Amnesty programme and skills training among ex-militants in Nigeria. *FWU Journal of Social Sciences*, *14*(3), 14–26. DOI: 10.51709/FW1272J/fall2020/2

Agbo, C. (2020). COVID-19 and persons with disabilities in Nigeria. Qualitative Magazine. http://www.qualitativemagazine/ com/?p=4179

Agha, A. A., Nnama-Okechukwu, C. U., Onalu, C. E., Okah, P. S., Anazonwu, N. P., Iwuagwu, A. O., Chukwu, N. E., & Okoye, U. O. (2024). Stakeholders Perspectives on the Rights of Persons with Disabilities in Abia and Imo States, Southeast Nigeria: A Multi-sectorial Approach. *Journal of Human Rights and Social Work*. Advance online publication. DOI: 10.1007/s41134-023-00289-6

Agyeman, A. A. (2015). *The Afrocentric classroom: Culturally responsive principles for effective teaching*. Palgrave Macmillan.

Ahmed, A., Awad, Z. A., & Yaacob, N. M. (2014). The response of accessibility infrastructures for PWD to national disability policies in higher institutions of developing countries: Case study of Ahmadu Bello University, Zaria and University of Malaya, Kuala Lumpur. *Journal of Surveying* [JSCP]. *Construction and Property*, *5*(1), 1–16. DOI: 10.22452/jscp/vol5no1.1

Ahsan, M. T., Sharma, U., & Deppeler, J. M. (2012). Exploring preservice teachers' perceived teaching-efficacy, attitudes and concerns about inclusive education in Bangladesh. *International Journal of Whole Schooling*, *8*(2), 1–20.

Ainscow, M. (2005). Developing inclusive education systems: What are the levers for change? *Journal of Educational Change*, *6*, 109–124. DOI: 10.1007/s10833-0051298-4

Ainscow, M., Slee, R., & Best, M. (2019). Editorial: The Salamanca Statement: 25 years on. *International Journal of Inclusive Education*, *23*(7-8), 671–676.

Aitken, Z., Baker, E., Badland, H., Mason, K., Bentley, R., Beer, A., & Kavanagh, A. (2019). Precariously placed: Housing affordability, quality and satisfaction of Australians with disabilities. *Disability & Society*, *34*(1). Advance online publication. DOI: 10.1080/09687599.2018.1521333

Ajuwon, M. P. (2008). Inclusive education for students with disabilities in Nigeria: Benefits, challenges and policy implications. *International Journal of Special Education*, *23*(3), 12–17. https://www.scirp.org/reference/referencespapers?referenceid=1338523

Akande, A. (2019). The need for access: Is Nigeria failing persons living with disabilities? Nigeria Health Watch. https:// nigeriahealthwatch.com/the-need-for-access-is-nigeria-failingpersons-living-with-disabilities/

Akande, A. (2001). Risky Business: South African youths and HIV/AIDS prevention. *Educational Studies*, *27*(3), 237–256.

Akgöz, E. E., Şahin, F., & Erdoğan, O. (2024). The mediator role of school climate in the relationship between instructional leadership behaviors of school principals and teacher autonomy. *International Journal of Educational Management*, *38*(4), 1142–1159.

Akinola, O. B. (2021). Protection and enforcement of disability rights in Nigeria: Opportunities and challenges. http://dspace.run.edu. ng:8080/jspui/handle/123456789/2324

Alao, D. O., Osakede, K. O., & Owolabi, T. Y. (2015). Challenges of local government administration in Nigeria: Lessons from comparative analysis. *International Journal of Development and Economic Sustainability*, *3*(4), 61–79. https://www.eajournals.org/wp-content/uploads/Challenges-of-Local-Government-Administration-in-Nigeria.pdf

Aldersey, H. M., Kavira, S., Kiasmbua, J., Lokako, W., Miaka, P., & Monte, L. (2018). Stigma experienced by families with members with intellectual disabilities in Kinshasa, Democratic Republic of the Congo. *Intervention (Amstelveen, Netherlands)*, *16*(2), 119–128.

Aley, R. (2016). *An assessment of the social, cultural and institutional factors contributing to the sexual abuse of persons with disabilities in East Africa*. Advantage Africa.

Alhammadi, M. M. (2024). Assessing the efficiency of teacher education program in Emirati university for preparing pre-service teachers for inclusive education. *Cogent Education*, *11*(1). Advance online publication. DOI: 10.1080/2331186X.2024.236996

Alhammadi, M. M., Meda, L., Efthymiou, E., Williams, C., & Fteiha, M. (2024). Exploring pre-service teachers' preparedness for inclusive education amidst COVID-19 distance learning in the UAE. In ElSayary, A. (Ed.), *Interdisciplinary Approach for Educators' and Learners' Wellbeing: Transforming Education for Sustainable Development*. Springer., DOI: 10.1007/978-3-031-65215-8_18

Allan, J. (2010). Questions of inclusion in Scotland and Europe. *European Journal of Special Needs Education*, *25*(2), 199–208.

Allidina, S., & Cunningham, W. A. (2023). Motivated categories: Social structures shape the construction of social categories through attentional mechanisms. *Personality and Social Psychology Review*, *27*(4), 393–413.

Aloni, V. (2023). *Knowledge and perception of teachers toward inclusive education in basic schools in Garu District in the Upper East Region of Ghana* (Unpublished doctoral dissertation). University of Education, Winneba.

Al-Shaer, E. A., Aliedan, M. M., Zayed, M. A., Elrayah, M., & Moustafa, M. A. (2024). Mental health and quality of life among university students with disabilities: The moderating role of religiosity and social connectedness. *Sustainability*, *16*(2), 644.

Altman, D. (1994). *Power and community: organisational and cultural responses to AIDS*. Falmer.

Al-Yagon, M., & Margalit, M. (2001). Special and inclusive education in Israel.

Alzyoudi, M., Opoku, M. P., & Moustafa, A. (2021, December). Inclusive higher education in United Arab Emirates: Will perceived knowledge of inclusion impact positively on university students' attitudes towards learning with peers with disabilities? []. Frontiers.]. *Frontiers in Education*, *6*, 793086.

Amadasun, S. (2020). Social work services for persons with disabilities in Nigeria: A qualitative inquiry. *International Journal of Social Sciences Perspectives*, *6*(2), 59–67. DOI: 10.33094/7.2017.2020.62.59.67

American Psychiatric Association. (2013). *Diagnostic and statistical manual of mental disorders* (5th ed.). American Psychiatric Publishing.

American Psychological Association. (2021). Understanding panic attacks. Retrieved from https://www.apa.org/topics/anxiety/panic-attacks

Anastasiou, D., & Kauffman, J. M. (2011). A social constructionist approach to disability: Implications for special education. *Exceptional Children*, *77*(3), 367–384.

Anazonwu, N., Okah, P., Chukwu, N., Agha, A., Iwuagwu, A., Onalu, C., Nnama-Okechukwu, C., & Okoye, U. (2022). Barriers to domestication and implementation of the Disability Act in Southeast Nigeria. *Journal of Social Work in Developing Societies*, *4*(1), 33–50. https://journals.aphriapub.com/index.php/JSWDS/article/view/1532/1459

Anderson, N.. (2004). National cross sectional study of views on sexual violence and risk of HIV infection and AIDS among South African school pupils. *BMJ (Clinical Research Ed.)*, •••, 329–952. PMID: 15485935

Anggraeni, D., Mustoip, S., & Hanifah, H. (2024). Analysis of Student Social Interaction in the Salted Egg Making Project in Elementary Schools. *EduBase: Journal of Basic Education*, *5*(2), 163–167.

Annie, P., & Chimuka, C. (2024). Effect of bullying on learners with Autism Spectrum Disorder: A case of a selected special unit at the mainstream in Kabwe, Zambia. *Education Journal*, *8*(1), 83–90.

Anyanwu, E. C., Maduka, C. P., Ayo-Farai, O., Okongwu, C. C., & Daraojimba, A. I. (2024). Maternal and child health policy: A global review of current practices and future directions. *World Journal of Advanced Research and Reviews*, *21*(2), 1770–1781.

Apanel, D. (2009). Oblicza edukacji integracyjnej w Polsce w opiniach i doświadczeniach nauczycieli. [Faces of integrated education in Poland in teachers' opinions and experiences] In Żółkowska, T., & Konopska, L. (Eds.), *W kręgu niepełnosprawności – teoretyczne i praktyczne aspekty poszukiwań w pedagogice specjalnej* [In the circle of disability - theoretical and practical aspects of research in special pedagogy]. (pp. 171–180).

Aranda, C. L. (2015). Targeting disability discrimination: Findings and reflections from the national study on housing discrimination against people who are deaf and people who use wheelchairs. *Cityscape: A Journal of Policy Development and Research, 17*(3), 103-122. https://www.jstor.org/stable/26326963

Arkansas Department of Education. (2008). Special education and related services 2.00 definitions.

Asante, M. K. (2016). Afrocentricity: The theory of social change.https://science .jrank.org/pages/8216/Afrocentricity-Afrocentricity-Its-Critics.html. https://doi.org/ DOI: 10.1002/9781118766804.wbiect128

Assaly, I., & Jabarin, A. (2021). Arab Israeli EFL teachers' perceptions and practices vis-à-vis teaching higher-order thinking skills: A complicated relationship. *Language Teaching Research, 28*(4), 1635–1655. DOI: 10.1177/13621688211032426

Assefa, E. A., & Zenebe, C. K. (2024). Fostering inclusive excellence: Strategies for effective diversity management in schools. *International Journal of Research in Education Humanities and Commerce*, *5*(2), 189–211.

Assembly, U. G. (2007). United Nations declaration on the rights of indigenous peoples. *UN Wash*, *12*, 1–18.

Auerbach, J.. (2005). Gender-based violence and HIV among women: Assessing the evidence. *AMFAR Aids Research*, *3*, 1–2.

Auvert, B.. (2005). Randomised, controlled intervention trial of male circumcision for reduction of HIV infection risk: The ANRS 1265 trial. *PLoS Medicine*, *2*(11), 1112–1122. PMID: 16231970

Avissar, G. (2012). Inclusive education in Israel from a curriculum perspective: An exploratory study. *European Journal of Special Needs Education*, *27*(1), 35–49.

Avramidis, E., Bayliss, P., & Burden, R. (2000). A survey into mainstream teachers' attitudes towards the inclusion of children with special educational needs in the ordinary school in one local educational authority. *Educational Psychology*, *20*(2), 191–211.

Avramidis, E., & Norwich, B. (2002). Teachers' attitudes towards integration / inclusion: A review of the literature. *European Journal of Special Needs Education*, *17*(2), 129–147. DOI: 10.1080/08856250210129056

Babbie, E., & Mouton, J. (2009). *The practice of social research*. Oxford University Press.

Badenhorst, M. G.. (2008). Trends in sexual behaviour among Free State University Students. *The Social Work Practitioner-Researcher, 20*(11), 106123.

Badimo, T. P., & Masisi, I. M. (2025). Educators' experiences and coping strategies in response to learner violence in Mopani district, Limpopo. *The Journal for Transdisciplinary Research in Southern Africa, 21*(1), 1527.

Badran, L., Amin, H., Gur, A., & Stein, M. (2023). I am an Arab Palestinian living in Israel with a disability: Marginalisation and the limits of human rights. *Disability & Society, 38*(1), 1–20. DOI: 10.1080/09687599.2023.2181764

Badr, H. M. (2019). Exploring UAE Teachers' Attitude towards the Successful Implementation of the General Rules in the" School for All" Initiative. *Journal of Language Teaching and Research, 10*(1), 92–103.

Badu, E. (2016). Experiences of children with intellectual disabilities in the Ashanti Region of Ghana. *Journal of Social Inclusion, 7*(1), 20–30.

Baffoe, M. (2013). Stigma, discrimination & marginalization: Gateways to oppression of persons with disabilities in Ghana, West Africa. *Journal of Educational and Social Research, 3*(1). Advance online publication. DOI: 10.5901/jesr.2013.v3n1p187

Baffoe, M. (2013). Stigma, discrimination and marginalisation: Gateway to oppression of persons with disabilities in Ghana, West Africa. *Journal of Educational and Social Research, 3*(1), 187–193.

Bakare, M. O., & Munir, K. M. (2011). Autism spectrum disorders (ASD) in Africa: A perspective. *The African Journal of Psychiatry, 14*(3), 208–210. DOI: 10.4314/ajpsy.v14i3.3

Bakioglu, A., Arikan, A., & Tezer, E. (2021). Teacher attitudes toward inclusive education: A systematic review of the literature. *Journal of Education and Training Studies, 9*(7), 12–23.

Baloyi, R. P. P. (2023). *School principals' ability to influence the improvement of learner performance in selected rural schools in Limpopo* (Unpublished doctoral dissertation). North-West University, South Africa.

Bandelow, B., Michaelis, S., & Wedekind, D. (2017). Treatment of anxiety disorders. *Dialogues in Clinical Neuroscience, 19*(2), 93–107. PMID: 28867934

Banks, L. M., Kelly, S. A., & Kyegombe, N.. (2017). If he could speak, he would be able to point out who does those things to him: Experiences of violence against children with disabilities in Uganda and Malawi. *PLoS One, 12*(9), e0183736. PMID: 28926598

Banks, L. M., Walsham, M., Neupane, S., Pradhananga, Y., Maharjan, M., Blanchet, K., & Kuper, H. (2019). Access to Social Protection Among People with Disabilities: Mixed Methods Research from Tanahun, Nepal. *European Journal of Development Research, 31*, 929–956. DOI: 10.1057/s41287-019-0194-3

Barbareschi, G., Carew, M. T., Johnson, E. A., Kopi, N., & Holloway, C. (2021). "When They See a Wheelchair, They've Not Even Seen Me"-Factors Shaping the Experience of Disability Stigma and Discrimination in Kenya. *International Journal of Environmental Research and Public Health, 18*(8), 4272. DOI: 10.3390/ijerph18084272

Barbareschi, G., & Holloway, C. (2020). Understanding independent wheelchair transfers. Perspectives from stakeholders. *Disability and Rehabilitation. Assistive Technology, 15*(5), 545–552. DOI: 10.1080/17483107.2019.1594407

Barnard, R. W., & Henn, R. H. (2023). Overcoming learning obstacles: Strategies for supporting students with diverse needs. *OAlib, 10*(8), 1–14.

Barrett, H. L. (2024). *Access to inclusive early childhood development and education services for refugee children who experience communication disability, in Rwanda* (Unpublished doctoral dissertation). Manchester Metropolitan University, UK.

Barrio, B., Miller, D., Ojeme, C., & Tamakloe, D. (2018). Teachers' and parents' knowledge about disabilities inclusion in Nigeria. *Journal of International Special Needs Education, 22*(1), 14–24. https://files.eric.ed.gov/fulltext/EJ1222118.pdf

Bateman, A. W., & Fonagy, P. (2016). Mentalization-based treatment for personality disorders. *World Psychiatry; Official Journal of the World Psychiatric Association (WPA), 15*(1), 38–42. PMID: 26833606

Bates, S. C. (2002). Good news for AIDS myths. *Missionalia, 30*(11), 93–108.

Bayer, R. (2008). Stigma and the ethics of public health: Not can we, but should we. *Social Science & Medicine, 67*(3), 463–472. PMID: 18502551

Beck, A. T. (2011). *Cognitive therapy: Basics and beyond.* Guilford Press.

Beer, A., Faulkner, C., Paris, C., & Clower, T. (2011). *Housing transitions through the life course: Aspirations, needs and policy.* Policy Press., DOI: 10.2307/j.ctt9qgq1p

Bekker, L. G., & Hosek, S. (2015). HIV and adolescents: Focus on young key populations. *Journal of the International AIDS Society, 18*(2), 100–130.

Bell, D. (2013). *Investigating teaching and learning support for students with hearing impairment at a university in the Western Cape.* (Doctoral dissertation, Stellenbosch: Stellenbosch University).

Bello, O. S. (2020). *The accusation of elderly women as witches in Nigeria. A project submitted in partial fulfilment of the requirements for obtaining the degree of Master of Arts in Development Studies*. International Institute of Social Studies.

Bełza, M. (2014). *Szkolnictwo specjalne w Polsce – różne formy organizacji* [Special education in Poland – different forms of organization]. University of Silesia.

Bender, W. N., Vail, C. O., & Scott, K. (1995). Teachers' attitudes toward increased mainstreaming: Implementing effective instruction for students with learning disabilities. *Journal of Learning Disabilities*, *28*(2), 87–94. PMID: 7884302

Ben-Yehuda, S., Leyser, Y., & Last, U. (2010). Teacher educational beliefs and sociometric status of special educational needs (SEN) students in inclusive classrooms. *International Journal of Inclusive Education*, *14*(1), 17–34.

Berk, M., & Dodd, S. (2005). Bipolar II disorder: A review. *Bipolar Disorders*, *7*, 11–21. PMID: 15654928

Bernard, H. R. (2002). *Research methods in anthropology: Qualitative and quantitative methods*. Altamira Press.

Bernays, S.. (2017). "Not taking it will just be like a sin": Young people living with HIV and the stigmatization of less-than-perfect adherence to antiretroviral therapy. *Medical Anthropology*, *36*(5), 485–499. PMID: 28379042

Berthé, A., Berthé-Sanou, L., Konaté, B., Hien, H., Tou, F., Somda, S., Bamba, I., Drabo, M., Badini-Kinda, F., & Macq, J. (2013). The unmet needs of the elderly living with functional disabilities in Bobo-Dioulasso (Burkina Faso) Rev. *D'epidemiol. Sante Publique*, *61*, 531–537. DOI: 10.1016/j.respe.2013.07.682

Bhardwaj, P. (2019). Types of sampling in research. *Journal of the Practice of Cardiovascular Sciences*, *5*(3), 157–157. https://go.gale.com/ps/i.do?p=HRCA&sw=w&issn=23955414&v=2.1&it=r&id=GALE%7CA609784775&sid=googleScholar&linkaccess=fulltext

Bhayiya, A. (2000). Women, HIV/AIDS and Poverty – Vulnerability and rights, theories and practices. (Paper presented at the GOOD Conference on Gender and HIV/AIDS, 11–13 September 2000. Oslo, Norway. Bollard, M. (2009). Promoting human rights approach for people with learning disabilities. *Primary Health Care*, *19*(9), 26–28.

BJPsych Open. (2023). Personality disorders: Latest insights and therapeutic advances. British Journal of Psychiatry Open. Available at: https://www.cambridge.org/core/journals/bjpsych-open

Black, M. (2000). The roots of child neglect. In Reece, R. M. (Ed.), *Treatment of child abuse: Common ground for mental health, medical, and legal practitioners* (pp. 157–164). Johns Hopkins University Press.

Boersma, J. M. F. (2008). *Violence against Ethiopian children with disabilities: The stories and perspectives of children* (Unpublished PhD thesis). University of Amsterdam, Netherlands. Retrieved from https://www.dcdd.nl

Bollard, M. (2009). Promoting human rights approach for people with learning disabilities. *Primary Health Care*, *19*(9), 26–28.

Bonaccio, S., Connelly, C. E., Gellatly, I. R., Jetha, A., & Martin-Ginis, K. A. (2020). The participation of people with disabilities in the workplace across the employment cycle: Employer concerns and research evidence. *Journal of Business and Psychology*, *35*(2), 135–158. DOI: 10.1007/s10869-018-9602-5

Bongabong, J. M. M., MEda, M. G. Q. D., & LPTb, W. E. C. (2023). Exploring the Real-Life Issues and Challenges in an Inclusive Classroom through the Lens of General Education Kindergarten Teachers and Parents: A Qualitative Study. *Exploring the Real-Life Issues and Challenges in an Inclusive Classroom through the Lens of General Education Kindergarten Teachers and Parents: A Qualitative Study, 115*(1), 25-25.

Bonsang, E., & Klein, T. J. (2012). Retirement and subjective well-being. *Journal of Economic Behaviour and Organization, 83(3),* 311-329. https://doi.org/.06.002DOI: 10.1016/j.jebo.2012

Bourgeault, I., Mantler, J., & Power, N. (2021). Mental health in academia: The challenges faculty face predate the pandemic and require systemic solutions. *Academic Matters*. https://academicmatters.ca/mental-health-in-academia/

Boyer, P. (2023). *The naturalness of religious ideas: A cognitive theory of religion*. University of California Press.

Boyle, C., Topping, K., & Jindal-Snape, D. (2013). Teachers' attitudes towards inclusion in high schools. *Teachers and Teaching*, *19*(5), 527–542.

Bradshaw, C., Atkinson, S., & Doody, O. (2017). Employing a qualitative descriptive approach in health care research. *Global Qualitative Nursing Research*, *4*(1), 1–8. PMID: 29204457

Brady, M (1999) Female genital mutilation: Complications and risk of HIV transmission. *AIDS Patients Care and STD'S* 13, pp. 121:709–716.

Brandt, A., Hansen, E. M., & Christensen, J. R. (2020). The effects of assistive technology service delivery processes and factors associated with positive outcomes-A systematic review. *Disability and Rehabilitation. Assistive Technology*, *15*(5), 590–603. DOI: 10.1080/17483107.2019.1682067

Brandt, S., Kidron, A., & Raviv, A. (2018). The effects of inclusive education on attitudes: A meta-analysis. *European Journal of Special Needs Education*, *33*(3), 358–373. DOI: 10.17977/um005v1i12017p025

Bremer, C. D., Clapper, A. T., Hitchcock, C., Hall, T., & Kachgal, M. (2002). *Universal Design: A Strategy to Support Students' Access to the General Education Curriculum*. Information Brief.

Bridgraj, A. (2000). AIDS threat to higher education. *The Teacher*, *25*, 9.

Briggs, D., Telford, L., Lloyd, A., & Ellis, A. (2023). *The new futures of exclusion: Life in the Covid-19 aftermath*. Springer Nature.

Browder, D. M., Jimenez, B. A., & Trela, K. (2012). Grade-aligned math instruction for secondary students with moderate intellectual disability. *Education and Training in Autism and Developmental Disabilities*, *47*, 373–388.

Brown, S. (2014). *Coping, Resolution and Advocacy in Parents of Children with Autism*. Purchase College, State University of New York.

Brugere, C., Bansal, T., Kruijssen, F., & Williams, M. (2023). Humanizing aquaculture development: Putting social and human concerns at the center of future aquaculture development. *Journal of the World Aquaculture Society*, *54*(2), 482–526.

Bryman, A., & Burgess, R. G. (2002). *Developments in qualitative data analysis: An introduction in analysing qualitative data*. Routledge.

Buchem, I. (2013). Diversität und Spaltung. [Diversity and division] In Ebner, M., & Schön, S. (Eds.), *Lehrbuch für lernen und lehren mit technologien* [Textbook for learning and teaching with technologies]. 2nd ed., pp. 387–395). Epubli GmbH.

Buenaventura, C., & Gaza, J. (2025). Guided Language and Science Learning Activity Booklet: An Interdisciplinary Educational Resource. *Dibon Journal of Education*, *1*(2), 134–150. DOI: 10.64169/dje.79

Buettgen, A., Lofts, K., & Tompa, E. (2024). Disability inclusion in the green economy: A scoping review of challenges, barriers and opportunities. *J. Green Econ. Low-Carbon Dev*, *3*(4), 208–222.

Bumma, F. N., Ayagere, S. A., Amakiri-Whyte, B. H., & Ubani, P. (2020). Urban public buildings and accessibility challenges in Nigeria. *International Journal of Research and Scientific Innovation*, *7*(5), 209–215. https://rsisinternational.org/journals/ijrsi/digital-library/volume-7-issue-5/209-215.pdf

Bunch, J. C. (2023). *Assistive technology life worlds: Inclusive qualitative methodological innovations for diverse body minds* (Unpublished doctoral dissertation). Arizona State University.

Bunning, K., Gona, J. K., Newton, C. R., & Hartley, S. (2017). The perception of disability by community groups: Stories of local understanding, beliefs and challenges in a rural part of Kenya. *PLoS One*, *12*(8), e0182214. PMID: 28771637

Burge, P., Ouellette-Kuntz, H., & Lysaght, R. (2007). Public views on employment of people with intellectual disabilities. *Journal of Vocational Rehabilitation*, *26*(1), 29–37. DOI: 10.3233/JVR-2007-00360

Burgess, D., Ding, Y., Hargreaves, M., van Ryn, M., & Phelan, S. (2008). The association between perceived discrimination and underutilization of needed medical and mental healthcare in a multi-ethnic community sample. *Journal of Health Care for the Poor and Underserved,* 19:894-911.https://www.ncbi.nlm.nih.gov/nlmcatalog?term=%22J+Health+Care+Poor+ Underserved%22%5BTitle+Abbreviation%5D

Byrne, L., Happell, B., Welch, T., & Moxham, L. J. (2013). 'Things you can't learn from books': Teaching recovery from a lived experience perspective. *International Journal of Mental Health Nursing*, *22*(3), 195–204. PMID: 23020070

Cage, E., & Troxell-Whitman, Z. (2019). Understanding the reasons, contexts and costs of camoufaging for autistic adults. *Journal of Autism and Developmental Disorders*, *49*(5), 1899–1911. DOI: 10.1007/s10803-018-03878-x

Caissie, R., & Wilson, E. (1995). Communication breakdown management during cooperative learning activities by mainstreamed students with hearing losses. *The Volta Review*.

California Department of Education. (1999). *Communication needs and quality of education for deaf and hard-of-hearing children: Advisory Task Force*. California Department of Education.

Calvo, R., Teasley, M., Goldback, J., McRoy, R., & Padilla, Y. (2018). Achieve equal opportunity and justice. In Fong, R., Lubben, J., & Barth, R. (Eds.), *Grand challenges for social work and society* (pp. 239–272). Oxford University Press.

Campbell, C.. (2005). 'I have an evil child at my house': Stigma and HIV/AIDS management in a South African community. *American Journal of Public Health, 95*(5), 808–815. PMID: 15855456

Campbell, C.. (2007). 'Dying twice': A multi-level model of the roots of AIDS stigma in two South African communities. *Journal of Health Psychology, 12*(3), 403–416. PMID: 17439992

Campbell, E. (2018). Reconstructing my identity: An autoethnographic exploration of depression and anxiety in academia. *Journal of Organizational Ethnography, 7*(3), 235–246. DOI: 10.1108/JOE-12-2017-0067

Carew, M. T., & Shakespeare, T. (2024). Beyond disability stigma: Examining tolerance and intolerance toward disability issues. *Scandinavian Journal of Disability Research, 26*(1).

Carhart-Harris, R. L.. (2018). Psilocybin with psychological support for treatment-resistant depression. *The Lancet. Psychiatry, 5*(7), 616–627. PMID: 27210031

Carnemolla, P., & Bridge, C. (2018). A scoping review of home modification interventions: Mapping the evidence base. *Indoor and Built Environment, 29*(3), 299–310. DOI: 10.1177/1420326X18761112

Carrington, S., Mavropoulou, S., Saggers, B., & Nepal, S. (2024). *Inclusive education in Australia: Policy review.* Autism CRC. autismcrc.com.au

Carrington, S., Deppeler, J., & Moss, J. (2010). Cultivating Teachers' Beliefs, Knowledge and Skills for Leading Change in Schools. *The Australian Journal of Teacher Education, 35*(1). Advance online publication. DOI: 10.14221/ajte.2010v35n1.1

Cassidy, S. A., Gould, K., Townsend, E., Pelton, M., Robertson, A. E., & Rodgers, J. (2020). Is Camouflaging Autistic Traits Associated with Suicidal Thoughts and Behaviours? *Expanding the Interpersonal Psychological Theory of Suicide in an Undergraduate Student SampleJ Autism Dev Disord, 50*(10), 3638–3648. DOI: 10.1007/s10803-019-04323-3

Catano, V., Francis, L., Haines, T., Kirpalani, H., Shannon, H., Stringer, B., & Lozanzki, L. (2010). Occupational stress in Canadian universities: A national survey. *International Journal of Stress Management, 17*(3), 232–258. DOI: 10.1037/a0018582

Centre for Citizens with Disabilities. (2021). Peoples with disabilities want domestication of Disability Act in all states. *The Guardian, March 17*. m.guardian. ng>news>pwds-want-dom... Cho, H., MacLachlan, M., Clarke, M., & Mannan, H. (2016). Accessible home environments for people with functional limitations: A systematic review. *International Journal of Environmental Research and Public Health, 13*(8), 826; https://doi.org/DOI: 10.3390/ ijerph13080826

Cerna, L., Mezzanotte, C., Rutigliano, A., Brussino, O., Santiago, P., Borgonovi, F., & Guthrie, C. (2021). Promoting inclusive education for diverse societies: A conceptual framework. *OECD Education Working Papers*, (260), 0_1-57.

Chapman, R. (2020). Neurodiversity, wellbeing, disability. In Rosquvist, H., Chown, N., Stenning, A. (Eds.), *Neurodiversity studies: A new critical paradigm (pp. 57–72).* New York, NY: Routledge Department of Education (DoE). (2016). *Policy on Inclusive Education*. Pretoria: Government Printer.

Chen, C. H. (2021). The roles of psychosocial developmental crisis and self-stigma in mental health among college students with disabilities. *International Journal of Disability Development and Education*, *68*(2), 287–302.

Chhabra, S., Srivastava, R., & Srivastava, I. (2010). Inclusive education in Botswana: The perceptions of school teachers. *Journal of Disability Policy Studies*, *20*(4), 219–228.

Chikore, J. (2000) Sexuality and Aids. (Paper presented at the GOOD Conference on Gender and HIV/AIDS, 11–13 September 2000. Oslo, Norway. Chileshe, M & Bond V.A. (2010) Barriers and outcomes: TB patients co-infected with HIV accessing antiretroviral therapy in Rural Zambia. *ART Special Issue. AIDS Care, Vol*. 22, pp. 51–59.

Chitiyo, M., Hughes, E. M., Changara, D. M., Chitiyo, G., & Montgomery, K. M. (2017). Special education professional development needs in Zimbabwe. *International Journal of Inclusive Education*, *21*(1), 48–62. DOI: 10.1080/13603116.2016.1184326

Chitiyo, M., Kumedzro, F. K., Hughes, E. M., & Ahmed, S. (2019). Teachers' Professional Development Needs Regarding Inclusive Education in Ghana. *International Journal of Whole Schooling*, *15*(2), 53–79. https://files.eric.ed.gov/fulltext/EJ1224611.pdf

Chodkowska, M., & Kazanowski, Z. (2007). *Socjopedagogiczne konteksty postaw nauczycieli wobec edukacji integracyjnej* [Socio-pedagogical contexts of teachers' attitudes towards integrated education]. Wydawnictwo UMCS.

Chopra, M., Lawn, J. E., Sanders, D., Barron, P., & Abdool Karim, S. S.. (2009). Achieving the health Millennium Development Goals for South Africa: Challenges and priorities. *Lancet*, *374*(9694), 1023–1031. PMID: 19709737

Chowdhury, J. S., Hatta, Z. A., & Singh, S. (2025). Phronesis as a Pathway for the Nature and Development of Pedagogical Content Knowledge (PCK): Seeing Through Indigenous Gnoseology. In Current Trends and Best Practices of Pedagogical Content Knowledge (PCK) (pp. 89-118). IGI Global Scientific Publishing.

Chowdhury, J. S., Vadevelu, K., Hatta, Z. A., Ashraf, M., & Bhaumik, A. (Eds.). (2024). *Reviving and re-writing ethics in social research for commoning the community*. IGI Global.

Chowdhury, J. S., Vadevelu, K., Singh, P. S. J., Saad, M. R. M., & Hatta, Z. A. (2024). *The Intersection of Faith, Culture, and Indigenous Community in Malaysia and Bangladesh*. Springer.

Christian Blind Mission. (2019). *Lessons from disability audit of Northeast Nigeria Transition to Development (NENTAD) humanitarian response. Nigeria briefing.* https://www.cbmuk.org.uk/wp-content/uploads/2019/07/Lessons-from-Disability-Audit-of-North-East-Nigeria-NENTAD-humanitarian-response.pdf

Chuene, D. M., & Teane, F. M. (2024). Resource inadequacy as a barrier to effective curriculum implementation by life sciences teachers in South Africa. *South African Journal of Education*, *44*(2).

Cimermanová, I. (2017). English language preservice and in-service teachers' self-efficacy and attitudes towards integration of students with learning difficulties. *Journal of Language and Cultural Education*, *5*(1), 20–38.

Cinamon, R. G., & Rich, Y. (2005). Work–family conflict among female teachers. *Teaching and Teacher Education*, *21*(4), 365–378. DOI: 10.1016/j.tate.2004.06.009

Clemente, K.A.P., Silva, S.V.D., Vieira, G.I., Bortoli, M.C., Toma, T.S., & Ramos, V.D., Brito, & C.M.M. (2022). Barriers to the access of people with disabilities to health services: A scoping review. *Revista de Saude Publica*, *56*, 64. DOI: 10.11606/s1518-8787.2022056003893

Coetsee, E. E. (2007) Culture and gender as risk factors in patterns of high-risk sexual behaviour among students on the main campus of the University of the Free State. Bloemfontein: University of the Free State (Master's thesis in Psychology of Education).

Coleman, C. (2024). Challenges faced by people with disabilities. https://lordslibrary.parliament.uk/ challenges-faced-by-people-with-disabilities/?cf_chl_f_tk=6laY-Ca7Ceh9HoiDp0EC_fK4a_rtsSK. wGQ7 kv64uPV0-1729728839-1.0.1.1-DhWQx8FNf771FdVJ9pleh14KU0.sQLtpF14Yu7c.7Tw

Collins, P. S. (2003). Inclusion reconsidered. *Philosophy of Education Archive*, 449-457.

Collins, A., Rentschler, R., Williams, K., & Azmat, F. (2022). Exploring barriers to social inclusion for disabled people: Perspectives from the performing arts. *Journal of Management & Organization*, *28*(2), 308–328.

Cooc, N. (2021). Disparities in general education inclusion for students of color with disabilities: Understanding when and why. *Journal of School Psychology*, *90*, 43–59. DOI: 10.1016/j.jsp.2021.10.002 PMID: 34969487

Coopes, A. (2016). Australian researchers declare an end to AIDS as a public health issue. *BMJ (Clinical Research Ed.)*, *354*, i3895. PMID: 27406234

Coovadia, H., Jewkes, R., Barron, P., Sanders, D., & McIntyre, D. (2009). The health and health system of South Africa: Historical roots of current public health challenges. *Lancet*, *374*(9692), 817–834. PMID: 19709728

Corker, M. (2000). The U.K. Disability Discrimination Act: Disabling language, justifying inequitable social participation. In Francis, L. P., & Silvers, A. (Eds.), *Americans with disabilities: Exploring implications of the law for individuals and institutions* (pp. 357–370). Routledge.

Cornelissen, G. M. (2005) HIV/AIDS Knowledge, awareness and perception of undergraduate students at the University of Stellenbosch. Stellenbosch: University of Stellenbosch (Master's thesis in Philosophy).

Cornoldi, C., Terreni, A., Scruggs, T. E., & Mastropieri, M. A. (1998). Teacher attitudes in Italy after twenty years of inclusion. *Remedial and Special Education*, *19*(6), 350–356.

Corrigan, P. W. (2004). How stigma interferes with mental health care. *The American Psychologist*, *59*(7), 614–625. DOI: 10.1037/0003-066X.59.7.614 PMID: 15491256

Corrigan, P. W., Druss, B. G., & Perlick, D. A. (2014). The impact of mental illness stigma on seeking and participating in mental health care. *PSPI*, *15*(2), 37–70. PMID: 26171956

Corrigan, P. W., Druss, B. G., & Perlick, D. A. (2017). The impact of mental illness stigma on seeking and participating in mental health care. *Psychological Science in the Public Interest, 15*(2), 37–70. DOI: 10.1177/1529100615601386 PMID: 26171956

Corrigan, P. W., Kerr, A., & Knudsen, L. (2005). The stigma of mental illness: Explanatory models and methods for change. *Applied & Preventive Psychology, 11*(3), 179–190.

Corrigan, P. W., & Shapiro, J. R. (2010). Measuring the impact of programs that challenge the public stigma of mental illness. *Clinical Psychology Review, 30*(8), 907–922. PMID: 20674114

Corrigan, P. W., & Watson, A. C. (2002). Understanding the impact of stigma on people with mental illness. *World Psychiatry; Official Journal of the World Psychiatric Association (WPA), 1*(1), 16–20. PMID: 16946807

Coughlan, F. J.. (1996). Where knowledge and attitudes separate: Adolescent HIV/AIDS knowledge survey as information for social work training. *Social Work, 32*(31), 255–261.

Council of the European Union. (2010, May 11). Council conclusions on the social dimension of education and training, 3013 Meeting of the Education, Youth and Culture Council. Author.

Courtenay, K., & Cooper, V. (2021). COVID-19: People with learning disabilities are highly vulnerable. *BMJ (Clinical Research Ed.), 374*, n1701. DOI: 10.1136/bmj.n1701 PMID: 34261641

Coyne, I. T. (1997). Sampling in qualitative research. Purposeful and theoretical sampling; merging or clear boundaries? *Journal of Advanced Nursing, 26*(3), 623–630. DOI: 10.1046/j.1365-2648.1997.t01-25-00999.x PMID: 9378886

Crawford, A., Hollingsworth, H. H., Morgan, K., & Gray, D. B. (2008). People with mobility impairments: Physical activity and quality of participation. *Disability and Health Journal, 1*, 7–13. https://pubmed.ncbi.nlm.nih.gov/21122706/

Crowley, P. E. (2016). Preventing abuse and neglect in the lives of children with disabilities. In Crowley, P. E. (Ed.), *Preventing abuse and neglect in the lives of children with disabilities* (pp. 239–266). Springer.

Cuijpers, P.. (2019). The efficacy of psychotherapy and pharmacotherapy in treating depression. *Psychological Medicine, 49*(4), 525–534.

Dawn, R. (2023). Role of culture and media in disability studies: A medium of social construction of disability. *Journal of Disability & Religion, 27*(1), 1–22.

de Andrade, T. B., & de Andrade, F. B. (2018). Unmet need for assistance with activities of daily life among older adults in Brazil. *Revista de Saude Publica, 52*, 75. DOI: 10.11606/S1518-8787.2018052000463

De Boer, A., Pijl, S. J., & Minnaert, A. (2011). Regular primary schoolteachers' attitudes towards inclusive education: A review of the literature. *International Journal of Inclusive Education, 15*(4), 331–353.

Deacon, H. (2006). Towards a sustainable theory of health-related stigma: Lessons from the HIV/AIDS literature. *Journal of Community & Applied Social Psychology, 16*(6), 418–425.

Deacon, H.. (2005). *Understanding HIV/AIDS stigma, a theoretical and methodological analysis*. Human Sciences Research Council.

Debasu, H., & Yitayew, A. (2024). Examining Elements of Designing and Managing of Creating Inclusive Learning Environment: Systematic Literature Review. *International Journal of Special Education, 39*(1), 33–43.

Denscombe, M. (2008). *The Good Research Guide for small-scale social research projects* (3rd ed.). Open University Press.

Department of Basic Education (DBE). (2015). *Report on the implementation of Education White Paper 6 on Inclusive Education: Overview for the period 2013–2015*. Government Printers.

Department of Education (DoE). (1995). *White Paper on Education and Training*. Retrieved on 16 October 2024 from: https://www.gov.za/sites/default/files/gcis_document/201409/16312gen1960.pdf

Department of Education (DoE). (1997). *Education White Paper 3: A Programme for the Transformation of Higher Education.*

Department of Education (DoE). (2001b). *Education White Paper 6: Special needs education: Building an inclusive education and training system*. Retrieved March 4 2024 from: https://www.vvob.org/files/publicaties/rsa_education_white_paper_6.pdf

Destyani, A. R., Ghazali, A. F., Harizta, A. D., & Nashori, H. F. (2019). Social support, gratitude and psychological wellbeing of persons with disabilities. ICRMH, September 18-19, Jakarta, Indonesia. https://doi: DOI: 10.4108/eai.18-9-2019.2293369

Deutsch, F. M. (2007). Undoing gender. *Gender & Society, 21*(1), 106–127. DOI: 10.1177/0891243206293577

Dev, S., George, M., Rafique, S., Vaddapalli, M., Nair, S., & Al Hameli, A. (2024). Sustainable inclusive framework studio for inclusive education—Perceptions of teachers, parents, and students in United Arab Emirates. *Sustainability, 16*(15), 6367.

Digest, I. (2007). https:www.unicef-irc.org/publications

Dilger, H. (2007). Healing the wounds of modernity: Salvation, community and care in a Neo-Pentecostal church in Dar Es Salaam, Tanzania. *Journal of Religion in Africa. Religion en Afrique, 2007*(37), 59–83.

Dizdarevic, A., Mujezinovic, A., & Memisevic, H. (2017). Comparison of teachers' attitudes towards inclusive education in Bosnia and Herzegovina and European Union. *Journal of Special Education and Rehabilitation, 18*(1-2), 92–108.

Dlamini, N. G., & Dlamini, N. D. (2024). Understanding the well-being challenges confronting academic staff in South African universities: A narrative review. *Discover Education, 3*(1), 1–10.

do Amaral Madureira, A. F., da Silva, M. R. G., & de Paula, L. D. (2020). Social identities, prejudices, and exclusion: The reproduction of social (in) visibility in school contexts. *Psychology as a Dialogical Science: Self and Culture Mutual Development*, 115-134.

Donald, A. (2010). *Introduction to Research in Education.* Wadsworth Cengage Learning.

Donnelly, V., & Watkins, A. (2011). Teacher education for inclusion in Europe. *Prospects, 41*(3), 341–353.

Donohue, D., & Bornman, J. (2014). The challenges of realising inclusive education in South Africa. *South African Journal of Education, 34*(2).

Dozono, T. (2023). Eugenic ideology and the world history curriculum: How eugenic beliefs structure narratives of development and modernity. *Theory and Research in Social Education, 51*(3), 408–437.

Du Plessis, A. B. (2006). *The academic self-concept of learners with hearing impairment in two South African public school contexts: Special and full-service inclusion schools.* (Doctoral dissertation, University of Pretoria).

Du Toit, L. (1996). An introduction to specialised education. In Engelbrecht, P., Kriegler, S. M., & Booysen, M. I. (Eds.), *Perspectives on learning difficulties: International concerns and South African realities* (pp. 5–19). Van Schaik.

Dube, T., Ncube, S. B., Mapuvire, C. C., Ndlovu, S., Ncube, C., & Mlotshwa, S. (2021). Interventions to reduce the exclusion of children with disabilities from education: A Zimbabwean perspective from the field. *Cogent Social Sciences*, *7*(1), 1913848.

Dwairy, M. A. (1998). *Cross-cultural counseling: The Arab-Palestinian case*. The Haworth Press.

East, M. (2024). The vital role of social workers in supporting individuals with intellectual and developmental disabilities. https://www.linkedin.com/pulse/vital-role-social-workers-supporting-individuals-matt-east-rfmnc

Ébalé, S., Benson, A., & Mulemi, T. (2023). The Ubuntu and African identity in the 21st century. *The International Journal of Humanities & Social Studies*, *11*(7), 47–62. DOI: 10.24940/ theijhss/2023/v11/i7/HS2307-006

Eden, C. A., Chisom, O. N., & Adeniyi, I. S. (2024). Promoting digital literacy and social equity in education: Lessons from successful initiatives. *International Journal of Management & Entrepreneurship Research*, *6*(3), 687–696.

Edström, K., Gardelli, V., & Backman, Y. (2024). Inclusion as participation: Mapping the participation model with four different levels of inclusive education. *International Journal of Inclusive Education*, *28*(12), 2940–2957.

Eiken, R. (2015). *Teacher attitudes toward the inclusion of students with disabilities in the general education classroom* [Doctoral dissertation, Northwest Missouri State University].

Ekpe, C., & Mamah, S. (1997). *Social Work in Nigeria: A colonial heritage*. Unik Oriental Prints Ltd.

Eleweke, C., & Ebenso, J. (2016). Barriers to accessing services by people with disabilities in Nigeria: Insights from a qualitative study. *Journal of Educational and Social Research*, *6*(2), 113–123. DOI: 10.5901/jear.2016.v6n2p113

Elias, M. J., Parker, R., & Weissberg, R. P. (2018). *Social and emotional learning: A framework for educating children*. Routledge.

Elliott, R., & Timulak, L. (2021). Essentials of descriptive-interpretive qualitative research: A generic approach. In *Essentials of descriptive-interpretive qualitative research: A generic approach*. American Psychological Association., DOI: 10.1037/0000224-000

Ellis, C., Adams, T. E., & Bochner, A. P. (2010). Autoethnography: An overview. *Historical Social Research (Köln), 36*(4), 273–290. https://www.jstor.org/stable/ 23032294

ElSayary, A., Mohebi, L., & Meda, L. (2022). The impact of the relationship of social/emotional, cognitive, and behavioral engagements on developing preservice teachers' digital competencies. *Journal of Information Technology Education, 21*, 269–295.

Engelbrecht, P. (2006). The implementation of inclusive education in South Africa after ten years of democracy. *European Journal of Psychology of Education, 21*(3), 253–264.

Engel, G. L. (1977). The need for a new medical model: A challenge for biomedicine. *Science, 196*(4286), 129–136. PMID: 847460

Enos, G. A. (2020). Support students, faculty members during pandemic. *Disability Compliance for Higher Education, 25*(12), 2–2. DOI: 10.1002/DHE.30869

Equality and Human Rights Commission. (2011). Hidden in plain sight: inquiry into disability-related harassment. https://www.equalityhumanrights.com/en/publication -download/ hiddenplain-sight- inquiry- disability- related- harassment.

Erenc, J. (2008). *Bycie innym. Problem wykluczenia i izolacji ludzi niepełnosprawnych* [Being different: The problem of exclusion and isolation of people with disabilities]. Wydawnictwo UG.

Essien, E. J. (1997). Cross-national HIV infection control practices and fear of AIDS: A comparison between Nigeria and the USA. *International J. STD & AIDS, Vol., 8*(12), 764–771. PMID: 9433951

Etajuri, E. A., Mohd, N. R., Naimie, Z., & Ahmad, N. A. (2022). Undergraduate dental students' perspective of online learning and their physical and mental health during COVID-19 pandemic. *PLoS ONE, 17*(6), e0270091. https://doi.org/ members' intent to stay: a structural equation modeling approach. Nurs. Health Sci.DOI: 10.1371/journal.pone.0270091faculty

Etieyibo, E. (2020). Rights of persons with disabilities in Nigeria. *Afrika Focus, 33*(1), 59–81. DOI: 10.1163/2031356X-03301005

European Agency for Development in Special Needs Education. (2010). Teacher education for inclusion: International literature review.

Evans, C., & Lewis, J. (2018). *Analysing semi-structured interviews using thematic analysis: Exploring voluntary civic participation among adults.* SAGE Publications, Ltd., DOI: 10.4135/9781526439284

Ezer, F., & Aksüt, S. (2021). Opinions of Graduate Students of Social Studies Education about Qualitative Research Method. *International Education Studies*, *14*(3), 15–32. DOI: 10.5539/ies.v14n3p15

Fakolade, O. A., Adeniyi, S. O., & Tella, A. (2009). Attitude of teachers towards the inclusion of special needs children in general education classroom: The case of teachers in some selected schools in Nigeria. *International Electronic Journal of Elementary Education*, *1*(3), 155–169.

Fakolade, O., Adeniyi, S., & Tella, A. (2009). Attitude of teachers towards the inclusion of special need children in general education classroom: The case of teachers in some selected schools in Nigeria. *International Electronic Journal of Elementary Education*, *1*(3), 155–169. https://files.eric.ed.gov/fulltext/EJ1052033.pdf

Farber, S., & Páez, A. (2010). Employment status and commute distance of Canadians with disabilities. *Transportation*, *37*(6), 931–952. DOI: 10.1007/s11116-010-9268-y

Faronbi, J. O., Faronbi, G. O., Ayamolowo, S. J., & Olaogun, A. A. (2019). Caring for the seniors with chronic illness: The lived experience of caregivers of older adults. *Archives of Gerontology and Geriatrics* 82: 8-14. https://doi.org/. archger.2019.01.013DOI: 10.1016/j

Farrelly, S., Jeffery, D., Rüsch, N., Williams, P., Thornicroft, G., & Clement, S. (2015). The link between mental health-related discrimination and suicidality: Service user perspectives. *Psychological Medicine*, *45*(10), 2013–2022. PMID: 25678059

Faurholt-Jepsen, M.. (2015). Electronic monitoring of mood for bipolar disorder. *International Journal of Bipolar Disorders*, *3*(1), 1–8. PMID: 26277270

Fawole, I.O. et al. (1999) A school-based AIDS education program for secondary school students in Nigeria: a review of effectiveness. *Health Edu, Res,* Vol. 14, 5), pp. 675–683.

Federal Republic of Nigeria. (2020). National Policy on Aging. https://fmic. gov.ng/fg-approves-national-policy-on-ageing-for-older-persons-in-nigeria/

Fernandes, J. K., & Myers, S. S. (2010). Inclusive deaf studies: Barriers and pathways. *Journal of Deaf Studies and Deaf Education*, *15*(1), 17–29. DOI: 10.1093/deafed/enp018 PMID: 19617377

Findley, M., Smith, S., Gorski, J., & O'neil, M. (2007). Safety climate differences among job positions in a nuclear decommissioning and demolition industry: Employees' self-reported safety attitudes and perceptions. *Safety Science*, *45*(8), 875–889. DOI: 10.1016/ j.ssci.2006.08.027

Finkelstein, V. (1980). *Attitudes and disabled people*. World Rehabilitation Fund.

Fiorilli, G., Iuliano, E., Aquino, G., Battaglia, C., Giombini, A., Calcagno, G., & de Cagno, A. (2013). Mental health and social participation skills of wheelchair basketball players: A controlled study. *Research in Developmental Disabilities*, *34*(11), 3679–3685.

First, M. B.. (2018). DSM-5 and clinical diagnosis. *Annual Review of Clinical Psychology*, *14*, 1–23. DOI: 10.1146/annurev-clinpsy-050817-084925

Fitrianto, I. (2024). Critical Reasoning Skills: Designing an Education Curriculum Relevant to Social and Economic Needs. *International Journal of Post Axial: Futuristic Teaching and Learning*, 245-258.

Flicker, S., & Nixon, S. A. (2014). The DEPICT model for participatory qualitative health promotion research analysis piloted in Canada, Zambia and South Africa. *Health Promotion International*, *2014*. Advance online publication. https://www .ncbi.nlm.nih.gov/pubmed/24418997. 10–1093

Flick, U. (2002). Qualitative research - state of the art. *Social Sciences Information. Information Sur les Sciences Sociales*, *40*(1), 5–24. DOI: 10.1177/0539018402041001001

Florian, V., & Katz, S. (1983). The impact of cultural, ethnic, and national variables on attitudes towards the disabled in Israel: A review. *International Journal of Intercultural Relations*, *7*, 167–179.

Forman, L. (2003) The constitutional imperative to treat: The South African government's constitutional obligations to provide antiretroviral medicines. Paper at the South African AIDS Conference; Durban. 3–6 August.2003.

Frank, C. (1999). *Ethnographic Eyes: A Teacher's Guide to Classroom Observation*. Heinemann.

Franklin, B. M. (Ed.). (1996). *Interpretación de la discapacidad: Teoría e historia de la educación especial* [Interpretation of disability: Theory and history of special education]. Ediciones Pomares-Corredor.

Freeman-Green, S., Williamson, P., & Cornelius, E., K. (2023). Promoting Inclusive Practices in Education: Bridging Gaps and Fostering Independence. *Teaching Exceptional Children, 56*(2), 68–69. DOI: 10.1177/00400599231223785

Freire, P. (1990). *Pedagogy of the oppressed.* Continuum.

Friend, M., & Bursuck, W. D. (2006). Including students with special needs: A practical guide for classroom teachers (4th ed.). Pearson & Allyn Bacon.

Fröjd, S. A., Nissinen, E. S., Pelkonen, M. U. I., Marttunen, M. J., Koivisto, A.-M., & Kaltiala-Heino, R. (2008). Depression and school performance in middle adolescent boys and girls. *Journal of Adolescence, 31*(4), 485–498. DOI: 10.1016/j.adolescence.2007.08.006 PMID: 17949806

Fullan, M. (1993). Innovation, reform and restructuring strategies. In Cawelti, G. (Ed.), *Challenges and achievements of American education* (pp. 116–133). Association for Supervision and Curriculum Development.

Fullick, M. (2011). "My grief lies all within" – PhD students, depression & attrition. *University Affairs*. https://www.universityaffairs.ca/opinion/in-my-opinion/my-grief-lies-all-within/

Gaad, E. (2004). Cross-cultural perspectives on the effect of cultural attitudes towards inclusion for children with intellectual disabilities. *International Journal of Inclusive Education, 8*(3), 311–328.

Gajdzica, Z. (2009). Codzienne wsparcie ucznia niepełnosprawnego w klasie integracyjnej [Daily support for disabled students in integrated classrooms]. Pedagogika. *Zeszyty Naukowe Wyższej Szkoły Humanitas, 4*, 67–76.

Gao, R. (2023). Promoting students' classroom participation in the context of inclusive education: A case study of students with autism. *International Journal of New Developments in Education, 5*(15).

Garuba, A. (2003). Inclusive education in the 21st century: Challenges and opportunities for Nigeria. *Asia Pacific Disability Rehabilitation Journal, 14*, 191–200.

Gavish, B., & Shimoni, S. (2011). Elementary school teachers' beliefs and perceptions about the inclusion of children with special needs in their classrooms. *Journal of International Special Needs Education, 14*(2), 49–60.

Gebremikael, L., Sicchia, S., Demi, S., & Rhoden, J. (2022). Afrocentric approaches to disrupting anti-Black racism in health care and promoting Black health in Canada. *Canadian Medical Association Journal, 194*(42), 89–105. DOI: 10.1503/cmaj.220456

Gentilini, U., & Omamo, S. W. (2011). Social protection: Exploring issues, evidence and debates in a globalizing world. *Food Policy*, *36*, 329–340. https://www.sciencedirect.com/science/article/pii/S0306-9192(11)00046-7

Gerbert, B.. (1991). The impact of who you know and where you live on opinions about AIDS and health care. *Social Science & Medicine*, *32*(6), 677–681. PMID: 2035043

Ghaemi, S. N., Bauer, M., Cassidy, F., Malhi, G. S., Mitchell, P., & Phelps, J.. (2008). Diagnostic guidelines for bipolar disorder: A summary of the International Society for Bipolar Disorders Diagnostic Guidelines Task Force report. [This is the summary statement for the Diagnosis Task Force of the International Society for Bipolar Disorders, completed in preparation for the DSM and ICD revisions.]. *Bipolar Disorders*, *10*, 117–128. PMID: 18199230

Ghergu , A. (2001). *Psihopedagogia persoanelor cu cerin e speciale: Strategii de educa ie integrată* [Psychopedagogy of persons with special needs: Integrated education strategies]. Polirom.

Ghergu , A. (2006). *Psihopedagogia persoanelor cu cerinţe educative speciale: Strategii diferenţiate şi incluzive în educaţie* [Psychopedagogy of persons with special educational needs: Differentiated and inclusive strategies in education]. Polirom.

Gibney, E. (2017). Teaching load could put female scientists at career disadvantage. *Nature News*. https://www.nature.com/news/teaching-load-could-put-female-scientists-at-career-disadvantage-1.21839

Goetz Fidler, C. J. (2023). *Stigma resistance versus self-stigma in university students with mental health problems* (Doctoral dissertation). Lakehead University.

Goffman, E. (2009). *Stigma: Notes on the management of spoiled identity*. Simon & Schuster.

Goldin, C. S. (1994). Stigmatization and AIDS: Critical issues in public health. *Social Science & Medicine*, *39*(9), 1359–1366. PMID: 7801171

Gona, J. K., Newton, C. R., & Rimba, K.. (2015). Parents' and professionals' perceptions on causes and treatment options for autism spectrum disorders in a multicultural context on the Kenyan coast. *PLoS One*, *12*(1), e0132729. PMID: 26267668

Goodwin, F. K., & Jamison, K. R. (2007). *Manic-depressive illness*. 2nd edition. New York: Oxford University Press. *This is the authoritative text on BMD, being a recent update of the most comprehensive discussion of BMD available.*

Goodwin, I., Davis, E., Winkler, D., Douglas, J., Wellecke, C., D'Cruz, K., Mulherin, P., & Liddicoat, S. (2022). Making homes more accessible for people with mobility impairment: A lived experience perspective. *The Australian Journal of Social Issues*, *57*(4), 956–969. DOI: 10.1002/ajs4.214

Gordon, C. (2018). Ubuntu: The impact of African philosophy on education. *Journal of Philosophy of Education*, *52*(4), 636–653.

Gordon, G. (2015). Ubuntu pedagogy: Cultural responsibility and community involvement. *Education as Change*, *19*(1), 102–115.

Gormaz-Lobos, D., Galarce-Miranda, C., Hortsch, H., & Vargas-Almonacid, C. (2021). Teacher Training's Needs in University Context: A Case Study of a Chilean University of Applied Sciences. [IJET]. *International Journal of Emerging Technologies in Learning*, *16*(09), 119–132. DOI: 10.3991/IJET.V16I09.21389

Goulden, M., Mason, M. A., & Frasch, K. (2011). Keeping women in the science pipeline. *The Annals of the American Academy of Political and Social Science*, *638*(1), 141–162. DOI: 10.1177/0002716211416925

Gous, G., & Wheatcroft, J. M. (2020). Directive leading questions and preparation technique effects on witness accuracy. *SAGE Open*, *10*(1), 2158244019899053.

Graham, L. J. (2020). Inclusive education in the 21st century. In Graham, L. J. (Ed.), *Inclusive Education for the 21st Century: Theory, Policy and Practice* (pp. 3–26). Routledge., DOI: 10.4324/9781003116073-2

Graham, L. J., & Slee, R. (2008). An illusory interiority: Interrogating the discourse/s of inclusion. *Educational Philosophy and Theory*, *40*(2), 277–293. DOI: 10.1111/j.1469-5812.2007.00331.x

Grande, I., Berk, M., Birmaher, B., & Vieta, E. (2016). Bipolar disorder. *Lancet*, *387*(10027), 1561–1572. DOI: 10.1016/S0140-6736(16)00200-8 PMID: 26388529

Greeff, M.. (2008). Disclosure of HIV status: Experiences and perceptions of persons living with HIV/AIDS and nurses involved in their care in Africa. *Qualitative Health Research*, *18*(3), 311–324. PMID: 18235155

Green, G. (1995). Attitudes towards people with HIV: Are they as stigmatizing as people with HIV perceive them to be? *Social Science and Medicine, Vol.*, *4*(4), 557–568. PMID: 7481950

Greenstein, L. (2017). *9 ways to fight mental health stigma*. National Alliance on Mental Illness. https://www.nami.org/blogs/nami-blog/october-2017/9-ways-to-fight-mental-health-stigma

Gregson, S. (2017) Documenting and explaining the HIV decline in east Zimbabwe: the Manicaland General Population Cohort., CA.BMJ Open. 2017 Oct 6;7(10):e015898. doi: : 28988165 Free PMC article.DOI: 10.1136/bmjopen-2017-015898.PMID

Grinker, R. R. (2020). Autism,"stigma," disability: A shifting historical terrain. *Current Anthropology*, *61*(S21), S55–S67.

Grove, S. J., & Fisk, R. P. (1992). Observational data collection methods for services marketing: An overview. *Journal of the Academy of Marketing Science*, *20*(3), 217–224. DOI: 10.1007/BF02723408

Grubic, N., Badovinac, S., & Johri, A. M. (2020). Student mental health in the midst of the COVID-19 pandemic: A call for further research and immediate solutions. *The International Journal of Social Psychiatry*, *66*(5), 517–518. DOI: 10.1177/0020764020925108 PMID: 32364039

Grue, J. (2023). The CRPD and the economic model of disability: Undue burdens and invisible work. *Disability & Society*, *39*(12), 3119–3135. DOI: 10.1080/09687599.2023.2255734

Grzegorzewska, M., & Wapiennik, E. (2008). Comparative policy brief status of intellectual disabilities in the Republic of Poland. *Journal of Policy and Practice in Intellectual Disabilities*, *5*(2), 137–141.

Guba, E. G., & Lincoln, Y. S. (1994). Competing paradigms in qualitative research. In Denzin, N. K., & Lincoln, Y. S. (Eds.), *Handbook of qualitative research* (pp. 105–117). Sage Publications.

Guddad, P. (2025). Challenges Faced by the Visually Impaired Students during Online Learning: Lessons for Teachers. *Dibon Journal of Education*, *1*(1), 1–12. DOI: 10.64169/dje.6

Guest, G., Namey, E., & Chen, M. (2020). A simple method to assess and report thematic saturation in qualitative research. *PLoS One*, *15*(5), e0232076. DOI: 10.1371/JOURNAL.PONE.0232076 PMID: 32369511

Guevara, A. (2024). How American Society and Law Continue to Undermine People with Disabilities Seeking Education and Employment. *UC Law Constitutional Quarterly*, *51*(1), 65.

Gumpel, T. P. (1999). Special education in Israel. In Reynolds, C. R., & Fletcher-Janzen, E. (Eds.), *Encyclopedia of special education* (Vol. 2, pp. 995–998). Wiley.

Gumpel, T. P., & Awartani, S. (2003). A comparison of special education in Israel and Palestine: Surface and deep structures. *The Journal of Special Education, 37*(1), 33–48.

Guojonsdottir, H., Cacciattolo, M., Dakich, E., Davies, A., Kelly, C., & Dalmau, M. C. (2008). Transformative pathways: Inclusive pedagogies in teacher education. *Journal of Research on Technology in Education, 40*(2), 165–182.

Hackett, R. A., Steptoe, A., Lang, R. P., & Jackson, S. E. (2020). Disability discrimination and well-being in the United Kingdom: A prospective cohort study. *BMJ Open, 10*(3), e035714. DOI: 10.1136/bmjopen-2019-035714

Hager, T., & Jabareen, Y. (2016). From marginalization to integration: Arab-Palestinians in Israeli academia. *International Journal of Inclusive Education, 20*(5), 455–473.

Haihambo, C., & Lightfoot, E. (2010). Cultural beliefs about disability in Namibia: Implications for inclusion of people with disabilities. *International Journal of Special Education, 25*(3), 76–87.

Hamra, M.. (2006). Relationship between expressed HIV/AIDS-related stigma and HIV-beliefs/knowledge and behaviour in families of HIV infected children in Kenya. *Tropical Medicine & International Health, 11*(4), 513–527. PMID: 16553935

Hanus, M., & Krause, U. (2025). Geography teachers' networks as platforms for continuous professional development: experience from the Netherlands and Czechia. In *Handbook of Geography Education* (pp. 723–750). Springer Nature Switzerland.

Happé, F., & Frith, U. (2020). Annual Research Review: Looking back to look forward – changes in the concept of autism and implications for future research. *Journal of Child Psychology and Psychiatry, and Allied Disciplines, 61*(3), 218–232. DOI: 10.1111/jcpp.13176

Hardman, K. (2008). The situation of physical education in schools: A European perspective. *Human Movement, 9*, 5–18.

Hargreaves, A. (2021). What the COVID-19 pandemic has taught us about teachers and teaching. *Facets, 6*(1), 1835–1863.

Harrower, J. K., & Dunlap, G. (2001). Including children with autism in general education classrooms: A review of effective strategies. *Behavior Modification, 25*(5), 762–784.

Haruna, M. A. (2017). The problems of living with disability in Nigeria. *Journal of Law, Policy andGlobalization, 6(5),* 103-113. https://iiste.org/Journals/index.php/ JLPG /article/view/3902 7.

Harvey, E. R. (2008). Deafness: A disability or a difference. *Health L. & Pol'y, 2,* 42.

Hassan, F. (2003) Treat the people ... now. Human rights and the law in the struggle for treatment. Paper at the South African AIDS Conference; Durban. 3–6 August 2003.

Healy, D. (2006). The latest mania: Selling bipolar disorder. *PLoS Medicine, 3,* e185. PMID: 16597178

Herek, GM. (2002) Thinking about AIDS and stigma: a psychologist's perspective. *J Law Med Ethics Winter,* Vol. 30, 4, pp. 594–607.

Herek, G. M. (2009). Hate crimes and stigma-related experiences among sexual minority adults in the United States: Prevalence estimates from a national probability sample. *J Interpers Violence, Vol., 24*(1), 54–74. PMID: 18391058

Herek, G. M., & Glunt, E. K. (1988). An epidemic of stigma: Public reactions to AIDS. *The American Psychologist, 43*(11), 886–891. PMID: 3063145

Herman, A. A., Stein, D. J., Seedat, S., Heeringa, S. G., Moomal, H., & Williams, D. R. (2009). The South African Stress and Health (SASH) study 12-month and lifetime prevalence of common mental disorders. *South African Medical Journal, 99*(5), 339–344. PMID: 19588796

Hernández-Torrano, D., Somerton, M., & Helmer, J. (2020). Mapping research on inclusive education since Salamanca Statement: A bibliometric review of the literature over 25 years. *International Journal of Inclusive Education, 16*(9), 1–20. DOI: 10.1080/13603116.2 020.1747555

Heto, P. P., & Mino, T. (2023). (Dis)ontinuity of African indigenous knowledge. AlterNative. *An International Journal of Indigenous Peoples, 19*(1), 71–79. DOI: 10.1177/ 11771801221138304

Hildebrandt-Wypych, D. (2022). Contrasting Narratives of the Israeli-Palestinian Conflict in Polish History Textbooks. *Frontiers in Education, 7,* 815830. DOI: 10.3389/feduc.2022.815830

Hilt, L. T. (2017). Education without a shared language: Dynamics of inclusion and exclusion in Norwegian introductory classes for newly arrived minority language students. *International Journal of Inclusive Education, 21*(6), 585–601. DOI: 10.1080/13603116.2016.122 3179

Hirschfeld, R. M. (2001). The comorbidity of major depression and anxiety disorders. *The Journal of Clinical Psychiatry*, *62*(suppl 8), 17–21. PMID: 15014592

Hodgson, T. F., & Khumalo, S. (2016). Too many children left behind: Exclusion in the South African inclusive education system, with a focus on the Umkhanyakude District, KwaZulu-Natal. *A Section 27 Report*. Retrieved March 17, 2024, from www.section27.org.za

Hodkinson, A., & Deverokonda, C. (2011). For pity's sake: Comparative conceptions of inclusion in England and India. *International Review of Qualitative Research.*

Hodkinson, A. (2009). Preservice teacher training and special educational needs in England 1970–2008: Is government learning the lessons of the past or is it experiencing a groundhog day*? European Journal of Special Needs Education*, *24*(3), 277–290.

Hodkinson, A., & Vickerman, P. (2009). Key issues in special needs and inclusion. *Sage (Atlanta, Ga.).*

Hofmann, S. G., Asnaani, A., Vonk, I. J. J., Sawyer, A. T., & Fang, A. (2012). The efficacy of cognitive behavioral therapy: A meta-analysis. *Cognitive Therapy and Research*, *36*(5), 427–440. DOI: 10.1007/s10608-012-9476-1 PMID: 23459093

Holt-Lundstad, J. (2017). The potential public health relevance of social isolation and loneliness: Prevalence, Epidemiology, and risk factors. *The Public Policy and Aging Report*, *27*(4), 127–130. DOI: 10.1093/ppar/prx030

Horner, R. H., Carr, E. G., Halle, J., McGee, G., Odom, S., & Wolery, M. (2005). The use of single-subject research to identify evidence-based practice in special education. *Exceptional Children*, *71*(2), 165–179. DOI: 10.1177/001440290507100203

Houshmand, K. (2015, September 18). How to avoid the destructive effects of competition at school. *HuffPost*. https://www.huffpost.com/archive/ca/entry/competition-students_b_8156376

Hugo, M. (2001). Mental health professionals' attitudes towards people who have experienced a mental health disorder. *Journal of Psychiatric and Mental Health Nursing*, *8*(5), 419–425. PMID: 11882162

Hulatt, L., & Freitas, G. (2024). Disability discrimination: Act, causes and effects. https://www.studysmarter.co.uk/explanations/social-studies/stratification-and-differentiation/disability-discrimination/

Hulek, A. (1992). *Uczeń niepełnosprawny w szkole masowej* [Disabled student in mainstream school].

Hull L, Mandy W, Lai M, Baron-Cohen S, Allison C, Smith P, & Petrides K V (2019). Development and Validation of the Camouflaging Autistic Traits Questionnaire (CAT-Q)J Autism Dev Disordr;49(3):819-833. doi: DOI: 10.1007/s10803-018-3792-6

Human Rights Watch. (2015). *Complicit in exclusion: South Africa's failure to guarantee an inclusive education for children with disabilities*. Human Rights Watch.

Hume-Nixon, M., & Kuper, H. (2018). The association between malnutrition and childhood disability in low- and middle-income countries: Systematic review and meta-analysis of observational studies. *Tropical Medicine & International Health, 23*(11), 1158–1175. DOI: 10.1111/tmi.13139

Hunt, X., Bradshaw, M., Vogel, S. L., Encalada, A. V., Eksteen, S., Schneider, M., Chunga, K., & Swartz, L. (2022). Community Support for Persons with Disabilities in Low- and Middle-Income Countries: A Scoping Review. *International Journal of Environmental Research and Public Health, 19*(14), 8269. DOI: 10.3390/ijerph19148269

Husband, G. (2020). Ethical Data Collection and Recognizing the Impact of Semi-Structured Interviews on Research Respondents. *Education Sciences 2020, Vol. 10, Page 206, 10*(8), 206. https://doi.org/DOI: 10.3390/EDUCSCI10080206

Hytten, K., & Bettez, S. C. (2011). Understanding education for social justice. *The Journal of Educational Foundations, 25*(1), 7–24.

Insel, T. (2017). Digital mental health and the future of care. *World Psychiatry; Official Journal of the World Psychiatric Association (WPA), 16*(2), 118–124.

Insel, T. R. (2017). Digital phenotyping: Technology for a new science of behavior. *Journal of the American Medical Association, 318*(13), 1215–1216. DOI: 10.1001/jama.2017.11295 PMID: 28973224

Institute of Development Studies. (2020). *Nigeria Situational Analysis Version II*. https://opendocs.ids.ac.uk/opendocs/bitstream/handle/20.500.12413/15561/DID%20SITAN%20Nigeria%20V2%20July%202020.pdf?sequence=1&isAllowed=y

Ipingbemi, O. (2015). Mobility challenges and transport safety of people with disabilities in Ibadan, Nigeria. *African Journal for the Psychological Study of Social Issues, 18*(3), 15–28. https://www.ajol.info/index.php/ajpssi/article/view/136989

Irshad, M. A., Amir, R. M., & Rafaqat, M. S. (2024). Towards Inclusive Classrooms: Identification of the Role of Teachers in Creating an Inclusive Learning Environment. *Journal of Asian Development Studies, 13*(3), 1323–1332.

Irwanto, Kasim, E.R., Fransiska, A., Lusli, M., & Siradj, O. (2010). Analisis situasi penyandang disabilitas di Indonesia: Sebuah desk-review. *Pusat Kajian Disabilitas Fisip UI*

Islam, K. M. A., & Bhuiyan, M. S. S. (2020). Growing importance of ICT in ELT for effective pedagogy during COVID-19 pandemic in Bangladesh. *Journal of ELT and Education*, *3*(3), 106–115.

Ismayilli, T., & Nuri, A. (2025). Applications that can be used in Mobile-Assisted Language Education. *Dibon Journal of Education*, *1*(2), 111–119. DOI: 10.64169/dje.82

Iwuagwu, A. O., & Kalu, M. E. (2021). Covid-19 and older adults: The paradox of physical distancing. *Ace Journal of Public Health and Community Medicine, 1(1)* 8-9. https://www.researchgate.net/publication/349992131_COVID-19_and_Nigerian_Older_Adults_The_Paradox_of_Physical_Distancing#fullTextFileContent

Jaarsma, E. A., Dijkstra, P. U., Geertzen, J. H. B., & Dekker, R. (2014). Barriers to and facilitators of sports participation for people with physical disabilities: A systematic review. *Scandinavian Journal of Medicine & Science in Sports*, (6), 871–881. DOI: 10.1111/sms.12218

Jain, D., Potluri, V., & Sharif, A. (2020, October). Navigating graduate school with a disability. In *Proceedings of the 22nd International ACM SIGACCESS Conference on Computers and Accessibility* (pp. 1-11).

Jaiyeola, G. D., Wong, A. Y., Bryck, R. L., Mills, C., & Hutt, S. (2025, March). One Size Does Not Fit All: Considerations when using Webcam-Based Eye Tracking to Models of Neurodivergent Learners' Attention and Comprehension. In *Proceedings of the 15th International Learning Analytics and Knowledge Conference* (pp. 24-35).

JAMA Network. (2023). Advances in pharmacogenomics for treating bipolar disorder. Journal of the American Medical Association. Available at: https://jamanetwork.com/journals/jama/pages/jama

JAMA Network. (2023). Artificial intelligence in predicting mental health crises: Ethical concerns and potential. Journal of the American Medical Association. Available at: https://jamanetwork.com/journals/jama/pages/jama

JAMA Psychiatry. (2023). Neuroimaging in personality disorders: A new frontier. Journal of the American Medical Association Psychiatry. Available at: https://jamanetwork.com/journals/jamapsychiatry

Jansson, J., Kerr, C. C., & Wilson, D. P. (2014). Predicting the population impact of increased HIV testing and treatment in Australia. *Sexual Health, 11*(2), 46–54. PMID: 24502838

Jardinez, M. J., & Natividad, L. R. (2024). The Advantages and Challenges of Inclusive Education: Striving for Equity in the Classroom. *Shanlax International Journal of Education, 12*(2), 57–65.

Jenkins, A. A., & Yoshimura, J. (2010). Not Another Inservice!: Meeting the Special Education Professional Development Needs of Elementary General Educators. *Teaching Exceptional Children, 42*(5), 36–43. DOI: 10.1177/004005991004200504

Jenkins, J. H., & Carpenter-Song, E. A. (2008). Stigma despite recovery. *Medical Anthropology Quarterly, 22*(4), 381–409. PMID: 19189724

Jenkins, K., & Kim Webster, A. (2021). Disability, impairment, and marginalised functioning. *Australasian Journal of Philosophy, 99*(4), 730–747.

Johnson, D. W., & Johnson, R. T. (2019). An educational psychology success story: Social interdependence theory and cooperative learning. *Educational Researcher, 38*(5), 365–379. DOI: 10.3102/0013189X09339057

Jones, L., Bellis, M. A., Wood, S., Hughes, K., McCoy, E., Eckley, L., Bates, G., Mikton, C., Shakespeare, T., & Officer, A. (2012). Prevalence and risk of violence against children with disabilities: A systematic review and meta-analysis of observational studies. *Lancet, 380*(9845), 899–907. DOI: 10.1016/S0140-6736(12)60692-8 PMID: 22795511

Jones, S. C., Gordon, C. S., Akram, M., Murphy, N., & Sharkie, F. (2022). Inclusion, exclusion and isolation of autistic people: Community attitudes and autistic people's experiences. *Journal of Autism and Developmental Disorders, 52*(3), 1131–1142.

Kahng, S. K., & Mowbray, C. T. (2005). What affects self-esteem of persons with psychiatric disabilities: The role of causal attributions of mental illnesses. *Psychiatric Rehabilitation Journal, 28*(4), 354–360. PMID: 15895919

Kaimara, P. (2023). Digital transformation stands alongside inclusive education: Lessons learned from a project called "Waking Up in the Morning." *Technology. Knowledge and Learning, 1*(1), 1–27. DOI: 10.1007/s10758-023-09427-w

Kakuma, R., Kleintjes, S., Lund, C., Drew, N., Green, A., & Flisher, A. J. (2010). Mental health stigma: What is being done to raise awareness and reduce stigma in South Africa? *The African Journal of Psychiatry, 13*(2), 112–124. PMID: 20473472

Kalichman, S. C.. (2005). Development of a brief scale to measure AIDS-related stigma in South Africa. *AIDS and Behaviour, Vol.*, *9*(2), 135–143. PMID: 15933833

Kalichman, S. C., & Simbayi, L. C. (2003). HIV testing attitudes, AIDS stigma, and voluntary HIV counseling and testing in a black township in Cape Town, South Africa. *Sexually Transmitted Infections*, *79*(6), 442–447. PMID: 14663117

Kalichman, S., & Simbayi, L. (2004). Traditional beliefs about the cause of AIDS and AIDS-related stigma in South Africa. *AIDS Care, Vol.*, *16*(5), 572–580. PMID: 15223526

Kapp, S. K., Gillespie-Lynch, K., Brooks, P. J., & Paradiz, M.. (2013). Growing up with autism: The developmental, conceptual, and personal narrative of neurodiversity. *Journal of Developmental Psychology.*, *49*(5), 540–550.

Karni, N., Reiter, S., & Bryen, D. N. (2011). Israeli Arab teachers' attitudes on inclusion of students with disabilities. *British Journal of Developmental Disabilities*, *57*(113), 123–132.

Kasler, J., & Jabareen, Y. T. (2017). Triple jeopardy: Special education for Palestinians in Israel. *International Journal of Inclusive Education*, *21*(12), 1261–1275.

Kassah, K. A., Kassah, B., & Abota, K. (2012). Abuse of disabled children in Ghana. *Disability & Society*, *25*(5), 1–13.

Katsui, H., & Kumpuvuori, J. (2008). Human Rights Based Approach in Development in Uganda. *Scandinavian Journal of Disability Research*, *10*(4), 227–236.

Kauffman, J. M., & Landrum, T. J. (2013). *Characteristics of emotional and behavioral disorders of children and youth*. Pearson.

Kavanagh, A., Krnjacki, L., Aitken, Z., LaMontagne, A., Beer, A., Baker, E., & Bentley, R. (2015). Intersections between disability, type of impairment, gender and socio-economic disadvantage in a nationally representative sample of 33,101 working-aged Australians. *Disability and Health Journal*, *8*(2), 191–199. DOI: 10.1016/j.dhjo.2014.08.008

Kavkler, M., Babuder, M. K., & Magajna, L. (2015). Inclusive education for children with specific learning difficulties: Analysis of opportunities and barriers in inclusive education in Slovenia. *Center for Educational Policy Studies Journal*, *5*(1), 31–52.

Keusch, G.T., Wilentz, J. & Kleinman, A. (2006). Stigma and global health: Developing a research agenda. *Lancet 2 367*(9509), 525-527.

Khaleel, N., Alhosani, M., & Duyar, I. (2021, April). The role of school principals in promoting inclusive schools: A teachers' perspective. *Frontiers in Education, 6*, 603241. DOI: 10.3389/feduc.2021.60324

Khan, F. (2024). Navigating the Gap: Disability Rights and Social Inclusion in a Changing World. *Social Science Review Archives, 1*(03), 1–9.

Kim, H. Jang, S, & Lim, J. (2022). Service Demand for and Awareness of a Primary Healthcare Pilot Project for People with Disabilities. *J Korean Med Sci. 1;37(30)*:e241https://doi. org/DOI: 10.3346/ jkms.2022.37.e241

Kim, J., Kim, J., Kim, Y., Han, A., & Nguyen, M. C. (2021). The contribution of physical and social activity participation to social support and happiness among people with physical disabilities. *Disability and Health Journal, 1*, 100974. DOI: 10.1016/j.dhjo.2020.100974

Kinchin, I. M. (2024). *How to mend a university: Towards a sustainable learning environment in higher education*. Bloomsbury.

King-Thorius, K. A., & Waitoller, F. R. (2017). Strategic coalitions against exclusion at the intersection of race and disability—A rejoinder. *Harvard Educational Review, 87*(2), 251–257.

Kippax, S., & Race, K. (2003). Sustaining safe practice: Twenty years on. *Social Science & Medicine, 57*(1), 1–12. PMID: 12753812

Kirkpatrick, D. L. (1975). *Evaluating training programs*. American Society for Training and Development.

Kirmayer, L. J.. (2016). Cultural contexts of mental health. *Lancet, 387*(10037), 918–929.

Kita, Y., Yasuda, S., & Gherghel, C. (2022). Online education and the mental health of faculty during the COVID-19 pandemic in Japan. *Scientific Reports, 12*(1), 8990. DOI: 10.1038/s41598-022-12985-6 PMID: 35637241

Kivunja, C., & Kuyini, A. B. (2017). Understanding and Applying Research Paradigms in Educational Contexts. *International Journal of Higher Education, 6*, 26–41. DOI: 10.5430/ijhe.v6n5p26

Kolleck, N., Schuster, J., Hartmann, U., & Gräsel, C. (2021). Teachers' professional collaboration and trust relationships: An inferential social network analysis of teacher teams. *Research in Education, 111*(1), 89–107. DOI: 10.1177/00345237211031585

Korlison, O. A. N. D. (2023). *The experience of special education teachers with dyslexic students: A case study* (Unpublished doctoral dissertation). Capella University.

Korndoerfer, K. M. (2023). What Does a Social Worker for Disability Services Do? https://www.google.com/search?q=What+Does+a+Social+Worker+for+Disability+Services+Do%3F&oq=What+Does+a+Social+Worker+for+Disability+Services+Do%3F&gs_lcrp=EgZjaHJvbWUyBggAEEUYOTIHCAEQIRiPAtIBCDEzNTZqMGo3qAIIsAIB8QVCdxFwWM2_2g&sourceid=chrome&ie=UTF-8

Koszela, K. (2013). The stigmatisation of disabilities in Africa and the developmental effects. *Independent Study Project (ISP) collection 1639*. University of Texas at Austin, US, Summer.

Koutsoklenis, A., & Papadimitriou, V. (2024). Special education provision in Greek mainstream classrooms: Teachers' characteristics and recruitment procedures in parallel support. *International Journal of Inclusive Education*, *28*(5), 561–576.

Kovačević, J., & Radovanovic, V. (2023). Social distance towards students with disabilities in inclusive education. *International Journal of Disability Development and Education*, *70*(1), 106–119.

Kowatch, R. A. (2005). Review and meta-analysis of the phenomenology and clinical characteristics of mania in children and adolescents. *Bipolar Disorders*, *7*, 483–496. PMID: 16403174

Kozleski, E. B., Artiles, A. J., & Waitoller, F. R. (2011). Introduction: Equity in inclusive education: Historical trajectories and theoretical commitments. In Artiles, A. J., Kozleski, E. B., & Waitoller, F. R. (Eds.), *Inclusive education*. Harvard University Press.

Krahn, G. L. (2011). WHO World Report on Disability: A review. *Disability and Health Journal*, *4*(3), 141–142. DOI: 10.1016/j.dhjo.2011.05.001

Kratt, D. (2018). Teachers' perspectives on educator mental health competencies: A qualitative case study. *American Journal of Qualitative Research*, *2*(1), 22–40.

Küçüksüleymanoğlu, R. (2025). Principles of Equality: Social Justice and Equal Opportunities. In *Creating Positive and Inclusive Change in Educational Environments* (pp. 23–52). IGI Global Scientific Publishing.

Kumari, S., Singh, A. R., Verma, A. N., Verma, P. K., & Chaudhury, S. (2009). Subjective burden on spouses of schizophrenia patients. *Indian Journal of Psychiatry*, *18*(2), 97–100. PMID: 21180485

Kurth, A. E. et al. (2015) HIV testing and linkage to services for youth. *Journal of the International AIDS Society*, 18, 19433 [PMC free article] [PubMed] [CrossRef] [Google Scholar Landefeld, C.C. et. al (2018) Prevention of Mother-to Child Transmission of HIV in Yaounde: Barrier to Care. *AIDS care*, Vol. 30, 1, pp. 116–120. DOI: 10.7448/IAS.18.2.19433

Kushwaha, R. K., Tripathi, A., Singh, C., & Yadav, M. K. (2024). *Inclusive Education*. Blue Rose Publishers.

Kusters, A. (2012). "The Gong Gong Was Beaten"—Adamorobe: A "Deaf Village" in Ghana and its marriage prohibition for deaf partners. *Sustainability*, *4*(10), 2765–2784.

Kuvalekar, K., Kamath, R., Ashok, L., Shetty, B., Mayya, S., & Chandrasekaran, V. (2015). Quality of life among persons with physical disability in Udupi Taluk: A cross sectional study. *Journal of Family Medicine and Primary Care*, *4*(1), 69–73. DOI: 10.4103/2249-4863.152258

Låftman, S. B., Almquist, Y. B., & Östberg, V. (2013). Students' accounts of school-performance stress: A qualitative analysis of a high-achieving setting in Stockholm, Sweden. *Journal of Youth Studies*, *16*(7), 932–949. DOI: 10.1080/13676261.2013.780126

Lambert, V. A., & Lambert, C. E. (2012). Qualitative descriptive research: An acceptable design. *Pacific Rim International Journal of Nursing*, *16*(4), 255–256.

Lamichhane, K. (2015). *Disability, education and employment in developing countries: From charity to investment*. University Press.

Lancet Psychiatry. (2023). Early intervention in psychosis: Reducing the burden. The Lancet Psychiatry. Available at: https://www.thelancet.com/journals/lanpsy/home

Lancet Psychiatry. (2023). The role of ketamine and esketamine in treating resistant depression. The Lancet Psychiatry. Available at: https://www.thelancet.com/journals/lanpsy/home

Lang, R., & Upah, L. (2008). Scoping study: Disability issues in Nigeria. https://studylib.net/doc/13390397/scoping-study--disability-issues-in-nigeria-final-report

Lawrie, S. M. (1999). Stigmatisation of psychiatric disorder. *Psychiatric Bulletin*, *23*(3), 129–131.

Lee, C. C. (Ed.). (1997). *Multicultural issues in counseling: New approaches to diversity* (2nd ed.). American Counseling Association.

Lee, H. J., Jeong, W., Chon, D., Kim, J. H., & Moon, J. Y. (2022). The Association between perceived discrimination and mental health of wage workers with disabilities: Findings from the panel survey of employment for the disabled 2016-2018. *International Journal of Environmental Research and Public Health, 19*(14), 8541. DOI: 10.3390/ijerph1914 8541

Levy, S. R., Gopang, M., Ramírez, L., Bernardo, A. B., Ruck, M. D., & Sternisko, A. (2024). A human rights-based approach to climate injustices at the local, national, and international levels: Program and policy recommendations. *Social Issues and Policy Review, 18*(1), 3–30.

Leyser, Y., & Romi, S. (2008). Religion and attitudes of college preservice teachers toward students with disabilities: Implications for higher education [in Hebrew]. *Higher Education, 55*(6), 703–717.

Lichtensztejn. (2006). Integracja: szansa czy zagrożenie? Warunki sensownej integracji [Integration: Opportunity or threat? Conditions for meaningful integration]. https://profesor.pl/mat/pd6/pd6_e_lichtensztejn_20060216.pdf

Lifshitz, H., & Glaubman, R. (2002). Self-efficacy and attitudes towards inclusion of religious and secular student teachers. *Journal of Intellectual Disability Research, 46*(5), 405–418. PMID: 12031023

Lindsay, S., Fuentes, K., Ragunathan, S., Li, Y., & Ross, T. (2024). Accessible independent housing for people with disabilities: A scoping review of promising practices, policies and interventions. *PLoS One, 19*(1), e0291228. DOI: 10.1371/journal.pone.0291228

Lindsey, R. B., Pond, A. J., & Lindsey, D. B. (2018). *Culturally Proficient Leadership: The Personal Journey Begins Within.* Corwin Press.

Link, B. G., & Phelan, J. C. (2001). Conceptualizing stigma. *Annual Review of Sociology, 27*(1), 363–385.

Link, B. G., & Phelan, J. C. (2006). Stigma and its public health implications. *Lancet, 367*(9509), 528–529. PMID: 16473129

Lin, L. C., & Hung, I. C., Kinshuk, & Chen, N. S. (2019). The impact of student engagement on learning outcomes in a cyber-flipped course. *Educational Technology Research and Development, 67*(6), 1573–1591. DOI: 10.1007/S11423-019-09698-9/METRICS

Littlewood, R. (1998). Cultural variation in the stigmatisation of mental illness. *Lancet, 352*(9133), 1056–1057. PMID: 9759770

Livingston, L. A., Shah, P., & Happé, F. (2019). Compensatory strategies below the behavioural surface in Autism: A qualitative study. *The Lancet. Psychiatry*, *6*(9), 766–777. DOI: 10.1016/ S2215-0366(19)30224-X

Loewen, G., & Pollard, W. (2010). The social justice perspective. *Journal of Post-secondary Education and Disability*, *23*(1), 5–18.

López, F., & Sleeter, C. E. (2023). *Critical race theory and its critics: Implications for research and teaching*. Teachers College Press.

Loreman, T., Deppeler, J., & Harvey, D. (2011). *Inclusive education: Supporting diversity in the classroom* (2nd ed.). Allen & Unwin.

Luckner, J. L., & Cooke, C. (2010). A summary of the vocabulary research with students who are deaf or hard of hearing. *American Annals of the Deaf*, *155*(1), 38–67. DOI: 10.1353/aad.0.0129 PMID: 20503907

Luckner, J. L., & Handley, C. M. (2008). A summary of the reading comprehension research undertaken with students who are deaf or hard of hearing. *American Annals of the Deaf*, *153*(1), 6–36. DOI: 10.1353/aad.0.0006 PMID: 18619066

Ludeman, R. B., & Schreiber, B. (2020). *Student Affairs and Services in Higher Education: Global Foundations, Issues, and Best Practices* (R. B. Ludeman & B. Schreiber (eds.); 3rd edition). International Association of Student Affairs and Services (IASAS) in cooperation with Deutsches Studentenwerk (DSW). https://www.studierendenwerke.de/fileadmin/api/files/210129_dsw_iasas_final_web.pdf

Lukas, B. A., & Yunus, M. M. (2021). ESL Teachers' Challenges in Implementing E-learning during COVID-19. *International Journal of Learning. Teaching and Educational Research*, *20*(2), 330–348.

Lundberg, U., & Cooper, C. L. (2010). *The science of occupational health: Stress, psychobiology, and the new world of work*. Wiley-Blackwell. mental health and gender in secondary school. Education Inquiry, https://www.tandfonline.com/doi/full/10.1080/20004508.2018.1558665

Lund, C., Kleintjes, S., Kakuma, R., & Flisher, A. J. (2010). Public sector mental health systems in South Africa: Inter-provincial comparisons and policy implications. *Social Psychiatry and Psychiatric Epidemiology*, *45*(3), 393–404. PMID: 19506789

Luo, X., Du, B., Gui, P., Zhang, D., & Hu, W. (2023). A Hunger Games search algorithm with opposition-based learning for solving multimodal medical image registration. *Neurocomputing*, *540*, 126204.

Lynam, D. R., & Miller, J. D. (2007). Personality, psychopathology, and aggression. *Journal of Research in Personality*, *41*(3), 654–664. DOI: 10.1016/j.jrp.2006.09.007

MacKenzie, A., Bower, C., & Owaineh, M. (2020). Gratitude versus children's rights: An exploration of mothers' attitudes towards disability and inclusive education in Palestine. *International Journal of Educational Research Open*, *1*, 100001.

MacKenzie, A., & Chiang, T. H. (2023). The human development and capability approach: A counter theory to human capital discourse in promoting low SES students' agency in education. *International Journal of Educational Research*, *117*, 102121.

Mackenzie, S., & Smith, L. (2016). Building inclusive communities for children with Autism Spectrum Disorders: An exploration of collaborative learning practices. *Journal of Autism Spectrum Disorders and Developmental Disorders*, *46*(3), 635–650.

Mackin, P., Targum, S. D., Kalali, A., Rom, D., & Young, A. H. (2006). Culture and assessment of manic symptoms. *The British Journal of Psychiatry*, *189*, 379–380. PMID: 17012663

Madar, N. K., & Danoch, A. (2021). Inclusive education in Israel: A study of policy impact on access to education. *International Journal of Inclusive Education*, *28*(1), 78–89. DOI: 10.1080/13603116.2021.1916109

Maguvhe, M. O. (2023). Unique African challenges in the provision of quality inclusive education in school education and training. In Maguvhe, M. O., & Masuku, M. M. (Eds.), *Using African Epistemologies in Shaping Inclusive Education Knowledge* (pp. 285–306). Springer Nature Switzerland., DOI: 10.1007/978-3-031-31115-4_16

Maguvhe, M. O. (2024). Inclusive education: Controversies, successes, and future prospects. In Maguvhe, M. O., Mpya, N. G., & Sadiki, M. C. (Eds.), *Handbook of research on inclusive and accessible education* (pp. 1–17). IGI Global.

Maguvhe, M. O. (2025). *Inclusive Education: Towards Social Justice, Achievement of Equality and Advancement of Human Rights*. BRILL.

Mahajan, A. P.. (2008). Stigma in the HIV/AIDS epidemic: A review of the literature and recommendations for the way forward. *AIDS, Vol.*, *22*(Suppl 2), S67–S79. PMID: 18641472

Mahammoda, S. A. (2022). *Educational reforms in Ethiopia: From the imperial era to the present* (Unpublished doctoral dissertation). Necmettin Erbakan University, Turkey.

Mahat-Shamir, M., Neimeyer, R. A., & Pitcho-Prelorentzos, S. (2021). Designing in-depth semi-structured interviews for revealing meaning reconstruction after loss. *Death Studies*, *45*(2), 83–90. DOI: 10.1080/07481187.2019.1617388 PMID: 31116652

Mahlangu, S. M., & Mtshali, T. I. (2024). Inclusive education strategies for knowledge development of teachers enrolled in the advanced vocational and training education program. *International Journal of Religion*, *5*(3), 166–174.

Makuyana, T. (2024). Proven African inclusive education strategies for educators to build a safe and diverse learner community. In Maguvhe, M. O., Mpya, N. G., & Sadiki, M. C. (Eds.), *Handbook of Research on Inclusive and Accessible Education* (pp. 140–156). IGI Global.

Makweya, P. P., & Sepadi, M. D. (2025). Inclusive Education and Lifelong Learning: Beyond School Walls. In *Global Practices in Inclusive Education Curriculum and Policy* (pp. 261-280). IGI Global.

Malinovskiy, S., Shibanova, E., & Movkebayeva, Z. (2024). Barriers and facilitators of access to higher education in a weakly institutionalised context: Perceptions of disabled students. *Disability & Society*, *39*(9), 2258–2280.

Mandy, W. (2019). Social camouflaging in Autism: Is it time to lose the mask? *Autism*, *23*(8), 1879–1881. DOI: 10.1177/1362361319878559

Maponya, T. J. (2020). The Instructional Leadership Role of the School Principal on Learners' Academic Achievement. *African Educational Research Journal*, *8*(2), 183–193.

Margalit, M. (2000). *Report of the committee on the implementation of special education law* [in Hebrew]. Ministry of Education.

Marshall, M. N. (1996). Sampling for qualitative research. *Family Practice*, *13*(6), 522–526. DOI: 10.1093/fampra/13.6.522 PMID: 9023528

Marshark, M., & Hauser, P. (2013). *How deaf children learn: What parents and teachers need to know*. Oxford University Press.

Martin Ginis, K. A., van der Ploeg, H. P., Foster, C., Lai, B., McBride, C. B., Ng, K., Pratt, M., Shirazipour, C. H., Smith, B., Vásquez, P. M., & Heath, G. W. (2021). Participation of people living with disabilities in physical activity: A global perspective. *Lancet*, *398*(10298), 443–455. DOI: 10.1016/S0140-6736(21)01164-8

Martinez, R., & Vemuru, V. (2020). Social inclusion of persons with disabilities in Nigeria: Challenges and opportunities. https://blogs.worldbank.org/nasikiliza/social-inclusion-persons-disabilities-nigeria-challenges-and-opportunities

Mayo Clinic Staff. (2017). *Mental health: Overcoming the stigma of mental illness.* https://www.mayoclinic.org/diseases-conditions/mental-illness/in-depth/mental-health/art-20046477

Mbago, M. C. Y. (2004). Socio-demographic correlates of desire for HIV testing in Tanzania. *Sexual Health, 1*, 13–21. PMID: 16335292

Mburu, S. (2017). Challenges faced by schools for disabled children in Kenya. *Kenyaplex, 15*(October), 3.

McCausland, D., McCallion, P., Carroll, R., & McCarron, M. (2021). The nature and quality of friendship for older adults with an intellectual disability in Ireland. *Journal of Applied Research in Intellectual Disabilities, 34*, 763–776. DOI: 10.1111/jar.12851

McDonald, M. (1993). The construction of difference: An anthropological approach to stereotypes. In Macdonald, S. (Ed.), *Inside European Identities: Ethnography in Western Europe* (pp. 219–236). Routledge.

McFall, M. T. (2016). Divine Hiddenness and Spiritual Autism. *Heythrop Journal. Heythrop Journal, 63*(4), n/a–n/a. DOI: 10.1111/heyj.12324

Meda, L., Efthymiou, E., AlHammadi, M., Williams, C., & Fteiha, M. (2023). Conceptualizing and Reimagining the Future of Inclusive Education in the UAE. *Open Education Studies, 5*(1), 20220205. DOI: 10.1515/edu-2022-0205

Meda, L., Mohebi, L., El Sayary, A., & Karaki, S. (2023). A Mutually Enriching Inclusive Education Teacher Professional Development Program: Mentors' and Mentees' Reflections'. *International Journal of Evidence Based Coaching and Mentoring, 21*(2), 51–62. DOI: 10.24384/fv45-1467

Meo, G. (2008). Curriculum planning for all learners: Applying universal design for learning (UDL) to a high school reading comprehension program. *Preventing School Failure, 52*(2), 21–30. DOI: 10.3200/PSFL.52.2.21-30

Mergler, A., Carrington, S., Kimber, M., & Bland, D. (2016). Inclusive values: Exploring the perspectives of pre-service teachers. *The Australian Journal of Teacher Education, 41*(4), 2. DOI: 10.14221/ajte.2016v41n4.2

Meyer, B. D., & Mok, W. K. C. (2019). Disability, earnings, income and consumption. *Journal of Public Economics, 171*(C), 51–69. DOI: 10.1016/j.jpubeco.2018.06.011

Meyer, B., & Asbrock, F. (2018). Disabled or cyborg? How bionics affect stereotypes toward people with physical disabilities. *Frontiers in Psychology*, *9*, 2251. DOI: 10.3389/ fpsyg.2018.02251

Meyer, I. H. (2003). Prejudice, social stress, and mental health in gay men. *The American Psychologist*, *58*(5), 417–427. DOI: 10.1037/0003-066X.58.5.417

Mhlongo M (2018), A framework for the integration of indigenous knowledge into libraries in South Africa IFLA Journal 47(3)

Miklowitz, D. J.. (2021). Psychosocial treatments for bipolar disorder. *The Lancet. Psychiatry*, *8*(3), 211–221.

Miller, A. N., & Rubin, D. L. (2007). Factors leading to self-disclosure of a positive HIV diagnosis in Nairobi, Kenya: People living with HIV/AIDS in the Sub-Sahara. *Qualitative Health Research*, *17*(5), 586–598. PMID: 17478642

Milner, H. R. (2017). Culturally Relevant Pedagogy in a Diverse Classroom. *Theory into Practice*, *56*(3), 243–250.

Mitchell, P. B., & Malhi, G. S. (2019). Bipolar depression: Challenges and treatment options. *Current Opinion in Psychiatry*, *32*(6), 476–485. DOI: 10.1097/ YCO.0000000000000543

Mitra, S., Posarac, A. & Vick, B. (2013). Disability and poverty in developing countries: A multidimensional study. *World Development* 41: 1-18. https://doi.org/ . 2012.05.024DOI: 10.1016/j.worlddev

Mittler, P. (1995). Education for all or for some? International principles and practice. *Australasian Journal of Special Education*, *19*(2), 5–15.

Mizunoya, S., Mitra, S., & Yamasaki, I. (2018). Disability and school attendance in 15 low- and middle-income countries. *World Development,* Elsevier, 104(C), 388-403. https://doi: : 388-403.DOI: 10.1016/j.worlddev.2017.12.001 104

Mizunoya, S., & Mitra, S. (2013). Is there a disability gap in employment rates in developing countries? *World Development*, *42*, 28–43. DOI: 10.1016/j.worlddev.2012.05.037

Mohammed, A. (2025). Developing Advanced Reading Skills Through Extensive Reading: Findings from Palestinian schools. *Dibon Journal of Education*, *1*(1), 56–68. DOI: 10.64169/dje.24

Molnár, T., Jenei, S., Moreno, E., Lakshmi, V. P., Malatyinszki, S., & Dávid, L. D. (2024). The Role of Lifelong Learning in Labour Market Competitiveness. *Journal of Ecohumanism*, *3*(8), 7743–7761.

Molto, M. (2003). Mainstream teachers' acceptance of instructional adaptations in Spain. *European Journal of Special Needs Education, 18*, 311–332.

Morgan, H. (2021). Mad studies and disability studies. In *The Routledge international handbook of Mad studies* (pp. 108–118). Routledge.

Moscoso-Porras, M., & Alvarado, G. (2018). Association between perceived discrimination and healthcare-seeking behaviour in people with a disability. *Disability and Health Journal,11*(1), 93-8. https://www.ncbi.nlm.nih.gov/nlmcatalog?term=%22Disabil+Health +J%22%5BTitle+Abbreviation%5D

Mou, M., & Albagmi, F. M. (2024). Merging critical disability theory with post-colonial hybridity theory: A widened lens and implications. *Disability & Society, 39*(9), 2344–2356.

Moury, C., & Escada, M. (2023). Understanding successful policy innovation: The case of Portuguese drug policy. *Addiction (Abingdon, England), 118*(5), 967–978.

Moustache, H. M., & Makhoba, M. (2024). Educators' experiences of teaching learners with hearing loss in inclusive classrooms. *South African Journal of Childhood Education, 14*(1), 13.

Moyi, P. (2017). School enrolment and attendance for children with disabilities in Kenya: An examination of household survey data. *Forum of International Research in Education, 4*(2), 1–21.

Mpofu, J. (2023) Understanding Autism: An African Perspective. In HR Maapola-Thobejane & M O Maguvhe (Eds) Handbook on Shifting Paradigms of Disabilities in the Schooling System. IGI Global book series Advances in Educational Technologies and Instructional Design (AETID) (ISSN: 2326-8905; eISSN: 2326-8913

Mpofu, J. (2020). Partnerships for Autism in Zimbabwean Inclusive Education System. In Sefa Dei, G. J., Phasha, N., & Mahlo, D. (Eds.), *Autism: Perspectives from Africa* (Vol. I, pp. 168–181). University of South Africa.

Mpofu, J. (2023). An afro-centric approach to inclusive education. In Maguvhe, M. O., & Masuku, M. M. (Eds.), *Using African epistemologies in shaping inclusive education knowledge*. Palgrave Macmillan., DOI: 10.1007/978-3-031-31115-4_5

Mpofu, J., & Molosiwa, S. (2017). Disability and inclusive education in Zimbabwe. In Sefa Dei, G. J., Phasha, N., & Mahlo, D. (Eds.), *Inclusive education in African contexts: Anti-colonial educational perspective for transformative change* (pp. 49–65). Sense Publishers.

Mrema, D., Ndayambaje, I., Ntawiha, P., & Ndabaga, E. (2024). The Practicability of Quality Assurance Mechanisms in Promoting Tanzanian Universities' Compliance. *European Journal of Educational Research, 13*(3).

Muchini, B.. (2011). Local perceptions of the forms, timing and causes of behavior change in response to the AIDS epidemic in Zimbabwe. *AIDS and Behavior, 15*(2), 487–498. PMID: 20803064

Muhammad, S. (2025). Integrating Social Studies Education to Tackle Socioeconomic Challenges in Nigeria: A Case Study of Selected Upper Basic Schools in Gusau Metropolis, Zamfara State. *Dibon Journal of Education, 1*(2), 85–100. DOI: 10.64169/dje.45

Munyayi, F. K., & van Wyk, B. E. (2024). Policy and programming towards addressing treatment gaps in adolescents living with HIV: A content analysis of policy and programme documents in Namibia. [JIAPAC]. *Journal of the International Association of Providers of AIDS Care, 23*, 23259582241236061.

Mupedziswa, R., Rankopo, M., & Mwansa, L. (2019). Ubuntu as a Pan-African philosophical framework for social work in Africa. In Twikirize, J. M., & Spitzer, H. (Eds.), *Social work practice in Africa: Indigenous and innovative approaches* (pp. 21–38). Fountain Publishers., DOI: 10.2307/j.ctv2tp73vt

Musengamana, I., Shaoan, M. M. R., Namanyane, T., Lafferty, N., & Uzochukwu, O. M. (2024). Teachers' Role in School Decision-Making Process: A Case Study of Teachers and School Leaders Perceptions in Rwanda Public Secondary School. *Asia Social Issues, 17*(4), e267161–e267161.

Musselman, C. (2000). How do children who can't hear learn to read an alphabetic script? A review of the literature on reading and deafness. *Journal of Deaf Studies and Deaf Education, 5*(1), 9–31. DOI: 10.1093/deafed/5.1.9 PMID: 15454515

Muthukrishna, N. (Ed.). (2008). *Educating for social justice and inclusion in an African context: Pathways and transitions*. Nova Science.

Muthukrishna, N., & Engelbrecht, P. (2018). Decolonising inclusive education in lower income southern African educational contexts. *South African Journal of Education, 38*(4), 1–11.

Muthukrishna, N., & Ramsuran, A. (2008). Editorial: HIV/AIDS, education, and childhood in the African context. *Journal of Psychology in Africa, 18*(3), 367–370.

Mwoma, T. (2017). Education for children with special needs in Kenya: A review of related literature. *Journal of Education and Practice, 8*(28), 188–200.

Myers, M. D. (2014). Overview of qualitative research. In M. Frenz, K. Nielsen, & G. Walters (Eds.), *Research methods in management* (pp. 87–98). Sage. Myint, L.L., Akkadechanunt, T., Sirakamon, S., Chitpakdee, B.: Factors influencing nursing

Namanyane, T., & Shaoan, M. R. (2021). Inclusive education: A literature review on definitions, attitudes and pedagogical challenges. *International Journal of Research and Innovation in Social Science*, *5*(3), 358–365.

Naqeeb, H. (2025). Intercultural Communicative Competence: Definition, Models, Measurement Instruments, and Empirical Practice in the EFL Classroom. *Dibon Journal of Education*, *1*(1), 23–41. DOI: 10.64169/dje.15

National Institute of Mental Health. (2024) Mental Illness—National Institute of Mental Health. https://www.nimh.nih.gov/health/statistics/mental-illness

Naude, A., Kang, L. J., Moretti, M., Rocha, A. D. S., Maxwell, G. R. D., & Bornman, J. (2024). Using the ICF to Guide Inclusion in the African Educational Context: A Scoping Review. *Education Sciences*, *14*(12), 1290.

Ndibalema, P. (2025). Perspectives on barriers to learning opportunities among deaf children in Tanzania. *International Journal of Educational Research Open*, *9*, 100468.

Ndlovu, S. (2023). Indigenous knowledge systems in Africa: Exclusion of students with disabilities in South African higher education. *Curriculum Perspectives*, *43*(Suppl 1), 127–140.

Neece, C., McIntyre, L. L., & Fenning, R. (2020). Examining the impact of COVID-19 in ethnically diverse families with young children with intellectual and developmental disabilities. *Journal of Intellectual Disability Research*, *64*(10), 739–749.

Neighbours, H. W., Caldwell, C., Williams, D. R., Nesse, R., Taylor, R. J., & Bullard, K. M.. (2007). Race, ethnicity, and the use of services for mental disorders: Results from the National Survey of American Life. *Archives of General Psychiatry*, *64*, 485–494. PMID: 17404125

Nel, C., Dieker, L., & Marais, E. (2024). The integration of mixed reality simulation into reading literacy modules. *Education Sciences*, *14*(10), 1128.

Neves, C., Almeida, A. P., & Ferreira, M. (2023). Headteachers and inclusion: Setting the tone for an inclusive school. *Education Sciences*, *13*(2), 129.

Newfield, D. (2011). Multimodality and children's participation in classrooms: Instances of research. *Perspectives in Education*, *29*(1), 27–35.

Ngema, Z., & D'amant, A. (2024). Implementation of inclusive education as experienced by immigrant learners of diverse backgrounds in South Africa. *South African Journal of Education, 44*(1), S1–S9.

Ngo, H., Shin, J. Y., Nhan, N. V., & Yang, L. H. (2012). Stigma and restriction on the social life of families of children with intellectual disabilities in Vietnam. *Singapore Medical Journal, 53*(7), 451–457. PMID: 22815013

Ngui, E. M. (2010). Mental disorders, health inequalities and ethics: A global perspective. *International Review of Psychiatry (Abingdon, England), 22*(3), 235–244. PMID: 20528652

NHS Digital. (2017). Mental health of children and young people in England 2017. https://files.digital. nhs.uk/A6/EA7D58/MHCYP%202017%20Summary.pdf

NHS Digital. (2020). Mental health of children and young people in England, 2020. https://files.digital. nhs.uk/AF/AECD6B/mhcyp_2020_rep_v2.pdf

Niehaus, I. (2006) Leprosy of a Deadlier Kind: Conceptions of AIDS, Sex and Death in the South African Lowveld; Paper presented at the Institute for Social and Economic Research; Rhodes University. October 2006.

Nielsen, J. V., Smedegaard, S., Klakk, H., & Skovgaard, T. (2023). Same, same but different: Comparing program fidelity at early versus late adopters of a successful long-term school-based physical activity intervention. *Health Promotion Practice, 24*(6), 1237–1245.

Nieuwenhuis, J. (2010). Analyzing qualitative data. In Maree, K. (Ed.), *First Steps in Research* (pp. 72–80). Van Schaik.

Nigeria Demographic and Health Survey. (2018). *2018 DHS key findings*. https:// www.microdata.worldbank.org>...>DHS

Nijakowska, J. (2014). Dyslexia in the European EFL teacher training context. In Pawlak, M., & Aronin, L. (Eds.), *Essential topics in applied linguistics and multilingualism: Studies in honor of David Singleton* (pp. 129–154). Springer., DOI: 10.1007/978-3-319-01414-2_8

Nind, M. (2014). Conducting qualitative research with people with learning, communication, and other disabilities: Methodologies, ethics, and the role of the researcher. *Disability & Society, 29*(3), 431–445.

Nirit, K. V., & Shunit, R. (2013). Attitudes towards autism among Israeli Arab teachers' college students. In *Recent advances in autism spectrum disorders* (Vol. II). IntechOpen.

Nkosi, T. (2015). *Expanding the Potential of Ubuntu in South Africa's Schools. Educational Philosophy and Theory*. Longman.

Nnama-Okechukwu, C. U., Chukwuka, P. N., & Okoye, U. O. (2020). Challenges with institutional support services for undergraduate students with visual impairment in University of Nigeria, Nsukka. *Evidence-Informed Social Work, 17*(6), 677–695.

Nseibo, J. K. (2021). Exploring the experiences of children and youth with mobility impairments in four basic educational settings in Ghana (Master's thesis, University of Oslo). University of Oslo Digital Repository. Mbaku, J. M. (2021). International law, corruption and the rights of children in Africa. *San Diego Int'l LJ, 23*, 195.

Ntuli, L. T. (2018). *Managing curriculum implementation at selected primary schools in the Sekhukhune district, Limpopo province* (Doctoral dissertation, Doctoral thesis. University of South Africa, Pretoria.

Obiakor, F., & Offor, M. (2011). Special education provision in Nigeria: Analysing contexts, problems and prospects. *International Journal of Special Education, 26*(1), 25–32. https://www.academia.edu/59362328/Special_Education_Provision_in_Nigeria_Analyzing_Contexts_Problems_and_Prospects

Obst, P., & Stafurik, J. (2010). Online we are all able bodied: Online psychological sense of community and social support found through membership of disability-specific websites promotes well-being for people living with a physical disability. *Journal of Community & Applied Social Psychology, 20*(6), 525–531. DOI: 10.1002/casp.1067

Odenbring, Y. (2019). Strong boys and supergirls? School professionals' perceptions of students'

Odero, C. A. (2024). *Falling through the cracks: Exploring parental struggles and experiences when accessing special education for children with disabilities in Kenya* (Unpublished Master's thesis). Bowling Green State University.

Oexle, N., Müller, M., Kawohl, W., Xu, Z., Viering, S., & Wyss, C.. (2017). Self-stigma as a barrier to recovery: A longitudinal study. *European Archives of Psychiatry and Clinical Neuroscience, 268*(2), 209–212. DOI: 10.1007/s00406-017-0773-2 PMID: 28188369

Ofuani, A. (2011). The right to economic empowerment of persons with disabilities in Nigeria: How enabled? *African Human Rights Law Journal, 11(2),* 639-658. https://www.ahrlj.up.ac. za /ofuani-ai-2011

Ogechi, N. O., & Ruto, S. J. (2002). Portrayal of disability through personal names and proverbs in Kenya: Evidence from Ekegusii and Nandi. *Stichproben. Wiener Zeitschrift für Kritische Afrikastudien, 3*(2).

Ogundipe, S. (2019). Buhari signs law banning discrimination against persons with disability. https://www.premiumtimesng.com/news/headlines/307474-buhari-signs-law-banning-discrimination-against-persons-with-disability.html?tztc=1

Okah, P., Chukwu, N., Agha, A., Onalu, C., Nnama-Okechukwu, C., Iwuagwu, A., Anazonwu, N., & Okoye, U. (2023a). Formal support services for People living With Disabilities (PWDs) in Southeast Nigeria. *Journal of Social Work in Developing Societies, 5*(2), 50–64. https://journals.aphriapub.com/index.php/JSWDS/article/view/2315

Okah, P., Onalu, C., & Okoye, U. (2023b). National Health Insurance Scheme in Nigeria: Exploring limitations to utilisation by adult enrollees. *Journal of Social Service Research, 49*(6), 715–730. DOI: 10.1080/01488376.2023.2265417

Okpa, J. T., Ilupeju, A. A., & Eshiotse, E. (2020). Cybercrime and socio-economic development of corporate organisations in Cross River State, Nigeria. *Asian Journal of Scientific Research, 13*(3), 205–213. DOI: 10.3923/ajsr.2020.205.213

Olawumi, K. B., & Mavuso, M. P. (2024). In-service teacher training programmes that promote education for sustainable development: A review of emerging literature. *Interdisciplinary Journal of Education Research, 6*, 1–20.

Oliver, M. (1996). *Understanding disability: From theory to practice*. Macmillan.

Omianowski, M. (2008). Dziecko niepełnosprawne na lekcji wychowania fizycznego w szkole masowej [Child with disability in physical education class in mainstream school]. http://wychowaniefizyczne.pl/userfiles/_download/inne_michniep.pdf

Omote, T. (2021). Ubuntu and Community Resilience: Reflections on collective responsibility in education. *Journal of African Cultural Studies, 33*(1), 99–113.

Onalu, C., & Nwafor, N. (2021). Social supports available to persons with disabilities in Nigeria. https://www.doi: DOI: 10.5772/intechopen.97790

Onalu, C., Chukwu, N., Nnama-Okechukwu, C. U., Iwuagwu, A., Agha, A., Okah, P., Anazonwu, P., & Okoye, U. (2023). An exploratory study of the situation of persons with disabilities in Nigeria: Practice consideration for social workers. *Journal of Evidence-Based Social Work*. Advance online publication. DOI: 10.1080/26408066.2023.2265920

Opoku, M. P., Mustafa, A., Anwahi, N., Alkatheeri, F., Alsuwaidi, N., Alqutaiti, A., & Belbase, S. (2024). Working as teacher assistants/aides in schools: Understanding experiences in an Arabian context using the wider pedagogical role model. *Cogent Education, 11*(1). Advance online publication. DOI: 10.1080/2331186X.2024.2319450

Opoku, M. P., Nketsia, W., Banye, M. A., Mprah, W. K., Dogbe, J. A., & Badu, E. (2020). Caregiving experiences and expectations of parents with in-school children with intellectual disability in Ghana. *Research in Developmental Disabilities, 96*. Advance online publication. DOI: 10.1016/j.ridd.2019.103524 PMID: 31739195

Oranga, J., Obuba, E., Sore, I., & Boinett, F. (2022). Parental involvement in the education of learners with intellectual disabilities in Kenya. *OAlib*, *9*(4), 1–18.

Osberg, D., & Biesta, G. (2010). The end/s of education: Complexity and the conundrum of the inclusive educational curriculum. *International Journal of Inclusive Education, 14*(6), 593–607. DOI: 10.1080/13603110802530684

Ostrowska, A. (2002). Społeczeństwo polskie wobec osób niepełnosprawnych. Przemiany postaw i dyskursu [Polish society towards disabled people: Changes in attitudes and discourse]. In J. Sikorska (Ed.), *Społeczne problemy osób niepełnosprawnych* [*Social problems of disabled people*] (pp. 51-64). IFiS PAN.

Pagán-Rodríguez, R. (2014). How do disabled individuals spend their leisure time? *Disability and Health Journal*, *7*(2), 196–205. DOI: 10.1016/j.dhjo.2014.01.001

Paley, J. (2002). The Cartesian melodrama in nursing. *Nursing Philosophy*, *3*(3), 189–192. DOI: 10. 1046/j.1466-769X.2002.00113.x

Pańczyk, J. (2002). Kompetencje pedagogów specjalnych jako wyraz oczekiwań, wyzwań rynku edukacyjnego, rehabilitacyjnego i resocjalizacyjnego XXI wieku. [Competencies of special educators as an expression of expectations and challenges of the 21st century educational, rehabilitation and resocialization market] In Górniewicz, E., & Krause, A. (Eds.), *Od tradycjonalizmu do ponowoczesności: dyskursy pedagogiki specjalnej* [*[From traditionalism to postmodernity: Discourses of special pedagogy*]]. (pp. 261–267). Wydawnictwo UWM.

Park, E., & Yi, S. (2025). Compulsory education enhances financial inclusion across socioeconomic groups: A global analysis. *Humanities & Social Sciences Communications*, *12*, 695. DOI: 10.1057/s41599-025-04911-y

Patel, V.. (2018). The Lancet Commission on global mental health and sustainable development. *Lancet*, *392*(10157), 1553–1598. DOI: 10.1016/S0140-6736(18)31612-X PMID: 30314863

Paz, D. (1997). *Implementation of the special education law, rationale and forming up* [Paper presentation]. Special Education Department Meeting, Ramat-Gan, Bar-Ilan University, School of Education.

Pedersen, H., & Söderström, S. (2024). The creation of cyborgs within a socially constructed understanding of disability and assistive activity technology use. *Disability & Society*, *39*(8), 1984–2006.

Persson, A. (2014). Transmission and prevention of HIV among heterosexual populations in Australia. *AIDS Education and Prevention*, *26*(3), 245–255. PMID: 24846487

Persson, B. (2006). Pathways to inclusion: A guide to staff development. *European Educational Research Journal*, *5*, 152–158.

Peruzzo, F. (2023). A certain kind of freedom, a certain subject of right: The disability dispositif of inclusion and the government of the disabled child in the Italian education system. In Beckett, M., & Callus, M. (Eds.), *The Routledge International Handbook of Children's Rights and Disability* (pp. 520–536). Routledge., DOI: 10.4324/9781003056737

Petersen, I., Bhana, A., Campbell-Hall, V., Mjadu, S., Lund, C., & Kleintjies, S.. (2009). Planning for district mental health services in South Africa: A situational analysis of a rural district site. *Health Policy and Planning*, *24*(2), 140–150. PMID: 19147698

Phasha, T. N., & Myaka, L. D. (2014). Sexuality and sexual abuse involving teenagers with intellectual disability: Community conceptions in a rural village of KwaZulu-Natal, South Africa. *Sexuality and Disability*, *32*(2), 153–165.

Phelan, J. C., Link, B. G., & Dovidio, J. F. (2008). Stigma and prejudice: One animal or two? *Social Science & Medicine*, *67*(3), 358–367. PMID: 18524444

Pinfold, V., Thornicroft, G., Huxley, P., & Farmer, P. (2005). Active ingredients in anti-stigma programmes in mental health. *International Review of Psychiatry (Abingdon, England)*, *17*(2), 123–131. PMID: 16194782

Pitpitan, E. V.. (2012). AIDS-related stigma, HIV testing, and transmission risk among patrons of informal drinking places in Cape Town, South Africa. *Annals of Behavioral Medicine, Vol.*, *43*(3), 362–371. PMID: 22367752

Popescu-Sarry, D. (2024). Discrimination without traits: From social construction to the politics of discrimination. *The American Political Science Review*, *118*(2), 890–902.

Potter, W. J. (1996). *An analysis of thinking and research about qualitative methods.* Arlbaum Associates.

Pradhan, K. C., & Naik, M. S. (2024). Inclusive education: A foundation for equality and empowerment at the elementary stage. *International Journal of Multidisciplinary Research in Arts. Science and Technology*, *2*(2), 1–8.

Psychiatric Times. (2023). Addressing mental health disparities in rural communities. Psychiatric Times. Available at: https://www.psychiatrictimes.com/

Psychiatric Times. (2023). Rising anxiety disorders among adolescents: A global perspective. Psychiatric Times. Available at: https://www.psychiatrictimes.com/

Qo'ldoshev, R., Dilova, N., & Hakimova, N. (2024). Guiding left-handed students to a healthy lifestyle during the period of adaptation to school education. In *BIO Web of Conferences* (Vol. 120, p. 01049). EDP Sciences.

Quesada-Pallarès, C., Rebollar-Sánchez, E. M., Fernández-de-Álava, M., & Ciraso, A. (2018). Is in-service teacher training useful? Applying the transfer of learning factors model in mexican schools. In Caudle, L. (Ed.), *Teachers and Teaching* (pp. 1–24).

Qvortrup, A., & Qvortrup, L. (2018). Inclusion: Dimensions of inclusion in education. *International Journal of Inclusive Education*, *22*(7), 803–817. DOI: 10.1080/13603116.2017.1412506

Ragin, C. C., Shulman, D., Weinberg, A., & Gran, B. (2003). Complexity, generality, and qualitative comparative analysis. *Field Methods*, *15*(4), 323–340. DOI: 10.1177/1525822X03257689

Rahim, R. (2024). Social workers' role in the provision of services for families with children and youth with disabilities in Latvia, Slovakia, and Portugal. SHS Web of Conferences 184, 01007. *Int. Conf. Society Health Welfare.* https://doi.org/DOI: 10.1051/shsconf/202418401007

Rakwar, J.. (1999). Cofactors for the acquisition of HIV-1 among heterosexual men: Prospective cohort study of trucking company workers in Kenya. *AIDS*, *13*, 607–614. PMID: 10203386

Ramasela S F (2022). An Afrocentric critique of the pitfalls of the African union in promoting unity, peace, and solidarity of African states Journal of African Union Studies Vol. 11, No. 2, 2022, pp. 19–33

Ramos, M. C. (1989). Some ethical implications of qualitative research. *Research in Nursing & Health*, *12*(1), 57–63. DOI: 10.1002/nur.4770120109 PMID: 2922491

Ranganathan, N., & Wadhwa, T. (2024). *Guidance and counselling in schools: Theory and practice*. Taylor & Francis.

Rankin, W. W.. (2005). The stigma of being HIV-positive in Africa. [PMC free article] [PubMed] [Google Scholar]. *PLoS Medicine*, *2*(8), e247. PMID: 16008508

Reavley, N. J., & Jorm, A. F. (2012). Stigmatising attitudes towards people with mental disorders: Changes in Australia over 8 years. *Psychiatry Research*, *197*(3), 302–326. PMID: 22417929

Reeves, P., Ng, S. L., Harris, M., & Phelan, S. K. (2022). The exclusionary effects of inclusion today:(re) production of disability in inclusive education settings. *Disability & Society*, *37*(4), 612–637.

Rehmat, S., Ahmed, S. Z., & Sultan, S. (2025). Intersectional Stigma's Consequences on Transgender Students' Mental Health, Motivation, and Academic Performance. *Social Science Review Archives*, *3*(1), 493–511.

Reimers, F. M. (2024). The sustainable development goals and education, achievements and opportunities. *International Journal of Educational Development*, *104*, 102965.

Republic of Kenya. (2001). *The Children's Act (No. 8)*. Nairobi: The National Council for Law Reporting with the Authority of the Attorney General. Retrieved from www.kenyalaw.org

Republic of Kenya. (2006). *The Sexual Offences Act (No. 3)*. Nairobi: The National Council for Law Reporting with the Authority of the Attorney General. Retrieved from www.kenyalaw.org

Republic of Kenya. (2010). *The Constitution*. Nairobi, Kenya: The National Council for Law Reporting with the Authority of the Attorney General. Retrieved from www.kenyalaw.org

Republic of Kenya. (2012). *The Task Force on the Re-alignment of the Education Sector to the Constitution of Kenya, 2010: Towards a globally competitive quality education for sustainable development*. Report of the Task Force. Nairobi: The National Council for Law Reporting with the Authority of the Attorney General. Retrieved from www.kenyalaw.org

Republic of South Africa. (1996). *Constitution of the Republic of South Africa*. Government Printer.

Reygan, F., & Steyn, M. (2017). Diversity in basic education in South Africa: Intersectionality and critical diversity literacy. *Africa Education Review*, *14*(2), 68–81.

Rhoades, E. A., Price, F., & Perigoe, C. B. (2004). The changing American family & ethnically diverse children with hearing loss and multiple needs. *The Volta Review, 104*(4), 285–305.

Rice, F., Ng-Knight, T., Riglin, L., Powell, V., Moore, G. F., McManus, I. C., & Frederickson, N. (2021). Pupil mental health, concerns and expectations about secondary school as predictors of adjustment across the transition to secondary school: A longitudinal multi-informant study. *School Mental Health, 13*, 279–298. DOI: 10.1007/s12310-021-09432-5

Riche, N. (2014). *Research Study on Children with Disabilities Living in Uganda Situational Analysis on the Rights of Children with Disabilities in Uganda* UNICEF Uganda. Available at:http://www.anppcanug.org/wp-content/uploads/Resource_Center/Research_Reports/research_report_11.pdf

Rimmer, J. H., Riley, B., Wang, E., Rauworth, A., & Jurkowski, J. (2004). Physical activity participation among persons with disabilities: Barriers and facilitators. *American Journal of Preventive Medicine, 26*(5), 419–425. DOI: 10.1016/j.amepre.2004.02.002

Rindels, J. (2021). *Competition, comparison, and pressure to perform: An analysis of the impact of the Advanced Placement program on suicidality among high-achieving adolescents* (Doctoral dissertation, University of Iowa). https://doi.org/ DOI: 10.17077/etd.0e6x2d1w

Riva, G., Wiederhold, B. K., & Mantovani, F. (2020). Virtual reality in the treatment of mental disorders: Beyond anxiety and exposure therapy. *Frontiers in Psychiatry, 11*, 179. DOI: 10.3389/fpsyt.2020.00179

Rizova, E., Keskinova, A., Georgievska, S., Stanojkovska Trajkovska, N., Demetriou, K., Borges, F., Vieira, R., & Lazova, L. (2023). *Research for Best Practices of Inclusion of Adults with Disabilities on the Labor Market*. Elena Rizova.

Roberson, L. (2001). Integration of computers and related technologies in deaf education teacher preparation programs. *American Annals of the Deaf, 146*(1), 60–66. PMID: 11355079

Robertson, S. M. (2010). Neurodiversity, Quality of Life, and Autistic Adults: Shifting Research and Professional Focuses onto Real-Life Challenges. *Disability Studies Quarterly, 30*(10).

Rodriguez, C. C., & Garro-Gil, N. (2014). Inclusion and integration on special education. *Procedia: Social and Behavioral Sciences, 191*, 1323–1327.

Roeser, R. W., Galloway, M., Casey-Cannon, S., Watson, C., Keller, L., & Tan, E. (2008). Identity representations in patterns of school achievement and well-being among early adolescent girls: Variable- and person-centered approaches. *The Journal of Early Adolescence*, *28*(1), 115–152. DOI: 10.1177/0272431607308676

Ronen, C. (2007). Issues and debates concerning mainstreaming and inclusioning educational settings. [in Hebrew] In Reiter, S., Leyser, Y., & Avissar, G. (Eds.), *Inclusiveness – learners with disabilities in education* (pp. 27–55). Ahva.

Rossler, W. (2016). The stigma of mental disorders: A millennia-long history of social exclusion and prejudices. *EMBO Reports*, *17*(9), 1250–1253. PMID: 27470237

Rüsch, N., Angermeyer, M. C., & Corrigan, P. W. (2005). Mental illness stigma: Concepts, consequences, and initiatives to reduce stigma. *European Psychiatry : the Journal of the Association of European Psychiatrists*, *20*(8), 529–539. PMID: 16171984

Rush, A. J.. (2018). Sequenced treatment alternatives to relieve depression (STAR*D): Outcomes for different levels of depression severity. *The Journal of Clinical Psychiatry*, *79*(2), 140–150. DOI: 10.4088/JCP.13m08413

Sachs, G. S. (2004). Strategies for improving treatment of bipolar disorder: Integration of measurement and management. *Acta Psychiatrica Scandinavica. Supplementum*, *422*, 7–17. PMID: 15330934

Sait, W. (2023). *An exploration of disability experiences and responses of disabled persons and their families within Muslim culture of the community of Strand, South Africa* (Unpublished doctoral dissertation). Stellenbosch University.

Salimzadeh, R., Saroyan, A., & Hall, N. C. (2017). Examining the factors impacting academics' psychological well-being: A review of research. *International Education Research*, *5*(1), 13–44.

Saloviita, T. (2005). Erityisopetus opettajankoulutuksen sisältöalueena. [Special education as a content area of teacher education] In Jakku-Sihvonen, R. (Ed.), *Uudenlaisia maistereita* [New kinds of masters]. (pp. 339–351). Otava.

Saloviita, T. (2020). Teacher attitudes towards the inclusion of students with support needs. *Journal of Research in Special Educational Needs*, *20*(1), 64–73. https://doi.org/https://doi.org/10.1111/1471-3802.12466

Sambo, A. (2016). Physically challenged students and their information needs. Library Philosophy and Practice (E-Journal), 1461. https://www.researchgate.net/publication/313615123

Samsari, E., Nikolaou, G., & Palaiologou, N. (2025). Multicultural Education and Students with Special Needs: A Case Study from Greece. *International Journal of Disability Development and Education*, *72*(1), 134–148.

Sandelowski, M. (2000). Focus on research methods-whatever happened to qualitative description? *Research in Nursing & Health*, *23*(4), 334–340. DOI: 10.1002/1098-240X(200008)23:43.0.CO;2-G PMID: 10940958

Sandler-loeff, A., & Shahak, Y. (2006). *People with disabilities in Arab society in Israel: An opportunity for social change*. JDC Israel, The Unit for Disabilities and Rehabilitation.

Santamaría Graff, C. (2021). Co-investigation and co-education in 'family as faculty'approaches: A repositioning of power. *Theory into Practice*, *60*(1), 39–50.

Santamaría, M. D., Mondragon, N. I., Santxo, N. B., & Ozamiz-Etxebarria, N. (2021). Teacher stress, anxiety and depression at the beginning of the academic year during the COVID-19 pandemic. *Global Mental Health (Cambridge, England)*, *8*, e14. DOI: 10.1017/gmh.2021.14 PMID: 34192001

Sartorius, N. (1998). Stigma: What can psychiatrists do about it? *Lancet*, *352*(9133), 1058–1059. PMID: 9759771

Sasson, I., & Miedijensky, S. (2020). Transfer skills in teacher training programs: The question of assessment. *Professional Development in Education*, *49*(2), 243–256. DOI: 10.1080/19415257.2020.1839783

Saunders, L., & Wong, M. A. (2020). Critical pedagogy: Challenging bias and creating inclusive classrooms. *Instruction in libraries and information centers.*

Save the Children. (2011). *Out of the shadows: Sexual violence against children with disabilities*. Save the Children.

Sayed, Y., Motala, S., & Hoffman, N. (2017). Decolonising initial teacher education in South African universities: More than an event. *Journal of Education*, *68*, 59–91.

Sayed, Y., Soudien, C., & Carrim, N. (2003). Discourses of exclusion and inclusion in the South: Limits and possibilities. *Journal of Educational Change*, *4*(3), 231–248. DOI: 10.1023/B:JEDU.0000006162.07375.aa

Sayyidah, A. N. (2015). Dinamika penyesuaian diri penyandang disabilitas di tempat magang kerja (studi deskriptif di balai rehabilitas terpadu penyandang disabilitas (BRTPD) Yogyakarta). *INKLUSI*, *2*(1), 64–86. DOI: 10.14421/ijds.020104

Scambler, G. (1998). Stigma and disease: Changing paradigms. *Lancet*, *352*(9133), 1054–1055. PMID: 9759769

Schechtman, Z., & Or, A. (1996). Applying counselling methods to challenge teacher beliefs with regard to classroom diversity and mainstreaming: An empirical study. *Teaching and Teacher Education.*

Scheetz, N. A. (1993). Closing the gap: Fostering a smooth transition toward independent living for the hearing impaired student entering the postsecondary setting. *Rural Special Education Quarterly, 12*(3), 36–41.

Schmidt, M., & Ksenja, V. (2015). Attitudes of teachers towards the inclusion of children with special needs in primary and secondary schools. *Hrvatska Revija za Rehabilitacijska Istraživanja, 51*(2), 16–30.

Schwab, S., Gebhardt, M., Hessels, M. G., Ellmeier, B., Gmeiner, S., & Rossmann, P. (2015). Does inclusive education change teachers' educational goals? A comparative analysis of two cross-sectional surveys in Austria. *Journal of Studies in Education, 5*(4), 114–130.

Schwartz, I. S.. (2019). *Partnerships for Inclusion: The Role of Family in the Education of with Autism. International Journal of Inclusive Education Shakespeare, T. (2013). Disability rights and wrongs revisited.* Routledge.

Scior, K. (2011). Public awareness, attitudes and beliefs regarding intellectual disability: A systematic review. *Research in Developmental Disabilities, 32*(6), 2164–2182. DOI: 10.1016/j.ridd.2011.07.005

Sedeto, M. H., & Dar, M. J. (2019). Socio-economic challenges of persons with disabilities: A Case Study of Ethiopia. *Global Journal of Human-Social Science: C Sociology & Culture, 19* (1), 1-9. https://globaljournals.org/GJHSS_Volume19/3-Socio-Economic-Challenges-of-Persons.pd

Sekulowicz, M., & Sekulowicz, A. (2015). The special education system in Poland: From segregation to inclusion. *Journal of the International Association of Special Education, 16*(1), 4.

Sendziuk, P. (2003). *Learning to trust: Australian responses to AIDS.* UNSW Press.

Sepadi, M. D. (2023). *Investigating the Content Knowledge of Teachers' Continuous Professional Development Programmes for the Implementation of Inclusive Education in Limpopo Province* (Doctoral dissertation, University of Limpopo).

Shabangu, B. (2021). *Investigating (possible) tensions and possibilities of decolonising History curriculum as a locus to foster inclusive education in South African schools* (Unpublished doctoral dissertation). University of the Witwatersrand.

Shakespeare, T. (2013). The social model of disability. In Davis, L. J. (Ed.), *The Disability Studies Reader* (4th ed., pp. 214–221). Routledge.

Shakespeare, T., & Watson, N. (2002). The social model of disability: An outdated ideology. *Research in Social Science and Disability*, *2*, 9–28.

Shannon, P., & Agorastou, M. (2006). Identifying children with developmental disability receiving child protection services: A national survey of child welfare administrators. *Families in Society*, *87*(3), 351–357.

Sharaga, D. (1986). Human rights in emergency situations under the European Convention on Human Rights. In Y. Dinstein (Ed.), *Israel yearbook on human rights* (Vol. 15, pp. 217-242). Tel Aviv University Press.

Sharma, G. (2017). Pros and cons of different sampling techniques. *International Journal of Applied Research*, *3*(7), 749–752.

Sharma, U., Forlin, C., & Loreman, T. (2008). Impact of training on preservice teachers' attitudes and concerns about inclusive education and sentiments about persons with disabilities. *Disability & Society*, *23*(7), 773–785. DOI: 10.1080/09687590802469271

Sheehan, L., Nieweglowski, K., & Corrigan, P. W. (2017). Structures and types of stigma. In Gaebel, W., Rossler, W., & Sartorius, N. (Eds.), *The stigma of mental illness – end of the story?* (pp. 43–66). Springer.

Shisana, O., ... (2008) South African national HIV prevalence, incidence, behaviour and communication survey, a turning tide among teenagers? South Africa: Human Science Research Council Press. 75 p. Available: http://www.hsrcpress.ac.za/product.php?productid=2264&cat=1&page=3. Accessed 16 August 2012. This is an open-access resource for more detailed information about HIV/AIDS in South Africa.

Sholanke, A. B. (2019). Compliance of academic buildings of selected universities in Ogun State, Nigeria with universal design parameters. Unpublished Ph.D Thesis, Covenant University, Ota, Ogun State, Nigeria. https://www.academia.edu/113763853/Compliance_of_High_rise_Buildings_Vertical_Accessibility_Components_with_Universal_Design_Strategies_A_Case_Study_of_Covenant_University_Ota_Nigeria

Shumba, A. (2006). Child abuse in schools and the law in Zimbabwe: Current issues and challenges in the new millennium. *Child Abuse and Neglect Research in South Africa*, *7*(4), 48–60.

Silberman, S. (2015). *Neurotribes: The Legacy of Autism and the Future of Neurodiversity*. Avery., DOI: 10.1353/anq.2015.0057

Simbayi, L. (2003). HIV testing attitudes, AIDS stigma, and voluntary HIV counselling and testing in a black township in Cape Town, South Africa. *Sexually Transmitted Infections, Vol., 79*(6), 442–447. PMID: 14663117

Siraz, J., Wahab, H. A., & Saad, R. M. (2020). Volunteering'as Praxis During COVID-19: Experiences from Bangladeshi Migrant Workers in Malaysia and Indigenous Communities of Bangladesh. *Eubios Journal of Asian and International Bioethics; EJAIB, 30*(8).

Skeggs, B. (2002). *Formations of class and gender: Becoming respectable* (2nd ed.). Sage.

Skinner, D. & Mfecane, S. (2004) Stigma, discrimination and implications for people living with HIV/AIDS in South Africa. *Journal of the Social Aspects of HIV/AIDS, Vol.* 1, 3, pp 157–164.

Souto-Manning, M., Martell, J., & Álvarez, B. (2024). *Reading, Writing, and Talk: Teaching for Equity and Justice in the Early Grades*. Teachers College Press.

Spencer, R., Walsh, J., Liang, B., Mousseau, A. M. D., & Lund, T. J. (2018). Having it all? A qualitative examination of affluent adolescent girls' perceptions of stress and their quests for success. *Journal of Adolescent Research, 33*(1), 3–33. DOI: 10.1177/0743558416670990

Srinivasa, D. K., & Trivedi, S. (1982). Knowledge and attitude of mental diseases in a rural community of South India. *Social Science & Medicine, 16*, 1635–1639. PMID: 7146940

Stallman, H. M. (2010). Psychological distress in university students: A comparison with general population data. *Australian Psychologist, 45*(4), 249–257. DOI: 10.1080/00050067.2010.482109

Starck, J. G., Hurd, K., Perez, M. J., & Marshburn, C. K. (2024). Interest convergence and the maintenance of racial advantage: The case of diversity in higher education. *The Journal of Social Issues, 80*(1), 272–307.

Starczewska, A., Hodkinson, A., & Adams, G. (2012). Conceptions of inclusion and inclusive education: A critical examination of the perspectives and practices of teachers in Poland. *Journal of Research in Special Educational Needs, 12*(3), 162–169.

Stentiford, L., Koutsouris, G., & Allan, A. (2023). Girls, mental health and academic achievement: A qualitative systematic review. *Educational Review, 75*(6), 1224–1254. DOI: 10.1080/00131911.2021.2010244

Stinson, M., & Antia, S. (1999). Considerations in educating deaf and hard-of-hearing students in inclusive settings. *Journal of Deaf Studies and Deaf Education, 4*(3), 163–175. PMID: 15579885

Stopler, L. (2007). *Hidden shame: Violence against children with disabilities in East Africa.* Terres des Hommes Nederlands.

Storbeck, C. (2009). Educating the deaf and hard of hearing learner. In Landsberg, L., Kruger, D., & Nel, N. (Eds.), *Addressing barriers to learning: A South African Perspective.* Van Schaik.

Sullivan, A. M., McCarthy, J., & Pierce, L. (2020). Building Inclusive Learning Communities: A Framework for Culturally Responsive Teaching. *International Journal of Inclusive Education, 24*(10), 1035–1051.

Sur, M. H., Jung, J., & Shapiro, D. R. (2022). Theory of planned behavior to promote physical activity of adults with physical disabilities: Meta-analytic structural equation modeling. *Disability and Health Journal, 15*(1), 101199. DOI: 10.1016/j.dhjo.2021.101199

Swartz, L., & Marchetti-Mercer, M. (2019). Migration, technology and care: What happens to the body? *Disability & Society, 34*, 407–420. DOI: 10.1080/09687599.2018.1519409

Szumski, G., Smogorzewska, J., & Karwowski, M. (2017). Academic achievement of students without special educational needs in inclusive classrooms: A meta-analysis. *Educational Research Review, 21*, 33–54. DOI: 10.1016/j.edurev.2017.02.004

Tangcharoensathien, V., Witthayapipopsakul, W., Viriyathorn, S., & Patcharanarumol, W. (2018). Improving access to assistive technologies: Challenges and solutions in low- and middle-income countries. *WHO South-East Asia Journal of Public Health, 7*(2), 84–89. DOI: 10.4103/2224-3151.239419

Tasneem, S. T. (2020, May 9). Think out of the box to ensure learning continuity. *The Daily Star.* https://www.thedailystar.net/opinion/news/think-out-the-box-ensure-learning-continuity-1898287

Teaching Excellence in Adult Literacy. (2010). TEAL *Fact Sheet No. 2: Universal design for learning,* Retrieved February 9, 2023 from: http://www. udlcenter.org/

Tedlock, B. (1991). From participant observation to the observation of participation: The emergence of narrative ethnography. *Journal of Anthropological Research, 47*(1), 69–94. DOI: 10.1086/jar.47.1.3630582

Temple, J. B., Kelaher, M., & Williams, R. (2018). Discrimination and avoidance due to disability in Australia: Evidence from a national cross-sectional survey. *BMC Public Health, 18*, 1347. DOI: 10.1186/s12889-018-6234-7

Temple, J., & Kelaher, M. (2018). Is disability exclusion associated with psychological distress? Australian evidence from a national cross-sectional survey. *BMJ Open, 8*, e020829. DOI: 10.1136/bmjopen-2017-020829

Temple, J., & Williams, R. (2018). Financial wellbeing of older Australians with multiple health conditions. *Australasian Journal on Ageing*. Advance online publication. DOI: 10.1111/ajag.12497

Tesch, R. (1990). *Qualitative Research: Analysis, Types and Software Tools*. Falmer.

Thackwray, B. (2013). Effective evaluation of training and development in higher education. In *Effective Evaluation of Training and Development in Higher Education*. Routledge., DOI: 10.4324/9781315041896

Thapaliya, M. A. (2016). Report on disability in Nepal. Sydney (Australia): Australian Himalayan Foundation (AHF), 1-24. https://www.australianhimalayanfoundation.org.au/wp-content/uploads/2017/08/2016_Nepal_Disability_Report.pdf

The Guardian. (2019). Next level for disability law in Nigeria, July 11. M.guardian.ng>opinion.next-level-for... Thomsen, F. K. (2017). *Discrimination: Oxford research encyclopedia of politics*. Oxford University Press; Oxford, UK. https://oxfordre.com/politics/display/10.1093/acrefore/9780190228637.001.0001/acrefore-9780190228637-e-202?d=%2F10.1093%2Facrefore%2F9780190228637.001.0001%2Facrefore-9780190228637-e-202&p=emailAG4hUJ.qDxj6E

The Lancet Editorial. (2016). The health crisis of mental health stigma. *Lancet, 387*, 1027. PMID: 27025171

Theurel, A., Witt, A., & Shankland, R. (2022). Promoting university students' mental health through an online multicomponent intervention during the COVID-19 pandemic. *International Journal of Environmental Research and Public Health, 19*(16), 10442. DOI: 10.3390/ijerph191610442 PMID: 36012078

Thomas, G., Walker, D., & Webb, J. (1997). *The making of the inclusive school*. Routledge Falmer.

Thornicroft, G., Brohan, E., Kassam, A., & Lewis-Holmes, E. (2008). Reducing stigma and discrimination: Candidate interventions. *International Journal of Mental Health Systems, 2*, 3–10. PMID: 18405393

Thornicroft, G., Brohan, E., Rose, D., Sartorius, N., & Leese, M. (2009). Global pattern of experienced and anticipated discrimination against people with schizophrenia: A cross-sectional survey. *Lancet, 373*(9661), 408–415. PMID: 19162314

Thulo, A. (2024). Teachers' perceptions on integration of information and communication technology in History teaching and learning at five high schools in Maseru (Master's thesis, National University of Lesotho).

Tiernan, B. (2021). Inclusion versus full inclusion: Implications for progressing inclusive education. *European Journal of Special Needs Education, 37*(5), 882–890. DOI: 10.1080/08856257.2021.1961197

Tilstone, C., Florian, L., & Rose, R. (1998). *Promoting inclusive practice*. Routledge Falmer.

Tiwari, D. N. (Ed.). (2023). *Towards inclusive societies: Psychological and sociological perspectives*. Taylor & Francis.

Tongco, M. D. C. (2007). Purposive sampling as a tool for informant selection. *Ethnobotany Research and Applications, 5*, 147–158.

Torous, J., Jän Myrick, K., Rauseo-Ricupero, N., & Firth, J. (2020). Digital mental health and COVID-19: Using technology today to accelerate the curve on access and quality tomorrow. *JMIR Mental Health, 7*(3), e18848. DOI: 10.2196/18848 PMID: 32213476

Townsend, R. C., Huntley, T., Cushion, C. J., & Fitzgerald, H. (2020). 'It's not about disability, I want to win as many medals as possible': The social construction of disability in high-performance coaching. *International Review for the Sociology of Sport, 55*(3), 344–360.

Tucci, D. L., Merson, M. H., & Wilson, B. S. (2010). A summary of the literature on global hearing impairment: Current status and priorities for action. *Otology & Neurotology, 31*(1), 31–41. DOI: 10.1097/mao.0b013e3181c0eaec PMID: 20050266

Tucker, R., Kelly, D., Johnson, L., De, J. U., & Watchorn, V. (2022). Housing at the fulcrum: A systems approach to uncovering built environment obstacles to city scale accessibility and inclusion. *Journal of Housing and the Built Environment, 37*, 1179–1197. https://hdl.handle. net/ 10536/DRO/DU:30154331

Tvingstedt, A. L. (1993). *Social Conditions of Hearing-Impaired Pupils in Regular Classes*. Reprints and Miniprints No. 773.

Ugalde, L., Santiago-Garabieta, M., Villarejo-Carballido, B., & Puigvert, L. (2021). Impact of interactive learning environments on learning and cognitive development of children with special educational needs: A literature review. *Frontiers in Psychology, 12*, 674033.

Ugwu, C.J., Ekere J.N., & Ohoh. C. (2013). Research paradigms and methodological choices in the research process. Journal of applied Information Science and Technology 14 (2)2021

Umeh, N., & Adeola, R. (2013). Country Reports: Nigeria. In: Ngwena, C., Plessis, H., Combrinck, H., & Kamga, S. (Eds.), *African Disability Rights Yearbook.* 1. https://www. adry.up.ac.za/images/adry/volume1_2013/adry_2013_1_full_text.pdf

Umoh, E., & Unaka, D. (2019). What needs to be done to enhance disability rights in Nigeria. Report on human rights violations based on real or perceived sexual orientation and gender identity in Nigeria, pp. 48-50. https://theinitiativeforequalrights .org/wp-content/uploads/2019/12/2019-Human-Rights-Violations-Reports-Based-on-SOGI.pdf

UNCRPD (United Nations Committee on the Rights of Persons with Disabilities). 2016. General Comment No. 4 (2016), Article 24: Right to Inclusive Education. https://www.refworld.org/docid/57c977e34.html

UNESCO. (1994). *The Salamanca statement and framework for action on special needs education.* Unesco.

UNESCO. (1994). The Salamanca statement and framework for action on special needs education. *World Conference on Special Needs Education: Access and Quality*, Salamanca, Spain.

UNESCO. (2009). Policy guidelines on inclusion in education.

UNESCO. (2015). *Rethinking Education: Towards a global common good?* Corporate author. UNESCO; DOI. https://doi.org/;DOI: 10.54675/MDZL5552ISBN. 978-92-3-100088-1

UNESCO. (2020). *Build back better: Education must change after COVID-19 to meet the climate crisis*. https://en.unesco.org/news/build-back-better-education-must -change-after-covid-19-meet-climate-crisis

UNESCO. (2020b). Towards inclusion in education: Status, trends and challenges. The UNESCO Salamanca Statement 25 years on. Paris: UNESCO. https://unesdoc .unesco.org/ark:/48223/pf0000374246

UNICEF. (2018). *In focus: Including children with disabilities.* UNICEF Europe and Central Asia Regional Office. Retrieved from www.unicef.org/eca

United Nations Educational Scientific and Cultural Organisation. (2009). Policy guidelines on inclusion in education. https://unesdoc.unesco.org/ark:/48223/pf0000177849

United Nations Educational, Scientific and Cultural Organization. (2018). *Education for all: Global monitoring report.* UNESCO. https://unesdoc.unesco.org/ark:/48223/pf0000265866

United Nations. (2006). *Conventions on the rights of persons with disabilities.* United Nations Department of Economic and Social Affairs.

United Nations. (2007). Convention on the rights of people with disabilities. www.publications.parliament.

United Nations. (2015). *Report of the Special Rapporteur on the rights of persons with disabilities. A/70/297.* United Nations.

UPIAS. (1976). Fundamental principles of disability. London: Union of the Physically Impaired Against Segregation. https://books.google.com.ng/books/about/Fundamental_Principles_ of_Disability.html?id=rS5BPQAACAAJ&redir_esc=y
Uromi, S., & Mazagwa, M. (2014). Challenges facing people with disabilities and possible solutions in Tanzania. Journal of Educational Policy and Entrepreneurial Research, 1(2), 158-165. https://core.ac.uk/download/pdf/234698127.pdf

Uteuova, K., & Amirbayeva, D. (2025). The Integration of the Eurasian Scientific Community and the Trilingual Education Policy. *Dibon Journal of Education, 1*(2), 101–110. DOI: 10.64169/dje.72

Utulu, S. N., & Lawoyin, T. O. (2007). Epidemiological features of HIV Infection among pregnant women in Markurdi, Benue State, Nigeria. *The Journal of Biological Sciences, 39*(3), 397–408. PMID: 16928285

Uwakwe, C. B. (2000). Systematized HIV/AIDS education for student nurses at the University of Ibadan, Nigeria: Impact on Knowledge, attitudes and compliance with universal precautions. *Journal of Advanced Nursing, 32*(2), 416–424. PMID: 10964190

Vahedi, L. TaleschianTabrizi, N., Kolahdouzan, K., Chavoshi, M., Rad, B., Soltani, S., & Ghojazadeh, M. (2014). Impact and amount of academic self-efficacy and stress on the mental and physical health of university students. *Research and Development in Medical Education, 3*(2), 99–104. https://doi.org/DOI: 10.5681/rdme.2014.022

van der Weele, S., & Bredewold, F. (2021). Shadowing as a qualitative research method for intellectual disability research: Opportunities and challenges. *Journal of Intellectual \& Developmental Disability, 46*(4), 340–350. https://doi.org/DOI: 10.3109/13668250.2021.1873752

Van Mieghem, A., Verschueren, K., Petry, K., & Struyf, E. (2020). An analysis of research on inclusive education: A systematic search and meta review. *International Journal of Inclusive Education, 24*(6), 675–689. DOI: 10.1080/13603116.2018.1482012

van Zyl, M. S. M. (2023). *Full-service school teachers' experiences of support* (Unpublished doctoral dissertation). Stellenbosch University.

Vanderstraeten, R. (2020). How does education function? *European Educational Research Journal, 14*(7), 49–56. DOI: 10.1177/1474904120948979

Vasquez, E. A. (2021). How can we best provide community supports in low- and middle-income countries? https://inclusive-policy.org/forum/how-can-we-best-provide-community-supports-in-low-and-middle-income-countries

Venkatapuram, S. (2014). Mental disability, human rights and capabilities approach. Searching for the foundations. *International Review of Psychiatry (Abingdon, England), 26*(4), 408–414. PMID: 25137106

Verdonschot, M. M., de Witte, L. P., Reichrath, E., Buntinx, W. H., & Curfs, L. M. (2009). Impact of environmental factors on community participation of persons with an intellectual disability: A systematic review. *Journal of Intellectual Disability Research, 53*(1), 54–64. DOI: 10.1111/j.1365-2788.2008.01128.x

Verza, E. (1995). Psihopedagogie specială [Special psychopedagogy]. Editura Didactică i Pedagogică.

Waghid, Y., & Engelbrecht, P. (2002). Inclusive education, policy and hope: Mapping democratic policy changes on inclusion in South Africa. *International Journal of Special Education, 17*(1), 20–25.

Waisath, W., McCormack, M., Stek, P., & Heymann, J. (2024). Dismantling barriers and advancing disability-inclusive education: An examination of national laws and policies across 193 countries. *International Journal of Inclusive Education, 28*(10), 2088–2103.

Walkerdine, V., Lucey, H., & Melody, J. (2001). *Growing up girl: Psychosocial explorations of gender and class*. Palgrave Macmillan.

Walton, E. (2023). Why inclusive education falters: A Bernsteinian analysis. *International Journal of Inclusive Education*, *27*(10), 1–15. DOI: 10.1080/13603116.2023.2241045

Wang, Z., Xu, X., Han, Q., Chen, Y., Jiang, J., & Ni, G. X. (2021). Factors associated with public attitudes towards persons with disabilities: A systematic review. *BMC Public Health*, *21*(1), 1058. DOI: 10.1186/s12889-021-11139-3

Wanjohi, A. M. (2019). Challenges facing inclusive education in Kenya. *Schools Net Kenya*, *3*(January), 1.

Wapiennik, E. (2008). Comparative policy brief: Status of intellectual disabilities in the Republic of Poland. *Journal of Policy and Practice in Intellectual Disabilities*, *5*(2), 137–141.

Warnes, E., Done, E. J., & Knowler, H. (2022). Mainstream teachers' concerns about inclusive education for children with special educational needs and disability in England under pre-pandemic conditions. *Journal of Research in Special Educational Needs*, *22*(1), 31–43.

Weissblei, E. (2011). The availability of resources for the community of children with special needs [in Hebrew]. Israel Knesset Report. Knesset Research and Information Center.

Were, A. R., Kioli, N. F., & Kurgat, S. G. (2016). Hidden shame: Sexual abuse against children with physical disabilities in rural Kenya. *International Journal of Sociology*, *4*(3), 82–87.

Wessels, M., & Rabinowitz, L. (2005). *Educator's guide to you, me & HIV*. Cold Spring Harbour Laboratory Press.

Whitehead, S. N. (2023). *Proposing clinician competency guidelines for the inclusion of disability in the undergraduate medical curriculum of South Africa: An exploratory study* (Doctoral dissertation, University of Cape Town).

Wiens, B., Karaki, S., & Mohebi, L. (2022). Teacher Training in Inclusive Education: Project Collaboration Between Al Jalila Foundation---Ta'alouf Program and Zayed University. In Coombe, C., Hiasat, L., & Daleure, G. (Eds.), *English Language and General Studies Education in the United Arab Emirates: Theoretical, Empirical and Practical Perspectives* (pp. 445–465). Springer Nature Singapore., DOI: 10.1007/978-981-16-8888-1_28

Wig, N. N.. (1980). Community reactions to mental disorders: A key informant study in three developing countries. *Acta Psychiatrica Scandinavica*, *61*, 111–126. PMID: 7361584

Wilczenski, F. L. (1995). Development of a scale to measure attitudes toward inclusive education. *Educational and Psychological Measurement, 55*(2), 291–299.

Willms, D. J. (2006). *Learning divides: Ten policy questions about the performance and equity of schools and schooling systems*. UNESCO Institute for Statistics.

Winter, J. A. (2003). The development of the disability rights movement as a social problem solver. *Disability Studies Quarterly, 23*(1). Advance online publication. DOI: 10.18061/dsq.v23i1.399.S2CID1429869 57

Winter, R., & Lavis, A. (2021). The impact of COVID-19 on young people's mental health in the UK: Key insights from social media using online ethnography. *International Journal of Environmental Research and Public Health, 19*(1), 352. DOI: 10.3390/ijerph19010352 PMID: 35010612

World Bank. (2020). *Disability inclusion.* https://www.worldbank.org/en/topic/disability#1

World Bank. (2020). *The COVID-19 Pandemic: Shocks to Education and Policy Responses*. World Bank., DOI: 10.1596/33696

World Health Organisation (WHO). (2017). *Prevention of deafness and hearing loss: 70th World Health Assembly, agenda item 15.8.* Retrieved May 23, 2023 from: https://apps.who.int/gb/ebwha/pdf_files/WHA70/A70_R13-en.pdf?ua=1

World Health Organisation. (2011). *World report on disability*. WHO/World Bank.

World Health Organisation. (2021). *Disability and Health.* https://www.who.int/news-room/fact-sheets/detail/disability-and-health

World Health Organization. (2018). *Improving access to assistive technology report by the director-general seventy-first world health assembly*. World Health Organization.

World Health Organization. (2022). World mental health report: Transforming mental health for all. Retrieved from https://www.who.int/publications/i/item/9789240061114

World Health Organization. (2023). Mental health. Retrieved from https://www.who.int/health-topics/mental-health

Xiao, J. J., & O'Neill, B. (2021). Disability type, financial capability, and Risky asset holding. *Journal of Disability Policy Studies, 32*(4). Advance online publication. DOI: 10.1177/1044207320981781

Yangdon, K., Sherab, K., Choezom, P., Passang, S., & Deki, S. (2021). Well-being and academic workload: Perceptions of science and technology students. *Educational Research Review, 16*(11), 418–427.

Yin, R. K. (1989). *Case Study Research: Design and Methods.* Sage.

Youngstrom, E. A.. (2005). Bipolar diagnoses in community mental health: Achenbach Child Behaviour Checklist profiles and patterns of comorbidity. *Biological Psychiatry, 2*(58), 569–575. PMID: 15950197

Yssel, N., Pak, N., & Beilke, J. (2016). A door must be opened: Perceptions of students with disabilities in higher education. *International Journal of Disability Development and Education, 63*(3), 384–394. DOI: 10.1080/1034912X.2015.1123232

Yusuf, M., Fakomogbon, M., & Issa, A. (2012). Availability of assistive technologies in Nigerian educational institutions. *International Journal of Social Sciences and Education, 2*(1), 44–55. http://ijsse.com/sites/default/files/issues/2012/volume%202%20issue%201%20Jan%202012/paper%204/paper-04.pdf

Zainal, Z. (2017). Case study as a research method. *Jurnal Kemanusiaan, 5*(1), 1–6.

Zaki, M. (2009). Validity and reliability of social support scale at the student of Isfahan Universities. *Majallah-i Ravanpizishki va Ravanshinasi-i Balini-i Iran, 14*(4), 439–446. https://core.ac.uk/download/pdf/33096621.pdf

Zermatten, J., & McCallum, R. (2011). Foreword. *Out from the Shadows: Sexual Violence against Children with Disabilities.* Handicap International: Save the Children, London.

Zvomuya, W. (2020). Ubuntuism as an international turning point for social work profession: New lenses from the African pot of knowledge. *African Journal of Social Work, 10*(1), 24–29. https://www.ajol.info/index.php/ajsw/article/view/194098

About the Contributors

Nareadi Phasha obtained her PhD from the University of Cambridge in the UK and her MEd degree in Special Education from Virginia State University in the US. She is a full professor of Inclusive Education and the founder and current lead of the UNISA Centre of Excellence in Disability. Previously, she served as the first Chair of the Department of Inclusive Education at the University of South Africa (UNISA). Prof. Phasha's work is closely aligned with South Africa's commitment to education for all. Her research investigates the challenges faced by learners in the current education system and addresses the high incidence of sexual victimization among school-age children and those with disabilities. In recognition of her significant contributions to research on violence against children and women, she was honored as a distinguished researcher by the former Minister of Higher Education, Mr. Derek Hanekom, during the Women in Research Awards in 2013. Prof. Phasha played a pivotal role as co-lead in a national project funded by the European Union, which involved the University of South Africa, the British Council, MiET-Africa, and the Department of Basic Education. This project focused on developing teacher education materials for inclusive teaching, which are now utilized by more than ten universities across South Africa. In January 2024, Prof. Phasha was appointed by the then Minister of Basic Education, Mrs. Angie Motshekga, to serve as a member of the Ministerial Task Team committee to review the South African White Paper 6 on Inclusive Education. Prof. Phasha has an extensive publication record in national and international peer-reviewed journals and has co-edited three books on Inclusive Education. She has supervised numerous PhD and Master's degree candidates and mentored several post-doctoral fellows.

***

Jihan Aloshi from Israel holds a PhD in Special Education Diagnosis of learning disabilities and dyslexia. Jihan research is on dyslexia and working memory. She works as Lecturer at Al-Qasemi Academic College & Ono Academic College in Israel. A mentor for teachers in the field of learning difficulties, learning strategies, and social-emotional learning.

Nkemdilim Anazonwu is a lecturer in the Department of Social Work, University of Nigeria, Nsukka with specialization in Disability and Vulnerable Groups

Noor Atieka bt Azmi Lecturer, Lincoln University, Malaysia Email: atiekaazmi@gmail.com

Jahid Siraz Chowdhury Associate Professor Lincoln University, Malaysia Email: jahid@lincoln.edu.my

Areej is an expert in STEAM education, teacher training, curriculum, teaching and learning, assessment, and school accreditation. She is an Approved Accreditation Lead Inspector from NEASC, CIS, and an approved visitor by CAEP accreditation. Furthermore, she was a Mental Health Ambassador at Zayed University and is a Certified AI Lead Assessor by IEEE. She was the graduate program coordinator at the College of Education at Zayed University and is currently an Associate Professor and Assistant Chair for the General Education Department at the College of Interdisciplinary Studies. Her research interests include educational technology, well-being, Human-computer interaction, entrepreneurship, innovation, STE(A)M, and assessment.

Islam A. Ismail, from Palestine, is the Editor-in-Chief of Dibon Journal of Education (ISSN: 2978-0586) and a Chief Executive at Dibon Publishing House in the United Kingdom. He holds a PhD in English Education and specialises in AI in education, educational technology, and teaching methods. At Dibon Journal of Education, he leads the strategic direction of the journal while maintaining its commitment to publishing high-quality research with global accessibility.

Enas Majadley, from Israel, holds a PhD in Special Education towards inclusion. Her research interests include students with learning difficulties, Integration, special education attitudes, hearing difficulties, autism, and mental disabilities. She works as a Lecturer at Al-Qasemi Academic College.

Andile Alfred Mdikana is currently employed as a Senior Lecturer at the University of South Africa in the Department of Inclusive Education since 1 November 2012 to date. He is currently mentoring colleagues who have PhD's on article writing for publication in peer reviewed journals. During his tenure at UNISA, he has developed modules on UNDERSTANDING INCLUSIVE EDUCATION AND ADVOCACY FOR PEOPLE WITH DISABILITIES. His academic citizenship includes the co-ordinatorship of the RESEARCH and MENTORSHIP committees and has been a member of the Higher Degrees in the Department of Inclusive Education. Furthermore, he has represented the department at college level in the Research and Higher Degrees committees. In addition to that he is also the primary lecturer and coordinator of the module called 'Addressing barriers to learning' and 'Advocacy for people with Disabilities'. Dr. A.A. Mdikana is a Registered Educational Psychologist since 2008. Prior to this appointment, he worked for Gauteng Department of Education as the Deputy Chief Education Specialist for Inclusion and Special Schools. It is worth noting that he spent four years running a private practice. He

Laila Mohebi stands out in the education sector, particularly in early childhood education and the role of technology in teaching. Holding a PhD from the British University in Dubai, her focus is on leadership and educational policy. As an associate professor at Zayed University, Dr. Mohebi is deeply involved in both teaching and research. Her scholarly contributions, highlighted by numerous publications in prestigious journals, center on utilizing technology in education, enhancing teacher training, and developing cutting-edge educational methods. Dr. Mohebi is dedicated to educational advancement, evidenced by her active participation in major projects and mentorship in teacher training initiatives. Her efforts are not just academic; they significantly influence future educational strategies and practices.

Jabulani Mpofu is a native African, and a Senior Lecturer in the department of Disability Studies and Special Needs Education at Zimbabwe Open University. Dr. Mpofu has more than twenty year's experience working with people with disabilities as an advocate for inclusive communities. Dr. Mpofu has published several research articles in peer-refereed journals, book chapters, and modules on disability issues. His primary teaching assignment at Zimbabwe Open University focuses on issues around Inclusive communities. Dr Mpofu's perception on disability and inclusive education is immersed in his professional preparation and work experience which values diversity in learners.

Chinwe Nnama-Okechukwu is a senior lecturer in the Department of Social Work, University of Nigeria, Nsukka with Specialization in Child Welfare Services

Doris Nyangoge Nyokangi is a highly accomplished Kenyan education specialist with a PhD in Inclusive Education from UNISA and a Master's in Education, Gender, and International Development from University College London. With extensive experience in leadership and research, she served as the

Chief Officer for Education in Kisii County (2018-2022) and held various roles at Egerton University, specializing in gender and development. Dr. Nyokangi has published numerous papers on gender-based violence, inclusive education, and women's empowerment. She is deeply involved in community outreach, including mentorship programs for girls in secondary schools and leading initiatives like the Rays of Hope Project. She has also served on several school management boards in Kisii County.

Paulinus Okah is a lecturer in the Department of Social Work, University of Nigeria, Nsukka, with specialization in Social Policy and Administration

Chinyere Onalu is a lecturer in the Department of Social Work, University of Nigeria, Nsukka, with specialization in public health

Maximus Sefotho is a Professor in the department of Educational Psychology ant University of Johannesburg

Index

A

B

C

D

E

F

G

H

I

K

L

M

N

P

R

S

T

U

V

W

www.ingramcontent.com/pod-product-compliance
Ingram Content Group UK Ltd.
Pitfield, Milton Keynes, MK11 3LW, UK
UKHW050844101026
15624UKWH00018B/512

9 798337 371634